1 GROUP:
SWIFT TO ATTACK

1 GROUP:
SWIFT TO ATTACK

*Bomber Command's
Unsung Heroes*

Patrick Otter

Pen & Sword
AVIATION

First published in Great Britain in 2012 by
PEN AND SWORD AVIATION
an imprint of
Pen and Sword Books Ltd
47 Church Street
Barnsley
South Yorkshire S70 2AS

ISBN 978 1 78159 094 2

A CIP record for this book is available from the British Library.

Printed and bound in England by
CPI Group (UK) Ltd, Croydon, CR0 4YY

Typeset in Plantin by CHIC GRAPHICS

Pen & Sword Books Ltd incorporates the imprints of
Pen & Sword Aviation, Pen & Sword Family History, Pen & Sword Maritime,
Pen & Sword Military, Pen & Sword Discovery, Wharncliffe Local History,
Wharncliffe True Crime, Wharncliffe Transport, Pen & Sword Select,
Pen & Sword Military Classics, Leo Cooper, Remember When,
The Praetorian Press, Seaforth Publishing and Frontline Publishing

For a complete list of Pen and Sword titles please contact
Pen and Sword Books Limited
47 Church Street, Barnsley, South Yorkshire, S70 2AS, England
E-mail: enquiries@pen-and-sword.co.uk
Website: www.pen-and-sword.co.uk

Contents

Foreword by Air Vice Marshal Stuart Atha...vii

Introduction ix

Acknowledgements... xii

Map of bases xvi

Chapter 1 Genesis 1

Chapter 2 The Leaders..11

Chapter 3 Enter the Wellington 17

Chapter 4 Expansion 38

Chapter 5 'Right on the Chin!' 47

Chapter 6 Enter the Heavies...62

Chapter 7 Happy Valley..74

Chapter 8 Fire and Brimstone..90

Chapter 9 Bigger and Better...101

Chapter 10 Confusion to the Enemy...106

Chapter 11 The Big City 115

Chapter 12 The Perfect Pilot..145

Chapter 13 Hard Times...153

Chapter 14 Learning the Ropes 175

Chapter 15 One Man's Story 188

Chapter 16 A Long Hot Summer..193

Chapter 17 The Highest Degree of Courage..................................218

Chapter 18 Where it Hurts Most 236

Chapter 19 'They Were All Mad Buggers!'....................................259

Chapter 20 Daylight at Last 271

Chapter 21 'Living in a Sea of Mud'..295

Chapter 22 The Veterans..317

Chapter 23 Aftermath..330

Chapter 24 The Airfields and Squadrons of 1 Group 334

Chapter 25 The Present Day 354

On Hallowed Ground 356

Bibliography 358

Index 360

Foreword

Today, the men and women of 1 Group are the RAF's primary warfighters and play the dominant role in the delivery of air power both at home and on operations overseas. In this invaluable record, however, Patrick Otter reminds us of a time when 1 Group was but one of many groups engaged in a war of national survival that required ordinary men and women to perform extraordinary feats. One cannot fail to be humbled and moved in equal measure by the tales of individual heroism and collective sacrifice as Patrick Otter vividly describes the human cost of war not in an abstract way but through the particular experiences of individual crews. The narrative is complemented by an impressive array of black and white photographs that add colour to the reader's understanding of the personal contribution. The faces look familiar, conveying conventional emotion in those who posed and much more profound feeling in those less poised. As the exceptional experience of the Bomber Command crews makes the inevitable transition from living history to the written word, Patrick Otter is to be congratulated for capturing in encyclopaedic detail the experiences of those within 1 Group. He has recorded for all time their contribution and, in doing so, has created a fitting tribute to their memory. 1 Group operations today, such as those over Libya or Afghanistan, may differ in terms of scale and the casualties incurred, but the character and quality of the men and women of 1 Group endures and there is much about those in 1 Group today that would appear familiar to those who served 70 years ago. Thanks to Patrick this book reminds us, to paraphrase the closing ode from Cedric Keith St George Roberts, how a very special generation gave all their tomorrows, and all they had to give, for our freedom. We who serve in 1 Group today, salute those who went before, honour their memory and are grateful to them for our hard won freedom.

Air Vice Marshal Stuart Atha DSO ADC
Air Officer Commanding 1 Group
December 2012

Introduction

This is the wartime story of 1 Group of RAF Bomber Command. It came into being in the summer of 1940, re-formed from the remnants of a light bomber force which had been all but destroyed in the month following the German invasion of the Low Countries and France. Five years later it was amongst the most powerful elements in Britain's armed forces, able to wreak destruction on an awesome scale with the greatest degree of accuracy then available.

1 Group's badge and motto.

1 Group was to fly from airfields in Lincolnshire, Yorkshire and Nottinghamshire and, in its five year war, was to lose almost 1,900 aircraft, the majority of them Lancasters, and the lives of 8,760 men, around one in seven of all those killed in Bomber Command operations. It flew at various times from 23 different airfields and, by the war's end, became one of the largest of all groups within Bomber Command.

How it began. Fairey Battles equipped the first 1 Group squadrons in the summer of 1940. (Author's collection)

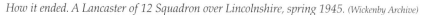

It lived to some degree in the shadow of its Lincolnshire neighbours in 5 Group, whose squadrons included the Dambusters of 617 and whose men included the likes of Guy Gibson, Leonard Cheshire and 'Babe' Learoyd. No VCs went to the men of 1 Group, although one young Wellington pilot was recommended for the medal only for the award to be downgraded to a CGM for what was purely geographic reasons. Yet their numbers included squadrons which flew the highest number of sorties, dropped the greatest number of bombs and suffered the highest casualties in the whole of Bomber Command. In all, 1 Group squadrons lost more than 1,500 aircraft in wartime operations, including over a thousand Lancasters, plus many more in accidents and in training. They were, very much, the unsung heroes of the bomber war.

There was nothing glamorous about the job they did. Crews were expected to fly 30 operations before they could think about survival. Until the later days of the war few managed to achieve that many. Their's was a cold, lonely and terrifying war, trapped in searchlights over the Ruhr, hounded by night-fighters over Berlin. Only German U-boat crews suffered higher casualties than the men of Bomber Command. Yet, when the war ended, there were to be no campaign medals for them although, belatedly, the remaining survivors are to finally receive recognition with the issue of a Special Bomber Command 'clasp'.

How it ended. A Lancaster of 12 Squadron over Lincolnshire, spring 1945. (Wickenby Archive)

INTRODUCTION

Lancasters en route for Germany, 1945. (Sir Guy Lawrence)

Churchill scarcely mentioned their contribution in his wartime memoirs. Yet without Bomber Command German industry would have been vastly more productive and huge numbers of men, guns and aircraft would have been released to fight elsewhere. Bomber Command fought Britain's Second Front from the summer of 1940 until the spring of 1944 and its efforts ensured the success of the Normandy invasion. That was something completely overlooked by the post-war apologists for Dresden, whose views did much to ensure that Bomber Command veterans never got the recognition their courage and sacrifice deserved.

For me, this is very much a personal story. My father was one of the 55,000 Bomber Command men who never came back, a 5 Group navigator killed over Berlin six months before I was born. My first playground was a disused 1 Group bomber airfield, my first toy a brass Spitfire cast from anti-aircraft shells.

1 Group's motto was 'Swift to Attack'. It was one they upheld magnificently. This is how they did it.

Patrick Otter
Lincolnshire 2013

Acknowledgements

It was a beautiful summer's day in the early 1980s when I first became fascinated by the story of Bomber Command's wartime 1 Group.

In my job as a Lincolnshire journalist I attended one of the annual services held by veterans of 625 Squadron, a former 1 Group squadron, on the site of their old airfield at Kelstern. It was one of those rare days on the Lincolnshire Wolds when there was little wind. The sun was shining brightly and that afternoon I got to meet a large group of men who, 40 years earlier, had taken off nightly from almost exactly the spot where we were standing. As I passed amongst them I realised that these were men with a very special bond holding them together. One was a solicitor, another was a shopkeeper, another worked as a mechanic, yet that afternoon they were all back in time at Kelstern circa 1944, all wearing the same uniforms, sharing the comradeship that only a bomber crew could experience and all facing the likelihood of imminent death.

They were willing to tell me about their experiences back then, about the hairy trips, the jaunts into Louth, a whole crew packed into an Austin Seven. They were, I realised, talking about a piece of history which had occurred just about in my lifetime and later, when I reflected on those conversations in the Lincolnshire sunshine, I felt it was time someone recorded their experiences so that their story could be told for future generations.

Over the next few months I began to research the history of wartime Bomber Command, and particularly that part which took place in my home county of Lincolnshire. It was something I found particularly poignant as my own father was among Bomber Command's 55,000 casualties.

It became clear to me that in the numerous books which appeared in the post-war years concerning Bomber Command's activities, the role of 1 Group appeared to be overshadowed, particularly by its south Lincolnshire neighbours, 5 Group. This was, to a degree, understandable: 5 Group was, for much of the war, the largest of the six groups which comprised Bomber Command's strike force. Its numbers included some of Bomber Command's elite squadrons, including the Dambusters of 617, and it was inevitable that when the bombing war was talked or written about, the spotlight would fall on 5 Group and its squadrons, including that which my father had served in. Then there was the East Anglian-based 3 Group which was amongst the first to operate four-engined 'heavies', 4 Group, which flew exclusively from Yorkshire and the all-Canadian 6 Group. Of 1 Group, however, little had been written.

ACKNOWLEDGEMENTS

In the late 1980s I wrote and had published through my then-employers a series of illustrated books under the umbrella title Maximum Effort telling the stories of some of those men who flew with 1 Group. It was not a definitive history, simply a journalist's take on what it must have been like to fly bombers from North Lincolnshire between 1940 and 1945. It was told largely through letters and interviews with large numbers of those who took part, both as aircrew and ground staff. I was fortunate in that my timing couldn't have been better: most of these men were approaching or just into retirement and a time of reflection in their lives. Many explained in their letters that they finally felt able to put down in words what they had experienced all those years ago. Supporting the stories were literally hundreds of photographs, willingly loaned to me by these extraordinary men and women.

This book is intended to take the story a stage further, weaving those recollections into a narrative covering the operational life of 1 Group from the day it was reformed in the summer of 1940 until the cessation of hostilities in Europe five years later.

Time marches on and most of those who contributed are now, unfortunately, no longer with us but my hope is that this account will keep their experiences and memories alive for future generations. I would like to take this opportunity to thank them all for what they did and trusting me with their recollections.

Many more have helped contribute to this story and, if I omit to mention anyone, I apologise now.

One man who deserves special thanks is David Irving, a Liverpool postman who began researching the story of George Ashplant during the 1990s as part of a project to discover what happened to the men whose names appear on the war memorial in Halewood. He generously turned over the fruits of his endeavours to me but sadly passed away before he could see the publication of this book.

When my researches began I was able to turn to the many squadron associations for help, people like Clem Koder, Percy Miller and Eric Thale at the 625 Association, who I had first met that afternoon at Kelstern. Others readily offered their assistance, including Vic Redfern, keeper of 101 Squadron's archives and albums, Edward Martin at the Wickenby Register, John Lamming of 103 Squadron, Shirley Westrup, guardian of the records of 103 and 576 Squadrons during their time at Elsham, Jim Wright, who ran the 166 Squadron Association, Zygmunt Bednarksi of 300 Squadron, Roland Hardy, who kept a wonderful collection of 550 Squadron photographs, Vernon Wilkes of 150, Freddie Fish of 170 Squadron and many, many more. Now the task of keeping the records of those squadrons has, in the main, passed to others and they have been just as helpful.

I must give a special word of thanks to David Fell, who now looks after the

Elsham Wolds Association and runs an excellent website. David is the font of all knowledge about Elsham and kindly supplied dozens of wonderful photographs. The Wickenby Register, which represented those who flew with 12 and 626 Squadrons, closed in 2011 but its spirit is kept alive by those volunteers who run the small museum there. One of their number is Anne Law who supplied a multitude of pictures, most of which have never been published before.

I also must thank David Briggs and Martin Nichols, who operate a superb website dedicated to RAF Fiskerton, both a 5 and 1 Group station, and without prompting put all their collection of 576 Squadron photographs at my disposal. They are part of a network of enthusiasts whose determination to keep alive the spirit of Bomber Command shows no sign of waning. Thanks also to Nic Lewis who is now the guardian of 625 Squadron memorabilia, the squadron which started it all for me and who also generously supplied photographs and gave me access to his late father's log book.

I must also thank the Holford family for their help in compiling the story of W/Cmdr David Holford. It was only thanks to the power of the internet (how did we manage before?) that I was to contact them and they supplied copious amounts of material to help tell the story of one of the most remarkable men to fly with 1 Group.

The spirit of 1 Group is kept alive in Australia by the surviving members of the 460 Squadron Association, including the indefatigable Laurie and Barbara Woods, and I'd like to thank them for their contribution. A special mention also to David Butler and his colleagues at the Real Aero Club at Breighton for their valuable help.

A special thanks, too, for my friends Martin Shiplee, Vince McDonagh, Peter Chapman, Brian Frith, Greg Brett and Derrick Rowbotham for providing additional sources of information. Dick Preston was incredibly helpful in providing material and illustrations on the development of the Rose turret, dipping deeply into the archives of Baker Perkins, which now owns the old Rose Brothers factory in Gainsborough. So, too, were all those other individuals who raided their own archives to willingly provide pictures for this book. Thanks, too, to my editor, Richard Gardner for his words of encouragement, and to Laura Hirst at Pen & Sword for all her invaluable assistance.

And then, of course, there's the man every aviation author turns to at times like this, Peter Green. I have known Peter now for over 30 years and I have never found him anything but generous in the extreme. He has an unrivalled collection of photographs and, I must say, knowledge of Bomber Command which far extends beyond mine. Peter is, and always has been, the ultimate enthusiast for all things linked to aviation but what sets him aside is his

ACKNOWLEDGEMENTS

willingness to share his collection with people like me. Despite advancing years, that enthusiasm still knows no bounds. I feel privileged to have been one of the many who have turned to Peter Green for assistance.

Finally, I would like to thank those who persuaded me to tackle this book, my wife Eva and son Chris, a better and more accomplished historian than I'll ever be. Without their encouragement this project would have still be nothing more than a folder in my computer's memory. I dedicate this book to them, the most important people in my life, along, of course, with our wonderful grandsons Nicholas and Sam.

Map of Bases

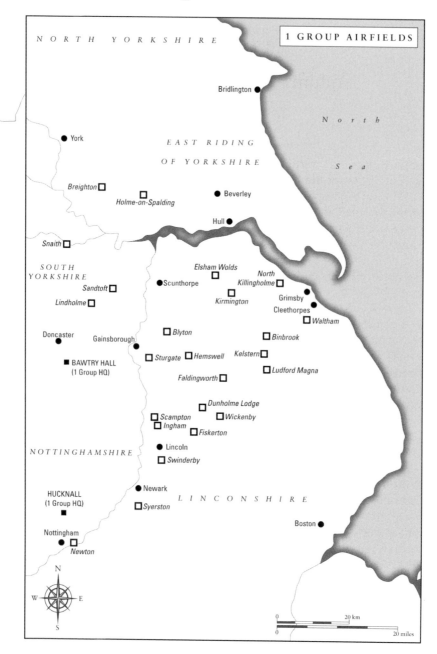

1 GROUP AIRFIELDS

N O R T H   Y O R K S H I R E

Bridlington ●

N o r t h

● York

E A S T   R I D I N G

O F   Y O R K S H I R E

S e a

Breighton □

Holme-on-Spalding □

● Beverley

Hull ●

Snaith □

SOUTH
YORKSHIRE

Elsham Wolds □

● Scunthorpe

North
Killingholme □

Sandtoft □

Kirmington □

Grimsby
Cleethorpes ●

Lindholme □

□ Waltham

Doncaster ●

Gainsborough ●

□ Blyton

□ Binbrook

■ BAWTRY HALL
(1 Group HQ)

□ Sturgate □ Hemswell

Kelstern □

□ Ludford Magna

Faldingworth □

□ Dunholme Lodge

□ Scampton   □ Wickenby
□ Ingham
  □ Fiskerton

NOTTINGHAMSHIRE

● Lincoln

□ Swinderby

HUCKNALL
(1 Group HQ)
■

● Newark

L I N C O N S H I R E

□ Syerston

Boston ●

Nottingham ●

□

Newton

N
W ● E
S

0   20 km
0   20 miles

Chapter 1

Genesis

Autumn 1939 – Autumn 1940

Bomber Command's wartime 1 Group was formed on the very day of France's final humiliation at the hands of Adolf Hitler, its leaders forced to sign an Armistice in the same railway carriage at the same spot on the forest of Compiègne where the Great War came to its conclusion.

Events at Hucknall to mark the reforming of 1 Group appear to have passed without such ceremony. Hucknall, five miles from Nottingham, was one of the oldest airfields in the country and before the war had been used by a variety of units, notably 104 Squadron which had flown the ill-fated Fairey Battle from there in 1938.

HQ 1 Group came into being officially on June 22, 1940 but it wasn't until five days later that it's first Air Officer Commanding, Air Commodore John Breen, arrived to take control of what was then a pitifully small command. It was made up of the remnants of four squadrons which had just returned from France where they had been horribly mauled in the air and on the ground by the Luftwaffe. They were scattered across the country awaiting new airfields from where, hopefully, they could be refitted and resume operations. It must have seemed a daunting task even for the most optimistic of those on the HQ staff.

The pre-war 1 Group, created when the RAF came into being in 1918, had been spread across the South Midlands and was equipped with Fairey Battles, single-engined light bombers which were obsolete even before they went into squadron service. In September 1939 it was formally disbanded and its 10 squadrons were formed into five wings of the grandiosely-titled Advanced Air Striking Force and sent to France under the control of Air Vice Marshal 'Pip' Playfield. The Battle crews were under no illusion about the inadequacy of their aircraft, a point bloodily brought home to them within days of arriving in France when four aircraft of 150 Squadron, later to be part of the new 1 Group, were shot down by Me 109s on a reconnaissance operation near Saarbrucken, five men being killed and a sixth, Sgt G. Springett, becoming one of the first RAF prisoners-of-war. A fifth aircraft was so badly damaged it crashed on return to the squadron's airfield at Challerange.

1

A Fairey Battle of 12 Squadron in France early in 1940. (Author's collection)

Sgt Rex Wheeldon was one of the men who flew Battles with the AASF in France and he later recalled: 'It was a responsive aeroplane and it had some agreeable qualities, but not as an operational machine. It simply lacked the guts to travel very quickly. I did once manage to get 300mph out of one, but that was in a dive over a bombing range. Normally, it stooged around at 160mph and any 109s around could leave us standing. It could only carry four 250lb bombs and it was far too slow if there were any fighters in the area.' Wheeldon was fortunate enough to be on leave when the Battle finally came up against the might of the Luftwaffe in May 1940, arriving back in France in time to see the end of the fighting there and to fly his 12 Squadron aircraft back to England.

That winter was to be a testing time for the AASF. Not only did their occasional brushes with the Luftwaffe show just how inadequate the Battle was, they had to endure a miserable time on the ground in bitterly cold conditions with many of the men having to sleep in tents. But that, it transpired, was the frozen calm before the fiery storm which was to descend on the Allied forces on May 10, 1940.

On that first day the AASF sent 32 Battles to help try to stem the German breakthrough in Belgium. Thirteen were shot down and several others so badly damaged they never flew again. Ten of those lost were from 12, 103, 142 and 150 squadrons, those which were later to form the nucleus of 1 Group.

Two days later came an operation that led to the award of the first RAF Victoria Crosses of the war. 12 Squadron was tasked with attempting to destroy

2

two bridges over the Albert Canal, which linked Antwerp and Liege and was a key defence line in Belgium. But it was a line which had already been breached and German armour was pouring over it. Five Battles, manned by volunteer crews, were sent, two to the bridge at Vroenhoven and three more to Veldwezelt. All five were shot down. Leading the attack on Veldwezelt was F/Lt Donald Garland, a 22-year-old Irishman. Despite the intense ground fire from an estimated 300 guns defending the bridge, he led a successful attack only for his aircraft to crash in flames just yards from the target. Just three men survived as prisoners-of-war from this attack and a month later the award of posthumous VCs were announced for Garland and his observer, Sgt Tom Gray. Astonishingly, there was no award for their 20-year-old wireless operator/gunner, LAC Lawrence Reynolds, who died with them in their flaming Fairey Battle, leading many to conclude that elitism still existed in the Royal Air Force. They were not wrong but that, along with many more pre-war shibboleths, were to vanish in the months and years ahead.

The rapid German advance saw the AASF squadrons being forced to move continually from airfield to airfield as the number of serviceable aircraft and available crews dwindled at an alarming rate. In the first 10 days the four squadrons lost 49 aircraft in operations or in bombing attacks on their airstrips, while 44 aircrew died, six were badly injured and 33 became prisoners. And it was far from being over.

The Battles were used in near-suicide missions during the Dunkirk evacuation and then continued to support Allied troops as the Germans pushed south of Paris and into Britanny.

Finally, on June 18, what was left of the Advanced Air Striking Force flew back to Britain with the ground crews being left to do what they could to get out from the few French ports not in German hands. In six weeks of fighting the AASF lost 159 Battles, 87 of them from 12, 103, 142 and 150 Squadrons. Suffering almost as badly were the Blenheims of 2 Group, some flying from England and others from France. In one raid alone on Gemblouz on May 17 82 Squadron, flying from Watton in Norfolk, lost 12 aircraft.

While all this was going on frantic work had been taking place back in England to reorganise the dwindling resources of Bomber Command, including plans to reform 1 Group. The RAF had at its disposal 2 Group operating Blenheims and 3 Group with Wellingtons in East Anglia, 4 Group with its Whitleys in Yorkshire and 5 Group flying Hampdens from Lincolnshire and Nottinghamshire.

In what was to prove a far-reaching decision, the Air Ministry decided to divide Lincolnshire in two, with 5 Group in the south and spilling over into Nottinghamshire and the new 1 Group in the north. The problem was that, at the time, there were only two operational bomber airfields north of Scampton: Hemswell, which was still occupied by 5 Group, and Binbrook, construction

This Battle of 12 Squadron came to grief after a heavy landing at Berry au Bac in France in the spring of 1940. It was later recovered, repaired and was flown briefly from Binbrook by the squadron. It was withdrawn from service in the early autumn and the following year was part of a consignment of Battles shipped to Canada where it was used by the No 8 Bombing and Gunnery School at Lethbridge, Alberta until 1945. (Wickenby Archive)

work on which was just about complete. A huge airfield expansion programme was being hastily drawn up and maps of much of eastern England were being pored over to find where best to put them but, in the meantime, it was a case of making do with what you had.

The four squadrons earmarked as the nucleus of 1 Group had arrived back in England with what Battles had survived the French debâcle just days before and were scattered far and wide awaiting orders. 12 Squadron went first to another 5 Group station, Finningley in South Yorkshire, only a few miles from where 1 Group HQ would later be based. There it remained until July 3 when, re-equipped with 18 Battles, it made the short flight to Binbrook, high on the Lincolnshire Wolds west of Grimsby where it was later joined by 142 Squadron. 103 Squadron's air contingent arrived at Abingdon on July 15, moving a day later to Honington in Suffolk before moving again on July 3 to Newton in Nottinghamshire. It was joined there on the same day by 150 Squadron which arrived via Abingdon and Stradishall in Suffolk.

Ground personnel from 103 and 150 Squadrons had escaped from France through the port of Brest and they were to join the air contingent at Newton, under the command of the popular W/Cmdr T.C. Dickens. Newton, although itself far from finished, was something of a revelation after the primitive conditions the squadrons had endured in France. It was remembered as 'a really comfortable place', with no shortage of fresh produce from local farms, plenty of attractive girls and just 10 miles from the delights of Nottingham.

It was W/Cmdr Dickens who led 103 on its first operation as a 1 Group Squadron, three aircraft leaving to attack targets around Rotterdam on the night of July 16, although one had to turn back with instrument failure. Further attacks followed but 103's first 'loss' was down to an over-enthusiastic member of its ground staff who, tired of waiting for a pilot to move a Battle out of a hangar, decided to do the job himself and ended up colliding with a second machine, both Battles being wrecked beyond repair. What happened to the hapless mechanic is not recorded.

142 Squadron had flown directly to Lincolnshire, landing at Waddington on July 16, before joining 12 Squadron at Binbrook on July 3.

A rare photograph of five of 103 Squadron's air gunners, pictured soon after the squadron converted to Wellingtons at Newton. All five had survived Fairey Battle operations with the squadron in the summer of 1940. (Elsham Wolds Association)

Among the first men to fly into Binbrook was LAC Les Frith, a wireless operator/gunner with 142 Squadron. He had joined the RAF in 1938 and had gone out to France with the AASF and later recalled that there were few of the old faces from the squadron's days at pre-war Bicester when they returned to England. All the wireless operator/air gunners had gone out to France as AC2s, the lowest rank in the Air Force. They had then become AC1s before, finally, becoming Leading Aircraftsmen. Imagine their surprise, therefore, to discover on their return that all trainee wireless operator/air gunners were now sergeants, with more pay and more privileges than those who had been doing the fighting! The returnees had to wait another few weeks for their promotions to go through.

When Frith and his crew arrived at Binbrook they found the place still occupied by civilian workers and it was only then that they learned that many of their ground crews and much of their equipment had been lost with the bombing and sinking of the converted liner *Lancastria* off St Nazaire on June 17 when an estimated 3,000 of the five thousand or more service personnel being evacuated from France were killed in what was Britain's worst maritime disaster. News of the sinking was kept quiet for some considerable time as it was judged the county had enough to digest without this latest disaster.

Their first job at Binbrook was to help prepare the airfield defences, which meant filling sandbags and mounting vintage Vickers K machine guns around the control tower and hangars. The men were all issued with tin helmets and gas masks and, as Les recalled in his memoirs, it felt more like being at the front line than on a Lincolnshire airfield. Much to the amusement of the airmen, two tanks which dated back to the First World War arrived at the airfield and they were hidden away in a nearby copse, emerging only occasionally for airfield defence exercises. Nine Hawker Hector army co-operation biplanes were also briefly stationed at Binbrook, from 613 Squadron which was in the process of converting to Lysanders.

The second operation mounted by 1 Group came on the night of July 21/22 when six Battles of 103 and 150 Squadrons left Newton to attack invasion barges in Dutch ports. The damage caused is not recorded but, given the tiny bomb load a Fairey Battle could carry over such a distance, it wasn't likely to have been much. The fact that the crews were untrained in night operations and were flying aircraft which were manifestly unsuited for such tasks is an indication of the desperate measures then being taken to forestall the threatened invasion.

Les Frith recalled that crews were nervous about flying more than 200 miles across the open sea in their single-engined Battles but the Merlin engines never missed a beat and there was not a single engine failure recorded. Over France they met some fierce anti-aircraft fire and the operations further exposed the Battle's severe limitations as a light bomber. For the crews it was dangerous, cold and uncomfortable but the Binbrook crews did gain some very valuable experience for what was to follow.

Further operations were carried on over the nights to come but the first casualties suffered by 1 Group came purely by accident. On July 27 150 Squadron had been prepared for another night raid when a bomb fell from the underwing mount on one of its aircraft at Newton, starting a fire. As a large group of airmen drawn from 150's ground crews and its HQ staff attempted to fight the blaze the bomb exploded, killing seven of them and badly injuring another four. Among the dead was F/O Walter Blom, who had survived operations in France with the squadron and had just been awarded a Distinguished Flying Cross.

Before the balloon went up: 12 Squadron personnel pictured under canvas in France in 1939. They are identified as Lofty Flay, Charlie Councell, Les Young, Tich Bowden and Jack Wright. (Wickenby Archive)

1 Group didn't have to wait long for its first losses in action. The following night six Battles left Binbrook, four from 142 and two from 12 Squadrons, to attack an airfield near Brussels. Two of the 142 aircraft failed to return. One, flown by P/O Matthew Kirdy, disappeared without trace and his name, along with those of his observer Sgt Norman Longcluse and wireless operator Sgt Bob Hettle, are now recorded on the Runnymede Memorial to those who have no known graves. They were the first men from 1 Group to die in action. The crew of the second Battle survived to become prisoners but two years later the pilot, F/Lt Robert Edwards, was shot while attempting to escape from a camp in Poland and is now buried in the Poznan War Cemetery. 12 Squadron's first loss came two nights later when a Battle returning from an abortive attack on the Channel ports was shot down by RAF Spitfires over The Wash. The bodies of the crew, F/O Brian Moss and Sgts Brian Conway and Tom Radley, were recovered from the sea and are now buried in St Mary's churchyard at Binbrook, the first of many war graves there.

As July slipped into August the threat of invasion grew. Aerial reconnaissance showed increasing number of improvised landing barges being assembled in North Sea and Channel ports and the meagre bomber force at the RAF's disposal directed its energies against these targets,

In mid-August 12 and 142 Squadrons left Binbrook briefly to operate from

Eastchurch in Kent where it shared what was to become one of the front-line Battle of Britain airfields with 266 Squadron's Spitfires. They were to remain there for three weeks during which time both squadrons mounted night attacks on the Channel ports which, by now, were only a short flight away, 142 Squadron losing two Battles in one night at a cost of three lives.

By the second week of September, with the Battle of Britain at its height, they were back at Binbrook where big changes would soon be afoot for both squadrons. The days of the Fairey Battle as a front-line aircraft were drawing to a close, and it couldn't come a moment too soon for those with the unenviable task of flying them.

Over at Newton 103 Squadron lost three of the five aircraft sent out on a night attack on Calais. Two of the crews were later reported to be PoWs while no trace was ever found of Sgt Fred Cooper's aircraft.

On October 1 both 103 and 150 Squadrons were told they were to convert to twin-engined Wellingtons and the following day the first of their new charges arrived. Each squadron was instructed to withdraw two Battles for each Wellington it received and within 10 days the last of the airworthy Battles had left. More men had been drafted in and would fly as second pilots and air-gunners in the six-man Wellington crews.

During the final months of the Battle's operational life two further squadrons joined the strength of 1 Group, 300 (Masovian) and 301 (Pomeranian), the first Polish bomber squadrons to operate within Bomber Command. They were soon joined by two further squadrons, 304 (Silesian) and 305 (Wielkopolska), and all were to serve with distinction, 300 remaining an integral part of 1 Group until the end of the war. 304 and 305 were largely made up of Poles who had joined the French Air Force after escaping from their homeland.

Polish airmen had begun arriving in considerable numbers in Britain in the winter of 1939/40 and they were joined that summer by very many more following the fall of France. Many had amazing stories to tell of escape from either the Germans or the Russians, long treks across Southern Europe and hazardous sea journeys, some initially to France where they served briefly with the French Air Force before escaping a second time to England. They were skilled airmen with a burning desire to fight the Germans and were just what an initially dubious RAF needed. They served with great distinction with Fighter Command and it was a Polish squadron, 303, which was amongst the most successful in the Battle of Britain. But many more were destined for bombers and it is interesting to note that in the pre-war Anglo-Polish treaty, which led Britain into the war in the first place, provision had been made for the creation of two Polish bomber squadrons under the command of the RAF.

Most of the early arrivals spent some time at Eastchurch where they were assessed before moving on either for further training on fighters or bombers.

The graves of the first three casualties from Binbrook, F/O Brian Moss, Sgt Brian Conway and Sgt Tom Radley, shot down in their Fairey Battle by RAF Spitfires on August 1, 1940. Theirs were the first of many wartime graves in St Mary's churchyard at Binbrook. (Author)

The pre-war agreement had envisaged the two Polish squadrons being equipped with Bomber Command's most up-to-date aircraft, the Vickers Wellington, but there simply were not enough to go around and, much to the Poles' dismay, they were told they would initially be equipped with the Battle. The station CO at Eastchurch, G/Capt A.P. Davison, a former military attaché at the British embassy in Warsaw, reported rather disingenuously in a memo: 'The Pole is an individualist and an aircraft like a Wellington, with a crew of six, is really not suited to their temperament.' How wrong he was proved to be, the Polish squadrons operating the Wellington with distinction and one of their number being the last to fly it in Bomber Command.

A formal agreement for the setting up of Polish bomber squadrons was signed in June 1940 with the Polish government-in-exile footing the bill via a loan from the British government. Polish airmen would wear RAF uniforms with a 'Poland' flash on their sleeves and would be subordinate to British station commanders and to King's Regulations. Their aircraft would be in RAF colours but with a red and white chequer on the fuselage and the Polish Air Force flag would fly at their airfields, albeit below the RAF standard.

300 and 301 were formed in July at Bramcote in Nottinghamshire, each with a joint Polish and RAF commanding officer, the latter in an 'advisory' capacity, and with a British adjutant and largely British technical staff.

In August they moved to the still-to-be completed airfield at Swinderby, alongside the Fosse Way, the old Roman road from Lincoln to Newark. Swinderby was one of the second tranche Expansion airfields and was still far from finished when the Poles arrived, which prompted Waclaw Makowski, the first CO of 300, to record: 'No chairs, no beds, no bar and no vodka!' There was such a shortage of everything that many personnel had to be accommodated temporarily at another nearly-finished airfield, Winthorpe, on the outskirts of Newark.

The Poles flew operationally for the first time on the night of September 14/15, sending no fewer than 32 Battles, the entire strength of the two squadrons, to attack invasion barges. Over the next few weeks they took part in several more attacks on the Channel ports, losing just two aircraft, one from 301 which was shot down and a second from 300 which crashed near Nottingham on its return from Calais, killing all three men on board.

304 and 305 Squadrons, in the meantime, were still working up on their Battles when the order came that they were to convert to Wellingtons, which meant their operational debut was to be delayed. Then came the order to move to the new airfield at Syerston, just off the Newark to Nottingham road, not far from Newton where 103 and 150 Squadrons were also in the process of converting to Wellingtons.

A new chapter in the wartime history of 1 Group was about to begin.

Chapter 2

The Leaders

1 Group's Commanding Officers

When the man charged with taking 1 Group to war strode into his office for the first time at the end of June 1940 he found he had little to command. That day 1 Group consisted of the battered remnants of four Fairey Battle squadrons, recently evacuated in great haste and without much of their equipment from France. It had only one airfield it could call its own and that still wasn't finished.

'Bomber' Harris , popularly known amongst his crews as 'Bert' or 'Butch'. (Author's records)

And yet the task facing Air Commodore John Breen was immense. Within weeks there was a very real possibility that German troops would be on British soil and somehow he had to forge together a bomber force to help stop them.

Breen was to be one of four men to lead 1 Group through the Second World War. He was a career airman who had been there on April 1, 1918 when the Royal Air Force came into being although, initially at least, he flew little more than a desk. In the post war years he was Director of Organisation and Staff at the Air Ministry, during which time he was promoted to squadron leader. But more exotic postings called and, after qualifying as a pilot with 24 Squadron at Northolt, he was posted to Iraq where he initially commanded the RAF's Armoured Car Wing, three companies of armoured cars which operated so successfully that they became the template for the formation of the RAF Regiment in the Second World War. Breen went on to command 84 Squadron in Iraq which was operating Wapiti light bombers before returning to England where he was appointed CO of 33 Squadron at Eastchurch. He then joined the Air Staff, serving initially in the Sudan before being appointed Senior Air Staff Officer at 4 Group, then led by Air Vice Marshal Arthur Harris, the man who was to lead Bomber Command for much of the Second World War.

Breen's tenure with 1 Group was to be a short one and he was succeeded at the end of November 1940 by Air Vice Marshal Robert Oxland. He had joined the RFC back in 1915 and had served as a meteorological officer in Iraq

Bawtry Hall, 1 Group's headquarters for much of the war. (Author's records)

in the 1920s followed by spells at Aldergrove in Northern Ireland and at Digby in Lincolnshire before becoming Director of Personnel Services at the Air Ministry in the 1930s. He had built a strong reputation as an organiser and it was this quality which Bomber Command was looking for as it began to rapidly expand.

It was AVM Oxland who oversaw the first major expansion of 1 Group. When he took over in the late autumn of 1940 he had just six squadrons, all of which had or were in the process of re-equipping with twin-engined Wellingtons. He was in charge when Group headquarters moved from Hucknall to Bawtry Hall, just south of Doncaster, in July, 1941 and when he left in February 1943 1 Group was a different beast and was on the verge of becoming the hugely powerful all-Lancaster bomber group which was to play such a vital role in the final 27 months of the war. So highly was Oxland rated that he left to become Senior Air Staff Officer at Bomber Command HQ before, in March 1944, becoming attached to the D-Day planning team in which he played a key role.

His successor at Bawtry was Air Vice Marshal Edward Rice, the man who was to lead 1 Group through the toughest period of the bomber war and by the time he handed over control in February 1945 the squadrons under his command had been forged into one of the most powerful bomber units in the world.

Rice was very much an airman's airman. He had joined the RFC as a pilot in 1915 and had served with distinction in France, first with 55 Squadron and then as a flight commander with 31 and 114 Squadrons before being given command of 97 Squadron in 1917 and 106 Squadron in the following May, by which time he had become a squadron leader in the new Royal Air Force. He ended the war in charge of 108 Squadron and later commanded 6 Squadron in Mesopotamia. Like many fellow officers Rice found himself surplus to requirements in the inter-war years before being brought back to run the RAF's 4 School of Technical Training. In September 1941 he was appointed as head of the RAF in West Africa, spending 18 months there before his appointment as AOC of 1 Group in February 1943. He ended the war commanding 7 (Operational Training) Group which was to include three former 1 Group units.

AVM Rice, a popular leader of 1 Group. (Grimsby Telegraph)

Edward Rice did not come from the same mould as many of the RAF's charismatic leaders but he was a man whose attention to detail and sheer determination to do the best for both the RAF and the men under his command won him widespread respect. It was Rice who was the driving force

Air Commodore 'Hoppy' Wray, the base commander at Binbrook for much of the war, talks to aircrew after a raid. Wray himself often flew with his men, both officially and unofficially. (Author's collection)

13

behind the innovative Rose rear turret which was fitted to 1 Group Lancasters in the later stages of the war, giving the aircraft much greater protection from German night fighters.

Rice was to prove an able and popular leader of 1 Group. He may have lacked the charisma of one or two of his contemporaries, but he was viewed as a man who would do his utmost to ensure the well-being of those who served under him. His popularity amongst air crews reached new heights in the autumn of 1944 when the Air Ministry decided to change the method of assessing the length of operational tours. In 1943 this had been fixed at 30 operations, a figure which relatively few were to live to achieve that year and during the spring of 1944. Things began to change following the Normandy invasion. Many operations were relatively short – support for military operations, attacks on French and Belgian rail targets, raids on flying bomb sites – and this meant tours which once took months to complete could now be over in a matter of weeks. Survival rates shot up but, at the same time, it meant the need for replacement crews increased substantially. The Air Ministry decided these 'soft targets' should actually only account for a third of an operational, meaning that potentially a bomber crew could have to fly on 90 raids before they were stood down.

Hugh Constantine, who was CO at Elsham when the station opened. He had previously commanded 214 Squadron and was a man held in high esteem by all those who served under him. He later became Senior Air Staff Officer at 1 Group HQ before a posting to Bomber Command headquarters. In 1945 he became Air Officer Commanding 5 Group and was to be knighted before his retirement from the RAF in 1964. (Elsham Wolds Association)

Rice was furious. He wrote to Harris that his crews were resentful and that the move could have a 'serious effect on morale'. He said that experienced bomber crews had always been prepared to take the rough with the smooth but this move was simply pushing them too far. 'They see the prospect of having to complete 90 raids during their tour and feel their likelihood of survival is slender,' he said, urging that the plan should be dropped immediately. Harris agreed and cancelled the order with immediate effect. Rice had won an important and life-saving battle for many of his men.

His successor and the final wartime AOC was Air Vice Marshal 'Bobby' Blucke, one of the outstanding men to serve with 1 Group in the war.

Robert Stewart Blucke had joined the Dorset Regiment as a second lieutenant in January 1915 and for a short period in the late spring of 1917 was acting commanding officer. Blucke joined the fledgling RAF in the spring of 1918 and served as an observer with 63 Squadron. The end of the war saw him transferred to the 'unemployed list' before he was recalled for pilot training, serving with 29 Squadron. He spent seven years in India before returning to Britain and a posting to RAE Farnborough where he was able to put to good use his fascination with the new world of electronics. It was Bobby Blucke who flew the Heyford bomber used in the first radar trials in 1935 and by 1940 he was in charge of the RAF's Blind Approach Training and Development Unit, which was to play a key role in the training of bomber pilots. He had a spell as officer commanding the Wireless Investigation Development Unit, helping produce counter measures for the Luftwaffe's Knickebein transmitters, which had been used so effectively for bombing operations over Britain in the early war years.

In 1942 came his first appointment within 1 Group as officer commanding Holme-on-Spalding Moor, one of the handful of airfields in East Yorkshire used by the group as a stop-gap until its new airfields in Lincolnshire were ready. The squadron at Holme was 101, which was in the process of converting to Lancasters, and it was to be the start of a long association between it and Bobby Blucke.

He was no desk-bound airman and flew whenever possible with the squadron, winning a DSO in September 1943 in a raid on Mannheim.

1 Group's final wartime leader Air Vice Marshal Blucke pictured in 1943 during his time as Base Commander at Ludford Magna. (Vic Redfern)

When 101 crossed the Humber to Ludford Magna Blucke went with them as AOC 14 Base, which took in the airfields and squadrons at Ludford, Wickenby and Faldingworth. It was at Ludford that his technical expertise came to the fore, the squadron being chosen as the first electronic counter measures squadron in Bomber Command and the airfield one of the first to be equipped with FIDO, the fog dispersal system which at first terrified many pilots faced with the task of landing between two strips of blazing petrol. Again it was Blucke leading from the front, showing crews just how to do it as he made a series of landings in the station's Airspeed Oxford.

101's role as an ECM squadron meant relentless pressure and led to high casualties but once more Blucke led from the front, flying frequently on operations despite strictures from Bomber Command.

In February 1945 he was 'Bomber' Harris's choice to take over as AOC of 1 Group and was to remain in charge until 1947. He later served as AOC of Transport Command before retiring in 1952 and died in 1988 at the age of 91, the last wartime leader of 1 Group and one of its most distinguished airmen.

Station commanders were sometimes left to pick up the pieces as this dramatic photograph from March 1945 shows. In the foreground is G/Capt Terrence Arbuthnot, the popular CO at Fiskerton, recovering .303 ammunition from the wreckage of a 1668 HCU Lancaster. It was on a cross-country exercise from Bottesford in neighbouring 5 Group when the pilot tried to make an emergency landing at Fiskerton, swung off the runway, crashed and caught fire. Two of the crew were badly injured. (Martin Nichol/David Briggs collection)

Chapter 3

Enter the Wellington

Start of the Onslaught:
Winter 1940–Winter 1941

On October 1, 1940 103 and 150 Squadrons heard the news all air crew at Newton had been waiting for – they were to re-equip with Vickers Wellingtons. On the same day similar orders went out to 300 and 301 Squadrons at Swinderby and to 304 and 305 Squadrons, whose aircrew were still in the midst of their Battle training, to prepare for conversion to Wellingtons.

At Binbrook, however, it was not until mid-November that similar orders came through. Wellington production had still not reached its peak but the object was to have all eight squadrons fully converted and operational for the start of 1941. Six of the squadrons were ready but the appalling winter of 1940 and the unserviceability of Binbrook's grass runways meant the two squadrons there had to wait until the spring of 1941 to make their Wellington debuts.

The Wellington was by no means a new aircraft. It had its origins in an Air Ministry specification of 1932 for a twin-engined heavy bomber capable of carrying 2,000lbs of bombs as far as Berlin. The first Wellington prototype flew in 1936 and it quickly proved itself to be easily the best British bomber of its day. Designed largely by Barnes Wallis, it was of a novel geodetic design, a lightweight grid-pattern covered with a fabric skin, which was both flexible (so much so that many wartime crews swore that no two Wellingtons were exactly the same shape) and strong.

The Mk I version, with which most 1 Group squadrons were first equipped, was good to fly, had an operating ceiling of 18,000ft (better than the early versions of both the four-engined Stirling and Halifax), a range of 1,540 miles and could carry 4,500lb of bombs. It had power-operated turrets, a crew of six and, operationally, was to considerably outlive its Bomber Command contemporaries, the Whitley and Hampden, finally being withdrawn from Bomber Command front line duties with 300 Squadron in the autumn of 1943. The early Mk Is delivered to 1 Group were powered by Bristol Pegasus engines while the later Mk IIs had Rolls-Royce Merlins. The Mk III had up-rated Bristol Hercules engines while the Mk IV was fitted with American-built Pratt

The crew of 12 Squadron's Wellington II PH-H W5419 pictured at Binbrook in the late spring of 1941. They are (left to right) wireless operator Sgt Philip 'Con' Ferebee, rear gunner Sgt Ted 'Jock' Porter, pilot F/Lt Bill Baxter (whose second name was, interestingly 'Bethune') navigator F/Sgt Glyn Mansal, front gunner Sgt Bryan Crocker, bomb aimer Sgt Bob Godfrey. The aircraft and crew with a different bomb aimer, was lost early in July, crashing in the sea after an attack on Bremen. (Wickenby Archive)

and Whitney Wasps, part of the original specification for a batch of Wellingtons due to be delivered to the French Air Force in late 1940.

The 'Wimpey' (a nick-name derived from the Popeye character J. Wellington-Wimpey) was the most numerous of all British wartime bombers, some 11,461 serving with no fewer than 45 different squadrons as well as the majority of Bomber Command's Operational Training Units, in the Middle East and in Coastal Command. Almost 1,400 were lost on operations, over 570 of them with 1 Group.

The first impact the Wellington had on 1 Group squadrons was on personnel, the new aircraft requiring a crew of six compared with the Battle's three. The Wellington carried a pilot, second pilot, navigator, wireless operator/air gunner, front gunner and rear gunner and this meant a big influx of new faces from OTUs. These were the days before the 'crewing-up' system of later years had evolved and it was up to aircraft captains to select their own men. It may have seemed haphazard but it worked well and within days the new crews were airborne as training grew in intensity.

At Newton the first Wellington arrived on October 2, 1940 and subsequent days saw further deliveries of more factory-fresh aircraft. The squadrons were instructed to withdraw two Battles for each new Wellington and by October 10 all the Battles had gone, either flown to maintenance units (many were sent to Canada where they were used in the Empire aircrew training scheme) or awaiting disposal.

It was a similar story with the Polish squadrons but 12 and 142 Squadrons at Binbrook had to wait another month for their first aircraft, with deliveries of new aircraft there continuing into December. Experienced Wellington pilots were posted in to Binbrook to help with the conversion. Among them was Sgt Handley Rogers who arrived from 149 Squadron at Mildenhall and was at the controls of Binbrook's very first Wimpey when it made a 30-minute test flight on November 14. Among the men he gave dual control to in those first few days was 12 Squadron's CO, W/Cmdr Vivian Blackden, along with S/Ldr Lowe and P/O Atkinson.

With both air and ground crews new to the Wellington and the prevailing weather conditions, it was a wonder there were fewer mishaps than there were. Sgt Rogers was flying with P/O Bilton's crew when their 142 Squadron Wellington crashed on take off following an engine failure. Three men, including Sgt Rogers, were injured. Sgt Rex Wheeldon managed to land a 12 Squadron Wellington in a field at Hawerby Hall, a few miles from the airfield, after thick fog descended on the airfield. Repairs, including an engine change – no mean feat in the middle of a Lincolnshire field - had to be carried out the following day before the aircraft was successfully flown back to Binbrook. Six months later this same Wellington was to be destroyed in a ground fire while it was being refuelled. At Newton another Wellington was badly damaged trying to land in fog while both aircraft were wrecked when a 150 Squadron

BH-O of 300 Squadron being 'bombed-up' at Swinderby, 1941. (Peter Green Collection)

Sgts Smith and Jones, pilots of a 103 Squadron Wellington, in the aircraft cockpit. (Elsham Wolds Association)

Wellington landed across the flare path during night training and hit a 103 Squadron machine, which itself had made a heavy landing 25 minutes earlier.

Finally, on December 22, 1940, 1 Group became operational on the Wellington, 103 and 150 Squadrons, each sending three aircraft to attack Ostend. All the aircraft returned safely, with optimistic reports of targets hit and 'extensive fires' left behind. A longer trip to the port of Bremen followed on the night of January 1/2 1941, this time as part of a much larger force of RAF bombers and real damage was done this time with the Focke-Wulf aircraft factory hit. Crews from Newton reported severe cold en route to the target

The damp demise of a 301 Squadron Wellington in a flooded field near Lindholme. (Peter Green Collection)

This 103 Squadron Wellington came to grief at Newton, making a wheels-up landing and ending in the station bomb dump. (Elsham Wolds Association)

and in one aircraft the handle to an auxiliary oil pump broke as the crew tried to pump frozen oil into an engine. Conditions like this were to become familiar to bomber crews over the next few years and were to become one of Bomber Command's greatest enemies. There were no Newton losses on the raid but two Wellingtons from Swinderby, both from 301, were lost, both crashing some hours apart south of Lincoln and initially were reported to have been shot down by German intruders. A search of Luftwaffe night fighter records show the first aircraft, piloted by S/Ldr S. Floryanowicz, was attacked by a Me 110 flown by Lt Rudolf Stradner of 1/NJG2 based at Gilze en Rijen, some 75Km east of Lowestoft, the Wellington finally coming down close to Digby airfield south of Lincoln. The second Wellington was attacked, again by a 110 of 1/NJG piloted by Uffz Helmut Arnold, 50Km east of Haisborough, and crashed near Wellingore, another Lincolnshire fighter airfield. As Digby and Wellingore were active airfields at the time it is likely both pilots were attempting to land their damaged aircraft when they crashed. There was just one survivor from the 12 men on board.

Losses in those first few months were mercifully small. The fledgling Luftwaffe night fighter force was still finding its feet let alone finding bombers in the night skies over Holland and Germany. There were few tactics on either side. Sgt Rex Wheeldon, who flew Wellingtons with 12 Squadron at Binbrook, recalled: 'We would be briefed on the raid we were to carry out, were given our bomb loads, fuel details and time of take off. The rest was up to us. We chose our own routes out, time over target and routes back again.'

A rare air-to-air shot of a 1 Group Wellington. PH-C was to be lost in 1942 while flying with 12 Squadron from Binbrook. (Wickenby Archive)

Navigation was the key to success and in these days was something of a black art. The only navigational aids available at this stage of the war were the sextant, compass, stop watch and slide rule. Later surveys were to find British bombing was wildly inaccurate, anything within five miles of the target being counted as a 'success'. In that first dark, bitterly cold winter finding the right country to attack was hard enough, as was finding your way home again.

A second attack on Bremen (port targets were thought easier to find because of their distinctive coastline) came early in January, by which time winter grade oil had been fitted to the Wellingtons. This time the target was covered by cloud and the bombing was scattered. On the way home some of the aircraft were buffeted by a severe thunderstorm. One of those aircraft, a 103 Squadron Wellington with Sgt W. R. Crich and his crew on board, became lost. The radio packed up, the compass was erratic and the aircraft could not break through the thick clouds to get an astro fix. The navigator, Sgt Les Waern, was sure they were over England but not exactly where. Crich, who had survived a crash landing in a Battle in France in May 1940, spotted a gap in the clouds and once through the crew were surprised to find they were over snow-topped mountains and wondered whether the navigator was wrong and that they were over Switzerland or the French Alps. At that moment the engines cut as the fuel ran out and it took all Crich's skill to land the aircraft in a field. As the aircraft came to a stop the crew jumped out only to find themselves surrounded by an excited crowd speaking a strange language. It transpired they had come down close to Abergavenny in South Wales. The six crew members were back at Newton three days later to find themselves down for ops the same night while their damaged aircraft was dismantled, taken away for repairs and later rejoined the squadron. This wasn't to be the end of the adventures enjoyed by the redoubtable Sgt Crich and his crew.

Meanwhile at Binbrook heavy snow was adding to the miseries of those stationed there. Some local roads were reported to have drifts 12 feet deep and the airfield was officially declared 'unserviceable' for a period of 16 days. When possible Wellingtons and their crews were sent to Tollerton, the pre-war Nottingham city airport where the grass runways were at least usable. It was during this period that 12 Squadron lost its first Wellington, the aircraft stalling soon after takeoff and crashing near Cotgrave, killing the crew of six plus a member of the ground crew, AC1 Jim Boxall, who was just 18 years old. Among the others killed was S/Ldr Philip Lawrence, one of 12 Squadron's senior flight commanders.

Sgts Coglon, Alan Mills and Whiting with a 103 Squadron Wellington. All were later to be shot down, Coglon and Whiting becoming prisoners of war while Sgt Mills escaped from the Vichy French. (Elsham Wolds Association)

Crashes also claimed the lives of men from 150 and 301 Squadrons although when two 300 Squadron Wellingtons crashed during training at Swinderby all on board walked away. Problems were being encountered at Swinderby in operating two full-strength Wellington squadrons and for a short period one of 301's flights moved to the newly-built airfield at Winthorpe. It was to be a temporary occupation: Winthorpe was far from finished and was later to become home to a 5 Group heavy conversion unit (today it is the home of the Newark Air Museum).

In the meantime Sgt Crich and his crew were back on operations at Newton. On the night of February 11 theirs was amongst six aircraft from 103 which took part in a raid involving 222 bombers on Hanover. Crich and his crew were on their way home when an engine failed over Holland. Steadily losing height, he managed to nurse the aircraft some way over the North Sea with the crew throwing out everything possible in an effort to lighten the aircraft. Finally, when it was clear they were not going to reach the coast, Crich ordered them to brace for ditching which he managed successfully. It was clear the aircraft would not stay afloat for long and the dinghy was released but unfortunately it emerged from the Wellington upside down and most of the

Air and ground crew with a 142 Squadron Wellington, Binbrook 1941. (Peter Green Collection)

survival gear was lost. The crew managed to right the dinghy, dragging on board rear gunner 'Jock' Cameron, who couldn't swim and had also suffered a broken collar bone in the ditching. They discovered what remained of the survival gear was just three partly-filled water bottles, a drogue, fluorescent dye and nine dinghy leak stoppers. Thankfully, the wireless operator, Sgt 'Chick' Layfield, had managed to get off an SOS with their approximate position just before the ditching. When daylight finally came all they could see were waves and an overcast sky. They were wet through, bitterly cold but managed to keep their spirits up by going through their repertoire of popular songs, helped by occasionally sips of water.

Later in the day they spotted a pair of Blenheims in the distance and then a Wellington flying a grid pattern, clearly looking for them or at least another crew in their predicament. Imagine their despair when the searching aircraft passed within 1,000ft of the dinghy but, despite their best efforts to attract the attention of the crew, they were not spotted. Another night passed and the six men shivered in the bitter cold and from the effects of sea sickness. On the morning of the second day of their ordeal they tied their scarves together to make a rudimentary sail and used their flying boots as paddles as they headed hopefully in the direction of England. As dusk approached they saw three ships in the distance and, much to their relief, the third, the *SS Tovelli*, spotted them. By this time Sgt Crich and his crew were in such a bad way that they were unable to scramble up the safety net onto the deck of the *Tovelli* and had to be hauled up by rope. They were later landed on the Isle of Sheppey and two of the crew required hospital treatment for the effects of their ordeal.

It was largely the result of their experiences that led to dinghies carried on RAF bombers to be adapted to include canopies to give downed airmen a better chance of survival. Crich and his crew were among the lucky ones. The North Sea was to claim the lives of countless bombers crews over the months and years to come. Another crew which did escape its clutches, however, was that of F/O Butkiewicz of 301 Squadron. His Wellington was on its way to Cologne when it was attacked by a Me110 40 miles off the English coast. The pilot took immediate evasive action while the rear gunner opened fire on the fighter. The Messerschmitt pilot was persistent and attacked again, setting fire to the Wellington. Both gunners managed to drive the 110 away but by this time the Wellington was in serious trouble with several fires blazing along the fuselage. The crew managed to get the fires out and the bombs were jettisoned in the sea but the undercarriage, flaps and emergency systems were out of action. But F/O Butkiewicz and his crew managed to get the badly damaged Wellington back to Swinderby where they made a successful emergency

A Wellington wireless operator in 'the office', 12 Squadron, Binbrook 1941. (Wickenby Archive)

This Wellington of 103 Squadron was shot down on the night of September 20, 1941 during a raid on Berlin. All six men on board were killed. (Elsham Wolds Association)

landing and were later commended for their actions by Air Marshal Sir Richard Peirse.

As the weather improved the pace of operations picked up but by now the main thrust of Bomber Command's attacks was directed at the growing menace posed to Britain's Atlantic life line by Germany's U-boat and surface fleet. Numerous attacks were carried out on U-boat pens and port installations along France's Atlantic coast in the spring of 1941 and 1 Group's Wellingtons found themselves in the thick of it. An attack on the battle cruisers *Scharnhorst* and *Gneisenau* cost 103 Squadron two Wellingtons, both crashing on their return. One hit a tree attempting an emergency landing near Yeovil and the pilot, the squadron's 32-year-old commanding officer, W/Cmdr Charles Littler, was killed. He had taken over the squadron a few months earlier after a staff posting at 1 Group HQ and was later buried in his home city of Liverpool.

Binbrook's Wellingtons finally became operational on the night of April 9-10 when four aircraft took part in an attack on Emden and it was to cost 12 Squadron its CO, W/Cmdr Vivian Blackden's Wellington being shot down by a night fighter over Holland, the aircraft exploding over the Ijselmeer after an engine caught fire. There were no survivors.

The Poles at Syerston also became operational at around the same time, three Wellingtons from 304 Squadron returning safely from an attack on Rotterdam. 305 were not so fortunate when they made their debut a week later, one of their aircraft falling to a night fighter over Emden, although four of the crew survived. These two squadrons were to lose nine more Wellingtons before a summer move to another temporary home, Lindholme in South Yorkshire. It is interesting to note that in an attack on Bremen on the night of May 8-9 each squadron lost an aircraft. The 305 Squadron Wellington was being flown by an RAF pilot while the aircraft lost by 304 Squadron had an all-RAF crew, an indication of how thinly spread were the resources of the Polish element within Bomber Command. Another 305 Squadron aircraft was lost in a tragic accident early in June when, during a training flight, it was hit by an Oxford of 25 FTS near Nottingham, at a cost of seven lives.

Wellingtons of 301 Squadron operated occasionally from Syerston in June and July and one of those operations, to Bremen on the night of July 3-4, an aircraft in which the Polish CO at Swinderby, G/Capt B. Stachon, was flying as second pilot failed to return, the third senior officer lost to 1 Group in a matter of weeks.

By now losses were mounting throughout Bomber Command as the intensity of the night bombing increased and German defences became ever more sophisticated. Hamburg, Brest, Mannheim, Kiel, Hamburg again, Cologne, Brest again, Mannheim once more, Bremen, Hanover, Cologne for a second time .... The targets came and went on the operations boards of squadrons throughout eastern England, and rare was the night when the BBC newsreader was able to announce 'all our aircraft returned safely'.

This was also a period of more changes for 1 Group. Early June saw the opening of Elsham Wolds in North Lincolnshire, the first of the new wartime stations to be allocated to the Group. On July 1 103 moved its Wellingtons

Sgt Kellaway at the controls of a 12 Squadron Wellington during an air test, Binbrook, 1941 (Wickenby Archive)

there, a move which was not at all popular with squadron personnel who liked the comforts of their Newton home, while 150 Squadron went to another brand new airfield, Snaith, just west of Goole in Yorkshire. These were the first of the new wartime-build airfields to be used by 1 Group and, while some work had still to be completed, each had three concrete runways which meant that no longer were operations dependent on the state of the grass strips. It also meant the Wellingtons could carry a bigger bomb load and more fuel, extending their range across Europe. It was to prove a hugely significant step for 1 Group and Bomber Command.

Early in July the four Polish squadrons were on the move, 300 and 301 to Hemswell and 304 and 305 to Lindholme. Hemswell had been in the front line of the bomber war since September 1939 and been used by Hampdens of 5 Group before its transfer to 1 Group. Lindholme, too, had been a 5 Group airfield and had also been used for the formation and training of the Canadian 408 Squadron. However, unlike Elsham and Snaith, both Hemswell and Lindholme still had grass runways which were to restrict their operational use in bad weather.

At Elsham, in the meantime, the early arrivals were in for something of a shock. G/Capt Hugh Constantine had been appointed the first station commander there and when he arrived he discovered that the hastily erected buildings were still without running water and electricity, other buildings and many of the roadways were still unfinished. Constantine, at 33 one of the youngest station commanders in the RAF, didn't stand on ceremony with the contractors and by the time 103 Squadron arrived Elsham was both operational and habitable. Constantine was to become a leading figure in the wartime history of 1 Group, something of an Elsham Wolds legend and left an abiding impression on all those who met him. He played rugby for both the RAF and Leicester and believed in keeping the men in his charge fit, often leading straggling lines of reluctant airmen on tough cross-country runs on non-flying days.

It wasn't just the cross-country running that came as such a shock to the men of 103. Newton had been a comfortable place from which to conduct their war but now they found themselves on a windy Lincolnshire plateau, some miles from the nearest pub and even further from the closest public cinema or dance hall. There was no central heating, their living quarters were rudimentary and everything seemed such a long way away, and that was just on the airfield. But nothing stood in the way of operations and on July 14, just three days after the squadron arrived, six aircraft left to attack Bremen, two later returning with mechanical defects.

The squadron's first operational loss from Elsham came ten days later when six Wellingtons took part in a daring daylight raid on the 26,000-ton pocket battleship *Gneisenau* which had recently arrived in dock at Brest. The attack involved a force of 79 Wellingtons drawn from 1 and 3 Groups and they

Wellington aircrew outside one of the camouflaged buildings at, Binbrook, 1941. (Wickenby Archive)

bombed from 15,000ft from a cloudless sky. Despite attempts to draw off the fighters by two separate groups of Fortresses and Hampdens, the Wellingtons had to face determined opposition from both fighters and flak and 10 Wellingtons failed to return, among them Sgt John Bucknole and his crew from 103. 12 Squadron also lost a Wellington in the raid, Sgt Harold Heald and his crew disappearing without trace off the French coast, one of four aircraft lost from Binbrook in a busy month for the crews of 12 and 142.

One of those flying that day was F/Lt Doug Gosman, a Fairey Battle veteran, and his 142 Squadron crew. His wireless operator Sgt Les Frith later recalled: 'Up to that point in the war I had never seen so much flak and, as we approached across the Cherbourg peninsular, the sky was one mass of thick black smoke. How on earth we were supposed to fly through that goodness only knows.

'Then it came to our turn to go in, flying straight and level with bomb doors down, the most dangerous time of all. Flak was bursting all around and, no sooner had we dropped our bombs, than the leading aircraft, flown by the CO, suddenly rose in the air sharply, having sustained damage under the front of the fuselage.'

A and B Flights with one of 103 Squadron's Wellingtons pose for this picture taken during the winter of 1941. (Holford family rrecords)

The radio in the CO's aircraft was out of action and Sgt Frith had to take on communications for the formation but found he couldn't use his own aircraft's trailing aerial. It was only when they returned to Binbrook that he discovered it had been shot away. Every aircraft that returned to Binbrook that day had been damaged by flak.

That month also saw 304 and 305 Squadrons begin operations from Lindholme. One aircraft failed to return from a raid on Emden at the end of the month and a week later a second aircraft piloted by one of 305's flight commanders, S/Ldr Scibor, came down in Belgium. Three of those on board managed to escape and two of them later made it back to England. There was a poignant moment at Lindholme on the afternoon of August 17 when the carrier pigeon which had accompanied a 305 Squadron crew on an attack of Cologne the night before arrived back at the make-shift pigeon loft on the

airfield. Of the Wellington and its six-man crew there was no trace, although later it was reported that four bodies of the crew had been found in the North Sea. At that stage of the war carrier pigeons were an integral part of a bomber crew's safety equipment and were intended to carry messages back to England when aircraft ditched in the sea. On this occasion there was no message, simply a very fortunate pigeon. The use of carrier pigeons was finally phased out at the end of 1943.

Another Wellington which failed to return to North Lincolnshire during August was QT-A of 142 Squadron, flown by F/Lt Gosman. His aircraft was caught in the beam of a master searchlight over Berlin and badly damaged by flak. Twenty minutes after leaving the target area the port engine began to overheat and had to be shut down. Despite the efforts of the crew to lighten the aircraft, the Wellington began to lose height steadily and finally Gosman gave the order to bail out. All six men escaped by parachute including the navigator F/Lt Durham and the wireless operator, Sgt Frith, both of whom had flown with Gosman in Battles in France, and were to spend the next few years 'in the bag'.

Poles line up their Wellington for a staged photograph at Hemswell in the summer of 1941.
(Grimsby Telegraph)

Two nights later Binbrook lost another Wellington following a raid on Rotterdam. A Luftwaffe Ju88 followed bombers back from the Belgian coast and attacked Sgt Cameron's aircraft over the Humber on its return. Two of the crew, Sgts Alan Wakeford and Ken Harrison, were killed virtually within sight of 12 Squadron's airfield.

At Snaith 150 Squadron lost five Wellingtons within a month of beginning operations from the Yorkshire airfield, including one aircraft which crashed near Edale in the Peak District after turning back with engine problems from an attack on Hamburg. Two of the losses came on a single night during an attack on Hanover. One 150 crew had two fortunate escapes within a short period in September 1941. On the night of the 2-3 Sgt Dickenson's crew left Snaith for at attack on Frankfurt but, less than half an hour later, the starboard propeller fell off their aircraft, Dickenson making an emergency landing at Kenley. Later in the month the same crew were returning from an attack on Berlin when their aircraft hit one of the barrage balloons guarding the Humber Estuary, the cable shearing off a propeller (this time the port one) and the Wellington crash landed on a sandbank not far from Spurn Point.

ENTER THE WELLINGTON

The first Australian bomber squadron to serve with Bomber Command was within 1 Group late in the summer of 1941. 458 (RAAF) Squadron was the first unit to use the new airfield at Holme-on-Spalding Moor, not far from Market Weighton in East Yorkshire. Led by W/Cmdr Norman Mulholland DFC, the squadron was to operate only briefly with 1 Group, sending 10 Wellingtons to Antwerp on the night of October 22-23, one aircraft failing to return. Five of those on board were British and the sixth, the second pilot, Sgt Peter Crittenden, was the first Australian to die flying with an RAAF unit in Bomber Command. 458 lost just three aircraft in a handful of operations before it was transferred to Malta early in February, 1942. During the transfer W/Cmdr Mulholland's aircraft crashed in the sea and his body was later recovered and buried in Sicily. (There appears to be some confusion as to whether 485 Squadron was attached to 1 or 4 Groups during its brief time at Holme-on-Spalding Moor. Some accounts show it part of 4 Group but all Australian ones indicate it definitely served with 1 Group. Additionally, Chris Blanchett, in his definitive 4 Group history, *From Hull, Hell and Halifax*, suggests 458 was never part of 4 Group).

Night fighters were becoming an increasing hazard for the North Lincolnshire Wellingtons, so much so that 1 Group's own Target Towing Flight was formed, initially being based at Goxhill (an airfield built for Bomber Command only for its approach from the north-east to be compromised by the balloon barrage in the Humber protecting the docks at Hull) before moving to Binbrook in November to replace 142 Squadron which moved to the new airfield at Waltham. The TTF initially used single-engined Lysanders to tow drogues but later used a collection of well-used Whitleys and Wellingtons in the towing role.

The TTF was intended to improve the quality of defensive gunnery within 1 Group as the threat from the Luftwaffe's growing night fighter force grew substantially as summer slipped into autumn in 1941. Flak and bad weather were the other main enemies of the Wellington crews and all three were to take their toll over the weeks and months to come. On the night of September 20-21 103 Squadron lost all four of the aircraft it contributed to a small-scale raid on Frankfurt. Shortly after take-off all the aircraft on this raid and a somewhat larger attack on Berlin (for which 103 provided another five aircraft) were recalled because of bad weather conditions but many of the crews did not pick up the message. One of the aircraft from 103 crashed near Holbeach trying to land in fog, another came down in Holland, a third was shot down over Germany and the fourth, low on fuel, was diverted to Linton-on-Ouse in Yorkshire but the pilot, P/O Ken Wallis, made an abortive attempt to land at Binbrook before both engines cut and he ordered the crew to bail out. Wallis himself finally got out when the stricken Wellington was less than 700ft above the ground and, during his brief descent, he was almost hit by his own aircraft as it came down virtually intact in a potato field near Market Rasen. All six crew members were picked up shortly afterwards from a pub in Caistor by 103's new CO, W/Cmdr Ryan. Although Wallis's crew escaped unscathed, that night cost 103 13 lives along with another man seriously injured and four men prisoners of war. The colourful Wallis himself survived the war and went on, among others things, to become a stunt pilot in the early James Bond films.

Another 103 crew had a fortunate escape when an engine on their Wellington caught fire soon after leaving Duisburg. P/O 'Taffy' Jones cut the power and used the graviner switch to extinguish the flames. The propeller continued to windmill until it finally flew off, hitting the fuselage, according to navigator Alan Mills, with a 'terrific clatter'. Losing height gradually, they managed to get across the North Sea, just missing the balloon barrage at Harwich, and headed for the Canadian fighter airfield at Martlesham Heath. Just as the pilot was trying to line the Wellington up for a landing the starboard engine misfired and died and he made a wheels-up landing on the edge of the airfield. The Wellington burst into flames immediately and five of the crew scrambled out but the rear gunner, Sgt Jack Edwards, was trapped. They had come down outside the ring of barbed wire which surrounded the airfield (a legacy of the invasion scare of 1940) and the station fire tender couldn't get to them. However, the aircraft had come down almost on top of an anti-aircraft gun site and the gun crew sergeant grabbed hold of the twin Brownings and gave an almighty tug, managing to pull the entire turret clear of the flames, which were then just three feet away, freeing Sgt Edwards.

At Binbrook 12 Squadron lost two flight commanders in a single night, S/Ldr Peter Edinger, who was killed along with four of his crew, and S/Ldr Fielden, whose entire crew became prisoners. The squadron lost two Wellingtons in an attack on Cologne the following month, one crashing in Holland with four of the crew being killed, while the second aircraft, which had turned back probably because of mechanical problems, crash-landed on the beach at Caister-on-Sea in Norfolk in the dark and tragically hit one of the anti-invasion mines and exploded, killing Sgt Frank Tothill and his crew.

Another tragedy for 12 Squadron occurred nearer home on the night of October 21 when Scotsman Sgt Jim Millar brought his Wellington back from Bremen unscathed only to hit one of the married quarters buildings at Binbrook as he attempted to land with only the rear gunner surviving the crash. A 142 Squadron aircraft failed to return from the same operation and is believed to have crashed in the sea off the Dutch coast.

On November 5 142 was given orders to begin its move to Grimsby, the airfield everyone known simply as 'Waltham'. It was a satellite of Binbrook and its concrete runways had been used by both 12 and 142 over the previous few weeks but now the move was to be permanent. As 142 moved out 12 Squadron stepped up a gear. More aircraft were delivered and more crews arrived and

F/Lt Doug Gosman (standing, extreme right) and his crew and the ground crew of Wellington QT-A of 142 Squadron pictured at Binbrook shortly before they were shot down on a Berlin raid in March 1941. All survived to spend the rest of the war behind wire. Les Frith, who flew Battles with Gosman in France, is pictured second from the left. (Brian Frith)

12 was able to form a third flight and marked the month by topping the 1 Group bombing tables, dropping 55 tons of bombs during 31 sorties. It was just as well for the weather closed in at the end of November and, for the second winter in succession, flying was severely restricted at Binbrook.

An advance party had moved into Waltham from Binbrook to prepare the way for 142's move. Among them was F/Sgt Alf Adams, a pre-war regular, who actually lived in Waltham village. He was a married man and when posted to Binbrook had found a house in Waltham and 'commuted' to Binbrook by bike – 'an hour going and half an hour back downhill!' – and was delighted to find himself in charge of the advance party for the squadron's move to an airfield five minute's walk from his house. He recalled trials being carried out on coating the main runway with wood chippings to help damaged aircraft make safer wheels-up landings. Unfortunately, the runway wasn't long enough but the system was later used at the emergency airfield at Carnaby, near

A Wellington of 12 Squadron being bombed-up at Binbrook, 1941. (Peter Green Collection)

Bridlington. Waltham was also one of two 1 Group airfields (the other was Elsham) where arrester gear was first fitted to help prevent runway overshoots.

1 Group's Polish squadrons were in the thick of the action that autumn and were, like their RAF counterparts, suffering increasing losses. An attack on Mannheim on the night of November 7-8 resulted in three Wellingtons from Hemswell, two from 300 and the third from 301 Squadrons, failing to return although, remarkably, all 18 men on board survived, two evading capture and making it back to England. One of the men taken prisoner, F/O Kolanowski of 301 Squadron, was to be murdered by the Gestapo following the 'Great Escape' in March 1944. By one of those coincidences of war, another of those to be shot in the same incident was P/O Mondschein, the pilot of a 304 Squadron Wellington lost from Lindholme on the same raid. The Mannheim attack also resulted in the loss of a Wellington and their crews from each of 103 and 150 Squadrons.

142's operational debut from its new home at Waltham came on the night of November 30-December 1 when nine Wellingtons took part in a raid on Hamburg involving 181 aircraft from Bomber Command. One turned back after problems were reported with the rear turret and another dropped its bombs on the Luftwaffe coastal airfield at Westerland on the island of Sylt. Two more failed to return, Sgt Alex Gilmour's Wellington going down in the Kiel area while 20-year-old Sgt Ken Barnfield's Wellington is believed to have crashed in the sea. All 12 men on board the two aircraft were killed. On board the missing 103 Wellington was navigator Sgt Alan Mills, who had escaped the crash on the Duisburg raid. He was the regular navigator for S/Ldr Ian Cross's crew but, when he wasn't flying, was the 'spare' navigator. That night he had been due to fly with a new crew but their operation was cancelled and instead went to Mannheim with Sgt Eric Lawson's crew. They were shot down near Nancy and he became something of a rarity at this stage of the war, an evader. He was interred for a while by the Vichy authorities but later managed to escape and made his way home via Gibraltar, arriving back in England 11 months after leaving Elsham. He later served with both Coastal and Transport Commands.

Operations continued as the year drew to a close but, inevitably, were restricted by bad weather which made those airfields without concrete runways unserviceable for short periods. An attack on Ostend on the night of December 16-17 cost each of the Lindholme squadrons a Wellington, one from 304 going down in the North Sea with no survivors while a second from 305 crashed on its return, badly injuring four of those on board. A week later 305 lost another aircraft, the Wellington crashing near Northampton not long after it took off for an attack on Cologne. The six men on board were to be the last from 1 Group to lose their lives in 1941.

The first full year of the bombing war had proved to be a tough one for the eight 1 Group squadrons. 1942 was to prove even tougher.

Chapter 4

Expansion

The Great Airfield Building Programme

When Britain declared war on September 3, 1939 there was just one operational bomber airfield in northern Lincolnshire, the area which was to become the home of 1 Group.

In the early 1930s there was a growing realisation that if a new war was to break out in Europe it would be dominated by the strategic bomber and Britain was singularly lacking in airfields to accommodate such a force, let alone the aircraft with which to prosecute such a conflict. It was this realisation that was the catalyst behind the large-scale Expansion Scheme for airfield construction which got under way in 1935. This scheme called for a chain of airfields stretching up the eastern side of Britain from Suffolk to North Yorkshire which, the argument went, would provide bases for a force capable of striking as far as Berlin. It proved to be astonishingly prescient.

QT-B of 142 Squadron pictured at Waltham in the winter of 1941-42. The aircraft crashed in the North Sea 70 miles east of Bridlington on the night of January 17-18, 1942 as it was returning from Bremen. No trace was ever found of the pilot, F/O Astley Pickett, and his crew. (Peter Green collection)

Another victim of the 1,000-bomber raid on Cologne, PH-C of 12 Squadron was shot down by flak and there were no survivors from F/Lt Tony Payne's crew. (Wickenby Archive)

Conventional thinking has it that Britain sleep-walked into the Second World War and was hugely under-prepared for the events which were to unfold in May 1940 and that is largely correct. But in terms of airfield construction that was not quite the case, although history was to prove that airfield expansion probably started a year later than it should have.

But by 1939 the first and second phases of the Expansion Scheme airfields were already operational and the third phase would be ready for use the following spring and summer.

Those early airfields were (and still are today) something to behold. They were built in the main by master craftsman, working to exacting designs and specifications. They featured enormous brick-built hangars which, given the size of bomber aircraft available at the time and even those envisaged, displayed a remarkable level of forward thinking on behalf of the body responsible.

The Air Ministry Works Directorate oversaw the planning and building of these early 'aerodromes' while the job of finding suitable airfield sites was the responsibility of the Air Ministry Aerodromes Board and the Air Ministry Lands Branch. Then, as now, they had to satisfy stringent conditions before work could begin. A standard architectural style was chosen and their work was monitored closely by the Society for the Preservation of Rural England and the Royal Fine Arts Commission. The new airfields were not only to be

Wellington pilots Sgts Bray and Spooner pictured at Elsham after nursing their badly damaged aircraft home after a serious fire. The remainder of their crew had bailed out but they got the fire under control and made it back to Lincolnshire. Both received DFMs for their efforts but both were later to be killed on operations. One of their crew members was later to be among the airmen shot during the Great Escape (Elsham Wolds Association)

proficient, they were to be pleasing on the eye too. A joiner who worked on the Expansion airfield at Manby in Lincolnshire recalled that when he fitted doors they had to close to the thickness of the cardboard in a cigarette packet. Those who served on some of the wartime-built airfields were lucky if they had a door to close at all, so many being scrounged to feed Nissen hut stoves.

The first stage of the programme saw the building of just one airfield in Lincolnshire (the rebuilt Waddington) and Linton-on-Ouse in Yorkshire, which, given the propensity of wartime airfields in both counties, seems somewhat strange looking back with the hindsight of history.

The second stage, however, did include Hemswell and Scampton in Lincolnshire and Finningley, Lindholme, Driffield, Leconfield and Dishforth in Yorkshire and Newton in Nottinghamshire and they opened from 1937 onwards. The final stage resulted in the building of Binbrook, Coningsby and Swinderby in Lincolnshire, Syerston in Nottinghamshire and Leeming, Middleton St George and Topcliffe in Yorkshire. Syerston and Swinderby were to come into use in 1939 and Binbrook and Coningsby the following year. They were all to be very well built places, designed to the highest standard of the day and providing accommodation for all ranks that was much superior to anything which had gone before or, in most cases, which came after. They had everything, except, that is, hardened runways. This was to be the Achilles heel for Bomber Command in the early days of the war. Grass landing strips had been acceptable for the aircraft of the 1930s, including the twin-engined Wellingtons, Whitleys and Hampdens. But once the rigours of war were imposed, with bombers expected to carry their maximum permitted bomb load and to operate in all weathers, the cracks, or at least the mud, began to appear. One example of this was Binbrook, high on the Lincolnshire Wolds. Its two resident squadrons, 12 and 142, exchanged their Fairey Battles for Wellingtons in the autumn of 1940 but, because of a particularly bad winter and poor drainage (the airfield was built in something resembling a saucer on top of the Lincolnshire Wolds), were not able to operate from their own airfield until the following April.

It wasn't until the next phase of airfield building, the great wartime programme, that hardened runways were included on most new construction projects. A standard three-runway layout in the familiar A-pattern emerged with the main runway extending to 1,400 yards and the subsidiaries to 1,100 yards was included in most new bomber airfields built after 1939 but, with the introduction of four-engined aircraft, these were extended to 2,000 yards and 1,400 yards respectively.

Aircrew of Wellington F-Firkin, 166 Squadron, at Kirmington. (Norman Ellis)

UV-K, a Mk IV Wellington of 460 Squadron, pictured at Breighton in 1942. The photograph was taken on a Kodak Box Brownie camera by pilot Bob Clark, who finished his tour with the squadron on this aircraft. (Author's collection)

The introduction of hardened runways was to lead to the temporary closure of many of the pre-war airfields for runway construction, mainly during 1943.

The wartime airfield building programme was probably the greatest feat of civil engineering ever undertaken in Lincolnshire. When the war began six bomber airfields had either been built or were nearing completion. By the end of 1943 another 25 would have been opened or were almost finished, and this was in addition to airfields for fighters, Coastal Command and training. It was a mammoth undertaking, particularly as Lincolnshire was only a part, albeit an important one, in the chain of wartime airfields stretching from one end of the country to the another.

As far as 1 Group was concerned, it was to occupy 18 of the county's airfields at one time or another together with two in Nottinghamshire and four in Yorkshire, 13 of which were wartime-built aerodromes.

Among the first of these was Grimsby, which, despite its official name, was known by all as Waltham, after the village it bordered. Before the war it had been Grimsby's municipal airport, home to various flying clubs and had been used extensively by the Civil Air Guard, which was to provide large numbers of young men for the RAF at the outbreak of war. By early 1940 the airfield was already being used by the Army and in April it was formally requisitioned from its owners, Grimsby Borough Council, by the Air Ministry for a fee of £1,200 a year, something of a bargain even in those days.

Tenders were immediately let for an airfield with three hardened runways, each 1,000 yards long and 50 yards wide, and associated buildings at an estimated cost of £500,000 and it went to Chapmans of Leicester. The contract stipulated that building priority must go to the runways and for labour Chapmans recruited many of the fish dock workers laid off in Grimsby after much of the port's fishing fleet was taken over by the Admiralty. The runways themselves were to have foundations three feet deep and work got under way immediately. Slag from the steelworks at Scunthorpe was brought in by lorry but, as the year went on, it was clear the work was falling behind schedule. Chapmans' contract was ended and Tarslag of Wolverhampton was brought in. Despite the harsh winter there was no let up in the work. Men worked 12-hour shifts and there was no respite at weekends. By now slag was being brought by train to Grimsby where it was unloaded by hand in sidings before being shovelled into a fleet of trucks and taken to Waltham. In January 1941 the contractors were ordered to extend the runways, one of 1,600 yards and the other two to 1,400 yards in line with the Air Ministry's new airfield specifications.

By the late summer of 1941 Wellington bombers of 142 Squadron at Binbrook began using the runways and dispersals at Waltham before eventually moving in officially in November. When they left a year later the runways were extended once again in time for the arrival of the Lancaster with this time limestone from local quarries being used in the construction.

It had taken some 18 months to build Waltham virtually from scratch. Within two years Lincolnshire airfields were being built far quicker. Ludford Magna, for example, took an optimistically-claimed 10 months to build and it was no ordinary airfield. At almost 430ft above sea level, it was the highest bomber airfield in the country and, because of the topography, the main runway had to be built north to south, instead of the usual south west-north east, a geographical abnormality which was later to cause problems for the pilots of Lancasters attempting landings there. Clearing the site before construction began proved a major task, including the complete demolition of all the buildings at Highfields Farm and taking the top off the village windmill as it lay in line with the main runway. It was a bleak, windswept place at the best of times yet the main contractors, George Wimpey & Co, had the place built in near record time, work starting in June 1942 and being completed by March the following year, although when the ground echelon of its one and only resident squadron arrived they found much work still to do, so much so that the camp cinema was used as sleeping quarters for the first six months of their time there. Ludford was never planned as anything other than a temporary airfield and Wimpey's £803,000 contract included the provision of a perimeter track, seven hangars (Ludford was earmarked as one of Bomber Command's new 'Base' stations), seven domestic sites, two messes, a communal site and sick quarters, sufficient to accommodate a maximum of 1,953 men and 305 women.

Flying control at Wickenby. The R/T operator is Mary Ormerod, (Wickenby Archive)

A month after starting work at Ludford Wimpeys also began construction on the neighbouring airfield at Kelstern which, if anything, was even bleaker than Ludford, lacking the proximity of a village, pub or main road. Kelstern was built on 400 acres of farmland and its construction involved the closure of a section of the Binbrook-South Elkington road, something which happened with some regularity during airfield construction. It, too, was an A-Class airfield, with the regulation 2,000- and two 1,400-yard runways, perimeter track, 36 hardstandings, three hangars and technical and domestic sites, with accommodation for 1,585 men and 346 women. Wimpey's contract for Kelstern was £810,000.

Virtually all the buildings on airfields like Kelstern and Ludford were prefabricated. Hangars were using either T2 or B1 specification (Ludford had both), and the technical and domestic sites were usually housed in Maycrete buildings or the ubiquitous Nissen huts, buildings which became almost synonymous with Lincolnshire during the war and immediate post-war years and many examples of which still survive.

It was estimated that the average three-runway airfield needed around a million cubic yards of excavation, 603,000 square yards of surfacing involving around 242,000 square yards of concrete. Add to that 34 miles of drainage, 10 miles of cable ducts and seven miles of water mains and it is easy to see how the scale of this work dwarfed anything which had gone before in Lincolnshire.

By the middle of 1942 virtually all airfield construction in Britain was in the hands of half a dozen of the country's largest construction companies. Between them they employed 127,000 men, many recruited from Ireland, using the latest machinery imported from the United States. A further 400,000 were employed on other airfield-associated work.

While the rate of building had increased enormously, the quality of the airfields decreased notably. Waltham was a far better built airfield than either Kelstern or Ludford and it showed particularly on the accommodation sites where foundations laid for Nissen huts were often seemed to follow the contours of the land rather than the bubble in a spirit level. But this was of little consequence in the rush to get the airfields built and the bomber squadrons flying and that is what contractors like Wimpeys and the men who worked for them did so spectacularly well.

As we have already seen, 1 Group began life on airfields designed and built in peace time, Newton, Binbrook and then Swinderby. It was to expand into others, Hemswell in Lincolnshire, Syerston in Nottinghamshire and Lindholme in South Yorkshire. It was also to take over Lincolnshire's most famous airfield at Scampton, but that was still a long way away.

The first wartime-build airfield allocated to 1 Group was Elsham Wolds, perched on the edge of the Wolds not far from the Humber. 103 Squadron went there in July 1941, at the height of summer when, according to the squadron historian 'the major drawbacks of the station were not readily apparent'. What was apparent was just how big the place was. There were no dispersals on pre-war stations. Bombers were parked on or around the aprons in front of hangars but at Elsham they were on the new frying pan-shaped concrete dispersals dotted around the perimeter and crews were no longer able to walk out to their aircraft. An internal 'bus service' started at Elsham while ground crew found it advisable to equip themselves with bikes.

One major change, however, was the introduction of concrete runways. Aircraft could now take off in all weathers with maximum bomb and fuel load and that fact alone was to alter altogether the nature of the air war over Europe.

After Elsham came Snaith, near Goole in Yorkshire. This was to be the new home of 150 Squadron, albeit on a temporary basis and was the first of a string of new airfields in Yorkshire to be used by 1 Group until its own Lincolnshire airfields were ready. Snaith, the remains of which today can still be seen from the M62, was later to become a 4 Group station.

Next came Waltham in November 1941, followed by another Yorkshire airfield, Breighton, in January 1942. That May saw the opening of Ingham as a satellite of Hemswell, the odd airfield out in all this. Ingham, which lay actually within the circuit of neighbouring Scampton, was opened with grass runways and was the only bomber station in Lincolnshire which was to remain so. It was from Ingham that the Poles of 300 Squadron were to fly the final operation in the Bomber Command career of the Wellington bomber.

A third Yorkshire airfield was transferred to 1 Group in September 1942. Holme-on-Spalding Moor near Market Weighton and it was to be the home of two 1 Group squadrons for the next nine months before reverting to 4 Group control. In the same month Wickenby opened as the new home of 12 Squadron.

Two further airfields opened before the end of the year, Kirmington and Blyton, the latter becoming one of 1 Group's major training bases.

Ludford and Kelstern both opened in the summer of 1943 and before the year ended the Group's final bomber airfield at North Killingholme was completed, becoming operational in the first few days of 1944. The final new airfield to join 1 Group's inventory was Sandtoft, which opened in February 1944. It was only ever used for heavy conversion training for new crews and later in the year was transferred, along with other HCUs, to the new 7 (Training) Group.

In the autumn of 1944 there was a major reorganisation of airfields in Lincolnshire which saw three 5 Group airfields, Scampton, Dunholme Lodge and Fiskerton, transferred to 1 Group, Dunholme operating only briefly before being closed to flying because of the intense pressure on air space around Lincoln.

Two further airfields worth a mention are Goxhill and Sturgate. Goxhill had been planned as a bomber airfield and, as such, would have been allocated to 1 Group but the proximity of the balloon barrage protecting the port of Hull meant that it was unsuitable for heavy aircraft and it eventually became a fighter training base for the USAAF. In its early days it did, however, house 1 Group's Target Towing Flight before that eventually moved to Binbrook. Sturgate was, perhaps, the state-of-the-art wartime airfield, complete with fog dispersal equipment but, by the time it opened in September 1944 was war had almost passed it by. Its runways were used occasionally by aircraft from 1 Group's Lancaster Finishing School at nearby Hemswell and it did house the 1 Group Aircrew School but it was never to become operational.

Wellington R1588 of 103 Squadron. It crashed into the North Sea in September 1942 while being operated by 22 OTU. (Elsham Wolds Association)

Chapter 5

'Right on the Chin!'

Spring and Summer 1942:
A Change of Tactics and Leadership

Thursday, 1 January 1942 dawned grey and cold across much of Lincolnshire and Yorkshire. It was the start of another year of war and, it has to be said, the spirit of optimism amongst the RAF's bomber squadrons had now been replaced by one of grim determination in the face of mounting losses and a growing realisation that the aerial assault on Germany was not going well. Despite all that 1941 had brought, it was clear that Hitler's industrial strength had been barely affected by the night bombing campaign. Photo reconnaissance of targets showed widely scattered bombing with little of the concentration needed to inflict serious damage. And, as if that wasn't enough, the evidence was there for all to see of the growing strength of the Luftwaffe's defensive capabilities. The result was a scaling back of attacks and the inevitable question: was Bomber Command worth the huge resources in both men and material being invested in it? It is interesting to note that at one stage of the war, a third of Britain's industrial capacity was, in one way or another, devoted to the bombing campaign.

In the autumn of 1940 Luftwaffe Generalmajor Josef Kammhuber had been put in charge of Germany's night fighter defences. It cannot have seemed to have been the most glamorous of jobs but Kammhuber was to prove to be perhaps the most effective of all the Luftwaffe's wartime commanders. He started by reorganising defences, building a chain of searchlights and acoustic detectors across Belgium and Holland, quickly dubbed the 'Kammhuber Line'. And in the Me110C, which had proved so vulnerable to RAF fighters in the Battle of Britain, Kammhuber found the ideal night fighter, sturdy, dependable and capable of packing a punch.

The Dornier 215 and the Luftwaffe's 'maid-of-all-work', the Ju88, were also redeveloped as even more effective night fighters.

German radar development was rapid and by early 1941 he had at his disposal a string of ground control radar sites, each equipped with a single *Freya* radar for detecting bombers and two *Wurzburg* sets for tracking aircraft. Night fighters operated in pre-determined boxes and, whenever a British

A very early picture of a 460 Squadron Wellington at Breighton. The Squadron's codes were later changed from UV to AR. (Keen collection)

bomber entered one of those boxes, ground controllers were able to direct the 110 towards their target. The major flaw with this system is that the controllers could only handle one target at a time but, with Bomber Command aircraft still flying individually, it had worked well throughout 1941. The Luftwaffe had also carried out successful trials with an airborne radar system, the *Lichenstein SN-2*, and towards the end of the year began rolling these out to their night fighter units, now partially re-equipped with superior Ju88s and Dornier 215s.

Just how successful this combination proved to be was demonstrated on the night of January 20-21 1942 when 20 1 and 3 Group Wellingtons and five Hampdens from 5 Group were sent to Emden. Standard practice was still for aircraft to be allotted take off times and crews were then free to plot their own routes to and from the target. The outward bound bombers were quickly picked up by German radar operators and Ju88Cs of 6/NJG2 of Dornier 215s of 11/NJG2, both based at Leeuwarden in Holland, were scrambled to intercept and in the space of just 69 minutes four of the attackers had been shot down, one of the Hampdens from 49 Squadron at Scampton, and three Wellingtons, one from 12 Squadron, another from 142 Squadron and the third from 101 Squadron (later to join 1 Group), then based at Oakington. All three of the Wellingtons fell to the guns of a single Ju88, flown by Oblt Ludwig Becker who was accompanied by his radio operator Fw Josef Straub. All three aircraft came down close to Terschelling in the Frisian Islands, the area covered by Becker's defensive box. Just four RAF crew survived, all from the 12 Squadron Wellington.

But changes were coming. Bomber Command tactics were already under review, a new leader was waiting in the wings and the first of the 'heavies', four-engined Halifaxes and Stirlings, were already in squadron service, although not with 1 Group squadrons which would have to soldier on with their Wellingtons for some considerable time yet.

The chain of events which were to lead to the first of those significant changes, new leadership, began that January when Sir Richard Peirse, was replaced at the head of Bomber Command with AVM Baldwin stepping in as temporary commander until, late in February, Sir Arthur Harris took over. Undoubtedly the most controversial figure in RAF history, Harris was to change the whole nature of the air war against Germany. Single minded to the point of ruthlessness, Harris drove his bomber force relentlessly over the next three years, doling out devastating blows to the enemy while suffering casualty figures surpassed only by German U-boat crews.

Yet the tactic that Harris was to become associated with, area bombing with all that it entailed, was not of his making, although it is clear it was one he took to with some relish. The directive which authorised area attacks itself was issued on February 14, 1942 and replaced the previous directive of the previous November ordering Bomber Command to conserve its forces following the mauling it had taken from German night fighters that autumn.

The directive, which had been drafted by the Deputy Chief of the Air Staff, AVM Norman Bottomley, stated: 'The primary objective of your operations should be focused on the morale of the enemy civil population and in particular the industrial worker.' Primary targets were to include the Ruhr cities of Cologne, Duisburg, Dusseldorf and Essen and Bomber Command was told: 'You are accordingly authorised to employ your forces without restriction.'

The gloves were off and the first major 'area' raid quickly followed on March 8-9 when Essen was the target.

Over the previous few months Bomber Command had spent much of its time attacking naval targets, U-boat pens, dock installations and, in particular, bases for German's large warships. They may have been few in number but their very presence was a major threat to Britain's fragile trans-Atlantic lifeline. For some time two of these warships, the *Scharnhorst* and the *Gneisenau*, together with the cruiser *Prinz Eugen*, had been effectively bottled up on France's Atlantic coast where they were subjective to frequent and heavy attacks by the RAF which had led to over 3,000 tons of bombs being dropped and had cost Bomber Command 127 aircraft.

However, early on the morning of February 12 all three ships left Brest on what was to become one of the Kriegsmarine's most audacious operations of the war. In poor weather conditions the three warships headed into the Channel and it wasn't until they had almost reached Calais that they were spotted by a patrolling Spitfire. The bad weather had led to most of Bomber Command being stood down for the day but, to its great credit, within two hours the RAF's largest daylight operation of the war was under way with some 272 aircraft attempting to stop the warships. Only a few managed to catch a glimpse of the two capital ships known collectively to bomber crews as 'Salmon and Gluck' (the firm of Salmon and Gluck Stein had once supplied copious amounts of tobacco products to the British armed forces), and even fewer managed to attack them. Two aircraft that did were a pair of Wellingtons from 103 Squadron flown by flight commander S/Ldr Ian Cross and his deputy, F/Lt David Holford. They attacked the ships at low level somewhere off the Dutch coast, Holford making it back to Elsham where he reported seeing the second Wellington, with his close friend Ian Cross at the controls, crash into the sea. Holford was later awarded the DSO for his actions while S/Ldr Cross and three other members of his crew survived and were picked up by the Germans. Just over two years later Cross was one of the escapees from Sagan PoW camp in eastern Germany in the breakout which became known as the Great Escape, only to be recaptured and shot by the Gestapo. Three other aircraft had joined in the hunt from Elsham. One, flown by F/Sgt Kitney, did locate the warships but was unable to attack while the others turned back having found nothing.

The 103 Squadron Wellington was the only aircraft lost by 1 Group that afternoon but several others were badly damaged as they attempted to attack the warships at low level and by German fighters. F/Lt Frank Campling (his first name was 'Eric' but he much preferred his second, Frank) of 142 Squadron made it back to Waltham with part of his starboard wing shot away, his turrets out of action and a huge hole in the rear fuselage and he was awarded an immediate DFC for his actions. He had flown part of the way at wave-top height, weaving continually before throwing off two pursuing German fighters. Campling went on to become a flight commander with 460 Squadron at Binbrook, where he won a DSO and a reputation as one of the most careful pilots on the squadron. There he once organised a competition to see who could get the best miles-per-gallon out of a Lancaster. He invariably won (his best figure was 1.1mpg!) but it meant his Lancaster was always last back from operations, which tempered somewhat his popularity with those who flew with him. He was later promoted wing commander and was to die while flying a Lancaster on a training exercise while commanding No. 1 Lancaster Finishing School at Hemswell. He was just 23 years old.

In the meantime, *Scharnhorst*, *Gneisenau* and *Prinz Eugen*, escaped in what became known as 'The Channel Dash', although both the larger vessels were damaged by mines dropped by 5 Group Hampdens. It was something of a humiliation for the British and the RAF in particular as the Germans slipped right beneath their noses. However, the warships now posed no serious threat to the vital Atlantic convoys and it meant Bomber Command was free to focus on striking targets in Germany.

300 Squadron Wellingtons pictured at Hemswell, early 1943. (Peter Green Collection)

Harris had been doing his homework and it was time to put his theories into practice. He believed the way to beat the German defensive system was simply to overwhelm it – instead of bombers going singly through the defensive boxes they would go in waves, in streams that would simply be too great for the defenders to cope with. It was a simple idea and, like many simple ideas, it worked brilliantly, at least until counter measures were introduced.

After another series of raids on Kiel, where the *Scharnhorst* and *Gneisenau* had taken refuge and in which the latter was hit and effectively put out of action, the RAF bombed the Renault factory at Billancourt on the outskirts of Paris in what was perhaps Bomber Command's most successful attack of the war so far. Two hundred and thirty-five bombers, flying in three waves, attacked from low level, the target being lit by flares in a raid that took less than two hours. Just one aircraft was lost and the factory, which was producing trucks for the German army, was out of action for over a month. The 1 Group crews were elated on their return. At Waltham F/Sgt Caldow reported bombing from little more than 1,500ft and seeing his bombs hit a gasometer and factory buildings.

The first wave of the attack at Billancourt had been led by some of Bomber Command's most experienced crews and the flares they dropped help guide the remainder of the force to the target. This was, in fact, the birth of the 'Pathfinders' and marked the start of yet another chapter in the bombing war.

A wonderful photograph of 12 Squadron's PH-C taken at sunset in February 1942. It was shot down over Denmark six hours after this photograph was taken. (Author's collection)

The night of March 8-9 saw the start of a series of concerted raids over three nights on Essen. They were not in themselves successful but saw the wide scale introduction of *Gee*, the first of the great navigational leaps the wartime RAF was to make. It worked by a bomber's navigator picking up pulse signals from at least two of a chain of *Gee* transmitting stations, enabling him to make a far more accurate fix on an aircraft's position. Limited trials had been carried out over the previous few months but the Essen raid marked its introduction on main force raids. The following night Essen was attacked again and among the aircraft shot down was a Wellington flown by S/Ldr John Nicholls of 150 Squadron at Snaith who died along with his crew. 12 Squadron lost a Wellington and five men on the same night while another of 'Shiny Twelve's' aircraft failed to return from the third Essen raid on March 9-10, the aircraft being hit by flak over Holland with the loss of three of those on board.

Early March saw the operational debut of 1 Group's newest squadron, 460 of the Royal Australian Air Force, the second Australian unit in Bomber Command. It had been formed on November 1, 1941 at Molesworth and moved to the new airfield at Breighton, near Selby, Yorkshire in early January where it formally became part of 1 Group. Breighton was barely finished by the time the Australians moved in and was another of the stop-gap airfields to be used by 1 Group until its own bases in Lincolnshire were ready for occupation. 460 would spend almost 18 months there and lost no time in getting down to business. The squadron was led by W/Cmdr A. L. G. Hubbard, one of the most experienced Australians in the RAF, with S/Ldrs Colin Gilbert and A.D. Frank as his flight commanders. They were a formidable team and drove their men hard and, by early March, determined the squadron was ready for operations. They had already lost one Wellington and its crew in a training accident but, with Gilbert and Frank leading, five aircraft from Breighton took part in a small scale raid on Emden on March 12-13. All returned safely although the accuracy of their bombing left much to be desired with later reconnaissance photographs showing the nearest fell five miles from the intended target. That was not unusual in early 1942. 460's first loss came a week later when one aircraft failed to return from an attack on Dunkirk with the loss of the entire crew, which comprised three Englishmen, two Australians and a New Zealander. Although officially an RAAF squadron and paid for by the Australian government, 460 was never to be entirely all-Australian. Their initial losses were heavy and there were some wild celebrations of the sort only the Australians could manage when later in the year two pilot officers, Bill Brill and Arthur Doubleday, became the first to finish tours of operations on the same day having previously served with other squadrons. The celebrations included sending buses to York hospital with instructions to the drivers to bring back as many nurses as possible!

There was little rest for the 1 Group crews. The Poles at Hemswell lost a Wellington and crew in a raid on Kiel while a 305 Squadron Wellington made it back from Cologne on the night of March 13-14 only to overshoot the runway at Lindholme, hit a building and burst into flames. Rescuers could only get to two of the men on board and one of those later died in hospital in Doncaster.

1 Group was back over Essen on the night of March 26-27, two 12 Squadron aircraft falling to the guns of a single night fighter over Holland. One of the aircraft was being flown by the squadron CO, W/Cmdr Albert Golding. In the same raid the Poles at Hemswell lost three aircraft and their crews, night fighters claiming a Wellington each from 300 and 301 Squadrons over Holland while a second 301 aircraft fell to flak. Just one man from the 18 on board survived to become a prisoner, losses the Polish squadrons could ill afford with so few replacements available.

Raids deeper and deeper into Germany brought the Poles at Hemswell and Lindholme closer and closer to their homeland. Aircrew at Hemswell are reported to have shouted for joy when first told they would be attacking Berlin and when the first of a series of attacks on the Hanseatic port of Rostock one crew made a slight diversion to ensure they flew over Polish territory before heading back to Lincolnshire.

It was another of the old Hanseatic League cities which 1 Group visited on the night of March 28-29 in what was so far the most devastating attack of the war so far. It was a crystal clear night, defences were weak and the *Gee-*

equipped aircraft in the first of three waves had no difficulty in locating their aiming point in the heart of the largely wooden city of Lübeck. One hundred and ninety aircraft, carrying a mixture of high explosive and incendiary bombs, hit the city centre and within a short period two-thirds of the city had been either destroyed or badly damaged. The raid was to cost 142 Squadron two aircraft while a third was lost from 305 Squadron at Lindholme. What happened to Lübeck was to lay down a marker for more devastating raids to come.

Continuing Wellington losses were putting an increasing strain on pilot training within Bomber Command. The aircraft had been designed to fly with a crew of six, including a second pilot, thus every loss meant that two pilots had to be replaced. At the end of March came the order from the Air Ministry that henceforth a Wellington crew would be made up of five men and aircraft would fly with a single pilot. It may have eased the strain on training but did little to lift the morale of crews.

In January 1942 a Wellington from 12 Squadron had been the first to carry and drop one of the new 4,000lb blast bombs and these weapons, usually carried in conjunction with containers of incendiary bombs, were causing increasing damage as area bombing began to leave its mark across Germany. The 4,000lb 'cookies', forerunners of even more destructive 8,000lb bombs, blew off roofs and opened the way for the incendiaries to get to work. It was a fearsome tactic, particularly when atmospheric conditions were right, and was to be later perfected over the cities of Hamburg and Dresden.

Essen was hit repeatedly during late spring and on the night of April 6-7 was again to be a target for Bomber Command. Among the squadrons taking part was 142 at Waltham. Alan Westwood drove a refuelling truck and had become friends with a particular pilot, 34-year-old F/Sgt Hayes, and was pleased when his pal completed his 30th operation and was screened from flying. However, his crew still had two more to go so that night volunteered to fly with them. 'The crew pressed him to stick with them until they had finished. I told him he was a bloody fool. He'd done his stint and should stay behind. But he wouldn't have it.' The Wellington never made it back to Waltham. It was hit by either flak or a fighter over Cologne, broke up and crashed on the outskirts of the city. There were no survivors.

The last of eight raids in five weeks on Essen on the night of April 12-13 cost Hemswell two more Wellingtons, one from 300 Squadron being shot down by a night fighter while a 301 Squadron aircraft force landed with battle damage in Norfolk, the crew escaping without injury. Some of the Poles seemed to have charmed lives. During the Rostock raid one aircraft from 301 Squadron had both engines damaged by flak and lost height rapidly. The pilot, F/O Nowacki, managed to regain control and, with no hope of making it back to England, headed across the Baltic before force landing in Sweden. He and his crew were repatriated the following year and were soon flying again. The following night another Hemswell Wellington, this time from 300, was shot down by a night fighter en route to Cologne. All the crew escaped by parachute and four of them managed to evade capture and made it back to England. The second pilot, P/O Wasik, had almost completed a second tour with 300 Squadron when he was shot down again. Once more he managed to escape to England and resumed flying.

In the meantime 300 had a new home, moving a few miles down the arrow-straight Ermine Street to Ingham, Hemswell's small satellite airfield which had been opened two years earlier before being upgraded to take bombers, albeit on grass runways. The squadron was to spend much of the next two years there.

A series of inconclusive attacks on Stuttgart in early May proved expensive for 1 Group. 460 lost its first aircraft and crews over Germany when two aircraft failed to return. One of the six men who died was one of the flight commanders, Colin Gilbert. The same raid cost 150 Squadron three aircraft. One crashed on take off, the crew escaping injury, while a second went down in the North Sea with the loss of all six men on board. The third was flown by Sgt Robert Baxter, a 24-year-old Australian. The port engine of his Wellington was damaged by flak over France but he managed to nurse the aircraft back to England only for the engine to fail when they were not far from home. It was clear the aircraft wouldn't make it back to Snaith and he opted for the nearest

P/O Ron Brooks and his Wellington crew of 142 Squadron at Waltham. Brooks was to win a DFC during a raid on Kassel. (D. Brooks)

airfield, which happened to be Blyton. The airfield was still far from finished but had usable runways so Baxter brought his Wellington in to land. It was still dark and what he couldn't see were the obstructions on the main runway left out by the contractors. The Wellington hit one of these and immediately burst into flames. Baxter and four of the other crew members got out through the pilot's escape hatch but it was only when they were clear of the burning aircraft that they spotted their wireless operator, who had become trapped, trying to get through the lower hatch. By this time ammunition and flares were exploding but Sgt Baxter immediately went back into the Wellington and managed to drag the wireless operator from the lower hatch and got him out of the pilot's escape hatch. He himself just got clear before the fuel tanks exploded, suffering extensive second degree burns to his hands and face.

For his actions Sgt Baxter was awarded the George Medal, the citation reading: 'The unselfish heroism displayed by this airman undoubtedly saved the life of his comrade.' But Robert Baxter did not live to receive his award from the King. On the day the award was announced, August 6, Sgt Baxter was one of a number of 150 Squadron crews selected for a raid on Duisburg. Shortly after his Wellington lifted off from Snaith at twenty-to-one the following morning the aircraft suddenly stalled and crashed into the ground, killing him along with four other members of his crew. He is now buried along side them in Selby cemetery.

As May wore on rumours began circulating airfields across North Lincolnshire and Yorkshire that 'something big' was about to happen. Quite how big no one could even guess.

The idea of sending 1,000 bombers to attack a single target, which would provide something of a propaganda coup for Bomber Command, emerged from discussions in April between Harris and his senior air staff officer and closest confidant AVM Robert Saundby. The main problem was that Bomber Command simply didn't have 1,000 bombers at its disposal but, in his preliminary planning, Saundby reckoned that by using aircraft from Training Command and from Coastal Command, it might be just possible.

The idea had great attraction for Harris. Not only would it be a huge boost to morale in a command which, before his arrival, was facing possibly being disbanded, it would prove once and for all that Bomber Command could play a major role in determining the outcome of the war. Harris believed that a series of 'knock-out blows' could so undermine morale in Germany that they would hasten the end of the war. And this, Operation Millennium, was to be the first of them. To ensure success the raid would have to be accurate and that meant one within range of *Gee*, and the planners suggested the two best options were Hamburg and Cologne. The idea was approved with some enthusiasm by Churchill and it was established that conditions would be ideal over a five-night period beginning on May 27.

There was a major set-back to the plan when Coastal Command refused to release aircraft for the attack, retribution perhaps for Bomber Command's reluctance to place some of its squadrons under Coastal's control for its operations against marauding U-boats. But Saundby was determined to make up the shortfall and squadrons were told to prepare every available aircraft, including clapped out 'hacks' and as many of those undergoing repair as possible, for operational duties. It was a mammoth undertaking but it worked. Bomber Command was able to assemble 678 aircraft (up from an original estimate of 490) while 91 and 92 Training groups provided a further 365 and Flying Training Command chipped in with another four to make a grand total of 1,047, not far short of Saunby's original estimate of 1,081. 1 Group's contribution was to be 156 Wellingtons, the second highest figure in Bomber Command. The operational order for the raid was issued on May 26 but bad weather over Germany meant a postponement until the night of May 30-31. Weather conditions over Germany also determined that Cologne would be the target.

There was frantic activity on airfields throughout the east of England to get aircraft ready. Sid Finn, who was a ground crew member at Elsham Wolds and later became 103's historian, later wrote of the 'common talk in the workshops, hangars and NAAFI' of a raid involving 1,000 aircraft. 'Extra bods were brought in to complete modifications,' he wrote, the modifications including the fitting of *Gee* equipment to the squadron's Wellingtons. 'We were trying to guess the target from the fuel and bomb loads...while some of the ground crews were working 24-hour shifts to get some of the old machines serviceable.' Speculation grew even further when 11 Wellingtons from 22 Operational Training Unit at Wellsbourne Mountford in Warwickshire flew into Elsham to take part in the raid.

It was a similar story at other 1 Group airfields. At Waltham the King's Head public house, which was not far from the station's main gate, was put out of bounds while work went on round the clock to get 22 Wellingtons prepared for the raid. At Binbrook 12 Squadron managed even more, a grand total of 28, the highest of any squadron in Bomber Command, plus three Whitleys of the station's 1481 Bomber and Gunnery Flight. The Poles at Hemswell and Lindholme were joined by crews from 18 OTU at Bramcote, the Poles' own training unit.

At briefings, crews were given detailed instructions of routes, turning points and the need for discipline in the bomber stream and, in particular, over the target itself. A personal message from 'Bomber' Harris was also read out to all crews in which he promised them the opportunity 'to strike a blow at the enemy which will...resound throughout the world.' He urged them to press home their attack with determination and resolution and added: 'Let him have it – right on the chin!' It was a message which went down well as crews realised that a new stage had been reached in the bomber war.

The raid itself was led by *Gee*-equipped Stirlings and Wellingtons of 3 Group with those 1 Group aircraft which had been modified to take *Gee* close behind. The attack itself was split into three waves, all the aircraft being scheduled to 'go through' the target in just 90 minutes. Cologne had been selected as the target primarily because it was expected to be cloud free, thus dramatically lessening the chance of mid-air collisions and none were reported. Of the aircraft which took off, many were to return early because of mechanical defects, more were shot down en route and others were forced back by battle damage. A total of 898 aircraft claimed to have bombed one of three aiming points in the city, although this was later revised down to 868, so the actual figure of 1,000 was not achieved, but that mattered little in the post-raid euphoria. 'A Thousand Bombers!' screamed the headlines the next day, and that was what really mattered. The raid itself was a great success for Bomber Command. The centre of Cologne was badly damaged, mainly by fire with two-thirds of the 1,455 tons of bombs dropped being incendiaries. That more damage on the scale of later raids on Hamburg and Dresden was not inflicted owed more to the modern street layout of Cologne than anything else. Almost 500 people died while thousands more were injured or bombed out of their houses.

For the RAF, too, it was a costly night, 41 aircraft failing to return. 12 Squadron at Binbrook suffered the highest losses in Bomber Command, three of its aircraft falling to flak and night fighters over Holland and Germany while a fourth blew up as it attempted an emergency landing in Norfolk. Two 'fresher' crews of their first operation were killed flying from Waltham while a 150 Squadron crew made it back only for their aircraft to crash near Faldingworth, killing all on board. Elsham lost a single Wellington but four of the 22 OTU aircraft failed to return with only one survivor from the 20 men on board. Several of those who died in those aircraft were highly experienced instructor including five men with DFMs, one with a DFC and a seventh, F/Lt Alwyn Hamman who had a DFC and Bar. There was a further tragedy in store for Elsham the following day. Sgt Les Flowers and his crew had been diverted to the new airfield at nearby Kirmington, which was still under construction, when they returned from Cologne. Later in the day they took off for the five-mile flight back to Elsham only for the port engine to fail, the Wellington crashing close to the airfield perimeter. Sgt Flowers died along with three other members of his crew and was later buried in Brigg cemetery. Although the losses were comparatively heavy they were nowhere near the 100 bombers Churchill thought the RAF could lose and proved that good though the German defences were, they could be overwhelmed.

Many senior officers flew with 1 Group that night. At Elsham the indefatigable station CO Hugh Constantine was at the controls of one of the first Wellingtons to take off. Another station commander taking part was

Some of those who didn't make it back. RAF prisoners at camp L3 during the summer of 1942 or 1943. The chalked notice on the hut tells us it is Officers versus NCOs in the Inter-Command Sports. (Greg Brett)

G/Capt Clayton Boyce at Binbrook (Boyce later became second in command of the Pathfinder force and was promoted to air vice marshal after the war). At Waltham the squadron CO W/Cmdr Don Simmons flew as a second pilot.

Handley Rogers, who had returned to Binbrook following his injuries in January 1941 (see *Enter the Wellington*), remembered the squadron also supplied three Wellingtons manned by scratch crews from OTUs. He was still medically unfit because of his injuries and was aerodrome control pilot that night. He had laid out the flare path on the (still grass) runway, watched as the aircraft left and remained at his post until they returned. One aircraft, a Whitley, was unaccounted for and he had just finished taking in the paraffin-filleds 'goose-neck' flares when he heard that the missing aircraft arrived on reduced power after engine problems which developed shortly after take-off. The pilot, Sgt Mead, had flown all the way to Cologne and back, bombing completely on his own.

The Cologne raid marked the biggest turning point of the bomber war and the all-out assault on Germany's industrial heartland. The bomber stream became the norm and, while the actual scale of that night's attack would not be surpassed until the war was in its final stages, the weight of that assault would expand dramatically as bigger and better aircraft came into the equation, particularly the Lancaster, of which just a handful flew on the night of May 30-31. The Germans, however, were quick learners and they were to adapt their defensive tactics to handle the bomber streams to the extent than losses on the Cologne scale were to be surpassed night after night.

With the 1,000-force still largely intact, a second assault was launched the following night, although this time only 956 aircraft were sent to Essen, a more difficult target in the heartland of the Ruhr and one which proved to be covered in haze. This time the bombing was scattered and little damage was caused, although the attackers lost another 31 aircraft. Among them was a 305 Squadron Wellington from Lindholme flown by the squadron CO W/Cmdr Hirzbandt, a former test pilot who had already won a DFC and been awarded an OBE. His second pilot was F/O Wieliczko who had been awarded the George Medal the previous year for rescuing a trapped tail gunner from a burning Wellington at 18 OTU, a Polish training unit which also took part in the Essen raid, one of its aircraft failing to return to Hemswell. Over at Breighton 460 lost two Wellingtons that night while another aircraft from 142 Squadron was lost when it turned back from the raid only to crash near Waltham, killing five of those on board.

Targets in the Ruhr and German ports were the main targets that month as Bomber Command returned to its 'bread and butter' attacks of around 200 aircraft at a time. But the same tactics were deployed, with the leading aircraft dropping flares to light the way for the main force. The Polish squadrons in 1 Group were to suffer particularly badly during this period. 300 Squadron, now flying from Ingham, lost its first aircraft from its new home in an attack on Bremen, although the crew were picked up by an air sea rescue launch after spending six hours in a dinghy off the Norfolk coast. Not so fortunate was the CO at Lindholme, G/Capt Stanislaw Skarzynski, who flew as second pilot in an attack on the same target at the end of the month. Four of the crew managed to escape and were picked up by the Royal Navy but the body of G/Capt Skarynski, who was 43 and a famous pre-war aviator in his native Poland, was later washed up on the Dutch island of Terschelling, where he was buried. This was to be the last operational loss from Lindholme, 305 moving to Hemswell while the South Yorkshire airfield had new runways laid in readiness for its new training role within 1 Group.

Despite the advent of new tactics casualties were rising amongst the 1 Group bomber crews. 460 at Breighton was amongst the worst affected, losing two aircraft at a time on eight occasions that summer and 23 in total before mid-September. One of those killed was S/Ldr Gilbert's replacement, S/Ldr John Leighton. At Waltham two flights from 142 Squadron were temporarily detached to Thruxton in an unsuccessful experiment to convert Wellingtons for paratroop use. Once they returned losses mounted as attacks on the Ruhr continued. Three aircraft failed to return from a series of attacks on Duisburg and three in a single night over Hamburg. 12 Squadron at Binbrook lost two in the same attack along with two Wellingtons the previous night which failed to make it back from Duisburg. A third turned back early with engine problems and crash-landed at the Coastal Command airfield at North Cotes, south of Cleethorpes. 150 at Snaith fared little better, losing 21 Wellingtons during the summer of 1942, including three in an attack on Bremen and another in a rare daylight raid. This involved just 10 aircraft which attempted to attack Essen at low level, the raid being aborted but not before the 150 Squadron Wellington was shot down by a flak ship off the Dutch coast, only the pilot surviving. Among 150's casualties that summer was one of its flight commanders, S/Ldr Lionel Cohen, whose Wellington crashed near Calais during an attack on Saarbrucken.

One man who was to see things at first hand that summer was Arthur Johnson, who flew as a gunner on P/O Ron Brooks' crew with 142 Squadron at Waltham. He had already served on Wellingtons in the Middle East but, on their return to the UK, the crew was broken up and he was eventually posted to Binbrook and then on to Waltham. He was pleasantly surprised by conditions there but when he entered his new quarters in a small hut just off Cheapside he was shocked to see orderlies clearing out the lockers of its last occupants, a crew missing from the previous night's operations. On their third operation to Frankfurt he saw a Wellington flying astern of their aircraft when there was suddenly a huge flash and he watched as debris rained down. The bomber, probably from 150 Squadron at Snaith, had taken a direct hit in its bomb bay. Arthur Johnson and his crew were to fly 12 operations from Waltham before returning to the Middle East with 142 Squadron later in 1942.

The summer was to see the peak of Wellington operations in 1 Group. A new era was about to begin and it would bring with it the first of the 'heavies', new squadrons and new airfields.

Chapter 6

Enter the Heavies

New Aircraft, New Squadrons, New Airfields:
Autumn – Winter 1942

It was only a week after the 1,000-bomber raid on Cologne that the introduction of four-engined aircraft to 1 Group began but it would be the end of the year before they would begin to make a meaningful contribution.

The change came amidst a re-organisation of 1 Group with new squadrons and several new airfields opening during the autumn as part of the huge expansion of Bomber Command.

In late September 101 Squadron was told to prepare for a move north from its base at Stradishall in Suffolk. It was 'to rearm with the Avro Lancaster' within 1 Group, news that was welcomed by 101 and by 1 Group alike. 101 Squadron had flown Blenheims in 2 Group before moving to Stradishall where

R/T in the control tower, a vital part of every bomber airfield. Pictured is Jessie Clarke, on the station staff at Wickenby. (Wickenby Archive)

F/Sgt Ken Berry with some of his Lancaster crew, Elsham early 1943. This crew had flown Halifaxes with 103 before the squadron re-equipped with Lancasters. He was awarded a DFM and returned to the squadron in 1944 only to be killed almost immediately. (Elsham Wolds Association)

A 460 Squadron Lancaster pictured shortly before the move to Binbrook. (D. Woods)

The way ahead. The entry of the Lancaster was to change the whole bomber war.
(Author's collection)

460 Squadron's G-George pictured with Australian air crew at Binbrook. It first flew operationally from Breighton on December 6, 1942 and went on to complete 90 operations with the squadron. *(Author's collection)*

A 460 Squadron Lancaster on an air test during the squadron's time at Breighton. *(Author's collection)*

Waltham May 1943 and Joe Clark and his crew are pictured with a brand new 100 Squadron Lancaster. *(Author's collection)*

it had operated Wellingtons as part of 3 Group. In its monthly summary, 1 Group announced the switch as 'excellent news' as the squadron had a 'fine record'. Now 101 was about to make a bit of history by becoming the first squadron in 1 Group to operate Lancasters.

Its new home was Holme-on-Spalding Moor in Yorkshire. The airfield had opened the previous year and had been used briefly by the Australians of 458 Squadron before it was transferred to the Middle East. 101 was to remain in Yorkshire until the following summer, at which point the airfield was allocated to 4 Group.

Two days after their arrival 10 of the squadron's Wellington crews were sent to 5 Group's 1654 Heavy Conversion Unit at Wigsley in Nottinghamshire to begin Lancaster training. There they were joined by a complement of flight engineers and mid-upper gunners to make up full Lancaster crews. The squadron received its first two Lancasters at Holme-on-Spalding Moor on October 11, a week before the men returned from Wigsley. 101's Wellington operations ceased at the end of October, by which time the squadron had 14 Lancasters and the remainder of its aircrew about to complete conversion onto the new bomber.

101's move to Yorkshire coincided with the opening 50 miles or so further south of another new airfield, Wickenby, mid-way between Market Rasen and Lincoln, 12 Squadron moving in from Binbrook on October 25. It, too, was

F/Sgt Leslie Naile of the Royal Australian Air Force and his crew pictured with their 100 Squadron Lancaster at Waltham in May 1943. A month later the aircraft was attacked by a night fighter during a raid on Gelsenkirchen and exploded. Only three bodies were ever recovered. The 27-year-old pilot's was not amongst them. (Author's collection)

Cliff Annis and crew at Elsham, 1943. Annis, a Lincolnshire man who ran his own aerial crop spraying business after the war, was later to be shot down, escaping when thrown through the roof of his Lancaster when it exploded. He spent the remainder of the war as a PoW (Elsham Wolds Association)

under orders to begin re-equipping with Lancasters. The following day Binbrook, 1 Group's first airfield in North Lincolnshire, was officially declared unserviceable and closed to flying to allow long-overdue work to begin on runway construction.

A third new airfield opened early in October at Kirmington and its first occupants were to be 150 Squadron which moved its Wellingtons and personnel from Snaith into Lincolnshire for the first time, Snaith immediately being transferred to 4 Group where it became the wartime home of 51 Squadron. The third new airfield to come on line that autumn was Blyton where a new squadron, 199, was formed on November 1942, the squadron taking over the relatively-new Wellington IIIs formerly used by 12 Squadron. Blyton had been used occasionally during the summer by B Flight of 18 (Polish) OTU, which was to continue to operate its Wellingtons from there alongside 199 Squadron until February 1943 when the airfield took on a new role as the home of a heavy conversion unit.

Earlier in the year a decision had been taken at Bomber Command HQ at High Wycombe to convert the all-Wellington 1 Group to heavy aircraft. By this stage of the war the first two of the RAF's triumvirate of four-engined 'heavies', the Stirling and the Halifax, were already in squadron service and the third, the Lancaster, was about to make its debut. The Lancaster was a design which had emerged from Roy Chadwick's drawing board following the enormous problems encountered by 5 Group with the twin-engined Manchester. It proved to be the greatest masterstroke of the bomber war, the Lancaster going on to become the outstanding aircraft of its generation and, eventually, the mainstay of Bomber Command. But much of this was unknown early in 1942 and there were very few Lancasters available anyway. The enormous Stirling had also proved a disappointment with poor performance and a worrying vulnerability. The Halifax, in the meantime, was judged to be better although some of the earlier variants were unforgiving to fly and could be catastrophic in the wrong hands. While the Lancaster was born great, the Halifax was only to achieve its successes later in the war when much-improved variants became available. The Halifax IIs and Vs destined for 1 Group, mainly in a training capacity, did not fall into that category.

103 Squadron at Elsham was first out of the blocks with the Halifax with the formation of the 103 Halifax Conversion Unit on June 7 1942. In charge was S/Ldr David Holford, still only 21 years old but with an impeccable record as a pilot behind him. He had already completed two tours of operations, had a DSO and DFC and Bar to his credit and, it seemed, a glittering career in the

Australian rear gunner Sgt Piper pictured at Elsham 1943 (Elsham Wolds Association)

67

A new 12 Squadron Lancaster at Wickenby draws some admirers. (Wickenby Archive)

RAF ahead of him. He was to go on to become the youngest wing commander in Bomber Command history only to meet his death in tragic circumstances 18 months later.

At Elsham his two instructors were P/O Potts and W/O Reg Fulbrook and they began work as soon as the first Halifax 11s arrived and by late July 103 was declared operational as a Halifax squadron. Their first operation was scheduled for the night of August 1-2 but the day was marked by an awful incident which underlined the problems with the Halifax 11. That morning 19-year-old pilot Sgt William Bagley took off on a short training flight in one of the Conversion Flight's aircraft. He had climbed out of Elsham and was returning when both port engines began misfiring and, as the Halifax approached the airfield, it suddenly stalled and spun into the ground. On board with Sgt Bagley were 11 other aircrew from 103 and all were killed instantly when the Halifax crashed just a matter of yards from the airfield boundary. Two days earlier one of the Halifaxes on the squadron's books had stalled and crashed between Grimsby and Louth, killing Sgt Stewart Stockford and his crew. Sudden stalls were one of the unnerving traits of the Halifax 11 and, no matter how experienced the pilot, they could prove lethal. That is exactly what happened to Reg Fulbrook on September 22, the senior instructor on the Conversion Flight. W/O Fulbrook, at 31 with a DFC to his name and a tour with 103 behind him, was practising three-engined landings when his aircraft suddenly stalled, turned on its back and dived into the ground killing everyone on board.

By comparison, 103's operational debut passed almost without incident. Seven aircraft, led by S/Ldr Holford, went to Düsseldorf and all returned safely, although Holford's aircraft sported 36 holes caused by flak. He had suffered engine problems on the way out and was unable to maintain height. He bombed from 8,000ft and then, on the way home, flew at low level over a Luftwaffe airfield while his gunners shot up a line of parked aircraft. The first operational loss came six days later when Sgt Joe Gilby's Halifax crashed into the Humber on its return from a raid on Duisburg. There were no survivors. 103 was to lose nine more Halifaxes and the lives of 46 men on operations before the order came towards the end of October to switch to Lancasters. Amongst the casualties was S/Ldr Sid Fox, who had won a DFM with 83 Squadron, and was into his second tour.

103 Squadron was to be the only unit in 1 Group to fly the Halifax operationally and it was also among the first to receive Lancasters. No sooner had the squadron been informed of the change than the first batch of factory-fresh Lancasters arrived, four of them being lost on operations within a matter of weeks.

The Australians of 460 got a new CO early in September when W/Cmdr Keith Kaufmann, one of six brothers serving in the Australian armed forces,

Canadian pilot Edgar Jones and his navigator Ted Hooke with some of the damage to their 103 Squadron Lancaster after an eventful trip to Berlin. Jones, then 20, was awarded an immediate DFC for getting the aircraft back to Elsham and was to receive a bar to the medal when he completed a tour with the squadron. He went on to become one of Canada's best-known naturalists, dying in 2011 at the age of 88 (Elsham Wolds Association)

Air and ground crew with 460 Squadron's A-Aussie at Binbrook, 1943 (John Kinghorn)

arrived to oversee Halifax conversion training at Breighton. The Australians lost one aircraft in a training accident at a cost of eight lives, before being told on October 20 that it was to receive Lancasters. (Kaufmann was a hugely popular figure at Breighton, legend having it that he announced his arrival by walking into the mess and announcing: 'I hear you blokes are pretty good drinkers. Let's get stuck in and see how good you are!') The squadron's conversion flight later moved to nearby Holme-on-Spalding Moor where its Halfaxes were replaced by four Lancasters and four Manchesters before returning to Breighton. There it was joined by 103's Conversion Flight and the two units merged to become 1656 Heavy Conversion Unit and moved to Lindholme. The role of the HCU was to do exactly what the term implied, training new crews on four-engined flying. This they would do on an initial mixture of Halifaxes, Manchesters (twin-engined but with some of the characteristics of the Lancaster) and the few Lancasters available. Later, as squadrons demanded every Lancaster coming off the production line, another link in the training chain was forged with the creation of Lancaster Finishing Schools. 1 LFS was formed at Hemswell early in 1944 and was in business for most of the year, providing the final training for crews before they were sent to 1 Group Lancaster squadrons.

1 Group's initial Lancaster conversion courses at Breighton proved far from satisfactory.

One of the young 101 Squadron pilots sent to Breighton was F/Sgt Marcel Fussell who later recorded that priority always appeared to be given to 460's crews. So frustrated was he that he cycled back to Holme-on-Spalding Moor (it was only seven miles away) and reported his frustrations to his CO. The following day one of the new conversion unit's Lancasters and an instructor arrived from Breighton to begin a conversion course for the remaining 101 Squadron men.

1 Group's fourth Lancaster squadron was to be 12. It moved from Binbrook to Wickenby in late September and continued to operate its Wellingtons 111s for another month before conversion work began. It was to spend most of that period on 'gardening' operations, dropping sea mines in enemy coastal waters. Each sector from the Baltic to the Bay of Biscay was named after a flower, hence 'gardening' trips, the mines often referred to as 'seeds'. These were mostly performed by a small number of aircraft, often operating at low level in areas protected by German flak ships. Unlike bombing, there was no spectacular conclusion but, just like bombing, it was highly dangerous work and losses were high and the chances of survival over the sea were minimal. In that month at Wickenby 12 Squadron lost five Wellingtons on mining operations with 17 men being killed and just one aircraft on a bombing operation.

The first Lancaster operation mounted by 1 Group came on the night of November 20 when 101 Squadron sent 12 aircraft as part of a force of 232 bombers which attacked Turin, the largest operation so far against an Italian target. The following night Lancasters from 103 Squadron each dropped four 1,500lb mines off Biarritz. The next night 12 Lancasters from Elsham were part of a force which attacked Stuttgart. Six nights later seven aircraft from 103 Squadron took part in an attack on Turin in northern Italy. All returned safely and the crews expressed delight with their new aircraft, which could now carry a greater bomb load over an increased distance at a greater height than anything that had gone before. While the Elsham Lancasters returned safely, two other 1 Group aircraft, Wellingtons from 142 and 150 Squadrons, did not make it back, one crashing while trying to land at Manston in Kent while the second was abandoned by its crew over France. Italian targets were beyond the range of Lincolnshire- and Yorkshire-based Wellingtons and the aircraft taking part in this attack had needed to 'stage' through airfields in East Anglia and, in 142's case, Kent. Even then many others made it back with little more than fumes in their fuel tanks.

Among the first Lancasters to be lost by 1 Group in 1942 was an aircraft tragically shot down by the anti-aircraft defences over Redcar. It was from 101 Squadron at Holme-on-Spalding Moor and was returning from a mining

A-Aussie of 460 Squadron ready to receive a 4,000lb cookie. (Laurie Wood)

operation. There were no survivors from the seven-man crew. The pilot was Marcel Fussell, the young man who had so shown such determination in ensuring his squadron received adequate conversion training to Lancasters only a few weeks earlier.

That autumn was a particularly tough one for the 1 Group Wellington squadrons. In the three-month period before the Turin raid, 142 lost 26 Wellingtons and the lives 85 men. Five Wellingtons were shot down in a single night in an attack on Kassel, all from 'B' Flight and a third of those that left Waltham, and three more in an attack on Essen. It was to take part in a series of raids on Italian targets, usually operating from Manston, and these were to cost another four aircraft. However, the Wellington lost on its return from Turin was to be 142's last from Waltham. Early in November several crews were posted to the new airfield at Blyton to form the nucleus of a new squadron, 199, and at the same time 142 was put on notice for posting to Egypt. The squadron's final Bomber Command operation came on the night of November 25-26 when five aircraft left to drop mines off Brest. Waltham was now set to join the Lancaster club.

Another squadron on the move that autumn was 150. It moved out of Snaith, which was to become a 4 Group airfield, for Kirmington which officially became a satellite of Elsham in October 1942. 150's stay there was to last a little over six weeks before it, too, was on its way to the Middle East. Kirmington had opened in January that year but had been loaned to 21 Group Flying Training Command and was used by 15 (P) AFU until October when personnel and aircraft were moved to the unit's parent base at Leconfield in East Yorkshire and Kirmington was readied for bomber operations. 150 Squadron was to fly a handful of operations from there in October and November, during which it lost nine aircraft before it finally stood down.

By the end of the year all that remained at Kirmington were the home echelons of 142 and 150 Squadrons and in January 1943 they were merged as the reformed 166 Squadron. 166 had been part of the new Independent Bomber Force formed in 1918, one of the first long-range bomber forces in the RAF. It was disbanded in 1919 but reformed again in 1936 and the outbreak of war saw the squadron operating Whitleys in a training role before being disbanded and its staff and aircraft absorbed into 10 OTU. Now it was back in the bombing business again and was to play a major role in the final two and a half years of the bombing war.

Elsham lost its first Lancaster on operations on the night of December 2-3 when F/O Bob Cumming's aircraft was shot down during an attack on Frankfurt. 1 Group squadrons were to lose seven more before the end of the year. By the conclusion of the war, however, another 1,207 of the group's Lancasters were lost in action or in flying accidents, almost exactly one third of all those lost during the war in Bomber Command service.

A rare picture of a Halifax II of 460 Squadron's Conversion Flight at Breighton in late 1942. (Frank Watson via the Real Aero Club, Breighton)

Chapter 7

Happy Valley

Assault on the Ruhr:
Spring and Summer 1943

The forecast was bleak…and that didn't just apply to the weather as another new year of war dawned. On airfields across North Lincolnshire and into Yorkshire the beginning of 1943 just promised a lot more of the same, heavier and more frequent operations and far more casualties. All those expectations were to be exceeded.

An operational tour for an aircrew involved completing 30 sorties against enemy targets although, at this stage of the war, some only counted as a half-sortie as attacks on some of the Channel ports and French targets were considered somewhat less dangerous than those on more distant operations over Germany. However, the effects of being trapped in a burning bomber over Boulogne were just as fatal as over Berlin and this policy was, fortunately for many, to be changed but, for now, bomber crews had to soldier on.

Aircrew got just six days' leave in every six week period of operations and, for many, it was a case of hanging on until the next spell of leave came up, hoping that their's would not be the next empty dispersal, their lockers being cleared out or their place empty in the mess. Life expectancy on an operational bomber squadron by 1943 had dropped to the level of a subaltern on the Somme in 1916 yet few were the men who cracked beneath the strain. Some, of course, didn't last long at all. F/O Nebojska Kujundzic was one of the few Yugoslav nationals to serve in Britain's armed forces. He was born in Belgrade and was at Leeds University, studying engineering when the war broke out. He joined the university's air squadron and from there graduated to the RAF. After pilot training at Pensacola in Florida he became part of a new Lancaster crew at Lindholme and joined 103 Squadron at Elsham on March 3, 1943. The following morning he and his crew were detailed to complete a standard cross country exercise and left Elsham soon after lunch. At 4pm as the aircraft was flying over Peterborough an engine burst into flames and the aircraft quickly became unstable. He ordered his crew to jump but there was insufficient time for him to escape and he perished when the bomber crashed near Yaxley, a little over 24 hours after he joined the squadron.

Huge national resources were being poured into the bombing campaign with factories working round the clock to produce new aircraft, dozens of new airfields under construction and the seemingly endless supply of new crews being turned out of the training schools in Britain and overseas, the Operational Training Units and Heavy Conversion Units. New navigational aids, target marking and radar were all playing, or about to play, their part yet the enemies remained the same and, it seemed, even more formidable than ever. Luftwaffe defences were learning to cope with the bomber streams with new tactics involving free-roaming single-engined fighters and upward-firing cannon mounted in twin-engined night fighters, better and more sophisticated radar-predicted flak and radar-controlled searchlights were taking their toll on the British bombers. And there was still the oldest enemy of all, the weather, and it was particularly pernicious in January 1943.

The attention of the bombing campaign was now focused very much on Germany and on the Ruhr Valley in particular. Here was the heart of Hitler's war machine and it was on this area that the wrath of Bomber Command would fall. But 'Happy Valley' was the most heavily defended area on earth and the attacks rained on it for much of 1943 were to cost the lives of countless British and Commonwealth lives. At the heart of the Ruhr was the city of Essen where the anti-aircraft defences were so strong that bomber crews claimed it was possible to walk on the flak. It was Essen which claimed 1 Group's first losses

P/O Saunders in the mid-upper turret of 12 Squadron's ED548 V-Victor in March 1943. This aircraft exploded and crashed in the Firth of Fourth in July 1943 killing S/Ldr Robert Baxter and his crew. (Wickenby Archive)

of the year on the night of January 4-5 when both 101 and 460 each lost a Lancaster and with them the lives of 14 men. 12 Squadron at Wickenby was to suffer more than most during the first few weeks of 1943, losing nine Lancasters and 56 men killed in just six weeks. The first of those, with a mixed British, Canadian and Australian crew vanished on a mining operation with a second following soon afterwards over Essen. Then an attack on Berlin on the night of January 17-18 cost the squadron four Lancasters, one crew surviving to become PoWs. During the same raid the radio operator of a 460 Squadron Lancaster was killed when his aircraft was abandoned when out of fuel over Flamborough Head. As he jumped from the aircraft, Sgt Dudley Corfe's radio leads snagged his parachute lines and he fell to his death. Among the 19 Lancasters lost on the raid were three from heavy conversion units, including one from 1656 HCU at Lindholme. The aircraft – which was used frequently on bombing operations during this period – was flown by New Zealander F/Lt Sefton Hood and the crew included five Australians and a British mid-upper gunner. All were killed.

Some squadrons were still soldiering on with Wellingtons, although they were being used less frequently on the more distant German targets. New to 1 Group in January was 166 Squadron which flew its first operation to Lorient on the night of January 29-30. Twelve aircraft left Kirmington but only six reached the target area, three turning back with severe icing problems, one crash-landed with engine problems at Colerne in Wiltshire, another turned back with faulty equipment and the final aircraft, piloted by W/O Bob Grey, failed to return.

The limitations of the Wellington to operate as an all-weather bomber were being exposed in 166 Squadron. Early in February they sent 11 aircraft to Hamburg but only one made it, the others all turning back with severe icing problems. Wellingtons were still in operation with the Polish squadrons at in 1 Group and with 199 Squadron, which moved into Ingham at the beginning of February. 300 Squadron moved back to Hemswell where, shortly afterwards, 301 Squadron was disbanded and its air and ground staff absorbed into 300, 301 losing its last Wellington to a night fighter while on a mining trip to the Frisians on the night of January 9-10. Losses amongst Polish aircrew could not be replaced as readily as those amongst British or Commonwealth squadrons. 300's squadron history records the unit being 'seriously under-manned', a situation which only improved when 301 was disbanded. At Hemswell 300 and 305 operated in tandem until the summer of 1943 before the airfield closed for runway construction and 300 went back to Ingham, 305 being transferred to the new Tactical Air Force. The move back to Ingham was not a popular one amongst 300 crews and personnel. Ingham had widely dispersed accommodation, unlike the excellent pre-war facilities at Hemswell, and aircrew found operating from the bumpy grass runways unpleasant.

Lancaster LM321 pictured soon after it was delivered to 12 Squadron in the spring of 1943. It later served with 460, 550 and 100 Squadrons before being lost over France flying from Waltham as HW-K in June 1944 when three of P/O Skinner's crew were killed. (Wickenby Archive).

One of the 305 Squadron Wellingtons lost from Hemswell ditched in the North Sea after turning back from Wilhelmshaven, the crew managing to get off a distress signal before the aircraft went down. They were picked up several hours later by an air-sea rescue launch but, in the meantime, six volunteer crews from 166 Squadron spent four hours scouring the North Sea for them. They saw nothing, save for some of the new air-sea rescue floats which had recently been moored in the sea, each providing shelter, food and radio equipment for downed bomber crews.

199 Squadron moved from Blyton to briefly join 300 at Ingham and flew operationally until June when it was transferred to 3 Group and converted to Stirlings. In its time at Ingham the squadron was to lose nine aircraft and the lives of 42 men.

While the winter months proved tough going for the Wellington crews, things were not much better for 103 in its new Lancasters. Despite the awful weather that January, the squadron went to Essen no fewer than six times along with two trips each to Düsseldorf and Berlin and a single visit to Hamburg. Four of the Essen raids came in quick succession and on each occasion the weather proved a major hurdle. Oil pipes and gun turrets froze, engines failed to start. On one occasion half the aircraft prepared for an attack failed to take off, on another half the aircraft that left Elsham turned back with problems.

And for those that did make the target area, the defenders were as resolute as ever, four Lancasters being lost from the Essen raids.

Two major advances in bombing technique came that month with the debut of the new Pathfinder Force in the raid on Essen on January 13-14 and the first use of H2S ground-mapping radar at the end of the month when Cologne was attacked. Neither, it must be said, proved an instant hit but were to become vital to the bombing campaign in the months to come. The use of the PFF force of initially Stirlings and Halifaxes meant that 1 Group Lancasters could bomb from a higher altitude than previously, something which was welcomed by crews at Elsham as it gave them another slight edge in avoiding flak and fighters. H2S was also initially fitted to PFF aircraft and it gave navigators the ability to building up a picture of what lay beneath a bomber. It was to be particularly useful against German targets beyond the range of *Gee* and the newer *Oboe* navigational systems although initially the 'picture' it provided lacked much detail, particularly over built-up areas, later versions were much more sophisticated and played a major part in improving the accuracy of bombing. The Germans, however, were quick to pick up on it. On only its second operation, an attack on Cologne early in February, a PFF Stirling crashed in Holland and engineers were able to rebuild the damaged H2S set and later develop the *Naxos* detector, which allowed night-fighters to home in on H2S transmissions. As ever, the sword Bomber Command had been handed was double-edged.

One of three 103 Squadron aircraft lost on operations in February crashed near Milan after being hit by a shower of incendiaries dropped by another Lancaster over the target area. Several of the 4lb bombs hit the area around the cockpit, killing the pilot, 31-year-old S/Ldr Walter Powdrell, who had been a flight commander with 103 since the introduction of the Lancasters. Three of his crew survived. Another experienced officer was lost at the end of the month when a B Flight aircraft on a fighter affiliation exercise over the airfield lost a rudder during a series of violent manoeuvres. The pilot, F/Lt Dick Stubbs, ordered the eight men on board to bail out but, before he could follow them the aircraft went out of control and crashed into the grounds of Elsham Hall. F/Lt Stubbs, who came from Hull, was on his second tour and had already won a DFC with the squadron to go with the DFM he won in 1941. One of those on board had a miraculous escape. He had grabbed a parachute when the order was given but as he jumped, the harness slipped from his shoulder only for his left leg to catch in the webbing. Hanging by his leg, he then fell 6,000ft, landing in a field and suffering only a mild dose of concussion from his spectacular descent.

The beginning of March 1943 saw a new man in charge at 1 Group HQ in Bawtry, with AVM Arthur Rice taking over from AVM Robert Oxland. One of Rice's first jobs was to visit Waltham to meet 1 Group's newest squadron.

These Elsham armourers always took it in turns to chalk one of their children's names on the 4,000lb 'cookies' being prepared for 103 Squadron Lancasters. This was Kath's contribution.
(Norman Storey)

100 Squadron was one of the RAF's oldest bombing squadrons but had suffered terribly at the hands of the Japanese, whose fighter pilots made short work of 100's elderly Vickers Vilderbeest torpedo bombers. The squadron was disbanded and then reformed at Waltham on December 15, 1942 with Lancasters and by the middle of January its first crews had arrived from 1656 HCU at Lindholme and began to take delivery of 18 new Lancaster IIIs, forming two flights of eight with two reserve aircraft. Ground crews had been sent to Elsham and Holme-on-Spalding Moor to work alongside the resident squadrons and gain experience of the new aircraft. Most of the newcomers liked what they found at Waltham, one of the better wartime-build airfields. It had been well built, the accommodation huts were, certainly by 1943 standards, comfortable and there was a pub just outside the main gate along with a bus service to nearby Grimsby and Cleethorpes. Not all the incoming crews were new to Waltham, seven being drawn from men who had served there with 142 Squadron.

100 was quickly into its stride and began an extensive training programme, losing one aircraft in an accident near the airfield on February 15, the pilot, 23-year-old F/Lt Norman Stent and four of his crew, dying in the crash. The squadron made its operational debut on the night of March 4-5 when eight

aircraft left to drop mines in the Bay of Biscay. It proved to be an inauspicious start with F/Lt Richard Curle's Lancaster being shot down over the target area with the loss of all seven on board. A second aircraft then crashed while attempting to land at Langar in Nottinghamshire, killing six of those on board. The remaining six aircraft were all forced to divert because of poor visibility at Waltham. Interestingly, the briefing for this raid was attended by a number of senior 1 Group officers, including G/Capt Hughie Edwards, an Australian who had just been appointed CO at Binbrook. Waltham was still a satellite of Binbrook and would not become a station in its own right until later in the year as part of 12 Base. Edwards had won the Victoria Cross earlier in the war while leading 105 Squadron in a daylight raid on Bremen. By the time he had arrived at Binbrook he also had a DFC and a DSO and was one of a band of truly inspirational officers within Bomber Command. His appointment as CO at Binbrook was a precursor to 460 Squadron's move from Breighton to Lincolnshire during the summer of 1943. Edwards was to remain as station commander at Binbrook until January 1945 by which time he had officially flown another 15 operations, although he is believed to have made almost as many again in an unofficial capacity.

What became known as the Battle of the Ruhr officially began on the night of March 5-6 when the huge Krupps' works, which covered several square miles of the industrial landscape in Essen, was again the target. It would last four months and would herald the start of Harris's all-out offensive on Germany. This is what the expansion of the previous few months had been about: Harris hoped for a series of devastating blows which would destabilise Germany; what happened was a ratcheting up of the war of attrition on a scale which would have been unimaginable only a year earlier.

In the previous four months the striking power of 1 Group alone had increased dramatically. New and bigger squadrons operating from all-weather airfields aided by accurate navigational aids (including *Oboe*-equipped Mosquitos which were now flying on major raids) and far more accurate target marking all played their part. But above all it was the advent of the four-engined bomber, and particularly the Lancaster with its enormous carrying capacity, which was to change the bombing war.

While the Ruhr Valley was to be the primary aim of the campaign, Bomber Command would keep the defenders guessing by varying the nightly target with targets as far afield as Turin, Berlin, St Nazaire and Pilsen visited before the conclusion of this phase of the offensive in July.

It was to prove a hugely costly period for both sides. The accuracy of RAF bombing had improved dramatically, so much so that huge areas of industrial Germany were devastated. But German defences had improved to the extent that the period covered by the Battle of the Ruhr cost Bomber Command 1,000 aircraft. 1 Group alone lost 129 of its new Lancasters and 49 Wellingtons with

F/Lt Bill Wedderburn with his crew and ground-crew. He flew an eventful two tours with 101 Squadron, starting at Holme-on-Spalding Moor. (Vic Redfern)

the loss of 940 men killed in addition to those destined the spend the rest of the war in PoW camps. Of the Wellington squadrons 166 at Kirmington fared by far the worst, losing 25 aircraft and 108 men while the Australians of 460 Squadron lost 31 Lancasters from Breighton and their new base at Binbrook and the lives of 177 men. But, despite losses on this scale (the death toll alone was the equivalent of losing more than six full squadrons) there was no let up. The bombing war was relentless and as soon as an aircraft was lost another arrived to replace it along with another crew fresh from training to fill the gap.

One of the first aircraft to be lost from 1 Group in the Ruhr campaign was a 300 Squadron Wellington from Hemswell, which was shot down in a raid on Essen early in March. Four of the crew survived, the only casualty being the navigator S/Ldr Jankowski, who had been 305 Squadron's first CO when it was formed in 1940. Another Wellington from 199 Squadron survived a series of determined attacks from a Fw190, which was eventually driven off by the rear gunner, Sgt Finlayson, who was later awarded a DFM for his efforts. A second raid on Essen a few nights later cost 1 Group three Lancasters, one each from Waltham, Elsham and Holme-on-Spalding Moor with the lives of all 21 men on board. A Wellington from 199 Squadron was also lost when it crashed near Lincoln on a pre-raid air test. When one 460 Squadron Lancaster arrived back at Breighton with flak damage to the nose the pilot reported that part of the anti-aircraft shell which caused the damage was lodged in the sole of one of his flying boots.

During March 1 Group was to lose aircraft on all but three of the nights it operated with the worst losses coming at the end of the month when three Lancasters, two of them from 460 Squadron, failed to return from an attack on Berlin while two of the 12 aircraft sent from Kirmington as part of all-Wellington raid on Bochum the same night were shot down. With a 101 Squadron Lancaster crashing during an air test, that particular night cost of the lives of 33 young men from 1 Group. But there was far worse to come over the next few weeks.

Attacks on successive nights on Duisburg early in April were made through thick cloud cover over the target area and, despite the claims of many 1 Group Lancaster crews, the bombing was very scattered. Two Wellingtons failed to return to Kirmington, one crashing because of the old problem of icing, while another was lost from 300 Squadron. Of the five Lancasters lost, one from 101 Squadron flown by 23-year-old Canadian W/O John Steele exploded with such force that debris hit the night fighter responsible, killing the pilot. One of two 166 Squadron aircraft lost in one of the attacks suffered an engine failure after leaving the target area and, faced by strong headwinds, the crew realised they had no chance of making it home. The pilot, New Zealander Sgt George Barclay, managed to nurse the aircraft back across France but, almost two hours later, with the aircraft down to 600 feet, he ordered his crew to bail out over North-West France. All got out safely, although Barclay himself suffered a dislocated ankle on landing and was quickly rounded up together with another member of his crew but the other three all managed to get away from the crash site with varying degrees of success. The wireless operator, Sgt Bob Hart, managed to evade capture for four days until walking into a group of German soldiers. The rear gunner, Sgt Ron Limmage, who had only joined the crew as a last-minute replacement, was picked up by the French Resistance underground escape network and made it as far as the Spanish border before being recaptured along with several other British airmen after 37 days on the run. The Canadian navigator, P/O Bernard Marion, was more successful, thanks in no small degree to his fluent French. He was also picked up by the Resistance and travelled via Paris, Toulouse and Perpignan before crossing into Spain and on to Gibraltar. Forty-seven days after leaving Kirmington he arrived back in England. Not so fortunate were the three crews lost from 166 Squadron in an attack on Frankfurt the night after the Duisburg raid, losses which meant that 166's strength had been reduced by a third in just two nights.

A raid on the northern Italian port of La Spezia cost 1 Group four more

Lancasters. One from 101 Squadron crashed near Holme-on-Spalding Moor after turning back early with engine problems, killing all the crew, who were on their first operation. One of the two lost from 103 Squadron ditched in the Channel after being hit by light flak after crossing the French coast and losing most of its remaining fuel. The crew quickly made it into their dinghy and were picked up within minutes. Their aircraft, in the meantime, continued to float and heroic efforts were made to salvage it which only came to an end when one of the small boats trying to tow it into Falmouth struck the Lancaster's tail causing it to sink. The 30 hours it remained afloat was probably the longest recorded for any RAF bomber. Two nights later a 166 Squadron crew had to ditch their Wellington in the Channel when it developed engine problems on its way to Mannheim. The sea was rough and the aircraft struck the water hard and quickly settled. The rear gunner, Sgt Eric Hadingham, got out by swinging his turret and managed to scramble into the dinghy. He then pulled the navigator, F/O Alan Lord, out of the water. Then, in the darkness, they heard the shouts of the American bomb aimer Sgt John Paul Merton and when they paddled over to him found him supporting the unconscious figure of the pilot, F/O Selwyn Lupton. After a tremendous effort they managed to get Merton on board but, by this time, the pilot had died and they let his body go. They searched in vain for the fifth member of the crew, Sgt Bill Whitfield, but decided he must have gone down with the aircraft. Their dinghy then developed a slight leak and the men found that most of the emergency rations and distress flares were missing. With Merton injured and drifting in an out of consciousness, the two men took turns pumping up and bailing out the dinghy while Alan Lord found some Ovaltine tablets and a bar of chocolate in his pocket. They also had a one pint tin of water between them. Those meagre rations had, astonishingly, to sustain them through the next five and a half days. By this time Sgt Merton had succumbed to his injuries and their dinghy had drifted to within a few miles of the English coastline which, agonisingly, they could just see but not reach. Finally they were spotted by an aircraft and a rescue launch picked them up, their epic ordeal later being recounted at some length in *The Sunday Pictorial*.

That same night 1 Group's Lancasters went to Pilsen in an unsuccessful attempt to destroy the Skoda factories with 101 and 103 each losing an aircraft while three from 460 failed to return with the loss of all 22 men on board. 460 was to lose another three four nights later when the Lancasters went on the 1,200-mile return trip to Stettin when, once again, there were no survivors. On the same night 100 Squadron lost two aircraft, including one flown by their CO W/Cmdr James Swain, while two failed to make it back to Wickenby and another to Elsham.

A major minelaying operation around the Elbe estuary on the night of April 28-29 cost 12 Squadron dearly with four of its Lancasters failing to return.

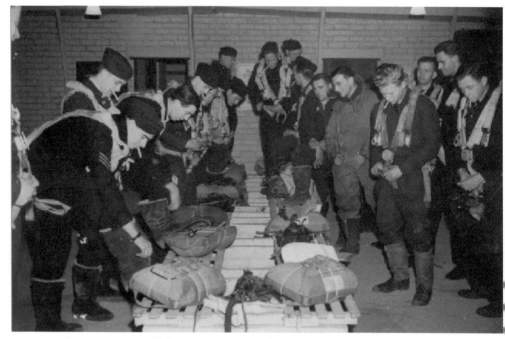

460 Squadron crews at Binbrook prepare for another operation. (Laurie Wood)

One was flown by one of the squadron's flight commanders, S/Ldr Edward Tyler, while another pilot lost was P/O Laurence Head, who had recently been awarded a DFM. But there was much worse to come for 101 Squadron a week later when no fewer than five of its aircraft failed to make it back to Holme-on-Spalding Moor from Dortmund and a sixth crashed on take off. One was shot down by a night fighter over Holland, another disappeared over the North Sea, a third crashed at Scorton airfield, near Richmond. Another aircraft crashed on its return to the airfield while the final aircraft crashed near North Cave, a few miles from the airfield. It had suffered severe flak damage and the 21-year-old pilot, W/O Gerald Hough, and his crew struggled to keep the aircraft flying, only to hit high ground when almost in sight of their airfield, the crash killing the pilot and two of the crew. That same raid claimed two Wellingtons from Kirmington and a Lancaster from 460 Squadron, their last operation from Breighton before they moved to Binbrook. All the aircraft sent by 103 Squadron returned safely that night, including a brand new Lancaster III, ED888, which was in the hands of W/O Nick Ross and crew. Little did they know it but it was to be the first of 140 operations this particular Lancaster would complete, the most by any RAF bomber.

460's move to Binbrook was done in some style, a fleet of Horsa gliders pulled by Albemarle tugs transporting the ground crew on the short hop across the Humber to their new home atop the Lincolnshire Wolds. After the basic facilities of Breighton, Binbrook came as something of a welcome relief to the Aussies. It was by no accident that they found themselves at the best of 1 Group's airfields. In agreeing to fund bomber squadrons to operate within the RAF, the Australian government had made the offer subject to their men getting the best accommodation where possible, hence 460 found itself at Binbrook and 467 in neighbouring 5 Group went to Waddington, perhaps the finest of all Lincolnshire bomber bases. Instead of Nissen huts (which there still were aplenty but mainly for ground crew), the Australian crews were allocated the station's solidly-built married quarters, one house per crew. They loved Binbrook and Binbrook loved them, quickly making themselves at home in the local pubs and striking up a relationship with the locals which was to last for decades to come.

Binbrook itself was now one of the new Base HQs which had been set up within Bomber Command to simplify. Each Base was to be commanded by an air commodore and would include the Base station and up to two satellites. Base stations themselves were also extended to provide additional engineering facilities to handle major work on aircraft and the system was designed to help ease the way for another major expansion of Bomber Command and of 1 Group later in the year.

460 became operational from Binbrook on the night of May 18-19 with an uneventful mining operation carried out by five aircraft. The second operation, against Dortmund on the night of May 23-24, cost 460 two more aircraft. This particular attack was mounted by 826 Bomber Command aircraft and, in terms of bombs dropped, was the heaviest of the war so far. The city was devastated but it cost the Lincolnshire bomber squadrons dearly, 166 losing another three Wellingtons while 300 and 199 each lost one aircraft. One Lancaster from 101 was shot down, another crashed on its return while a 12 Squadron Lancaster was also lost. Two nights later Düsseldorf was attacked and the raid marked the second trip for 100 Squadron's newly-formed C Flight but one of the two aircraft which failed to make it back to Waltham was that flown by flight commander S/Ldr Philip Turgel.

Among the 826 aircraft attacking Dortmund was Lancaster ED995, PH-X of 12 Squadron. It had arrived at Wickenby only a few days before and was allocated to a new crew headed by F/O Jimmy Smith. He and most of his crew were to complete a full tour at Wickenby and, remarkably, every operation they flew was in PH-X, which carried the name 'Sarah' on its fuselage. Their only casualty was their original wireless operator, F/Sgt Tom Routledge, who died after failing to reconnect his oxygen supply properly on their second operation to Düsseldorf. F/O Smith's crew completed their tour in October when they returned safely from Frankfurt. ED995 was then allocated to F/Sgt Ron Collins and crew who were all new arrivals from Lindholme. Three nights after ED995 brought Jimmy Smith's crew safely back to Lincolnshire the Lancaster was shot down near Hamelin and six of those on board were killed.

At Holme-on-Spalding Moor F/Lt Bill Wedderburn's 101 Squadron crew had a lucky escape in a raid on Bochum, their third operation. They were late arriving and decided to take a 'short-cut' over Essen, thus finding themselves the only aircraft over the most heavily defended city in the world. They were coned by searchlights and bracketed by flak bursts but, by diving steeply, they managed to escape and, despite the damage suffered to their aircraft, N-Nuts, bombed the target and limped back to Yorkshire. So badly damaged was their aircraft it was struck off and ten nights later they flew in a new N-Nuts and went on to become the first complete Lancaster crew to finish a tour in 101, flying their final operation to Munich in September.

Bad weather gave the bomber crews and the citizens of the Ruhr some respite in early June but Düsseldorf was the target for another huge raid on the night of June 11-12. It was to be another bad night for the men of 12 Squadron with five Lancasters being shot down and only three men out of the 35 on board surviving. 100 Squadron lost two of the 26 aircraft it sent and another flight commander, S/Ldr Jim Manahan, a Canadian who was serving with the RAF. Another aircraft lost that night was a Wellington from 199 Squadron. Two nights later P/O Bill Sawdy and his crew failed to return to Ingham from a mining trip, the squadron's last casualties in its time with 1 Group. Within a matter of days it had moved out to Lakenheath where it joined 3 Group and converted to Stirlings. It was replaced at Ingham by 305 Squadron, which moved in from Hemswell, which was closing for runway construction.

Another squadron on the move was 101 which flew its final operation from Holme-on-Spalding Moor to Bochum on the night of June 12-13, losing one Lancaster in the process. The expansion of the all-Canadian 6 Group meant a reallocation of airfields in Yorkshire, the remaining 1 Group squadrons all moving south into Lincolnshire. Two days later the squadron's 32 Lancasters (101 was by now a three-flight squadron) were used as flying removal trucks, everything possible being packed in for the trip across the Humber to Ludford Magna. Holme had never been a popular spot for 101's air and ground crews but, if anything, first impressions of Ludford were that it was even worse. Ludford sits at almost the highest point on the Lincolnshire Wolds astride the Market Rasen-Louth road. It was still far from finished and F/Sgt Dick Schofield, who had joined the squadron in May, later recalled that when they arrived no perimeter or runway lights had been installed and initially crews had to rely on flares for taking off and landing with a few glim lights in place at 'dangerous corners' on the perimeter track, which aircraft had to negotiate using their landing lights and by shining Aldis lamps out of the bomb aimer's window. On some occasions the transport section was called upon to illuminate

103 Squadron's flamboyant Belgian pilot, F/Lt Victor Van Rolleghem, received an immediate Distinguished Flying Cross from 1 Group's AOC, AVM Rice, at a ceremony at Elsham. Van Rolleghem was an extraordinary character who completed 70 operations in two spells with 103 Squadron, winning a bar to his DFC and a Distinguished Service Order. On a more prosaic note, the trophy was to go to the station's soccer team, winner of the inter-group tournament.
(Elsham Wolds Association)

runways with the headlights of their vehicles. Accommodation was just as bad in the first few weeks, with some of the ground crew sleeping in tents while the lucky ones bedded down in the building destined to become the camp cinema. What Nissen huts that were ready were found to be infested with earwigs, the only cure being a thick coating of engine oil 'painted' around the hut bases. Ludford was to become notorious for its mud and duckboards abounded. Shortages or not, 101 was quickly back in business and flew to Cologne on June 16-17, losing its first aircraft from Ludford a few nights later over Krefeld. The squadron was to lose two more aircraft in an attack on Gelsenkirchen, six men from one aircraft drowning after bailing out over the Dutch coast only for the wind to blow their parachutes out to sea, and two more early in July in the second of a series of three attacks on Cologne. The flight engineer on one of these aircraft was Sgt Arthur Sharman who, at 39, was one of the oldest members of 101's aircrew. The flight engineer in the second, Sgt Glyn Lloyd, was just 17 and one of the youngest men to be killed on Bomber Command operations.

It was during these Cologne raids that the Luftwaffe introduced new tactics,

460's Squadron K2 – The Nazi Killer, pictured at Binbrook. (Author's collection)

introducing single-engined fighters in what became known as *Wilde Sau* operations, the fighters being given the freedom to operate high above target cities where they hoped to spot bombers illuminated below by target indicators and fires. In the areas they operated flak was limited to 15,000 feet giving them the chance to attack bombers as they crossed the target area.

Five 1 Group aircraft were lost on a raid on Gelsenkirchen on the night of June 25-26, three from 101 and two each from 166 and 103 Squadrons. There was only one survivor from the 101 Squadron aircraft and two from the pair of 166 Squadron Wellingtons lost. Remarkably, eight of the 14 men on the two Lancasters from Elsham were to survive, among them a man who was to find post-war fame as an actor and singer. Cy Grant was born in British Guiana and joined the RAF in 1941, one of 400 men from the West Indies who enlisted during a recruiting drive aimed at filling gaps in the ranks of the air force. He trained as a navigator and joined 103 Squadron as a pilot officer in May, 1943. He was part of F/Lt Alton Langille's crew and they were on their fourth operation when the Lancaster was attacked by a night fighter over Holland.

The rear gunner, Sgt Joe Addison, had shouted a warning but the fighter got in a sustained burst which set one of the engines on fire. F/Lt Langille put the Lancaster into a dive in an attempt to extinguish the fire but the flames spread. By the time they reached the Dutch coast it was clear they were not going to be able to get back across the North Sea in the face of a strong head wind so the pilot turned the aircraft round and ordered his crew to bail out. As they scrambled to get clear the Lancaster blew up, killing Joe Addison and the flight engineer, Sgt Ron Hollywood. Grant landed in a cornfield and spent most of the next day hiding and planning what he hoped would be his escape to Spain. But he realised that, as a 6ft 2ins West Indian, his chances were limited. He was later helped by a Dutch farm worker and his wife only to be turned over to the Germans by a policeman who spotted him near the farm. He was to spend the rest of the war in a series of PoW camps and was once pictured in a German newspaper, the caption sourly describing him as an RAF flier of 'indeterminate race'.

There was drama at Binbrook early in July as 460 prepared to send 26 Lancasters to Cologne. All the aircraft had been fuelled and bombs loaded when a final inspection was made. It was during this that an electrical fault caused the entire bomb load involving a 4,000lb 'cookie', two 500lb bombs and numerous canisters of incendiaries to fall from one of the Lancasters. A working party tried to move the incendiaries away from the aircraft and the blast bomb but by then some of the incendiaries had ignited and set fire to the aircraft. It was far too dangerous to try to salvage the Lancaster and everyone was ordered to clear the area. The station tannoy was used to warn all personnel to take cover and shortly afterwards the 4,000lb bomb exploded, destroying the burning aircraft and another nearby. Ivan Heath, a British rear gunner with the squadron, was checking his turret when he spotted the burning Lancaster which was on an adjoining dispersal. Realising what was about to happen, he ran for his life and had just made it to an old bomb crater on the edge of the airfield when the bombs exploded. Seven other aircraft were damaged and some minor damage was caused to station buildings. Once the area was declared safe every spare hand was brought in to clear debris and the squadron managed to get 17 aircraft away. Before they were due to return a bomb disposal unit arrived from Digby to make safe the two 500lb bombs. One of the 17 aircraft which did manage to take off failed to return, P/O Clifford Edwards and his mixed Australian-British crew disappearing without trace on what was their first operation.

The Ruhr offensive drew to a close in mid-July as Bomber Command switched its attention to other targets and, in particular, to the ancient city of Hamburg.

Chapter 8

Fire and Brimstone
Hamburg and Peenemünde

Shortly after 10pm on the night of Sunday July 25 1943 the first of 27 Lancasters of 103 Squadron took off from Elsham Wolds. They were bound for Germany's second city, Hamburg, a raid which was to prove yet another turning point in the bombing war.

On board those Lancasters, and on the other 764 RAF bombers that would aim for Hamburg that night, were thousands of packages of thin aluminium strips each measuring 30cm x 1.5cm, matching exactly the frequency of the radar sets which controlled German night fighters, anti-aircraft guns and searchlight batteries. 'Window' had arrived.

This top secret device had been developed by scientists a year earlier but its use had been withheld for fears that the Luftwaffe might copy it and use it on bombing raids on Britain. It was a decision which was to cost the RAF perhaps hundreds of aircraft and countless lives for the Hamburg raid that night was to prove that Window worked, and worked dramatically, even though the resourceful Germans would eventually find a way of dealing with it.

Window came in bundles of 2,200 strips and most aircraft carried at least 50, with crews being instructed to push out one bundle every 30 seconds as they approached the target area. Some of the aircraft flying that night had been modified with a special chute fitted near the bomb aimer's position to enable him to push out the bundles as they approached the German coast (this idea had been first developed by 460 Squadron air and ground crews at Binbrook and had been demonstrated to AVM Harris when he visited the airfield that summer). But the vast majority of aircraft had to use their flare chutes, usually situated in mid-fuselage, with usually the bomb aimer designated as the 'pusher-outer' while other crew members lent a hand. As the bundles opened and fell they reflected back radar images to Luftwaffe controllers so that the skies seemed full of British bombers. One estimate had it that the Window dropped that night presented radar images equivalent to an approaching force of 11,000 aircraft. The key *Wurzburg* radar system was immediately rendered impotent, *Lichtenstein* sets fitted to night fighters were filled with impenetrable images, radar-controlled searchlights and radar-predicted flak became virtually impotent. Of the 791 aircraft which flew to Hamburg just 12 were lost.

That attack was to be the first of a series of four, later collectively known as 'The Battle of Hamburg', aimed at destroying Germany's second city. It was an aim which came near to being realised, creating the first great 'fire storm' and killing 40,000 people. The fire storm created during the second raid was not a deliberate act by the British. The number of incendiaries used was no different to any other raid of a similar magnitude, nor was Hamburg particularly vulnerable. Most of its wooden buildings had been destroyed in a fire a century earlier. It was simply a matter of fate, the bombing coming at a time when various meteorological and atmospheric conditions combined for a disaster on a Biblical scale. Not for nothing were the Hamburg raids code named 'Operation Gomorrah'.

The 27 Lancasters provided by 103 Squadron was the highest number from any bomber squadron on any of the raids and they were to suffer the highest casualties, three aircraft – a quarter of all those lost – failed to make it back to Elsham. Lancasters flown by W/O Gordon Hardman and W/O Felix O'Hanlon had the misfortune to be found by night fighters, both crashing in the North Sea while the third, flown by F/Sgt Bob Moore, disappeared without trace. Another Lancaster was lost from 460 Squadron, which provided 26 aircraft, the second highest squadron total, for the raid and was led by the station commander Hughie Edwards, while 166 Squadron lost W/O George Ashplant and his crew, whose aircraft was unlucky enough to be caught by a searchlight over Hamburg and then coned by many more before it was shot down (for the story of George Ashplant see *The Highest Degree of Courage*). Another Wellington from 305 Squadron at Ingham ran out of fuel and crash landed at Trusthorpe on the Lincolnshire coast.

12 Squadron's 'Blitz 'Em Blondie' at Wickenby in the summer of 1943. (Wickenby Archive)

Meticulous planning went into that first raid, as it did into all Bomber Command operations by this stage of the war. Aircraft from 1 and 5 Groups assembled over Mablethorpe before heading out across the North Sea to a point off Heligoland where they joined aircraft from 4 and 6 Groups from Yorkshire and 3 and 8 (Pathfinder) Groups from East Anglia before turning in six waves to cross the Elbe estuary and across Hamburg. Precisely 42 minutes after crossing the German coast the bombers were back out across the North Sea. The bombing was concentrated and had been planned so that the inevitable 'creepback' itself inflicted huge damage.

When the raid was over there were muted celebrations back at bomber bases, although not perhaps at Elsham where three dispersals stood empty. The squadron historian later noted the night was 'a blow' to 103 Squadron.

There was to be no respite for 103, the remainder of Bomber Command nor, for that matter, the Germans. The following night over 700 aircraft bombed Essen. Hamburg had originally been chosen as the target but the city was still covered in some smoke from the previous Bomber Command raid and a daylight attack by the American Eighth Air Force so it was to be Essen's turn yet again. Window was again used to great effect although losses were higher, particularly among Halifax and Stirling squadrons, unable to fly at the altitude reached by the Lancasters. But 103 was to suffer again, losing two more aircraft, while a Wellington from 300 Squadron failed to return to Ingham and a 460 Squadron Lancaster, which had been hit by incendiaries over the target area, was wrecked on its return to Binbrook.

The following night came the raid for which the name 'Hamburg' will ever be associated with. It was a hot, dry night in the city, fires were still burning from the previous attacks, water supplies were low and many roads were blocked by rubble, hampering fire fighters. As the raid progressed the concentrated bombing led to a series of major fires which then joined together, sucking in oxygen and creating storm force winds which, in turn, increased the intensity of the conflagration. The firestorm was to last for some three hours during which time an estimated 40,000 people in the city died, many through carbon monoxide poisoning as the air was sucked from their shelters.

Bomber crews from Lincolnshire could see the flames over 100 miles from the target. One bomb aimer from Binbrook reported seeing a 'sea of flames' so bright that he could read his maps by their light. Aiming points had vanished and aircraft simply bombed the burning area, adding to the devastation below. F/Lt Wedderburn of 101 Squadron noted with some pleasure that Hamburg's defences were 'feeble in the extreme' thanks to Window.

Other returning aircrew spoke of the area looking like 'an active volcano', of columns of smoke reaching to over 20,000ft. It was a sight those who flew over Hamburg would never forget and many were the RAF airmen who felt pity for those on the ground. The raid itself cost 1 Group three Lancasters,

This was what did the damage. A Binbrook Lancaster's bomb load of high explosive and incendiaries, packed into canisters. (Peter Green Collection)

one each from 12, 100 and 101 Squadrons with just one man surviving.

Bomber Harris had promised to destroy Hamburg and he was a man of his word. The following night the city was bombed yet again, with over 700 aircraft targeting the few areas so far relatively undamaged. Again 1 Group lost three aircraft, two Lancasters from Binbrook and a 166 Squadron Wellington flown by F/O Eric Birbeck, who was on his fourth operation. His bomb aimer was F/Lt Jim Brind, the squadron's bombing leader. The pilot of one of the Binbrook Lancasters was P/O Herbert Fuhrmann who, along with his navigator P/O Charles Anderson, had won a DFM and a DFC respectively during a raid on Stettin earlier in the year. Their aircraft was lost over the North Sea and the entire crew is remembered on the Runnymede Memorial.

The fourth and final attack turned out to be a disaster for the attackers. And the enemy was an old one – the weather. Met officers had noted a large thunderstorm with clouds reaching up to 30,000 feet around Oldenburg, not far from the track the bombers would be taking but far enough for Harris to gamble on the raid going ahead. He got it wrong. Some were recalled while many crews were forced to turn back or to bomb other targets, at least four aircraft crashed because of severe icing or turbulence. It was to prove a terrifying experience for those who flew through it and one man flying with 460 Squadron that night was later to tell the author: 'It was as though God had decided we had done enough to Hamburg'.

Another man who flew that night was Sgt Cec Bryant, the rear gunner in a 166 Squadron Wellington. It was his crew's fourth trip to the city and the memories of it were to remain with him for the rest of his life.

This is how he remembered it: 'August 2 was a lovely day. It was Bank Holiday Monday but there was to be no rest for us. We had planned to take the bus from Kirmington into Cleethorpes and were just about to board in our best uniforms when the duty runner came to tell us that all flying personnel had to report to the flight office by 14.00 hours. Ops were on again.

'For once the ground crew were not sure about the target and their opinion was that it could be Cologne. But they were wrong and it was Hamburg again. The briefing was short and the Met officer told us it would be hot, even at 15,000 feet. Nevertheless, I decided to put my Sidcot suit on, just in case.

'Take-off would be late but it was difficult to get any rest. The CO and the padre were down in the changing room to wish everyone good luck and they were there again beside the runway as the first Wellington left. We were sent off at one minute intervals and once again we were climbing out over the Humber heading for Hamburg. Over Holland it was clear the flak boys were on their toes. Over to port a Wellington was coned by the lights and the last we saw he was going down, ablaze from end to end.

'A few miles inland the bomb-aimer told the pilot that dead ahead was a large bank of thick black cloud. This hadn't been mentioned by the Met people but it was there and had to be contended with. The pilot headed for a gap in the cloud but by the time we got there it had disappeared and we found ourselves in thick cloud at 14,000 feet. It was clear we couldn't maintain that for long as ice began forming on the wings and in seconds we were blacked out. All I could see were blue flashes coming off the gun barrels and parts of the aircraft. The wireless was out of action but the weather hadn't stopped the ack-ack.

'There was an extra large bang and Charlie *(their aircraft was numbered AS-C)*, still covered in ice, turned over. One moment I was conscious and the next half way to heaven. Goodbye mum, I shall never see England again. But then I began to come round and I could hear voices. We had dived out of control from 14,000 feet to just 3,000 feet before the pilot and bomb aimer had got the engines restarted. The hot night had melted the ice and Charlie was now under control. There was a warning sign on the main spar in the middle of the fuselage that the aircraft must not be dived at more than 280mph. We had just pulled out at 360mph and we were still flying.

'The flak was much more intense now we were low down but Hamburg was ahead of us. There was no time for a bomb run, it was a case of pressing the tit and getting the hell out of there. We were still 400 miles from home and the pilot decided to stay at a thousand feet and the tension kept us alert on that ride back. A few small guns had a go at us and then it was across the water, next stop Lincolnshire.

'The pilot contacted the duty controller at Kirmington and we received permission to land. We thought we must be the first back. As we came in I eased off my helmet and found blood on my ear. It seemed I had hit something hard in the hammering we took.

'In the funnel Charlie seemed to be going a bit fast but the skipper was lined up correctly. Half way down the runway we discovered we had lost a wheel, the flaps were badly buckled and the brakes had gone. At times like this you have to make decisions very quickly and our pilot was no slouch. We ran off the runway onto the grass and into a ploughed field. There was a crunch and we came to a halt. I was first out, running round to open the doors for the others. Fire was always a risk but there wasn't much petrol left and all the bombs had gone down in Hamburg.

'We stood there looking at Charlie thinking we had lost a friend. He would never fly with us again. With a broken wing and props, bent flaps and most of the bottom torn away, he looked a mess. But he was later repaired and flew again with an OTU.

'Back in the briefing room, the CO demanded to know where the hell we'd been. We told him we'd been to Hamburg. You must be joking, he told us. Hadn't we heard the recall message? We hadn't and we told him we were sure we'd reached Hamburg and hoped the camera in the aircraft had survived and the photograph would prove us right. We were anxious to see that photograph

F/O Eric Milliken of Springfield, New Zealand, at the controls of his 100 Squadron Lancaster, summer 1943. (Author's collection)

and we were not to be disappointed. It was a beautiful picture, showing our bombs falling in the Hamburg docks area.

'We had succeeded against all the odds but I think we had a guardian angel with us that night. When people asked me if I believe in God, I always tell them that I do. I flew with him to Hamburg on the night of August 2-3, 1943.'

Cec Bryant and his crew went on to complete their tour with 166 and he was to complete a second tour with 199 Squadron later in the war. His pilot received a DFM for his actions that night. The Wellington he saw shot down may well have been a second from 166, flown by Sgt Harold Nash, although official records indicate it was downed by a night fighter not flak. It was one of 11 aircraft from 1 Group lost that night including another 166 Squadron Wellington which had been tasked with using the raid as cover to lay mines in the Elbe. The Battle of Hamburg's final tally for 1 Group was 20 aircraft and the lives of 126 men, the greatest number of losses in Bomber Command.

The Wellingtons were now approaching the end of their operational life, although 166 Squadron was to lose seven in August with an eighth written off in a crash. All but two of those losses occurred on mining operations. Among them was F/O Bill McGinn and crew. The 20-year-old pilot and three of his previous crew had survived in June when they had bailed out of their aircraft over Skegness after an engine caught fire soon after take off. This time they were not so fortunate. 166's last operation in Wellingtons came on the night of August 30-31 on Mönchengladbach when two aircraft failed to return. A third flown by F/Sgt Pat Knight suffered an engine failure shortly after leaving the target area. The aircraft was then attacked by a night fighter, coned by search lights and hit by anti-aircraft fire as it crossed the Dutch coast at 1,000 feet. The crew threw everything possible out of the aircraft to keep it airborne as the pilot struggled to keep the Wellington flying. It was then discovered that the pilot had been wounded in the foot and the wireless operator, Jack Toper, had to use part of a harness to tie the pilot's injured foot to the rudder pedal. Eventually the aircraft made it back to England, crossing the coast at 300 feet, at which point the remaining engine burst into flames. F/Sgt Knight immediately ordered his crew to brace for a crash and put the aircraft down onto what turned out to be the playing fields at Clacton County High School. The force of the crash threw the pilot through the windscreen, breaking his left arm, left leg and several ribs. The rear gunner and bomb aimer scrambled clear but a parachute, which had opened accidentally during the crash, hampered both the navigator and wireless operator. The navigator had just managed to get clear when an oxygen bottle exploded severely burning the wireless operator, Jack Toper. He fell from the aircraft in flames and was saved by a soldier who quickly wrapped him in a greatcoat. Both he and the pilot, neither of whom were decorated for their actions, were to spend many months in hospital recovering from their ordeal, Jack Toper at the RAF's famed burns unit at East Grinstead.

Only the Poles at Ingham were still operating Wellingtons in 1 Group and they were to be reduced to a single squadron when 305 Squadron flew its last operation to Hamburg before moving south to join the 2nd Tactical Air Force. 300 Squadron was to lose an aircraft and crew to a night fighter on the Mönchengladbach raid. Earlier in the month three Wellingtons left Ingham to drop mines off the Frisian Islands. Over the North Sea an engine caught fire but the pilot, F/Sgt Rech, decided to continue with the operational. Shortly afterwards they were found by a night fighter and shot down into the sea. F/Sgt Rech and his wireless operator, F/Sgt Poddany, managed to escape from the aircraft and were to spend the next eight days in their dinghy before being picked up by the German navy, a remarkable testament to them and their survival equipment.

That August saw the 1 Group Lancasters visiting Italy four times as well as German targets, including two trips to Berlin, a precursor to what was to come in the months ahead. Those two raids were to cost the group nine aircraft, 100 Squadron at Waltham losing four in a single night with a fifth aircraft being wrecked on take off. Twenty-four aircraft were due to take part in the attack and several aircraft had managed to lift off before F/Sgt Don Dripps' aircraft came to grief. As it thundered down the runway the heavily laden Lancaster started to swing and, as the pilot attempted to correct it, the undercarriage collapsed and it skidded to a halt in a shower of metal shards and sparks. Fortunately the bombs did not explode and, after a delay, the remaining aircraft were rerouted to the shorter runway and just managed to make it over the airfield boundary fence. Five men did manage to survive from one of the four lost, bailing out after the aircraft was badly damaged by flak over Holland. Both the pilot, W/O Francis Preston, one of a number of Australian pilots with 100 Squadron, and his flight engineer, Sgt Harry Chadwick, were killed. Another aircraft flown by P/O Tom Collins crashed in the Baltic, while the third aircraft flown by F/Lt John Anderton crashed in Berlin, with one of the crew surviving. The fourth aircraft, flown by F/Sgt Lance Needs, disappeared without trace.

This was a period of heavy losses in 1 Group and at 460 Squadron in particular. F/Sgt Ivan Heath, rear gunner in a mixed British-Australian crew, had arrived at the squadron in June. New arrivals had their name put at the very bottom of the flight list but, within less than a month, his crew found themselves at the top of that same list. He had a close friend who he had met in training and they both joined the squadron at the same time. 'We had a two bob bet on who would survive the longest,' he later recalled. 'I won as he got the chop after 13 ops.' He also remembered nights out in Grimsby where he would often see girls waiting outside the town's Savoy Cinema in Victoria Street for Binbrook aircrew who had gone missing the night before. F/Sgt Heath and his crew did manage to complete their tour and he later went on to fly another 46 with two 8 Group Pathfinder squadrons.

During August 1 Group crews got the opportunity to meet the King and Queen during their visit to Binbrook. Crews from 12, 100 and 460 Squadrons assembled at Binbrook for the visit, during which the Royal party were shown round the airfield, inspected a Lancaster and had the opportunity to talk to some of the men who flew them. One was a young Canadian wireless operator from Wickenby, F/Sgt Bert Cruse. During a recent operation to lay mines off Danzig, their aircraft had been badly damaged by a night fighter and both gunners had been injured. When the aircraft finally landed at Coltishall an unexploded 20mm cannon shell was found lodged in the hydraulic reservoir just above F/Sgt Cruse's position in the aircraft, and he kept it as a souvenir. He was introduced to the King and Queen during the visit and was holding the shell. The Queen asked him about it and, after she heard the story, remarked: 'What a terrifying object', Bert replying: 'Yes Ma'am, it certainly put the sh….' at which pointed he stopped. The Queen, with a smile on her face, replied: 'I can well imagine it did, young man.'

Lancasters from 1 Group were among the 596 aircraft which attacked the German's secret rocket testing station at Peenemünde on the Baltic coast on the night of August 17/18. It was a raid Bomber Command was ordered to make and so serious was the threat of the development of flying bombs and long range rockets that crews were told that if they didn't hit it the first time they would have to go back again and again until they did.

This was to be an attack like no other so far in the war. It would be done in moonlight from relatively low level to ensure accuracy and it would be controlled for the first time by a Master Bomber, whose job would be to stay over the target to direct aircraft onto the correct aiming point. It was to be the template for many more successful bombing raids. It would also be the first time the German defenders would make use of night fighters fitted with twin upward firing cannon, *Schräge Musik*, 'jazz music'. Two aircraft fitted with these weapons are believed to have accounted for six of the 40 bombers lost by the RAF that night.

1 Group was to be spared the heavy losses of particularly 5 Group. The 1 Group Lancasters were in the first wave of the attack and, under the director of the Master Bomber, G/Capt John Searby of 83 Squadron, they hit several of the production sites. 103 Squadron records talk of a 'first class' attack and

Debrief at Ludford: a 101 Squadron crew go through the details of a raid back at base, late summer 1943. (Vic Redfern)

there was much agreement that the Master Bomber technique had been a great assistance. There was little fighter opposition to the 1 Group aircraft, the bulk of the German night fighters being lured away by a spoof raid on Berlin mounted by just eight Mosquitoes. However, the Luftwaffe fighters made it back to the Baltic to catch the later stages of the raid when most of the RAF bombers were lost. Just three aircraft failed to make it back to 1 Group airfields. One of the aircraft was flown by S/Ldr Fraser Slade, a hugely popular flight commander at Wickenby. He had previously served in the Middle East but had joined 12 Squadron earlier in the summer and had already flown on at least 20 operations. His aircraft was caught by a night fighter over the sea and is believed to have crashed off the Danish coast. A month later a notice appeared in the *London Gazette* announcing the award of the DSO to S/Ldr Slade. It read: 'Since returning to this country S/Ldr Slade has undertaken numerous sorties against varying targets in Germany and Italy. His ideal leadership and unconquerable spirit have set an example worthy of the highest regard.' The other 1 Group casualties that night were a 100 Squadron Lancaster flown by F/O Howard Spiers, a New Zealander, which came down near Peenemünde, and another from Elsham captained by Sgt Peter O'Donnell, which crashed in Denmark. The raid also saw 460 Squadron become the first in Bomber Command to complete 1,000 Lancaster sorties, a remarkable achievement and not the last the Aussies at Binbrook were to record. It was marked by a wild party on Cleethorpes Pier, an evening when, according to legend, beer was served in fire buckets and at least one young Australian had to be rescued from the sea.

Chapter 9

Bigger and Better

New Airfields and New Squadrons

Three years on from being able to muster only a handful of Fairey Battle squadrons, 1 Group had become a force to be reckoned with by September 1943. It was able to provide around 130 Lancasters plus one remaining Wellington squadron for operations and this figure was to increase still further in the months to come.

It was an autumn in which Bomber Command was to batter German targets unmercifully leading to the crescendo of attacks on Berlin. It was also to be a period of great change for the North Lincolnshire-based 1 Group.

September saw the full implementation of a command-wide reorganisation

S/Ldr Hinds, his crew and ground crew of M-Mother, 626 Squadron, 1943. Note the makeshift shack on the left where the ground crew took shelter in bad weather. (Wickenby Archive)

of control and administration. It was hardly the stuff of headlines but it was to further increase the efficiency of front-line squadrons and was to help Bomber Command to become one of the mightiest arms of warfare Britain has ever produced.

What happened was the full establishment of what became known as the 'Base' system which began to be implemented in March 1943. Previously airfields such as Binbrook or Elsham had smaller satellites, Waltham and Kirmington. The station commanders and their staff had control over their satellites but, inevitably, there was much duplication of administration and technical support. This was all swept away with the advent of the base system. Each base station would be controlled by an Air Commodore with a group captain commanding each station and a wing commander each squadron.

There were further refinements to the system that September, including the renumbering of the bases with the first being the Group's training base. The line

12 Squadron's Jerry Jones and Paddy Groves with a pair of .303 guns. (Wickenby Archive).

up in 1 Group was: No 11 Base: Lindholme, Blyton and Faldingworth (Faldingworth was later to become an operational station) with Sandtoft and Sturgate being added in 1944; No 12 Base: Binbrook, Waltham and Kelstern; No 13 Base: Elsham Wolds, Kirmington and North Killingholme (Ingham and Hemswell were added in 1944); No 14 Base: Ludford Magna, Wickenby and, from February 1944, Faldingworth. A fifth base was to be added in October 1944 when the airfields at Scampton, Fiskerton and Dunholme Lodge were added to 1 Group in its final wartime expansion.

One immediate effect of the system was the expansion of facilities at base HQ stations, including the erection of additional hangars. This enabled all major technical work to be concentrated on one airfield and it meant a concentration of RAF personnel there too. At Binbrook, for instance, the station complement stood at 2,200 personnel in addition to the Base commander's own staff. This included 743 men and women on the station HQ staff, 664 with 460 Squadron, 287 with 1481 (Bomber) Gunnery Flight, 191 with 2842 Light Anti-Aircraft Squadron, 136 with 460's Servicing Echelon, 151 with 12 Base Servicing Echelon and an additional 28 WAAFs.

In the case of Ludford Magna, it led to the airfield being extended to provide additional hangars and facilities on the western side of the Caistor-Horncastle road. This led to further restrictions on the public use of roads in an area already affected by the setting up of roadside bomb dumps fed from the railhead at nearby Stenigot.

The base system also allowed for flexibility of aircraft availability. If, for instance, 166 Squadron at Kirmington offered 18 aircraft for an operation and then one went unserviceable after an air test and no replacement was available, a spare could be provided from amongst the 13 Base squadrons, thus ensuring that the raid went ahead with the requisite number of aircraft. A base navigation officer also made sure that navigators' briefings were co-ordinated to make sure all squadrons received exactly the same information which, in turn, helped keep bombing concentrated. His job also involved selecting the best crews to provide updates on weather and wind conditions (the so-call 'wind-finders') during attacks.

It was not a perfect system but it was a very good one and it helped ensure that Bomber Command got the best out of each Group.

The three new airfields which were opened in the autumn and winter of 1943 were all to play a significant part in the future operations of 1 Group. First off the stocks was Kelstern, perched high on the Lincolnshire Wolds six miles from Louth. Neighbouring Ludford Magna could lay claim to be the highest

100 Squadron's M-Mother, ED583, pictured at Waltham in the early autumn of 1943 when it had already flown 42 operations. In the bomb-aimer's position is Sgt Harry Ferdinand. It was destroyed early in October when it broke up in the air near the airfield, killing all six on board including the pilot, W/O John Goozee. (Jimmy Flynn)

An unidentified 100 Squadron Lancaster alongside Waltham's becalmed wind-sock, summer 1943. (Author's collection)

operational bomber airfield in Britain at 428ft above sea level, but Kelstern was only a few feet lower and even more exposed to winds coming in from the North Sea. Ludford was also built alongside a large village served by the main Louth-Market Rasen road and boasting two excellent pubs. Kelstern had none of those attributes but was, nevertheless, becoming one of the most popular postings for all those who served there. It was hastily built, with some truly awful examples of how not to erect accommodation huts for those forced to spend winters on the Lincolnshire Wolds. But it was to be a well-run station, lacking the 'bull' found elsewhere with a first rate *esprit de corps* amongst those who served with its one and only squadron, 625. Much of the credit for all this went to G/Capt R.H. Donkin, a vastly experienced officer who had commanded 97 Squadron before the war, and was to remain in charge at Kelstern until just before the station closed in April 1945. Notes in the station records indicate in just how much regard he was held by those who served at Kelstern. The airfield had been commissioned by Air Commodore Arthur Wray, the base commander at Binbrook and it was Wray, another man held in the highest regard by those who served under him, who personally delivered the first Lancaster to Kelstern on October 7, 1943. 625 Squadron had been formed from 'C' Flight of 100 Squadron at Waltham and moved in to Kelstern a week later.

Faldingworth had opened in the late summer as a satellite of Lindholme and was initially earmarked for training purposes. 1667 HCU was formed at Lindholme on June 1 and a detachment moved to Faldingworth on August 8, with the entire conversion unit arriving two months later. Its formation meant that 1 Group now had three conversion units, the other two being 1656 at Lindholme and 1662 at Blyton. At the time 1667 operated a mixed force of Halifaxes and Lancasters and new crews would spend a large part of their course on Halifaxes before a final spell on Lancasters, the aircraft they would operate when posted to 1 Group squadrons. During the autumn of 1943 it was decided to concentrate all Lancaster training in special units, Lancaster Finishing Schools. Headquarters of 1 LFS was set up at Lindholme on November 21 with three flights being created, A Flight at Lindholme, B Flight at Blyton and C Flight at Faldingworth, all three moving to Hemswell early in 1944. This enabled 1667 at Faldingworth to become an all-Halifax unit. Most of the Halifaxes used here and at other training establishments were hand-me-downs, mainly from 4 Group squadrons. Earlier versions could be brutes to fly and lethal in inexperienced hands. Crews going through 1667 at Faldingworth were more fortunate as the unit had mainly Halifax Vs which were marginally more forgiving. Nevertheless, four aircraft were lost, along with a Lancaster in the pre-LFS days, killing 24 men. Training was sometimes almost as perilous as operation flying.

A long way from home P/O Eric Milliken of Springfield, New Zealand and his navigator, Sgt Bill George, of St James, Manitoba, Canada, during their time with 100 Squadron at Waltham. (Eric Milliken)

Sandtoft, which lay just over the Lincolnshire border a few miles from Lindholme, had opened in February 1944 and 1667 moved there for the remainder of the war, freeing up Faldingworth to become an operational station. It was to be the final home of the war of much-travelled 300 Squadron. The Poles had finally given up their trusty Wellingtons, the last squadron to fly them in Bomber Command, and had converted to Lancasters and, as ever, were to operate with great distinction until hostilities ceased. Their old home at Ingham, was occupied by 1481 Bomber and Gunnery Flight which moved in from Binbrook, later to be renamed 1687 Bomber Defence Training Flight. This unit was to provide invaluable training, towing targets over the ranges for gunners to hone their skills. After being formed at Binbrook in November 1941 from 1 Target Towing Flight, 1481 had become virtually a small squadron in its own right and by the end of 1943 had a complement of over 280 men and 24 aircraft, 10 Wellingtons, 13 single-engined Martinets and a Tiger Moth.

Four further squadrons joined the strength of 1 Group in November 1943. At Wickenby, 12 Squadron's C Flight was detached to form the nucleus of 626 Squadron and, at the same time, C Flight of 103 Squadron at Elsham became 576 Squadron. At the end of the month 100 Squadron's C Flight formed 550 Squadron, which was to remain at Waltham until the start of the new year when it moved to the last of 1 Group's wartime airfields at North Killingholme. 166 Squadron had converted to Lancasters earlier in the autumn with the formation of a third flight and, with 300 Squadron not far from following suit, 1 Group was reaching a new peak in its power.

Chapter 10

Confusion to the Enemy

101 Squadron and Electronic Counter Measures

On September 3, 1943 ground crews at Ludford Magna began preparing Lancasters for operations that night. From the fuel and bomb loads they guessed it was to be a long trip, and they were not wrong. It was to be Berlin.

As they worked they heard the sound of aircraft approaching and soon the first of two new Lancasters IIIs destined for service with 101 Squadron was touching down. They were factory fresh but they differed from the rest of the squadron's aircraft by sporting two seven-foot long aerials, one under the nose and another on top of the fuselage with a shorter aerial further back. Missing from the aircraft was the H2S dome with which most new Lancaster were fitted. A third aircraft arrived the following day, again fitted with the strange aerials. For weeks now rumours had been circulating Ludford that 'something

101 Squadron rear gunners wearing American-style body armour, Ludford Magna 1944. (Bill Churchley)

'McNamara's Band' of 101 Squadron in one of the station's hangars, late 1943 (Peter Green Collection)

big' was on the cards and this was yet more evidence that the rumours had some foundations. Earlier, crates of new radio equipment had begun arriving and a number of additional air crew had arrived at Ludford, all wireless operators.

Earlier in the summer a number of new measures concerning tackling the growing menace from Luftwaffe night fighters had been discussed at a series of high level meeting at Bomber Command HQ and the Air Ministry. One had been the introduction of Window, which had succeeded spectacularly over Hamburg but which, no doubt, the Germans would find a way round. The second measure was a device known by the codename 'Airborne Cigar' or ABC for short. It was designed to locate and disrupt night fighter communications and involved fitting three 50 watt transmitters inside a Lancaster, each capable of sending out frequency-modulated jamming signals. The idea was that the operator would locate and then lock on to transmissions and then use the transmitters to jam the signals through that array of aerials on the Lancasters. It involved fitting a range of bulky equipment weighing more than 600lbs in the mid-section of a Lancaster plus adding accommodation for an eighth crew member, who would be known as the 'special operator'. Aircraft carrying ABC later had a G suffix added to the serial number indicating access was limited

A carefully staged photograph at Ludford Magna in the summer of 1944 (one of the camp's photograph section had worked for the Daily Mirror before the war) The aircraft in the background is 101's Mike-Squared and just visible under the nose is one of the ABC aerials.
(Vic Redfern, via Peter Green)

to the aircraft while on the ground and that they should always be under armed guard.

101 Squadron was to become the RAF's very first electronic counter measures squadron. 100 Squadron at Waltham had originally been selected to fly ABC aircraft which, because of the additional equipment, would operate without H2S equipment and the under-fuselage dome. However, delays in producing the jamming equipment meant that by the time it was ready, 100 Squadron's aircraft had been converted to operate with H2S, leaving 101 Squadron, which was still without the new radar equipment, as the next in line. On such little matters the fate of so many men was decided.

Within a few days of the introduction of Window the Germans had responded by co-ordinating the commentaries of several controllers at different locations and by giving command of night fighters in a specific area to a master controller who could then guide them towards the bomber stream, thus restricting the effect of the aluminium strips. Even before this happened work on ABC had been completed at the Telecommunications Research Establishment at Malvern and was ready for trials to begin. The original code name was 'Jostle' but had changed to Airborne Cigar (earlier they had developed a ground-based jamming device which was designed to operate from

15 transmitters which would have been sites in East Anglia but it was limited to a range of 140 miles. The code-name selected was Ground Cigar – hence the adaptation of *Airborne*) by the time the first three Lancasters had been adapted by the RAF's Signals Intelligence Unit and flown to Ludford.

ABC had a range of 50 miles and its three transmitters were designed to operate on the wave bands between 39.3 and 42.5 MHz, which would cover all German night fighter transmissions.

There was to be no delay in testing the equipment. F/Lt Frank Collins, a radar specialist on secondment from Bomber Command HQ, was at Ludford to complete the installation work and test the equipment and the job of flying the trials was handed to F/Lt W. D. Austin. Initial trials took place on September 4, 5 and 6 and during the night of September 8 F/Lt Austin took an ABC-equipped aircraft on a four and a half-hour test flight to within 10 miles of the German coast. Aircraft had their H2S equipment removed at Ludford and were later sent to St Athan and Defford in the Midlands, the centre for RAF radar research, where more equipment was picked up and flown back to Ludford in readiness for the next stage of the trial work.

The special operators themselves had to understand German though not necessarily speak the language. They had to be able to identify transmissions

The dorsal ABC aerial is just visible on the right of this crew photograph from Ludford taken in 1944. Those on the picture are identified simply as Alec, George, Stan, Smithy, Jock, Bill and Ron. (P. Holway)

SR-O with its ABC aerials just visible, Ludford, 1943. (Vic Redfern)

and be skilful enough in the use of the equipment to change frequencies rapidly as Luftwaffe controllers sought to get around the jamming. In particular, they had to recognise German code words and log transmission to pass on to intelligence officers. They were all recruited from various trades but were given little information about exactly what they would be doing when they arrived at Ludford.

Among those who volunteered was Ron Chafer. He had trained as a signaller at the RAF's signals school at Madeley, Herefordshire and it was during this course that he happened to mention to one of the instructors that he had had some lessons in German before he joined up. He thought no more about it and, after completing the course, was promoted to sergeant and packed his bags ready to enjoy a spell of leave.

He was then told his leave had been cancelled and he was posted to 1656 Heavy Conversion Unit at Lindholme from where he was taken to Boston Park just south of the airfield where he was issued with new flying kit to replace the equipment he had been given at Madeley. A few days later he was taken by car to Hemswell, by then home of No 1 Lancaster Finishing School, where he met three other newly-promoted sergeants, all, like Ron, somewhat mystified about what they were doing there.

The next day all four were told to go to a hut on the airfield where they were met by a flight sergeant. He pointed to a door inside the building and told them: 'Through that door is something top secret. If you go through it you will commit yourself to going on operations. If you wish to withdraw, do so now and you'll not be considered LMF (lack of moral fibre, the worst label you could acquire in the wartime RAF). All four went through the door to become ABC operators. Ron Chafer was the only one to survive a tour of operations with 101 Squadron.

Another of those who volunteered was Sgt Harry van Geffen who later recalled: 'All that was really necessary was the ability to recognise an R/T transmission as definitely German, rather than Russian, Czech or Polish but obviously some special operators were more fluent in German than others.' He was sent on a course at the 1 Group Lancaster Finishing School at Hemswell (earlier courses were run at Lindholme or at Kingsdown in Kent) before arriving at Ludford where they were given further training in searching for

The ground crew of T-Tommy of 101 Squadron. Apart from strange aerials, most of the squadron's aircraft sported lurid nose art. (Vic Redfern)

German transmissions and back-tuning the ABC transmitters in order to jam it. 'Once we were able to do this in 30 seconds we were ready for business, although we often had to fly with another crew if our own was unserviceable.'

Many of the special operators who arrived at Ludford were men who had fled to Britain either to escape Nazi oppression before the war or from countries invaded by the Germans. There were a number of German-speaking Jewish refugees amongst them and many were given English-sounding names to help protect them if they were forced to bail out over enemy territory. Among them was F/Sgt Reuben Herscovitz from Manchester who flew under the name 'Ron Hurst' and never went on operations without a pair of civilian shoes around his neck in case he found himself on the run in Germany. He was to become something of an institution at Ludford, completing a full tour as a special operator and then volunteering for a second. Another specialist operator of German origin who flew with the squadron was 19-year-old Sgt Hans Schwarz, who served as 'Sgt Blake'. He was killed on a raid on Brunswick in August 1944 and is buried in the British war cemetery in Hanover under his real name. Many of the Jewish airmen who did fly did so designated as members of the Royal Canadian Air Force in an attempt to further fool their captors. One of the first special operators to be killed at Ludford, F/Sgt George Herman, died as a member of the RCAF although he was officially a British Jew.

Lancaster crews were usually tightly-knit units, men who had come together at OTUs, and many were to look upon the special operators as 'outsiders'. As a result the special operators found themselves often flying with several different crews, certainly in the early days of ABC. It was perhaps because of this and the bond they shared as 'specialists' the operators tended to form their own little groups within the squadron. They were not billeted with crews and the story went around that their work was so secret the authorities were afraid they might talk in their sleep! Some did, however, fly regularly with the same crew. W/O Les Temple completed a tour of 30 operations as an ABC operator in 1944 with 101 and flew most of them as part of the crew of F/O Erik Nielsen, who later became an MP and minister in the Canadian Government. He was the younger brother of the actor and film star Leslie Nielsen. Another special duties operator, Yorkshireman Peter Holway, also completed a full tour with the same crew and was treated as 'one of the boys' by P/O Hames and the other aircrew members.

The first extended trial took place on the night of September 22-23 when two ABC-equipped Lancaster took part in an attack on Hanover. Both returned (although a non-ABC aircraft from 101 was shot down) and the delighted special operator later reported the first German words he heard were: 'Achtung, English bastards coming!', a remark which has gone down in 101 legend. The following night three ABC Lancasters went to Mannheim on yet

A heavily doctored photograph from Ludford in the late spring of 1944. Blanked out are the ABC aerials on SR-G which is running up its engines ready for take-off. Note the FIDO pipes alongside the runway. (Terry Hancock via Peter Green)

another trial but this time one of them, flown by 20-year-olds F/O Don Turner, was attacked by a night fighter and exploded over France. Two of the crew managed to escape but the special operator, F/O Arthur Stafford, who had won a DFM with 97 Squadron, was among the six who died. A further trial was flown, again to Hanover, at the end of September and another ABC aircraft was lost, this time being shot down by an intruder near Lincoln. There were no survivors.

The first full-scale operation of ABC came on the night of October 7-8 when 343 Lancasters raided Stuttgart and only four were lost. There was little fighter opposition, due perhaps to a diversionary raid on Munich but helped, perhaps, by 101's special operators.

By October 6 half the Lancasters on 101's strength had been converted to ABC. These aircraft had their maximum bomb load reduced by 1,000lbs to take account of the equipment and the extra crew member. The special operator's position in the aircraft was close to the main spar and outside the heated area of a Lancaster meaning he had to wear one of the bulky heated suits issued to gunners. The conversion programme was a mammoth task for the ground crews at Ludford, each aircraft taking some 3,000 man hours to adapt. To help with the work six additional wireless mechanics were posted in along with, eventually, 33 special operators.

The ABC Lancasters from Ludford were now expected to fly on all Main Force raids at least eight aircraft flying at eight-mile intervals in bomber streams to give the maximum coverage to the jamming equipment. On nights when 1

Group was stood down at least six ABC Lancasters were tasked to fly with other groups. There was to be little rest for the bomber crews at Ludford.

Losses were high amongst the ABC aircraft. Two were lost in an attack on Hanover, including one with nine men on board, two more over Düsseldorf early in November and four in two raids on Berlin, three of them ABC aircraft. There began to be growing concern among some crews that the Germans were able to lock on to ABC transmissions, although there was no hard evidence of this. The Germans were able to examine the ABC equipment on the Lancaster of P/O Charles McManus, which was shot down over Holland during an attack on Berlin in November but there is nothing to suggest that night fighter tactics were changed as a result of this discovery. That didn't stop some 101 Squadron crews looking on their special operators as 'Jonah's'.

Sometimes the fates were kinder to the special operators than they were to other crew members. Sgt van Geffen's first crew at Ludford left to join a Pathfinder squadron after his first three operations. He then joined a second crew only for their aircraft to be ruled unserviceable on the morning of an attack on Pforzeim. The spare aircraft was a non-ABC Lancaster and Sgt van Geffen was left behind. The aircraft was one of two from 101 which failed to return.

Two weeks later his pilot was taken ill before an attack on Dessau and he was switched to fly with the stand-by crew, whose own special operator, 19-year-old Sgt Rudy Mahr, another British Jew flying as a Canadian, had been switched to S/Ldr Monty Gibbons' crew, who were short of a 'spec op'. Gibbons' aircraft disappeared without trace. Five days later he volunteered to fly on a daylight raid over Dortmund as a passenger. On their way back the Lancaster developed engine problems and was diverted to the emergency airfield at Carnaby, near Bridlington where they remained for four days until repairs could be carried out. Back at Ludford he learned that a previous regular skipper, S/Ldr Ian Macleod-Selkirk, had asked for Sgt van Heffen to be reassigned to his crew for a daylight attack on Dahlbruch but, because he was still at Carnaby, Sgt Johnny Toy, another 19-year-old special operator, volunteered to take his place. Theirs was the only aircraft lost on the raid.

Harry van Geffen was one of the lucky ones. 101 was to fly 2,477 sorties with ABC from Ludford, losing 171 Lancasters with1,040 men killed and 178 ending the war as prisoners, one of the highest loss rates in the whole of Bomber Command.

Chapter 11

The Big City

The Assault on Berlin
1943 – 1944

Early on the afternoon of Thursday November 18, 1943 crews at Wickenby crowded into the briefing room. They had been told ops were on again that night after a stand down of almost two weeks and were noticeably quiet as the curtain covering the map of the target was drawn back. Then there was a collective groan. It was Berlin, the 'Big City', and the red ribbons stretched tight across the map indicating the route they would have to take meant it was going to be tough. They were to be routed across Holland, passing north of Hanover and then onto the German capital. They would then turn south briefly before heading back across Germany, passing north of Leipzig, south of Cologne and out over Belgium. They were told that this was to give them the advantage of a diversionary raid on Ludwigshafen which would draw off the fighters. At least, that was the plan.

This was to become the opening encounter of what later became known as the Battle of Berlin, a series of 16 heavy raids on the capital between November 18 and the end of March 1944. Some historians suggest three earlier attacks in August and September should be included, but it mattered little to those men at Wickenby on that cold November Thursday. They knew they had a long night ahead of them.

Bomber Command crews were no strangers to Berlin. The city was attacked no fewer than 47 times in 1940 and 1941 although comparatively little damage was done. It was a distant target for the twin-engined Wellingtons, Hampdens and Whitleys then forming the bulk of the bomber inventory. It was only the arrival of the four-engined bombers, initially Stirlings and Halifaxes, which made Berlin more of a viable target. But it was the arrival of the Lancaster, with its superior performance and carrying capacity, that heralded the start of the true assault on Berlin. Air Chief Marshal Harris had been urged throughout the year to launch his attack on the German capital. He needed little encouragement to do this but he knew only too well that he had to conserve his forces until he had sufficient Lancasters to deal what he hoped would be a

Eric Parker and his 626 Squadron crew with a cookie destined for Berlin. (Wickenby Archive)

knock-out blow. In a famous memorandum he sent to Churchill early in November 1943 he wrote: 'We can wreck Berlin from end to end if the Americans will come in on it. It will cost us between 400 and 500 aircraft. It will cost Germany the war.' He was wrong. The Americans didn't come in, Bomber Command's losses on the 16 attacks amounted to 569 aircraft and the lives of 2,938 airmen. And it didn't cost Germany the war. Post-war accounts of men who took part speak of their disappointment and frustration that all the sacrifices made by Bomber Command failed to bring a speedy end to the conflict. Berlin was a huge, sprawling target, enormous damage was done and heavy, mainly civilian, casualties inflicted but the city, like London before it, survived to fight another day.

1 Group's contribution to the Battle of Berlin was to be a significant one. Its squadrons flew the second highest number of sorties in Bomber Command, lost the highest number of aircraft and suffered the most casualties. 460 Squadron at Binbrook flew the most sorties of any Bomber Command squadron and suffered the highest losses of any non-Pathfinder squadron. The squadron with the second highest number of sorties was 101 at Ludford, just along the road from Binbrook. And those men in the briefing room at Wickenby were to suffer almost as badly, with more than half their number amongst the missing over the next few months.

The Australians at Binbrook lost five aircraft in the three Berlin attacks in late August and early September, 22 men being killed, nine becoming prisoners and three being interred in Sweden. The latter included F/O Randall and two of the crew from his aircraft which crashed in Denmark on the night of September 3-4 after being hit by flak and then finished off by a night fighter. All seven men got out of the aircraft but it is believed the navigator, F/Sgt Norman Conway, drowned. Two of the crew were picked up by a Swedish ship and another managed to make his way to Sweden where the pilot joined them. 101 Squadron also lost five aircraft but only three of the 35 men on board survived. Two Lancasters were also lost from Elsham.

103 was to lose another couple of Lancasters a few nights later during an attack on Mannheim but this time all 14 men survived and, even more remarkably, half of them escaped captivity.

W/O Bob Cant and his crew had taken off from Elsham shortly after 7.30pm in 103's S-Sugar on their second operation. They were hit by flak and all bailed out over Luxemburg, landing safely. Cant along with his flight engineer F/Sgt Dicky Dickson and mid-upper gunner Sgt Bill Milburn made it to Switzerland thanks in no small way to the many French people who risked their lives on their behalf. The rear gunner, Sgt Bob Parkinson, and wireless operator Sgt Syd Horton managed to reach Paris where a priest arranged for them to reach the coast, the pair later crossing the Channel in a fishing boat. The bomb aimer, Sgt Denys Teare, met up with members of the French Resistance and, during the next year, took part in a number of operations against the Germans before finally meeting up with invading Allied troops. The

P/O Ellis, one of the founder members of 625 Squadron, pictured soon after the squadron moved there in the autumn of 1943. His flight engineer, Sgt Mortimer, is just visible behind him. (625 Squadron Association)

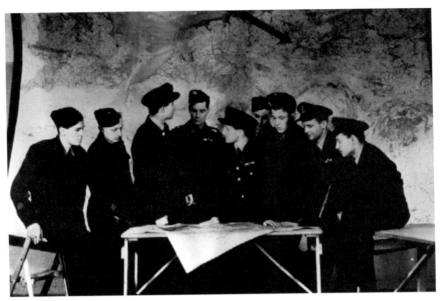

Briefing for Berlin: 626 Squadron aircrew pictured before the Black Thursday attack on Berlin in December 1943. They include – pilot W/O J. Butcher, W/O A.H. Rew, pilot S/Ldr J. Spiller, S/Ldr J.A. Neilson, F/Sgt Jacques (PoW 1944), pilot F/O R. Wellum, F/O Jack Hutchinson (killed Schweinfurt February 24/25, 1944). (Wickenby Archive)

only member of the crew not to make it back was the navigator, Sgt Tommy Thomas, who was captured in the Pyrenees in December, virtually within sight of the Spanish border. He was later accused of spying and spent some time in Fresnes prison in Paris before eventually being transferred to a PoW camp. Bob Cant's crew later discovered they were the most successful evaders of any wartime Bomber Command crew at that stage of the war. The second aircraft lost from Elsham that night was abandoned out of fuel by its crew in the Cherbourg area after becoming lost in bad weather. Six became prisoners, but the seventh, F/Sgt Bawden, also made it back to England.

Losses throughout 1 Group were high that September. 166 suffered its first Lancaster losses on the night of September 27-28 when three aircraft failed to make it back from Hanover. One returned early and crashed just outside Caistor, killing W/O Cecil Boone and his crew. A second, flown by W/O Paul Chesterton, crashed in Germany killing all but two of the eight on board, including the squadron signals leader F/Lt Henry McGhie. The third aircraft was shot down by a night fighter with three of the nine men on board being killed. The survivors included a two-man cine unit from the Ministry of Information.

An attack on Hanover on the night of October 8-9 marked the final bombing operation for 300 Squadron in its Wellingtons. They were joined by Wellingtons from 432 Squadron in 4 Group in the attack and all made it home safely. 300 hadn't quite finished with its Wellingtons. They were used solely for mining operations and the Poles at Ingham were to lose five on these operations before finally being stood down after an operation to St Nazaire on the night of February 20-21, 1944 when F/Sgt Kabacinski and his crew became the last Wellington operational casualties in Bomber Command. By that time a number of 300 Squadron crews had moved to Ludford to train on Lancasters before the squadron's final move of the war to Faldingworth.

The Poles, who had relished their first opportunity to bomb Berlin back in 1941, felt somewhat left out that autumn as bigger and bigger raids were mounted on German cities while they were tasked to carry out difficult and often dangerous mining operations in aircraft which were so much inferior to the Lancasters equipping other 1 Group squadrons. 300's squadron historian notes that the crews became 'browned off' by these thankless and arduous operations and never lost the hope of doing something 'useful' with their talents. On one occasion the squadron received a signal from Bomber Command HQ stressing how valuable their work was, not just in sowing mines, but in providing information. On this particular occasion in October, as they returned from a mining operation off the French coast, 300 crews had spotted

626 Squadron, aircrew, armourers and a WAAF enjoying the sunshine at Wickenby later 1943. (Wickenby Archive)

Time for tea: radar mechanics of 626 Squadron take a break when the tea wagon arrives, Wickenby 1944. (Wickenby Archive)

Briefing for Berlin. This pictures dates from December 1943 and shows crews of 460 Squadron at Binbrook. (Laurie Wood)

a number of enemy ships. Thanks to the information they provided, a surprise attack by 25 E-boats on a British convoy was thwarted, four E-boats sunk and another seven damaged.

In November the squadron laid its 2,000th mine, a Bomber Command record. There was a 48-hour pass plus a bottle of spirits for the crew responsible and a message from Air Chief Marshal Harris which read: 'Heartiest congratulations to the whole personnel of 300 Squadron of laying last night, in good and painstaking fashion, their 2,000th mine. It is a most valuable contribution towards winning the war with Germany and affords further proof of the splendid spirit of co-operation between both our air forces. I am proud to be in command of you!' It was a message that went down well with the Poles, but not half as well as the news that they would soon get Lancasters, a new airfield and the opportunity to bomb Germany themselves.

The Hanover raid of October 8-9 proved another tough night for 12 Squadron. Three of their aircraft failed to return and one of them was being flown by their new CO, W/Cmdr Bob Norman. He was an Australian who had already flown one tour with 460 Squadron and flew with a new crew from Wickenby on what would be his first and last operation from the airfield. His aircraft, which ironically had been supplied by 460 Squadron under the Base system when a 12 Squadron Lancaster was not available, was shot down over Germany but he survived along with two other members of the crew. There was only one survivor from the other two crews lost that night.

A second attack on Hanover nine days later cost 103 another three aircraft, all 21 crew members being killed. During the same raid two ABC Lancasters were lost from Ludford with just one man of the 16 on board surviving. Two nights later there was another long operation for the 1 Group Lancasters, this time to Leipzig. Among the aircraft lost that night was a Lancaster from 625 Squadron at Kelstern, the first operational loss from the station. It was flown by 20-year-old P/O Bill Cameron, one of three Canadians on board. There were no survivors.

The pilot of a 100 Squadron Lancaster, W/O Claude White, won a Conspicuous Gallantry Medal on the Leipzig operation. Not long after the aircraft had left Waltham the intercom system failed. Then, as they were crossing the Dutch coast, the port outer engine caught fire and the extinguisher built into the engine failed to put out the flames, which were now bright enough to illuminate much of the aircraft. In spite of this, W/O White decided to press on and, despite presenting a target for both fighters and flak, bombed Leipzig and turned for home, with flames still coming from the engine. With few instruments working, the navigator, Sgt Les Dowdell, displayed exceptional skill in plotting a course back to Waltham. Theirs was the last of 100 Squadron's aircraft to return from the raid, another landing on three engines while a second had landed at Bardney with technical problems. Just as Claude White's aircraft arrived over Waltham, with flames still visible in the port wing, an SOS was received at the airfield from a 61 Squadron Lancaster which was almost out of fuel. White was asked if he wanted to make an emergency landing but replied that 'another few minutes wouldn't make any difference' and flew round the circuit again. When he finally landed four minutes later, flames threatened to engulf the aircraft but he remained at the controls until the other crew members got out.

His citation concluded: 'In serious circumstances, this gallant pilot displayed skill, coolness and tenacity, which inspired all.' Sgt Dowdell was awarded a DFM for the 'valiant' support of his captain. Their crew went on to complete their tour at Waltham.

Two nights later and it was Kassel. Forty-three aircraft were lost that night, the highest figure of the autumn campaign. The Germans had changed tactics again and it was paying dividends for them. Thanks to their Window counter-measures, fighters were now freed from the shackles imposed on them by the old 'box' system and were now acting independently. Just as single engined fighters had been allowed to 'freelance' over the illuminated target areas, 'tame boar' twin-engined night fighters were now given their head to follow bomber streams both to and from targets and, with the aid of flares and radar which was able to pick up H2S transmissions, they were to have a devastating effect. The RAF countered this by using Mosquito night fighters equipped with *Serrate* radar. They were to prove effective but not enough to prevent almost 400 German night fighters wreaking havoc among the bomber streams over the coming weeks and months. Among the losses were another three Lancasters from Elsham, the casualties including another experienced flight commander, S/Ldr Clifford Wood. Two aircraft failed to make it back to Waltham, one being shot down over Germany and the second, flown by P/O Peter Andrews, hit a hillside at North Elkington, near Louth, killing the pilot, mid-upper gunner and bomb aimer. The crew was returning from their 23rd operation with 100 Squadron. An attack on Düsseldorf on the night of November 3-4 saw 18 Bomber Command aircraft lost, five of them from 1 Group. 12 Squadron at Wickenby lost two that night while two ABC Lancasters failed to return to Ludford and 625 Squadron suffered its second loss.

There then followed a two-week break from attacks on German targets for the Lancaster force. There was one long range operation for experienced crews to attack marshalling yards and the entrance to the Mont Ceris railway tunnel at Modane in the French Alps. It was an outstanding success with all aircraft returning safely. In their authoritative *Bomber Command War Diaries* Martin Middlebrook and Chris Everitt record this as an attack by 5 and 8 Group Lancasters alone, but squadron records show that 1 Group was also a participant that night, with aircraft from Elsham, Waltham, Ludford, Binbrook and Wickenby all taking part.

Lancasters ready for bombing up, 460 Squadron Binbrook. (Laurie Wood)

Crews were then given a week-long rest before the first of the 16 winter attacks on Berlin. This came on the night of November 18-19 and it proved to be something of an anti-climax for both sides. The German capital was covered in thick cloud and the 440 Lancasters taking part had to bomb on blind markers. Damage was limited and only nine bombers were lost, one each from 101, 460 and 100 Squadron failing to return, with a second from Waltham crashing when the crew bailed out over Surrey with the aircraft out of fuel. 1 Group was to escape lightly when the second raid took place on November 22-23. Bad weather kept many night fighters on the ground and Berlin was once again covered in cloud. But this time the PFF marking was remarkably accurate as was most of the bombing. A large area of the city was badly damaged in what was later reckoned to be the most effective attack of the war on Berlin. Twenty-six British aircraft were lost, more than half of them Halifaxes and Stirlings which were shortly to be withdrawn from attacks on the German capital. A 101 Squadron Lancaster was also wrecked in an accident while attempting to take off.

At Kirmington Sgt Stan Miller and his crew were on their first operation and bombed successfully through the clouds before turning for home. However, they strayed off course and, losing the protection of Window, were hit by radar-predicted flak, which damaged the port wing and rear turret. They were then picked up by a formation of no fewer than eight Ju88s and, after briefly exchanging fire, dropped into the cloud and made good their escape.

Alan Bodger and his 576 Squadron crew pictured at a snowy Elsham dispersal early in 1944. Note the four .303 guns in the back of the truck. (Elsham Wolds Association)

Fifteen minutes later Sgt Miller brought the Lancaster up through the overcast only to be attacked again. Once more he dropped into the cloud and this time stayed there until he knew they were safe. Sgt Frank Taylor's Lancaster was hit by flak over the Dutch coast but pressed on. However, it soon became clear they were not going to make it to Berlin and back so bombed the alternative target, Brunswick, before turning for home and once again were hit by flak over Rotterdam. Another crew on their first operation were lucky to make it back to England after running the gauntlet of flak batteries. Sgt Bill Butler's aircraft ran into bad weather and arrived over Berlin 10 minutes after the raid finished. They bombed without opposition but were then subjected to a ferocious barrage of anti-aircraft fire. They were fired on again over Hanover and lost their port inner engine only to be hit by more flak as they passed close to Rotterdam. Over the North Sea they lost another engine and sent out an SOS believing they would have to ditch. However, Sgt Butler managed to nurse the aircraft back to land and they made a wheels-up landing at Bradwell Bay in Essex. All three of the 166 Squadron pilots failed to complete their tours, Stan Miller being killed in a crash on returning from Berlin a month later, Bill Butler being killed over Brunswick in January and Frank Taylor becoming a prisoner at the end of March 1944.

There was to be no let up for the Lancaster crews or Berlin. Operations were on again the following day and, once again, the red ribbons on the target maps stretched to the German capital. It was to be a smaller-scale raid this time, involving 383 aircraft, the lowest number on any of the attacks, and, as on the previous night, it was to be a matter of 'straight in and straight out' with no feints to fox the defenders. 166 lost an aircraft, with both gunners being killed in night fighter attacks, while F/O Charles Jones and his crew failed to return to Wickenby where another 12 Squadron aircraft had earlier being wrecked in an accident. A 460 Squadron aircraft crashed at Kelstern during a pre-raid air test, killing two members of the crew, while two aircraft from the squadron were lost on the operation itself. The pilot of a 100 Squadron Lancaster which was brought down over Berlin was later rescued from one of the many lakes surrounding the city and was taken prisoner along with three other members of his crew.

Elsham intelligence officer Lucette Edwards with pilot Geoff Maddern on the flight deck of his Lancaster. (Elsham Wolds Association)

The MT Section outside Elsham's main hangar. Note the Lancaster in the background undergoing an engine change. (Elsham Wolds Association)

103 Squadron lost one Lancaster during that attack but when Berlin was visited again on the night of November 26-27 it was to lose three over the target with another written off with battle damage after a crash landing at the 6 Group airfield at Croft in North Yorkshire. A fourth aircraft, flown by F/O Robert Brevitt, was diverted to another Yorkshire airfield along with several other aircraft as visibility dropped at Elsham. As F/O Brevitt arrived in the circuit at his diversionary airfield, Middleton St George, his Lancaster was in collision with a Halifax II of 428 Squadron and crashed two miles from the airfield. Only one of the crew survived while all seven men in the Halifax, which was returning from an attack on Stuttgart, died. That night 103 Squadron had set a new Bomber Command record by supplying 30 of the 443 Lancasters on the raid.

It was a bad night all round for 1 Group. Three aircraft from 101 Squadron, two of them ABC-equipped, failed to return, while 550 Squadron, making its operational debut from Waltham before its move to North Killingholme, suffered its first loss, F/Lt Peter Prangley's Lancaster crashing on the outskirts of the city. His aircraft had been set alight by anti-aircraft fire and he remained at the controls after giving the order to bail out. It is believed at least four men

126

got out of the aircraft before it went out of control, two surviving while the body of a third, flight engineer Sgt Alan Ward, was found in the River Havel. No trace was ever found of the navigator, F/O Geoffrey Harris. 12 Squadron had one aircraft wrecked on take off and another on landing with battle damage, although both crews escaped, that of Sgt Arthur Twitchett being killed on a Berlin raid a few weeks later. Not so fortunate were the new boys of 626 Squadron at Wickenby, the squadron losing one aircraft over Berlin while a second crashed near the airfield on its return. This involved F/Lt Wood's crew and their Lancaster actually came down in the middle of the station's WAAF site close to the village of Holton Beckering. The aircraft tore through the site, narrowly missing one hut before its nose was torn off and the aircraft slithered to a halt in a field just short of the airfield, the crew walking away unscathed. This was the final operation of the crew's tour and they were determined to land at Wickenby, despite other aircraft being diverted. They opted to land on instruments, unaware that the beam approach was wrongly calibrated. A third Lancaster from the squadron, flown by F/Sgt Keith Windus RAAF, crashed trying to land at Marham, killing all on board. There were other losses that night for 460 and 166, two of its Lancasters failing to return.

A third Lancaster from Kirmington was attacked by a fighter over France which raked the full length of the aircraft, wounding the Canadian rear gunner Sgt George Meadows in the back and temporarily putting both turrets out of

A snow-covered A Flight dispersal Kelstern before an air test, winter 1944. (Eric Thale)

operation. The fighter then made a second attack, this time a cannon shell exploding in the cockpit. The elevators were damaged and the pilot, F/Sgt Roy Fennell, jettisoned the bomb load and ordered the crew to bail out. The bomb aimer, Sgt Ron Moodey, jumped but at that point F/Sgt Fennell managed to regain control and turned for home. The aircraft was to be attacked again several times by fighters but were driven off by fire from the rear turret where, despite his wounds and loss of blood, George Meadows refused to leave his position. F/Sgt Fennell managed to land the aircraft at Ford in Hampshire and it was only then that the severity of the wounds suffered by the rear gunner became known. Sgt Meadows was to receive an immediate award of the Conspicuous Gallantry Medal but was to spend some considerable time in hospital recovering from his injuries. The body of the bomb aimer was later found in France, his parachute unopened. Sgt Fennell and his crew, minus Sgt Meadows, were to be killed on the final raid in the Battle of Berlin in March, 1944.

The air battles over Berlin were now reaching their full fury. On the night of December 2-3 Berlin was hit yet again with another major raid, a force of 458 aircraft, mainly Lancasters, again taking the direct route. The fighters were waiting for them and of the 40 which failed to return, 18 were from 1 Group with another aircraft crash-landing on its return to Kelstern. It was a particularly black night for the Australians at Binbrook, with five of their aircraft being shot down. Among the 28 men who died that night in 460's Lancasters were two journalists, Norman Stockton of the *Sydney Sun* and Capt Nordahl Grieg, a Norwegian war correspondent, poet and relative of the famous composer. They had arrived at Binbrook five days earlier along with Colin Bendall, the air correspondent of the *Daily Mail* with the object of reporting at first hand on the bombing of Berlin. Capt Grieg was amongst his country's best known writers and had spent time in China reporting on the civil war. He was an avowed anti-fascist and escaped to England on the same ship which carried the Norwegian royal family in 1940. He was commissioned into the Norwegian Armed Forces as a war correspondent and was one of a number of journalists given permission to fly with Bomber Command that night, Ed Murrow of CBS and Lowell Bennett, another American who was working for the *Daily Express*, flew with 50 Squadron from Skellingthorpe, near Lincoln.

Grieg flew from Binbrook with the crew of F/O Alan Mitchell, their aircraft crashing some 40 miles from Berlin. The body of the Norwegian was never found. Norman Stockton went to Berlin with F/O James English and his crew, their aircraft exploding after being attacked by a night fighter near the target

S/Ldr Canham (centre) and his crew with H-Harry of 625 Squadron at Kelstern late 1943. They had originally been with 100 Squadron and brought their Lancaster with them. It was lost over Berlin with a different crew at the end of January 1944. (Author's collection)

area. Colin Bendall was more fortunate and made it back safely. Ed Murrow was also to return to Skellingthorpe but the Lancaster carrying Lowell Bennett was another casualty that night although Bennett himself escaped by parachute and spent the remainder of the war in a PoW camp. Binbrook's other casualties that night included the crew of S/Ldr Ted Corser, a popular flight commander with 460 Squadron.

Four of the Lancasters which left Wickenby during the late afternoon of December 2 were lost, three from 12 Squadron and a fourth from 626, flown by S/Ldr George Roden DFC. 101 Squadron lost three ABC Lancasters and among the men who died were F/Lt George Frazer-Hollins DFC and his special operator, F/O Arthur Weldon, both men being on their second tours, Weldon having flown earlier as a wireless operator. The third crew survived to spend the remainder of the war in captivity. At Elsham four full crews were lost, three from 103 and one from 576, flown by F/Sgt John Booth, a 20-year-old Australian. At Waltham, always regarded as one of the 'lucky' stations in Bomber Command, all but one of the 27 Lancasters sent by 100 and 550 Squadrons made it home, W/O Alan Collier's aircraft being hit by flak near Hanover. One of 100 Squadron's Lancasters had a fierce battle with a night fighter over the target and the rear gunner, Sgt Johnny Knox, was killed. Another man lost that night was S/Ldr John Garlick, who had won a DFC with 12 Squadron at Binbrook back in 1942. He was flying a 97 Squadron Pathfinder aircraft which was attacked by a night fighter and remained at the controls of the burning aircraft to give his crew the chance to escape.

Despite the awful losses Lancasters from 1 Group were sent on another long trip to Leipzig the following night. A diversionary attack on Berlin by Mosquitos drew off the bulk of the Luftwaffe night fighter force and losses were reduced with only two failing to return. P/O Charles Plumridge's 100 Squadron aircraft was shot down by a pair of night fighters near the target which then collided and crashed in flames, much to the satisfaction of the four crew members who got out of the Lancaster. The other loss was at Elsham where a 576 Squadron aircraft failed to return. There was also a very lucky escape for two other crews, one from 100 Squadron the other from 460 which collided over the target. The port wing of the Binbrook aircraft struck the underneath of the fuselage of the 100 Squadron Lancaster. Both aircraft were damaged but managed to make it home. The two crews then planned a night out together in Grimsby to celebrate their good fortune but it was never to taken place, the 460 Squadron crew failing to return from their next operation.

Bad weather and adverse moon conditions gave the weary aircrews the opportunity of some rest over the next two weeks. This came to an abrupt end on the morning of Thursday December 16 when the teleprinters at 1 Group HQ at Bawtry began to chatter. Operations were on again and, once more, the target was Berlin. This was a day which was to go down in Bomber Command

550 Squadron's O-Oboe showing the scars of a battle with a night-fighter over Berlin at the end of January 1944. Both turrets were wrecked and the gunners killed and parts of the fuselage shredded by cannon fire but O-Oboe made it back to the emergency airfield at Woodbridge where this photograph was taken. The aircraft was so badly damaged it had to be scrapped. (Roland Hardy)

annals as Black Thursday, not particularly because of the losses over Germany, bad though they were, but of the return of an old adversary, the weather which proved disastrous for many of the returning bombers. It was a misty day but the Met men were confident that visibility would improve and that conditions over Germany would keep much of the night fighter force on the ground. Neither forecast proved to be correct.

The raid got off to a bad start, with two Lancasters from Elsham, one from 103 and the other from 576, collided over the village of Ulceby minutes after taking off. The collision, or at least the tremendous explosion as the bomb load went off, was seen by many people on the ground, including children on their way home from schools in the villages stretching from Ulceby to Barton. There were no survivors. Over the target itself 1 Group lost a further five aircraft but it was when the attackers began to arrive back over Lincolnshire that the real problems began. The cloud base had come down, in some areas, almost to ground level. Worst affected was Waltham where four aircraft were to be lost, two in a collision in the circuit and two more in crashes near the airfield. Three

F/O Len Young DFC at the controls of D-Dog of 103 Squadron, December 1943. (Norman Storey)

460 Squadron aircraft crashed along with two each from Ludford and Kirmington. Among the Binbrook casualties was the crew of F/O Francis Randall DFC, the 21-year-old Australian pilot who had escaped that mid-air collision during the Leipzig raid. He circled in the gloom for 45 minutes before apparently running out of fuel and crashing into trees surrounding the bomb dump at Market Stainton. All those on board were killed but the crews of the other two from 460 survived. In all 1 Group lost 13 aircraft as tired crews tried to land in awful visibility, killing 59 men. The highest profile casualty was 22-year-old W/Cmdr David Holford, the man who won a DSO with 103 Squadron in 1942 and who led the first four-engined bomber raid of the war in 1 Group. He had recently taken over as CO at 100 Squadron and had opted to lead the squadron that night, only to die in the most tragic circumstances *(See a full account of David Holford's story in the following chapter).*

Another man who flew from Waltham that night was W/Cmdr Jimmy Bennett, the CO of 550 Squadron, and a close friend of David Holford. He was flying with 'Bluey' Graham and crew that night and, in an interview with the author, was later to recall: 'Our take off was early, about 4.40 in the afternoon, and even then the visibility wasn't very good and it was plain we were not going to be in for a very pleasant journey.'

The cloud cover cleared slightly over the North Sea and there was far more fighter activity than they had hoped to see but they dropped their bombs and got away with no trouble although they did see a few aircraft in flames, caught by either fighters or flak.

He went on: 'However, coming back the cloud started to increase again and it was clear that by the time we reached England it would be right down on the deck. Bluey decided to come down through the cloud while we were over the sea, always a wise practice in conditions like those. Lincolnshire may have been fairly flat, but there were places where it wasn't and there were always a few of what we called "stuffed clouds", which contained something hard, like a hill.

'We dropped down into the mist and Bluey picked up the outer circle of sodium lights at Waltham, stuck his port wing on them and followed them round until he found the funnel and put her down. We rolled along the runway to the far hedge and we were already aware that planes were coming down all around us, landing at the first opportunity, so we decided it would be a lot safer to leave the Lanc where it was and walk the rest of the way.'

As they did so he looked up and saw what appeared to be the red starboard wing tip light on a Lancaster. It appeared to be going the wrong way round the circuit. Then there was an almighty crash as it collided with another bomber going in the opposite direction.

Later he accompanied the station commander at Waltham, G/Capt Nick Carter, to Fulstow where the village hall had had been requisitioned as a temporary mortuary where the bodies of between over 30 1 Group airmen were laid out in straight lines. It was a sight which was to remain with him for the rest of his life. Later, he had the awful job of going to the Ship Hotel in Grimsby to break the news of David Holford's death to his widow, Joan. The couple had been staying there until they found a home near the airfield.

Canadian bomb aimer F/Sgt Bill Kondra, who was a member of F/O Tommy Heyes' crew, also witnessed the collision over Waltham. He and his crew had just made it back from Berlin and were thanking their lucky stars they had got down safely when they saw the flash and heard the sounds of a collision. 'It was something I will never forget," he was later to recall.

F/Sgt Pat Doyle's 625 Squadron crew never made it to Berlin that night. On the outward leg they ran into a severe thunderstorm and icing on the aircraft became so severe that their engines began to surge and the Lancaster started to lose height. They jettisoned their bombs and turned for home, St Elmo's Fire flickering from the wings. It was a frightening experience made even worse when the navigator, Sgt Dave Winlow, announced they were close to Kelstern but they couldn't make out anything in the murk below. Then, just as the skipper told the crew to be prepared to bail out, they saw a flicker of light. Down they went and found themselves over Ludford Magna, only a few miles from home, where they landed safely. This was one of four 'early returns' at Kelstern while, of the others dispatched on the raid, only two Lancasters would make it back safely that night. Nine were diverted, six of them to Blyton and the others to Ludford. W/O Don Baker's aircraft was shot down near Hanover with only one of the crew surviving while American pilot Arnold Woolley's Lancaster crash-landed at Gayton-le-Wold, not far from the airfield, killing two of the crew and injuring the survivors. Another Lancaster, flown by W/O Ellis, overshot on its return and then made a spectacular belly-landing on the airfield.

Eight of 101's Lancasters were diverted to Lindholme on their return. Another was diverted to Faldingworth but, unable to find the ground, the crew bailed out safely. Another, flown by 20-year-old Sgt Norman Cooper, crashed near Eastrington in East Yorkshire while attempting to divert to Holme-on-Spalding Moor while two others, the aircraft of F/Sgt Peter Head and Canadian F/O Ron MacFarlane, failed to return.

At Elsham two aircraft were diverted, one to Lindholme, the other to Kirmington, while another made an emergency landing in a field near Barton-on-Humber. Two 166 Squadron aircraft crashed on their return, Sgt Stan Miller's Lancaster hitting high ground near Caistor while F/Sgt Arthur Brown's machine came down near Barton. There were no survivors from either aircraft. F/O Peter Pollett and crew failed to return from the raid.

The visibility had been a fickle opponent that night. At Wickenby all the aircraft sent by 12 and 626 returned safely and landed with no problems. It was the same story on 5 Group airfields yet further south at Bourn in Cambridgeshire 97 Squadron lost seven aircraft in crashes, while another made a safe landing on the grass runway at Ingham, one of the few times a Lancaster landed there. The 1 Group Summary for December spoke of the need for crews to 'master the elements' and, while admitting conditions were 'vile and unexpected' stressed that 136 aircraft had landed safely, adding 'We must continue to strive for better airmanship and more effective ground control'.

The RAF had carried out the first successful test of fog dispersal equipment a month earlier when four Halifaxes of 35 (PFF) Squadron landed at Graveley in Cambridgeshire in poor visibility. The device that helped them get down was FIDO, the acronym for 'fog investigation dispersal operation', a system which had been developed at Birmingham University and involved burning huge quantities of petrol in special burners on each side of the runway, the heat generated dispersing the fog. It was an enormously expensive system which could burn more than 100,000 gallons of fuel an hour but it worked and it went on to save the lives of many RAF crew. Several crews did use FIDO to get down at Graveley but it was March before a 1 Group was to get the device, burners being laid alongside the main runway at Ludford Magna.

A Berlin survivor, JB555 flew to 'The Big City' on at least 10 occasions, first with 103 Squadron and then with 576. (Norman Storey)

FIDO was to be installed at a number of other airfields, including both Metheringham and Fiskerton (later to become part of 1 Group), along with the three special emergency airfields at Manston, Woodbridge and Carnaby in East Yorkshire, all of which had specially lengthened runways. It was also installed at the airfield at Sturgate, near Gainsborough, which was planned for 1 Group but was never used operationally.

Berlin was attacked again on the night of December 23-24 and once again tragedy struck at Waltham. It was almost midnight before most of the Lancasters of 100 and 550 got away from the airfield, the operation being delayed because of bad weather, and shortly after midnight reports came through that a Lancaster from Waltham had crashed at Fulstow, just off the Louth road. It was only discovered later that in fact two aircraft had collided after take off and crashed. There were no survivors from either F/Sgt William Cooper's 100 Squadron aircraft or from Sgt Hubert Woods' 550 Squadron Lancaster. Two other aircraft failed to return, one flown by P/O Don Dripps, a popular Australian whose crew were on their 23rd operation. Three aircraft were also lost from Elsham, two of them from 576 Squadron, while another, flown by Sgt Geoff Clark, failed to return to Kelstern.

One Kelstern crew had to thank the skill of their pilot, W/O Ted Ellis, for making it home. Their aircraft was hit by flak near Berlin and the rear turret damaged. They went on to drop their bombs but, as they did so, were attacked by a night fighter, both gunners being injured by cannon shell fragments. The aircraft by now had no hydraulics, intercom, the bomb doors were jammed open and there was considerable damage to the wings and fuselage, but W/O Ellis managed to get the aircraft and his crew home, an action for which he was to be awarded a Conspicuous Gallantry Medal.

There was to be one more major attack on Berlin before the year ended, five 1 Group Lancasters being lost on the night of December 29-30. Eighteen members of the crews of three of them, from 12,101 and 103 Squadrons, survived to become prisoners, an unusually high percentage, but only one man lived from the two aircraft lost by 460 Squadron.

If crews thought that 1944 was to bring a different direction they were mistaken. Early on January 1 orders came through for another 'maximum effort' and, once more, the target was Berlin although, once again, it was to be midnight before most of the 421 Lancasters taking part actually got away. A quarter of the 28 aircraft lost came from 1 Group, two of them ABC Lancasters from Ludford Magna. One crashed in Belgium while the second vanished without trace. This was flown by S/Ldr Ian Robertson who had won a DFC in a raid on Nuremburg the previous August. Also decorated in that operation was his flight engineer Sgt Tom Calvert and navigator F/O Sid Kennedy. His special operator that night was F/Lt Alf Duringer, who had won a DFM while flying as a wireless operator with 150 Squadron at Snaith and had later added a DFC while with 101. 550 Squadron also lost two aircraft that night others were lost from 12 and 626 at Wickenby and from 460 Squadron.

Berlin was attacked yet again the following night. This time only four 1 Group aircraft were lost while a fifth, flown by F/Lt Barrington Knyvett, crashed on take off from Binbrook, killing all seven men on board. Two nights later it was an even longer haul for the Lancasters, this time to Stettin. A diversionary raid on Berlin drew off many of the fighters and only 16 aircraft were lost, six of which were from 1 Group with 12 Squadron losing two. One was shot down over the target while the second force-landed in Sweden with battle damage, the crew, which included three Canadians, being interred. Three failed to make it back to Elsham, two of them from 576 Squadron, while a 626 Squadron Lancaster ditched in the North Sea not far from the Yorkshire coast at Withernsea. The aircraft had taken off from Wickenby shortly before midnight but it was almost 10am the following day that the aircraft came down on the sea, out of fuel. Australian pilot F/Lt Bill Belford and his crew were quickly picked up and were landed at Yarmouth, weary and glad to be alive after an eventful night. They were taken to a nearby USAAF airfield where Wickenby's Station Commander, G/Capt Crummy, was waiting to fly them 'home' in one of the squadron's Lancasters. Their reprieve was to be only

The ground crew of 625 Squadron's H-Harry, which was lost over Berlin at the end of January 1944. The aircraft had previously flown with 100 Squadron. (Author's collection)

temporary, six of the crew being killed and the seventh, navigator Sgt Alan Lee, becoming a prisoner of war when their aircraft was lost over Berlin later in the month.

The next major target for Bomber Command was Brunswick on the night of January 14-15 and it was to cost 166 Squadron its commanding officer. W/Cmdr Colin Scragg was an American who joined the RAF in the 1930s and flew fighters before being posted back to Canada as a flying instructor. Like many others in his position he was desperate to get back to Britain to take part in the real war and he finally achieved this in the summer of 1943, dropping a rank and eventually found himself at 18 OTU at Finningley before a spell at 1656 HCU at Lindholme, where he became a friend of W/Cmdr Holford, the 100 Squadron CO killed a few weeks earlier. In October 1943 he was finally on operations as A Flight commander at 103 Squadron and two months later promoted back to wing commander and appointed CO at 166 Squadron. That night he flew as pilot in S/Ldr Pip Papes' crew. Hampered by intercom problems, they bombed the target before being attacked by a night fighter. The aircraft went into a steep dive and Scragg ordered his crew to jump before unfastening his own straps. He managed to break the starboard window and squeezed through. Seconds after pulling the ripcord he landed on the ground, hid his parachute and began to walk. He hid up for the day in a hay loft before spending the next night heading, he hoped, for the Dutch border. Next morning brought him to the small town of Vienenburg in Lower Saxony and there he hid in the town's railway station, first in an outbuilding and then in the ladies lavatories. When night came he tried to board a train, only to be immediately spotted and surrounded by soldiers. He was to spend the remainder of the war as a prisoner and was the only survivor from his aircraft. His was one of two aircraft lost that night from Kirmington. Three Lancasters, all fitted with ABC, were lost from Ludford, only one man surviving. Among the other aircraft lost was that flown by F/O David Cobbin of 550 Squadron, their first operational loss from their new airfield at North Killingholme. Six of the crew died. 576 Squadron also suffered two more losses as did 626 Squadron.

1 Group's losses were to be small on the next two major attacks of the campaign, three aircraft being lost in attacks on Berlin and Magdeburg, one of those a 460 Squadron Lancaster which crashed on Whitegate Hill in Caistor, not far from the airfield, all the crew being injured.

Bomber Command had still not finished with Berlin and three more heavy raids were staged on successive nights before the end of January. The first was to cost 1 Group 12 of the 33 Lancasters lost. One from 625 Squadron at Kelstern was hit by flak on the return journey. The pilot, P/O Roy Cook, who had won a DFM and promotion earlier in the month, managed to keep the burning aircraft in the air for almost an hour before it crashed, killing him and the rear gunner, 37-year-old Sgt Jack Ringwood, one of the oldest men to serve with 625 Squadron. The others on board all managed to escape. 460 Squadron at Binbrook lost three aircraft but 10 of those on board survived to become prisoners. Another three were lost by 12 Squadron who were even more fortunate with casualties, six men being killed, 11 being taken prisoner and four more evading capture after coming down in Belgium where they were picked up by the Resistance and found their way to Spain and home. Another loss from Wickenby was the Lancaster of 23-year-old Australian F/Lt Bill Belford and crew, the survivors of the ditching earlier in the month.

It was Berlin again the following night as the Halifax squadrons of 4 and 6 Group were committed once again alongside the Lancasters of 1, 3 and 5 Groups, only to suffer disproportionate losses. Just four 1 Group Lancasters were lost, from 576, 625 and two from 166 Squadron, the pilot and navigator of one being blown clear when the aircraft exploded after a mid-air collision. The third wave of the attack saw three Lancasters lost of 16 sent from 100 Squadron at Waltham, with just two men surviving. All three aircraft were acting as PFF supporters and it was at this stage in the attack that many of the losses occurred as fighters got amongst the bomber stream.

The penultimate raid in the Battle of Berlin came a little over two weeks later in what was the heaviest raid so far on the German capital, 891 Lancasters and Halifaxes with 27 Lancasters and 17 Halifaxes being lost. One of the six lost from 1 Group was a 12 Squadron Lancaster which lost all four engines when it was hit by flak over the target area. The crew all bailed out but the unfortunate flight engineer, 19-year-old Sgt Eric Auty was killed when his parachute became entangled in the tail plane of the aircraft and he was dragged to his death. There were many bad ways of being killed in the air war but that must have been amongst the worst. Another aircraft that failed to return was flown by F/Lt Ken Berry of 103 Squadron. He was just 20 yet had won a DFM with the squadron a year earlier, was later promoted and was on his second tour. He and his crew died when their aircraft was shot down by a night fighter over Holland. His navigator was S/Ldr Harold Lindo DFC, a 27-year-old Jamaican who had joined the Royal Canadian Air Force in 1940. He had won his DFC in 1942 after he completed 21 operations in Wellingtons with the squadron. He was an outstanding navigator who became the squadron's Bombing Leader and survived a North Sea ditching in August 1941 when the Wellington he was in ran out of fuel 40 miles off the Yorkshire coast. S/Ldr Lindo was among a number of highly-decorated Jamaican officers who flew with Bomber Command and, after his death, his father sent a number of gold watches to the squadron to be awarded to the pilots who had completed the highest number of operations to Berlin.

There was now just one more raid on Berlin to come in the battle, but another six weeks were to pass before Bomber Command went back to the German capital. In between came a number of heavy raids on other German targets which were to cost Bomber Command, and 1 Group, dearly. The first of these was to Leipzig on the night of February 19-20 when the RAF lost a staggering 78 of the 823 aircraft sent. Seventeen of those lost were from North Lincolnshire, with two more being written off in crashes.

Two Lancasters from 103 were lost over Germany and two more in a mid-air collision during landing, one getting down safely while the second crashed with the loss of five lives. 625 Squadron at Kelstern was also badly affected, losing three aircraft and the lives of 18 men. The casualties included P/O Jim Aspin who was on his 13th operation. He had been awarded the DFM in one of the squadron's first operations shortly after it was formed. Three Lancasters from Kirmington were also shot down while a fourth flown by P/O Jim Catlin was attacked over the target by two Me110s and badly damaged with four of the crew being wounded. The rear gunner, Sgt Bill Birch, fought a running battle with one of the night fighters and was later to claim one as a 'probable'. His turret, in the meantime, had been virtually wrecked but he still managed to drive the second night fighter away. The flight engineer, Sgt Barry Wright, was badly injured and lost a lot of blood but, showing enormous determination,

Snow clearing at Ludford Magna, February 1944. The airfield was almost completely snow-bound for a week. (Vic Redfern)

managed to nurse the engines and help keep the Lancaster flying. With the bomb doors stuck open, the hydraulics gone and the trim controls stuck, the pilot struggled to keep the aircraft level as they painstakingly headed back for England where they managed an almost perfect landing at Kirmington after hand-cranking the undercarriage down only to discover both tyres were flat. Sgt Wright was later awarded the Conspicuous Gallantry Medal for his endeavours, while there were DFCs for P/O Catlin, the navigator P/O Tony Pragnell and the bomb aimer, P/O Frank Sim, and DFMs for Sgt Birch, the mid-upper Sgt Tom Powers and the wireless operator Sgt Tom Hall.

At Wickenby, three Lancasters failed to return, two of them from 12 Squadron. Two more were lost from Binbrook, another from 576 at Elsham and one from Ludford. It had been a very bad night indeed.

Berlin may have got some respite over the next few weeks but Bomber Command did not with seven more deep penetration operations over Germany. Stuttgart was the next to be hit, 1 Group losing a single Lancaster, the 460 Squadron aircraft being written off in a crash. Two nights later the bombers went to Schweinfurt as part of the Anglo-American assault on Germany's ball bearing production. Bomber Command lost 33 aircraft, far fewer than an earlier USAAF attack, with nine of the losses coming from 1 Group squadrons. Worst hit was 100 Squadron at Waltham which lost three aircraft, one of them with the squadron commander at the controls. W/Cmdr John Dilworth, who had only taken over the squadron after the death of W/Cmdr Holford just before Christmas, flew as second pilot in the crew of 20-year-old Sgt Arthur Merricks on what was to be their first and last operation. Two of the crew survived as they did from the second 100 Squadron aircraft, flown by F/O Vernon Jones, which was brought down by flak over France.

Waltham's third loss that night was the Lancaster of F/Sgt Francis Wadge. Only a few days earlier F/Sgt Wadge had been awarded an immediate DFM after his Lancaster collided with what may have been a German night fighter during the attack on Stuttgart. The collision tore away part of the port wing, wrecked the mid-upper turret, damaged the fuselage and bent the starboard rudder. The mid-upper gunner was injured in the collision and, with the engines vibrating badly, it took all the skill of the pilot, aided by his crew, to keep the Lancaster flying until they were able to make an emergency landing at Ford in Hampshire. Two nights later F/Sgt Wadge was on the battle order again for the attack on Schweinfurt. Flying with only two of his original crew, he turned back after reporting he was feeling ill and when his aircraft returned to Waltham he was ordered to fly out to sea and jettison some fuel. He returned to report that the jettison equipment would not work. He was then told to go back out to sea again and dump the bomb load. This he did but after that nothing more was heard from F/Sgt Wadge's Lancaster. No trace of it or its seven-man crew was ever found.

In an attack on Augsburg on the night of February 25-26, F/Lt Bill Eddy's 103 Squadron Lancaster was hit by flak in the target area and a small fire started in the fuselage. Worst still, fuel pipes had been fractured and an engine failed as they turned for home. By the time they had reached the Vosges area two more engines had failed and the pilot ordered the crew to bail out, fully aware that his own parachute had been destroyed in the fire. Somehow, F/Lt Eddy managed to land the badly damage Lancaster on a snow-covered field. Bill Eddy spoke both Spanish and French fluently (before the war he had lived in Argentina where he owned a cattle station) and fancied his chances of getting home again. After walking some time he made contact with the Resistance and within a few weeks found himself in Spain. He returned to England from Gibraltar in a destroyer and arrived back at Elsham with numerous bottles of wine and, best of all, a crate of oranges. Bill Eddy was then screened from operations but, after pulling some strings, was posted back to a Mosquito Pathfinder squadron in which he went on to complete a further 60 operations, adding a DFC and Bar to his DSO.

Stuttgart was attacked twice more at the beginning of March and again a fortnight later. There were no 1 Group losses in the first of these but on the second three Lancaster from Kelstern were among the seven aircraft from the Group which failed to return. Losses on this scale were felt particularly badly on recently formed squadrons like 625 and on tightly-knit airfield communities like Kelstern. P/O Derrick Gigger's Lancaster crashed in the sea off the French coast while the aircraft of F/Sgt Frank Hodgkins was attacked by a night fighter and exploded over Germany. The third Lancaster, flown by Canadian F/Sgt John Bulger collided with a Waddington-based 463 Squadron aircraft near Lincoln on its return. There were no survivors from either Lancaster. 625 was to lose another aircraft when Frankfurt was attacked two nights later, while Lancasters were also lost from101, 166 and 103 Squadrons. Four more were lost on a second raid on Frankfurt two nights later before what was to turn out to be the final major Bomber Command raid on Berlin of the war.

The German capital was to be attacked again on many occasions but never on the scale of that of the night of March 24-25 when 811 aircraft took part. Yet again, the weather was to have a say in the outcome and was to help cost Bomber Command dearly, 44 Lancasters failing to return, 20 of them from 1 Group alone. Twenty-eight Halifaxes were also lost.

Fierce winds battered the bomber stream as it headed across Europe, much stronger than had been forecast and so bad that the stream became scattered and many aircraft strayed over known flak belts, so much so that the majority of the losses fell to anti-aircraft gunners. Six of the aircraft lost were from Wickenby, four from 12 Squadron alone. Three members of F/O Galton de Marigny's crew survived to become prisoners while Sgt Alan Keveren, the bomb aimer in F/O Fred Hentsch's crew evaded capture and made it back to England. There were no survivors from F/Lt John Bracewell's crew but the pilot of the fourth aircraft, F/Sgt Colin Bates, managed to bail out along with his wireless operator. 626 Squadron lost its CO, W/Cmdr Quentin Ross's aircraft being shot down by a night fighter. There were no survivors from his aircraft or that of F/Sgt Keith Margetts, another victim of a night fighter. Kelstern had another bad night with three aircraft lost, although four of those who survived evaded capture and made it back to England. Another night fighter victim was P/O Alfryn Jenkins' 100 Squadron Lancaster.

Four Lancasters were also lost from 166 Squadron with only five men surviving while two were lost by 460 Squadron, including the Lancaster flown by F/Lt Allan McKinnon DFC, who was well into his second tour with the squadron. At Elsham four aircraft were shot down or wrecked, two from each of the resident squadrons. One of the 103 Squadron aircraft was flown by S/Ldr Ken Bickers, who was just 21, a flight commander and on the third operation of his second tour. The second aircraft made it back to England but only thanks to the remarkable efforts of its crew, who were on their fourth operation.

Coffee, a tot of rum and a chat with the padre. A 101 Squadron crew pictured on their return from Berlin, winter 1943. The notices on the wall remind crews to empty their pockets before leaving on operations as 'the smallest item of personal property might provide valuable information to the enemy', a further chilling reminder to crews that they might not make it back. (Vic Redfern)

P/O Fred Brownings' Lancaster was attacked by a night fighter over Denmark, but, after beating off the attack, continued towards their target, where they were due to act as a PFF supporter. At this time they estimated the tail wind had reached a speed of 80mph, which meant they had to fly a zigzag course to ensure they didn't arrive too early. Even so they did reach Berlin fractionally ahead of the main body of the Pathfinders and stirred up a hornet's nest from the city's defences. As they were turning away they were attacked by an Fw190, which made three passes, raking their M-Mother with cannon fire. The intercom was out of action, the mid-upper turret damaged while the rear gunner, Sgt Bob Thomas, had been killed. There was also a five-foot wide hole in the port wing and the flaps and tail trimmers were damaged. The aircraft had become so difficult to handle that the pilot had to use his knees and all his considerable strength in an effort to keep the Lancaster level. The parlous state of the aircraft and their remaining fuel meant they had to risk everything and fly through flak belts. As they approached one the wireless operator, F/Sgt Jack Spark, remembered seeing a night fighter coned in searchlights firing red and white Verey lights as a means of identification. There were some similar flares on board so he fired them and suddenly the searchlights went out and the anti-aircraft fire stopped. Once out over the North Sea the flight engineer P/O Arthur Richardson estimated they had just 20 minutes' worth of fuel left, just enough to reach the Sussex coast. Firing off what remaining Verey cartridges they had left, they reached the airfield at Dunsfold, south of Guildford (the airfield later used as a test track in TV's *Top Gear*). The landing lights were switched on for them and, after going round once, Fred Brownings finally got M-Mother onto the runway. With no flaps to slow them, they hurtled down the runway before hitting the wreckage of an American B-17 which had crash landed there a few days earlier. Brownings was awarded an immediate DFC along with Arthur Richardson, the navigator Ron Walker, the bomb aimer Norman Barker and there was a DFM for Jack Spark. Their luck held and all six who climbed out of M-Mother at Dunsfold survived the war.

Although the M-Mother's survivors didn't know it, the Battle of Berlin was over. It had been hugely costly but there was to be an even bigger price to pay in the weeks to come as Bomber Command turned its attention largely away from Germany.

Chapter 12

The Perfect Pilot

Wing Commander David Holford
DSO DFC and Bar

The attack on Berlin during the night of December 16-17, 1943, Bomber Command's 'Black Thursday', cost the lives of 296 aircrew, more than half that of the number of RAF pilots killed in the entire three months of the Battle of Britain.

The highest-ranking airman who died that night was the 22-year-old pilot of Lancaster JB560, HW-N of 100 Squadron, which had only been at Waltham for less than three weeks. His name was David Holford. He was the youngest wing commander and squadron commanding officer in Bomber Command history. He was regarded as one of the best young officers ever to serve with 1 Group and was to be killed in freak circumstances at the end of a raid in which he had, as usual, flown with the greatest degree of courage and with the utmost skill. This is his story.

David Holford was born in Kingston-on-Thames in 1921. He was the nephew of S/Ldr D'Arcy Grieg, a World War One pilot and part of the RAF team which won the Schneider Trophy in 1929 and, from that point on, there was only to be one career his eight-year-old nephew would pursue.

In 1938 David, then just 17, began his flying training at Harwell in Berkshire and by March 1940 had completed courses on Harts, Oxfords, Ansons and finally Wellingtons, being assessed as 'above average' on each. In March that year he was posted to 99 Squadron at Newmarket where he was to fly 11 operations as a second pilot, six of them with F/Lt Percy Pickard, the man who would star as the fictional S/Ldr Dickson, skipper of F-Freddie in the hugely popular 1941 film, *Target for Tonight*, and would be killed in his Mosquito leading the Amiens prison raid in 1944.

'He was a bright young lad,' remembered Norman Didwell of Leighton Buzzard, who was a rigger on 99 Squadron and was part of Pickard's ground crew. 'Ground crew never really formed a close relationship with temporary aircrew, we had a more firm relationship with our regular aircrew. However, I do remember P/O Holford and I know that Percy Pickard really rated him as a pilot.'

David Holford (left), still a flight lieutenant, pictured at Elsham on the day he won his DSO.
(Elsham Wolds Association)

At 19, P/O Holford was initially judged too young to have an aircraft of his own but by June 1940 he had done enough to persuade those in command of 99 Squadron of his capabilities and he became an aircraft captain in his own right, completing a further 15 operations. On July 31, 1940 his Wellington was part of a small force sent to attack an aircraft factory near Hamburg. When he arrived over the target, the area was covered in thick cloud and he went on to bomb the alternative target, marshalling yards at Oldenburg. Over the target area his aircraft was caught by searchlights and badly damaged by anti-aircraft fire which knocked out one engine. However, he managed to nurse the damaged aircraft back to Newmarket and was to receive a Mentioned in Despatches for his efforts. Shortly after this he was awarded a DFC and, as a mark of his abilities, was posted as an instructor to the newly-created 11 Operational Training Unit at Bassingbourn and was promoted to flying officer.

David Holford was to spend almost 14 months with 11 OTU and was again rated as 'above average' as an instructor but he saw his real role in the war as a bomber pilot. He did manage to fly one operation during his time there, a diversionary attack on Châlons in June, 1941, and was finally to get his wish to return to a front line squadron when he was posted to 103 Squadron at Elsham in North Lincolnshire on October 3, 1941, by now with the rank of flight lieutenant. His first operation was to Dunkirk later in the month and eight nights later he and his crew were part of an attack on Frankfurt and his bombs were seen to hit the city's main railway station. However, they were lucky to make it back after hitting a barrage balloon cable near Cardiff and having to make an emergency landing at Colerne in Wiltshire.

Undeterred, he and his crew reported seeing large fires in Hamburg on their next raid. They went on to complete 29 operations, one of them the daylight attack on the *Scharnhorst* and *Gneisenau* on February 12, 1942, Operation Fuller, which was to earn F/Lt Holford his DSO. (The two battle cruisers, plus the light cruiser *Prinz Eugen*, had been bottled up in the port of Brest where they had been subjected to repeated Bomber Command attacks over a three month period in operations which had cost the RAF 127 aircraft. On February 11, the three ships slipped out of Brest under cover of heavy cloud and were not spotted until they were off Boulogne early the next day. RAF bomber squadrons had been stood down because of the weather but, over the next few hours, 240 sorties were flown by Bomber Command and many more by Fighter Command and Fleet Air Arm aircraft in a bid to attack the ships. Only a handful of aircraft located the warships and even fewer were able to mount attacks and no hits were reported in what was the RAF's largest daylight bomber operation of the war so far. The German ships, however, did not escape unscathed; both *Scharnhorst* and *Prinz Eugen* later struck mines laid by 5 Group Hampdens near the Frisian Islands)

A few weeks earlier he had met a young WAAF officer, Joan, who worked in Intelligence/Operations at Elsham. Their friendship had started to develop and she was to watch the events of that day unfold with heightened concerns for the 103 Squadron crews involved.

'I happened to be alone in the Ops room when a call came through to say that the *Scharnhorst* and *Gneisenau* had escaped from Brest and had been seen in the Straits of Dover,' she told the author. 'All aircraft were to attack them as soon as possible and I lost no time in informing the station commander, G/Cpt Hugh Constantine, and all the others who needed to be informed.'

Unfortunately, the squadron had been stood down after a series of almost non-stop attacks on Brest and only two pilots were immediately available, S/Ldr Ian Cross and F/Lt David Holford. Three other Wellingtons were to take off later from Elsham. Two turned back with their bombs, unable to locate the warships while the third was unable to attack because of low cloud over the North Sea.

'David and Ian rushed out to help their ground crews to make their aircraft ready with the utmost speed. They took off together and flew side by side until they saw the two ships and, wishing each other luck, attacked separately,' said Joan.

'David shadowed them, in and out of the cloud, for over an hour, experiencing intense flak from both of them. His crew told me later that it was a really terrifying experience as their aircraft was frequently hit. David gritted his teeth so hard that he actually loosened one of them and it came out a few weeks later!

'He finally dropped his bombs and hoped they had caused some damage. Fortunately the flak did not hit anything vital, but the plane was full of holes when they returned to Elsham and David was awarded the DSO for his actions.

'Sadly, Ian Cross was shot down and we later learned he was rescued and sent to Stalag Luft 3. He was one of the men who later escaped through the tunnels they had made, but was caught and was one of the 50 men shot on Hitler's orders.'

Ian Cross had been one of 103's flight commanders and David Holford was promoted to squadron leader and took over his duties.

On June 8, 1942 S/Ldr Holford completed his second tour of operations on June 8, 1942 at the age of just 21. He didn't have to wait long for his next posting. 103 Squadron was to be the first to fly 'heavies' in 1 Group and he was going to command the conversion unit based at Elsham. In the meantime, he and Joan were married in Leigh-on-Sea in September and rented a small cottage in the nearby village of Elsham.

103 was to get Halifaxes and, aided by two experienced instructors, David Holford threw himself into his new task. By the end of July sufficient crews had been trained and enough new aircraft had arrived for the Halifaxes of 103 Squadron to make their operational debut. This came on the night of August 1-2 when seven aircraft took part in an attack on Düsseldorf. They were led, naturally, by S/Ldr David Holford, his aircraft returning with 36 flak holes in it. The squadron was to fly only a handful of operations with its Halifax IIs before the aircraft were replaced following a Bomber Command decision to equip all 1 Group squadrons with Lancasters.

103's Conversion Flight was later to merge with 460 Squadron Conversion Flight, then based at Breighton in East Yorkshire, and together they moved to

Lindholme to form 1656 Heavy Conversion Unit and in October 1942 David Holford was appointed officer commander B Flight. He was to remain there for well over a year but did manage to fly at least one operation, taking a Lancaster to Berlin on the night of January 17, 1943, in a raid when a number of HCU aircraft were involved.

One man who flew with him at both Elsham and Lindholme was Sgt Johnny Johnson, a young Australian flight engineer whose family came from Scotland.

He was later to write: 'At times during the war, a Bomber Command squadron suffered high losses and shaken morale. This was the case in 103 Squadron, Elsham Wolds, in 1942. As ever, when things seem bleakest, a leader emerged from the pack, in this case, David Holford.

'On first impressions he was a typical, neatly dressed RAF aircrew officer, smallish in stature, softly spoken, inconspicuous amongst the more animated, exuberant personalities. On meeting him, though, this first assessment proved wrong. Perhaps his charisma is best caught in the late Don Charlwood's book, *No Moon Tonight*: "Of his words I remember little, but his dark, staring eyes I have never forgotten. I felt they had looked on the worst and, on looking beyond, had found serenity".'

Johnny Johnson recalled that during his time at Elsham, David Holford had been selected to represent 1 Group aircrew at an informal meeting with the Chief of the Air Staff, Sir Charles Portal in January 1943, to regularise the length of a bomber crew's tour of operations. Among the other men at the meeting were two who were to become Bomber Command legends, W/Cmdr Willie Tait and W/Cmdr Hamish Mahaddie. The outcome was a recommendation that a tour should consist of 30 sorties followed by nine months at an Operational Training Unit, followed by a second tour of no more than 20 sorties.

'I flew with him three times on operations as his flight engineer and many times as an instructor on training flights. On operations he had one idiosyncrasy. After the normal: "All set boys? Here we go!" he would sing "I've got spurs that jingle, jangle, jingle, as we ride merrily along" until wheels-up was ordered. I never asked him why. Maybe that's how he saw life at that time, a bunch of cowboys in the sky, riding off to shoot up some German town.'

He remembered David Holford as rarely happier than when he was flying, particularly when he found himself weighed down by the administration work of a flight commander and later officer commanding the conversion unit.

'Once or twice a week he would stick his head into my office with the call: "Get your helmet, Johnny!" With only two of us in a Lancaster, ostensibly for a test flight, we would take to the skies over the Humber. Alone above the earth, David Holford's commanding officer-façade vanished. I soon learned that unlike other pilots who struggled to subdue a heavy bomber, an aircraft became part of him from the moment he reached the cockpit. Instead of finding myself flying with a stuffy officer, I discovered in his place a devil-may-care person determined to dissipate frustrations.

'Most often he would seek out fat cumulous masses and then dive down cloud valleys, banking round their curves as he whooped with sheer élan, Another trick was to practice two-engines-out-on-one-side landings on the flat, white stratus, checking minimum speeds and reactions.

'On one occasion we were over Mablethorpe and we feathered three engines to see if it was possible to glide back to base. We managed it with just 3,000 feet to spare.

'Sometimes we would fly over to Hemswell, where David would challenge some of the Polish fighter boys there to come up and get him if they could, and then demonstrated what was vintage David Holford. I was relegated to the rear turret on those occasions to give evasive directions and some days I had the huge red spinner of a Hurricane less than ten feet from where I was seated, with a wild fighter pilot making obscene gestures. Away we would go, with a happy-go-lucky pilot at the other end, twisting and turning over the sugar beet fields.'

Johnny Johnson also recalled the inspiration crews fresh from OTUs found when they listened and watched David Holford. He would always go out of his way to help crews reach operational standard and no condemnation of them ever escaped his lips. But some things he would not tolerate: lack of punctuality, crew members forgetting equipment and thus putting others at risk, and lack of respect for ground crews, with whom he had the greatest affinity.

In March 1943 Johnny Johnson went back to 103 to resume operations. 'You lucky b★★★★★!' was David Holford's reaction. In June that year Sgt Johnson bailed out of his Lancaster after it was involved in a collision over Gelsenkirchen and it was while he was a prisoner that he learned of David Holford's death. In April 1945 he slipped away from his prison camp in the company of a Canadian airman and, after a tough march, they made it to Allied lines. As he sipped his first cup of British tea for two years his thoughts turned to David Holford. 'He would have been proud of me! And his memory, plus the inspiration it provoked, must have reminded many aircrew of their pride in Bomber Command.'

In February 1943, just four days before his 22nd birthday, David Holford was promoted to wing commander, the youngest man to hold this rank in Bomber Command and one of the youngest in the history of the Royal Air Force. On November 21 he was posted to Waltham to take command of 100 Squadron and, on the same day, a message was sent from 11 Base HQ at nearby Binbrook to Bomber Command headquarters marked for the attention of Air Chief Marshal Harris. It read: 'All is now set for the Big Push. It is confirmed Wing Commander Holford is taking over 100 Squadron.'

On the morning of December 16 the squadron was ordered to prepare for a raid on Berlin and W/Cmdr Holford decided to put himself on the battle order as pilot of a crew which had had a particularly tough time. His wireless operator, Sgt Eric Mackay, later told the story of that operation to W/Cmdr Holford's widow.

'They were attacked by a night fighter on the way to Berlin and the damage the aircraft sustained slowed them down and they fell well behind the main bomber stream.

'They were attacked again on the way back, a lone aircraft was a tempting target for the fighters. When they got back to base there was thick fog and several aircraft in the circuit were trying to get down. David was late back, but delayed landing to let some of the less experienced crews try first.

'Eventually, running out of fuel, with a damaged aircraft and no visibility, he made an attempt to land, but hit rising ground with the tail and crashed. The rear turret broke clean away and the rear gunner was hurt, but not too badly. The wireless operator was also thrown clear and was uninjured.' Their aircraft had hit high ground a few miles west of the airfield, not far from Kelstern,

'There was thick snow on the ground and it was bitterly cold and Sgt Mackay stumbled around and found David lying clear of the aircraft. He found a parachute and managed to wrap it around him against the cold.

'David was conscious and kept saying: "The crew? Are the crew all right?" It was typical of him, I think, that even in those circumstances his thoughts were for the others and not for himself.

'It was a long time before any help came as the ambulances were already out dealing with all the crashes around Waltham. When they finally arrived he was dead. I have often wondered whether he died of exposure for his injuries were so slight, a small cut on his forehead and his legs broken just above the ankles.' Four of his crew also died in the crash.

He was later buried alongside many of the other casualties of that awful night in the Cambridge Military Cemetery. On his gravestone is written: *'Pass not this stone with sorrow, but with pride and strive to live as nobly as he died.'* Shortly after his death W/Cmdr Holford was awarded a second Mentioned in Despatches.

John Bratton was nine years old at the time. His family farmed land a couple of miles from the crash site and, like lots of small boys in Lincolnshire at the time, he was a keen collector of parts of wrecked aircraft, particularly Perspex which could be melted down to make all sorts of useful things. When he heard about the Lancaster coming down he set out across the fields to see the wreckage for himself. The aircraft had struck high ground before coming to rest in a valley less than three-quarters of a mile from the nearest dispersal at Kelstern and had broken into three pieces. It was close to what was locally known as Christmas Tree Wood and he remembers there was about six inches of snow on the ground and the Lancaster was 'pretty well mashed up'. It was being guarded by a number of airmen, one of whom smashed part of the rear turret to give him some pieces of the prizes Perspex. His elder brother later used the farm tractor to help recover the Lancaster's undercarriage, which had been torn off some distance from the crash site.

David Holford's wife was to receive many tributes to her husband. Don Charlwood wrote to her: 'He was the personification of all that was best in the Royal Air Force.' S/Ldr Colin Scragg wrote: 'He was capable of big things and his charm of manner, scrupulous fairness and unquestionable courage made him an outstanding leader of men.'

From F/Lt Nettleton: 'He was the finest boy I have ever met' and F/Lt Huxtable said: 'I have never encountered anything like the devotion David inspired in everyone.'

G/Capt Carter, the station commander at Waltham, said the RAF had lost an 'outstanding personality and squadron commander' while a WAAF at Elsham, Section Officer Cookson, wrote to say: 'I think he was one of the loveliest people I've ever known and I am so proud I knew him.'

From a PoW camp in Germany came a letter from Sgt Johnny Johnson saying 'I shall remember him as the finest gentleman I shall ever know' and the local doctor at Elsham, Dr T.H. Kirk, wrote to say: 'I don't think this ghastly war has done any more miserable thing than taking David Holford. The only tiny bit of comfort to you is that he did such wonderful things with his life in the short time he had.'

One man who flew with him at Elsham was S/Ldr Leonard Pipkin, who himself was to be killed in a bizarre accident while out shooting rabbits at Wymeswold in the summer of 1944.

He wrote: 'I don't think one could meet another man who would give so much confidence to a squadron before operations. He always chose the tough jobs. I can remember his last trip with 103, to Hamburg, always a tough target. David gave his usual piano solo and everyone was in high spirits in a short time. He would always press home the attacks, because he was true British and knew no fear. He was the perfect pilot.'

Chapter 13

Hard Times

Springtime Disasters and the Road to Normandy

The Battle of Berlin may have been over and what became known as the Transportation Plan, in which Bomber Command would divert its attention to the disruption of rail and road links across France in readiness for the invasion, was about to begin but Harris hadn't quite finished with long-distance German targets just yet.

During the early spring of 1944 he had come under increasing pressure to divert the growing strength away from area bombing to attacking targets vital to Germany's so far little-diminished industrial strength. It was what the Americans were striving to do, at some considerable cost to themselves. But Harris was convinced the road he had set his forces on was the right one; smashing German cities would bring the enemy to its knees, of that he was sure. But even Harris, with all his single-mindedness and drive which was to border on ruthlessness, would have to come to heel eventually as the momentum for the invasion of Europe increased and he had set a date, April 1, when he would bow to the inevitable. His parting shot was to be an attack on Nuremberg, on the night of March 30-31, a city with key industries and one closely associated with the rise of the Nazis, and also a largely undamaged target on his lengthy area bombing list.

There would be a half moon, which would normally mean no long-distance bomber operations, but early Met indications were that that there would be high cloud protecting the bombers on the outward leg while the return would be made after the moon had set. American fighter sweeps were also expected to hit night-fighter airfields so Harris decided to gamble and go for Nuremberg. Even when a revised meteorological forecast was presented to him, suggesting the cloud cover may not be as extensive as at first thought, he refused to cancel the raid. It was, said Martin Middlebrook in his 1973 seminal work *The Nuremberg Raid*, yet another gamble. Generals, Middlebrook argued, fought perhaps half a dozen battles in their careers while Harris fought one every night and, as all military men will admit, every battle involved a gamble on one scale

A 626 Squadron crew at Wickenby. They are (left to right) flight engineer E. Groom, bomb aimer W. Lamb, wireless operator P. Moore, pilot R. Wellham, navigator N. Knight,. Rear gunner J. Atherston and mid-upper J. Egan. They all survived their tour. (Wickenby Archive)

or another. But this was to be one that Arthur Harris was to lose and it was to cost his command dearly, 95 Lancasters and Halifaxes being shot down, another 10 destroyed in crashes largely due to battle damage while 48 returned showing the scars of flak or fighters. Worst still, 540 men were killed and another 148 became prisoners. Nine more managed to evade capture while 23 were wounded and three more injured in crashes. It was Bomber Command's greatest defeat and it was the squadrons of 1 Group which were to suffer most. The raid itself was largely unsuccessful with many of the aircraft which reached the target area bombing Schweinfurt, some 55 miles away, by error, although the damage there to the city's ball bearing industry proved to be more extensive than that caused in Nuremburg.

Nowhere were the losses felt more keenly than at Ludford Magna. 101 had sent 26 ABC-equipped aircraft on the raid and six were shot down and another crashed back in England, costing the lives of 45 of the 56 men on board those seven Lancasters. The surviving aircraft started arriving back at Ludford shortly after 5.30am on the morning of March 31 and it was only then that the crews began to tell their stories of the route to Nuremberg being marked by a trail of blazing aircraft. Within an hour or so 19 Lancasters were back, all but seven of them damaged by either flak or fighter shells, and the full horror of the night now began to unfold. Checks were made with other airfields in case the missing Lancasters had diverted but it soon became evident that 101 had suffered its worst night of the war and the worst of almost every squadron in Bomber Command.

When returning crews arrived in the messes for breakfast they were told to sit closer together for the sake of morale amongst ground personnel. Crews were asked to help themselves to their bacon and eggs as the WAAFS were too upset to serve them. One 101 Squadron pilot later recalled: 'We waited and waited and waited. We were an experienced crew and accustomed to losing the odd one or two aircraft. But with nearly a third of the squadron missing, this was a big kick in the guts to us all. We waited up until nearly mid-day before going to our huts, stunned, shocked and silent.' There was a silver-tinted lining for some: wireless operator John Allison had recently joined the squadron as part of the crew of 'Mac' McHattie and remembered that the loss of so many men that night meant their leave was brought forward.

Hopes had been much higher at 9.15pm the previous night when the first

Sgt Hannah and F/Sgt McDevitt pictured in front of the ubiquitous Nissen huts at Wickenby.
(Wickenby Archive)

F/O Bailey and crew, 625 Squadron, Kelstern. With them are two members of the ground crew of their aircraft, Wee Wally Wallaby. (Clem Koder)

of the 795 aircraft taking part in the raid took off from Elsham Wolds but by the time the front of the bomber stream reached the Belgian border the promised cloud cover had disappeared and the Lancasters and Halifaxes were bathed in moonlight. Worst still their route took them directly over two of the radio beacons over which 'Tame Boar' night fighters were circling. 1 Group aircraft had also been briefed to fly at a lower altitude, between 16,000 and 19,000 feet, than the rest of the bomber stream on the outward leg. Group policy by now was to fly with the maximum possible bomb load (tests had been carried out by 550 Squadron at North Killingholme to find out exactly how much a Lancaster could carry and it far exceeded what the designers had expected) and it was hoped the cloud cover would protect its heavily laden bombers. That decision was to cost its squadrons dearly.

Most of the victims fell to night fighters, although one of the first 101 casualties, the aircraft of P/O Bill Adamson DFC and his crew, who were on their 29th operation, was mistakenly shot down by a 4 Group Halifax. Sgt Don Brinkhurst, the aircraft's mid-upper gunner and one of three survivors, saw the Halifax about 300ft below them before there was a burst of tracer which set the Lancaster alight. Sgt Brinkhurst escaped capture, later flying on another 20 operations with 101. Four of the other losses at Ludford were attributed to fighters, while F/Sgt Gerald Tivey's Lancaster was destroyed by flak. The

A lucky escape. S/Ldr Hugh Grant-Dalton's Lancaster Q-Queenie of 550 Squadron showing marks of a brush with a German night-fighter fitted with upward firing cannon after a raid on Stuttgart, March 1-2, 1944. (Author's collection)

P/O John Carter and his 12 Squadron crew with their Lancaster Hellzapoppin who were lost on the Mailly-le-Camp raid. (Wickenby Register)

squadron's final loss was the aircraft of F/Sgt Edwin Thomas which crashed near Welford, Berkshire as it was returning to Lincolnshire, the Lancaster diving into the ground before exploding, killing all those on board.

At Kirmington four of the 20 Lancasters 166 Squadron sent to Nuremberg failed to return. All four were experienced crews. F/Lt Gordon Procter had taken along a new pilot for experience on what was his crew's 22nd operation, all eight men being killed when they were shot down by a fighter. F/Lt Frank Taylor was the only pilot to survive. He, too, was carrying a new pilot on what was known as a 'second dickey' trip, Sgt Allen Hughes, who had only recently arrived at Kirmington. He was killed along with the flight engineer, Sgt Eric Whitfield, but the others all became prisoners on what was their 18th operation.

460 Squadron at Binbrook had contributed 24 aircraft to the raid but three failed to return. One was flown by the vastly experienced S/Ldr Eric Utz DFC and Bar. He was on his 48th operation when it is believed his aircraft was hit by fire from a night fighter and exploded, the only survivor being his navigator who was blown clear. Utz was a flight commander with the squadron and was

remembered as an efficient and confident pilot whose loss was taken particularly badly by the Australians at Binbrook. Another 1 Group flight commander lost that night was S/Ldr Tom Nicholls of 625 Squadron. He was on his 21st operation and, like many before and after, fell victim to a night fighter, the only loss from Kelstern that night.

At Elsham two of the 16 aircraft sent by 103 Squadron were lost, including that of F/O James Johnson, whose Lancaster, N-Nan, had been the very first to take off on the raid. He was killed along with five other members of his crew. The squadron's other casualties were P/O Robert Tate's crew, shot down on their first operation. A 576 Squadron aircraft was also lost from Elsham.

At North Killingholme two of 550's Lancasters failed to return. One, flown by New Zealander F/Sgt Charles Foster, was caught by searchlights over Schweinfurt and brought down by flak. There were no survivors. The second aircraft lost from North Killingholme was flown by F/Sgt Arthur Jefferies, a colourful character who was on his 29th operation and had just been awarded a Conspicuous Gallantry Medal (see chapter entitled *An Outstanding Act of Courage*). Of the 1 Group squadrons operating that night only 100 at Waltham and 626 at Wickenby saw all their aircraft return although many came back

A typical load for 20 Lancasters. This staged 101 Squadron photograph was taken for Illustrated magazine. The photograph itself is believed to have been taken at the still-unfinished airfield at Faldingworth to keep Ludford's ABC Lancasters under wraps. (Vic Redfern)

Target for tonight is.... This picture dates from early 1944 at a pre-op briefing at North Killingholme. (Roland Hardy)

with battle damage. Crews from both squadrons reported seeing numerous losses and when they heard the doleful announcement by the BBC newsreader: 'Last night our bombers attacked Nuremberg and 96 of our aircraft failed to return' they realised the full extent of what they had witnessed. At Waltham stories of destruction were disbelieved at the post-op briefing and were put down to crews seeing German 'scarecrows', special flares which were supposed to imitate exploding bombers. It was only some time later that it was realised the Germans possessed no such thing as 'scarecrow' flares, what crews were seeing were indeed exploding bombers. Not all crews saw what was happening. One bomb aimer from Waltham noted in his diary: 'Quiet trip though lots of fighters and flares.'

Nuremberg marked the nadir of Bomber Command's operations and the zenith of the effectiveness of the Luftwaffe night fighter force. There would be other bad nights, including one in which 1 Group was to lose 28 aircraft, but a switch in targets and the terrible attrition wrought on the Luftwaffe by Allied, and particularly American, fighter operations, were to change to nature of the bomber war.

The main task of Bomber Command was now to support the coming invasion and over the next few weeks their primary role would be to attack marshalling yards, ammunition dumps and gun batteries, bombing raids which required multiple smaller scale attacks, accurate marking and precision bombing, two qualities which were now very much achievable.

When operations resumed on the night of April 9-10 1 Group aircraft were involved in attacks on two different targets in addition to a costly mining operation in the Baltic. 100 Squadron aircraft were amongst 40 Lancasters to attack railway yards in Lille while other squadrons attacked yards in Villeneuve-St-George, near Paris, one Binbrook Lancaster failing to return. 166 Squadron contributed just two aircraft to the second of the railway attacks but the remainder of the squadron was sent on the 1,600-mile round trip to lay mines in Gydnia Bay in the Baltic. This was an operation carried out once again in bright moonlight and was to cost 1 Group six aircraft, three of them from Binbrook with one each from 12, 103 and 166 Squadrons. There was little wonder crews particularly detested these so-called 'gardening' sorties.

The following night there was an all-1 Group attack on the rail yards at Aulnoye. It was another costly night with seven of the 132 Lancasters sent failing to return. An eighth aircraft was destroyed in spectacular fashion at Kirmington where 22 aircraft had been prepared for the raid by 166 Squadron.

Ready for Düsseldorf. S/Ldr J.G. Woolatt's crew prepares to board their 12 Squadron aircraft before a raid in April 1944. This Lancaster was to be lost in June that year with a different crew, four of those on board surviving (Wickenby Archive)

Four Lancasters had taken off before P/O Dudley Gibbons' aircraft swung as it was gathering speed and the undercarriage collapsed in a shower of sparks. It burst into flames and the crew got out quickly, fearing the bomb load may explode. The squadron commander, W/Cmdr Frank Powley, who was to be killed a year later while flying from Scampton, led the fire-fighting operations but, seeing what was about to happen, ordered everyone clear. With that at least nine of the 14 1,000lb bombs on board exploded, shattering windows in the surrounding area and blowing a crater 50ft wide in the middle of the main runway. The blast also damaged four other aircraft. There was no possibility of the other 17 aircraft getting away and the four that did had to land at North Killingholme after the raid. But, with a superhuman effort led by W/Cmdr Powley, the runway was repaired during the night and the following morning Kirmington was declared operational again.

The marking for the Aulnoye attack was carried out by Mosquitos from 8 (PFF) Group but plans were now well advanced for the two Lincolnshire-based groups to operate more independently. 5 Group had managed to prize two PFF squadrons, 83 and 97, away from 8 Group and they moved to Coningsby in April as the group's own marking squadrons. 1 Group's own pathfinders were somewhat more modest. Earlier that month S/Ldr Harold 'Bill' Breakspear, an outstanding flight commander at 100 Squadron, was asked to form a new unit, 1 Group Special Duties Flight, and given the choice of just five further 1 Group crews to man it. He went for F/Lt Bill Hull at 101, F/Lt F. Gillan (100 Squadron), F/Lt G. Russel-Fry (103), F/O J. Stewart (626) and P/O J. Marks (625). They all moved to Binbrook where they were to operate as a separate unit alongside 460 Squadron and began training immediately, using the bombing range at Misson, not far from 1 Group HQ at Bawtry, to practice marking techniques.

1 SDF, as it was officially designated, was to have a brief but successful spell of operations, opening with an attack on an ammunition dump at Maintenon at the end of April. With S/Ldr Breakspear directing operations as the Master Bomber, it proved a huge success. 100 Squadron's records note the bombing resulted a 'terrific fireworks display…a brilliant success of the whole show' and, in a congratulatory note, Air Vice Marshal Rice, OC 1 Group, commended Breakspear on some 'magnificent work', adding: 'The job was done with precision and complete efficiency.' The Special Duties Flight was to operate throughout the summer of 1944 but was disbanded at the end of August when, because of Allied advances, suitable targets were hard to find and its crews were released for normal duties. 1 Group's Operational report added: 'The magnificent marking carried out on some of the marshalling yards of France has been amply rewarded by the chaotic state of the enemy's lines of communications.'

John Jenkinson was a flight engineer with 103 Squadron at Elsham and his

A wonderfully evocative shot at an icy dispersal at Elsham Wolds in March 1944. The WAAF alongside the Lancaster is Rose Hammond. (Elsham Wolds Association)

crew were posted to the SDF during the summer of 1944 when they were told the flight was being used for 'visual marking of lightly defended targets in France'. Some of those who had flown earlier with the flight might have taken exception to the words 'lightly defended'.

Another man who later flew with the Special Duties Flight was Mike Stedman, whose 103 Squadron crew spent some weeks at Binbrook. He particularly remembered the training regime during which he had to fly at low level wearing blacked out goggles while his bomb aimer and flight engineer guided him around high ground and electricity pylons. It was, he said, great fun!

The Poles of 300 Squadron were to resume bombing on the night of April 18-19, attacking railway targets near Cologne and Rouen. They had moved into their new home at Faldingworth on March 1, delighted at last to have a 'real' airfield to call their own and to finally get their hands on Lancasters. The squadron historian notes that while Faldingworth was a rudimentary airfield with cold Nissen huts and little in the way of amenities, it did have long concrete runways and that meant 300 Squadron could finally convert from Wellingtons to Lancasters.

Earlier in the year the squadron's A Flight had continued mining operations while the remainder of the aircrew began Lancaster training, initially at Ludford, under the experienced leadership of S/Ldr Pozyczka. Their airfield at Ingham was too small to cope with Lancaster operations and the squadron also suffered from a chronic shortage of ground crews. Eventually part of their training was transferred to Hemswell where the Poles flew alongside the aircraft of 1 Group's Lancaster Finishing School until they were deemed ready for operations. Once at Faldingworth more Lancasters began to arrive and S/Ldr Pozyczka was promoted to wing commander and took command of 300, quickly bringing the squadron up to operational readiness. 300's former airfield, Ingham, became the new home of 1481 and 1687 Bomber Training Flights and was destined to end the war as 1 Group's only airfield still with grass runways.

The raid on Rouen was part of the rail strategy and one of the aircraft lost was a Lancaster from 625 Squadron, shot down by an intruder as it prepared to land. The destruction of this aircraft was witnessed by a 101 Squadron crew as they waited in the Binbrook-Ludford-Kelstern 'stack'. Wireless operator John Allison remembered their rear gunner shouting that the fighter was dropping flares, only to realise it was a burning Lancaster crashing onto the Lincolnshire Wolds. Almost throughout the war Luftwaffe intruders had provided a deadly reminder to bomber crews that they were not safe until they were actually on the ground and they would continue to do this until the closing weeks of the war.

Railway targets may have had priority but a number of German targets were also hit in April, including Düsseldorf, Karlsruhe and Essen. 101 Squadron's ABC aircraft also operated on other attacks on Munich, Brunswick and Schweinfurt. The Karlsruhe attack cost 1 Group nine aircraft, including the first two Lancaster losses for 300 Squadron. 103 Squadron also lost two although there were no casualties. One was damaged over the target by a night fighter and the pilot, F/Sgt Cecil Ogden, managed to ditch the aircraft in Sandwich Bay while the second was hit by incendiaries falling from another Lancaster over the target. The crew was ordered to bail out but the pilot quickly managed to regain control but not before the mid-upper gunner had already jumped. The aircraft managed to return to Elsham but was so badly damaged it was struck off charge. F/Sgt Ogden and crew were to be killed on operations shortly afterwards but 40 years after their ditching the remains of their aircraft were revealed off the Kent coast during an exceptionally low tide. That same operation was also to cost 626 Squadron dearly, with three aircraft failing to return to Wickenby. There were no survivors from the Lancasters of F/Sgt Fred Baker or from those flown by Canadian warrant officers Murray McPherson and Victor Bernyk.

Ready for ops, a 626 Squadron crew, 1944. They are (back row, left to right) bomb aimer F/Sgt Leo Curtain, pilot F/O Johnny Oram, wireless operator W/O E. Just, flight engineer F/Sgt Trevor Jenkins; front: mid-upper F/Sgt 'Logger' Wood, navigator F/O John Bright, and the rear gunner, Sgt 'Spider' Webb. Both gunners were later to be killed. (Wickenby Archive)

101 lost a highly decorated crew when supporting a 5 Group attack on Schweinfurt, F/O Philip Rowe's Lancaster being shot down over France. The pilot had recently been awarded a DFC and the other seven members of his crew DFMs for a recent operation. None of the eight men lived to receive their decorations. The squadron was to lose another two crews during a successful attack on tank production factories in Friedrichshafen, close to the Swiss border. The bombers had managed to evade the night fighters until they were leaving the target area when W/O Bert Noble's Lancaster was hit by cannon fire and exploded. The aircraft actually came down in Switzerland and the two surviving members of the crew were interred. A second 101 Lancaster came down on the other side of the border and the five survivors became prisoners.

The same raid was to cost 166 and 460 Squadrons three Lancasters each. There was only one survivor from the Binbrook Lancasters, one of which was flown by one of the flight commander, S/Ldr Eric Jarman DFC, a very popular man amongst his fellow Australians. The day before Jarman and his crew had posed for a portrait at Binbrook by the Australian artist, Stella Bowen. Today, that portrait hangs in the Australian War Memorial Museum. Interestingly, one

P/O Bob Eadie and one of his crew atop their Lancaster 'Nulli Secundus' (Second to None) at Elsham, autumn 1943. This Lancaster and crew both helped form the nucleus of 576 Squadron at the airfield soon afterwards. Nulli Secundus was lost over Berlin with a different crew on Christmas Eve that year. (Elsham Wolds Association)

of the other Binbrook crews, that of F/O George Brown, were all British, a sign perhaps that there were not enough Australian air crew coming through to fill the gaps in what was a very large squadron. At Kirmington one aircraft, Q-Queenie, was badly damaged in a battle with a night fighter in which the rear gunner, Glaswegian Sgt Lockhart Little, was killed. P/O Len Hunt continued his bombing run only for the aircraft to be attacked again. The aircraft was very difficult to handle but P/O Hunt and his flight engineer, Sgt Saunders, who had made no mention of being wounded in the second attack, had to use all their strength to stop the aircraft going into a fatal drive. Finally they used cable from the aircraft's trailing aerial to lash the control column back and eventually made it back to the emergency airfield at Woodbridge where they landed the aircraft on just one wheel. There was an immediate DFC for the pilot and a DFM for the flight engineer, who had to be hospitalised with his wounds.

One of the other aircraft lost from 166 Squadron also came down in Switzerland and the two survivors both later contended it was Swiss anti-aircraft fire and not a night fighter as shown in the official records which was the cause of their destruction. They wouldn't be the first or last RAF crew to suffer at the hands of the neutral Swiss.

On the night of May 3-4 crews from 1 and 5 Groups were briefed for an attack on a German military depot at Mailly-le-Camp, about 60 miles east of Paris. At Kirmington, crews were shown a scale model of the depot and were assured the attack would be 'a piece of cake, just like falling off a log'. What it turned out to be was the worst night of the war for 1 Group, a night in which they were to lose 137 men killed and 28 Lancasters with a 29th crashing on return, a loss rate exceeding 15%.

For the men who had been to Berlin and endured Nuremberg it seemed a straight forward operation. Because of the proximity of the village of Mailly, bombing would be from 5,000 feet with Mosquitoes from 5 Group marking the target, the whole raid being 'conducted' by W/Cmdr Leonard Cheshire, who would act as Master Bomber. The attack was due to open just after midnight with aiming points at either end of the barrack buildings and a third on nearby tank workshops. W/Cmdr Cheshire was to lead four Mosquitoes which would drop markers on the first aiming point and the area would then be illuminated by 83 and 97 Squadrons allowing 140 5 Group Lancasters to bomb. After a further 10 minutes, W/Cmdr Cheshire would mark the second aiming point which would be bombed by another 140 Lancasters from 1 Group. The third aiming point, the tank workshops, was close to the village and the intention was that it would be marked by 1 Group's Special Duties Flight and then attacked by the remaining 30 1 Group aircraft.

The aircraft began leaving Lincolnshire shortly after 10pm and, after crossing the French coast near Dieppe, descended to the bombing height. Phase one went almost exactly to plan. W/Cmdr Cheshire's markers were only slightly off target but a second load, dropped from 400ft by W/Cmdr Dave Shannon, was in precisely the right spot and the first wave were called in by the main force controller, W/Cmdr L.C. Deane of 83 Squadron. They were currently orbiting a point 15 miles away, waiting for the order to bomb and this was when things started to go horribly wrong. Only a few crews heard the order as Deane's transmission was suddenly drowned out by an American Forces Broadcasting Service station which suddenly broke into the bombers' frequency. One Lancaster crew member later recalled: 'All I could hear was the tune *Deep in the Heart of Texas* followed by hand clapping and a noise like a party going on. There was other garbled talk in the background but it was drowned out by the music.'

The crews that heard Deane's message went in to bomb while a few others used their initiative and followed them and the resulting bombing was very accurate. W/Cmdr Cheshire, in the meantime, realised what was happening and ordered in the final markers with the hope they would be spotted by the circling bombers and they would take it as a signal to attack.

By this time the 170 1 Group Lancasters had arrived and began circling their own holding point, which was marked by burning yellow Target Indicators. Their arrival coincided almost exactly with the first of the German night fighters and within minutes many more turned up, finding easy targets amongst the bombers silhouetted again the flares below. With still no clear instructions, some pilots moved away from the main area while others stuck to their orders and it was amongst the latter that the heaviest casualties occurred.

Finally markers were dropped on the second aiming point and then 1 Group aircraft were ordered to go in and bomb. What happened next was later described as 'like the starting gate at the Derby' as Lancasters streamed in to drop their bombs, again with great accuracy. 1 Group SDF had had problems locating its target but, rather than risk bombs falling on the village, S/Ldr Breakspear ordered his aircraft to attack the main target.

Bombers were still crashing in flames all around the area. One of those shot down was an ABC Lancaster from Ludford flown by F/Lt John Keard. It was hit by the upward-firing guns of a night fighter and exploded, the aircraft breaking into three parts. The rear gunner, 19-year-old Sgt Jack Worsford, was trapped in the rear section without his parachute. He had been wounded in the attack and lost consciousness as the rear section of his Lancaster spun down like a sycamore seed some 7,500ft to the ground. It is believed the tail section of the aircraft hit some high tension cables and then landed in trees, both helping soften the fall and making Jack Worsford one of the luckiest men in Bomber Command. The wreckage had come down near the village of Aubeterre and he was found by a group of people from the village who had walked across some fields to examine the wreckage. They were astounded to find anyone alive. Apart from the wound in his neck he had a broken leg and cuts and bruises. They carried him back to the village but it was clear he needed hospital treatment and so the Germans were called. Sgt Worsford was one of

P/O Roy Whalley and his 576 Squadron crew, pictured shortly before their aircraft was shot down over Mailly-le-Camp, only the flight engineer and navigator surviving. (Elsham Wolds Association)

only two survivors from four 101 Squadron aircraft lost in the raid. Many of the men who died were replacements for the crews killed only a month ago over Nuremburg.

Worst hit of all was 460 Squadron at Binbrook which lost six Lancasters and the lives of 39 men. Amongst them was F/Lt Bill Hull's all-British crew who were on their 30th operation, most of which they had flown with 101 Squadron before joining the Special Duties Flight at Binbrook, transferring to 460 to finish their tour. Hull had already won a DFC and three of his all-sergeant crew had DFMs. 460 was becoming an increasingly cosmopolitan squadron and F/Sgt George Gritty was the only Australian in his crew when they arrived at Binbrook as replacements in mid-April. Mailly was their first and last operation. Sgt Bill Williams, the crew's bomb aimer, later recalled how excited the crew were to reach the target area when they would finally begin to put to good use the two years' training they had received. They were ordered

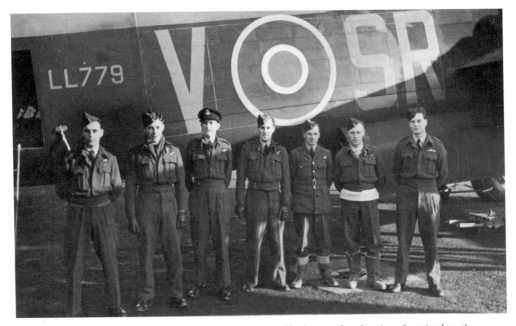

An ABC Lancaster of 101 Squadron pictured at Ludford soon after the aircraft arrived on the squadron in spring 1944. It was to be lost on ABC duties on July 21, 1944 when it was shot down over Holland during an attack on the fuel plant at Homberg in the Ruhr. (Dennis Smith)

to orbit a yellow marker and he then heard a series of rattling noises on the fuselage. It was cannon fire from a night fighter and the crew was ordered to bail out. Sgt Williams was one of three men to get clear of the aircraft before it went down. All three evaded capture, along with 13 other men who flew to Mailly-le-Camp that night, one of the highest figures of the war so far. Another who evaded capture was Australian F/Sgt Ralph Watson, one of five men to make it home from the crew of 166 Squadron's Z-Zebra. He was back in England by early August. The flight engineer in the same aircraft, Sgt Jack Marsden, landed with only one strap of his parachute intact. He was later picked up by members of the Maquis and reunited with his pilot, P/O Gerald Harrison. As both were being moved a car carrying Sgt Marsden was fired on by the Germans and he was wounded and taken to a nearby hospital. Later, as he was about to be moved to a PoW camp in Germany he was rescued by three heroic Resistance members who hoped to get him to Normandy where he could reach Allied lines. His health deteriorated and it wasn't until late August that he was finally handed over to the Americans. Back in England he was to spend four years in hospital recovering from his ordeal.

Z-Zebra was one of three Lancasters which failed to make it back to

Kirmington that night. Things were even worse at Wickenby where four aircraft from 12 Squadron and three from 626 were shot down. Five members of F/O Maxwell's 12 Squadron crew, including the pilot, made it back to England thanks to the help of local population. A sixth, Sgt Jim Davidson, was shot while hiding in the nearby town of Troyes and died of his wounds at the end of June. Of the squadron's other three losses only one man survived from the crews of P/O John Carter, F/O Jim Ormrod and F/Sgt Sydney Payne. Over at 626 all 21 men on board the three lost aircraft were killed. The bomb load on P/O David Jackson's Lancaster exploded as it was approaching the target and only two bodies, including that of the pilot, were ever found. One of 625 Squadron's flight commander, S/Ldr Gray, was one of only two survivors from the three Lancasters lost from Kelstern. His mid-upper gunner, Sgt Peter Johnson, was another who managed to evade capture after their aircraft was shot down, some time after leaving the Mailly-le-Camp area. Another crew lost from Kelstern was that of F/Sgt Neil McGaw. They were on their 15th operation and their navigator, 23-year-old Sgt Fred Clarke, was a Lincolnshire man. His family home was at Hackthorn, only 15 miles from Kelstern.

Three 103 Squadron Lancasters were lost from Elsham, the casualties including one of the oldest men to die on the raid, 32-year-old S/Ldr Jock Swanston, and one of the youngest, 20-year-old P/O John Holden. A Lancaster from 576 Squadron was badly damaged and just made it home, the rear gunner, Sgt Alf Hodson, being killed in a night fighter attack. 550 Squadron lost a single aircraft, flown by F/Lt Arthur Grain DFM, who was on his second tour. Flying with him that night was an Army officer, Major Sydney Whipp of the 7th Battalion, Duke of Wellington's Regiment, one of the few soldiers to be killed on bomber operations.

Once again 100 Squadron's luck held, with all its aircraft making it back to Waltham, although three arrived back with varying degrees of damage. Waltham was still a lucky place to serve, and it was only going to get luckier as the year progressed.

There were many recriminations when the survivors returned. At Kirmington the senior officer who had promised the operation would be 'a piece of cake' came in for particular attention while there was much criticism elsewhere at the communications failure and the hesitation shown by those in charge of the raid in keeping the bombers orbiting as the fighters got amongst them. One man who flew from Kelstern that night told the author: 'Mailly was a gigantic cock-up. If only we had been allowed to have gone in and bombed straight away many of those lads lost that night would have returned. As it was, I thank God we saw what was happening and decided to stay clear of those target indicators around which everyone was orbiting.'

The squadrons were given a couple of day's rest before operations were on again, this time 52 1 Group aircraft destroying an ammunition dump at

Aubigne. Just one aircraft, from 576 Squadron at Elsham, was lost but it was to cause much consternation amongst those planning the D-Day operation for, flying as second pilot, was Elsham's base commander, Air Commodore Ronald Ivelaw-Chapman, who had flown as an observer and as a bomber pilot in the First World War. He had arrived at Elsham six months earlier from a staff job in Whitehall where he was closely involved in planning Operation Neptune, the airborne element of the coming invasion. He was flying with F/Lt James Shearer's crew when they were attacked by a night fighter and managed to bail out along with the bomb aimer, Sgt Joe Ford, one of four Australians in the crew. They were on the run for several days before they became separated and it was after that when A/Cmdr Ivelaw-Chapman was captured.

When news of the loss of his aircraft reached SHEAF headquarters and the Air Ministry there was alarm and some anger that an officer of his seniority and with his involvement in 'Neptune' was flying at all (the air commodore was later to stress that his flight had been authorised, even though he was listed as 'additional aircrew'). Crews of all squadrons involved were questioned and they reported seeing at least two men bail out of the 576 Squadron aircraft. Then news came through from a Resistance group that A/Cmdr Ivelaw-Chapman had landed safely and was in their hands, although it was feared that a German agent had infiltrated that particular group. SOE was ordered to make every effort to get him back to England and a Lysander aircraft was scheduled to pick him up on the night of June 8th but hours before the Gestapo raided the house he was hiding in. He was later to relate that all they appeared interested in was how he had come by his French identity papers and the strength of Bomber Command. Never once did they ask the highest ranking RAF officer to fall into their hands about any involvement he might have had in the invasion planning.

Aubigne was one of a series of tactical targets hit by 1 Group during the month. Another, an attack on rail yards at Hasselt, was to prove costly, five aircraft being lost in a raid hampered by mist which covered the target. One of them was being flown by 103 Squadron's South African CO, W/Cmdr Hubert Goodman, the second senior officer to be lost from Elsham during May. Flying with the squadron CO was the crew of S/Ldr Vincent Van Rolleghem, a much-decorated Belgian pilot who had been taken to hospital suffering from a duodenal ulcer just before the operation. He was on his second tour with the squadron and in August 1943 the whole station was assembled to watch him being decorated with a DSO, DFC and Belgian Croix de Guerre by the AOC of 1 Group, AVM Rice. There were no survivors from either of the 103 Squadron aircraft. A replacement CO, W/Cmdr J. R. St John, a New Zealander who had flown a tour of operations on Stirlings, arrived at Elsham within a matter of days.

German targets were also hit later in the months and 1 Group was to lose

A wonderful shot of 576 Squadron's dispersals in the spring of 1944. The unnamed flight engineer was part of F/Lt Woods' crew. The aircraft in the background is ED888, Elsham's record-breaking Lancaster. (Elsham Wolds Association)

another 12 Lancasters over Dortmund and the same number in an attack on Duisburg. 100 Squadron's good fortune ran out over Duisburg when two aircraft were lost, with just one man surviving. 550 Squadron was hit hardest on that raid, losing three Lancasters and the lives of 21 men, all to night fighters. 100 Squadron was to lose another two in the Dortmund attack while one of two lost from 103 Squadron was flown by F/Lt Godfrey Morrison, who had recently been awarded a DSO. 300 Squadron also lost a Lancaster that night when it crashed in the Ruhr Valley. A second, carrying a crew of eight, turned back with engine trouble but, as it tried to land at Faldingworth, the aircraft struck the gunnery butts, killing two of the crew and injuring the remainder, one of whom died later in hospital. Another casualty that night was a Lancaster from 626 Squadron which crashed in Belgium, killing six of the crew. The only survivor was the Canadian bomb-aimer Sgt Ken McCoy. He managed to escape capture and made it back to Lincolnshire where he was posted to 153 Squadron at Scampton where he was to be killed in March 1945 on a mining operation in a largely Canadian crew.

Before May ended 1 Group mounted an inconclusive attack on railway yards at Aachen, going back again two nights later to finish the task. The two attacks cost the Group 14 aircraft, including three from 166 Squadron. One man who made it back to Kirmington from that raid was C Flight commander S/Ldr 'Mack' Mackie. It was the last of his tour with 166 and, remarkably, his 97th of the war. He was regarded by all who served with him as one of the bravest and coolest men who served with the squadron, and also one of the most superstitious. He always insisted that he fly an aircraft lettered M-Mike, the 13th letter of the alphabet. After leaving Kirmington he and his navigator, P/O Jack Stent, joined 139 Squadron flying Mosquitoes. Both survived the war.

As May drew to a close the Lancasters of 1 Group were used exclusively to soften up defences along the French coast and early in June they were to play a key part in supporting the greatest invasion in history. One of the Group's Lancasters was, in fact, to write itself into Operation Overlord by dropping the bombs which marked the beginning of D-Day.

Chapter 14

Learning the Ropes

Bomber Training in 1 Group

In the summer of 1944 18 heavy bombers and 43 lives were lost from Sandtoft in North Lincolnshire. Sandtoft's resident unit was not a bomber squadron, it was 1667 Heavy Conversion Unit, whose task was to train crews in the handling of four-engined aircraft. Training was to prove a dangerous business, almost as dangerous as operational flying, both for the novice crews and their instructors, most of whom had already flown at least one tour.

1 Group had three heavy conversion units. 1656 was at Lindholme in South Yorkshire, home also to the headquarters of Group training, 1662 was at Blyton while 1667 flew initially from Lindholme, moving to Faldingworth before finally settling at the new airfield at Sandtoft, on the northern edge of what is known as the Isle of Axholme, close to Lincolnshire's border with South Yorkshire.

Bomber crews' initial training was on operational training units – OTUs – where the nucleus of future bomber crews formed and did their initial training mainly on twin-engined Wellingtons. Before the advent of the heavies, there was a natural progression to squadrons and operational flying. But once the Stirlings, Halifaxes and Lancasters began to enter service there was a need for conversion training, to learn the intricacies of four-engined flying. Additional crew members were needed – in the case of a Lancaster, a flight engineer, whose job was vital in support of his pilot, and a mid-upper gunner.

In the early days, squadrons had their own conversion flights but it quickly became clear that this was a wholly inadequate system and something new was needed, hence the introductions of HCUs.

By the spring of 1942 plans were already under way for the conversion of 1 Group's squadrons from Wellingtons to Halifaxes, which were already going into service in Yorkshire with 4 Group. The first squadron scheduled to get the new aircraft was 103 at Elsham, with two others pencilled in for Halifaxes, the newly-formed 460 RAAF at Breighton and 101, which had just moved to Holme-on-Spalding Moor from Stradishall after being transferred from 3 Group.

A Halifax II of the type used extensively for the training of 1 Group crews. This particular picture shows an aircraft of 1658 HCU of 4 Group in which the pilot, S/Ldr Dobson, is demonstrating single-engined flying. (Sir Guy Lawrence via Peter Green)

The first conversion flight was 103, formed at Elsham under the command of S/Ldr David Holford, on May 3, 1942, although another month was to elapse before the first aircraft arrived. They were Halifax Mk IIs, already operational north of the Humber and an aircraft which was to earn itself an awful reputation, along with its sister, the Mk V. It wasn't until major modifications to the rudder and introduction of new and more powerful engines in the guise of the Mk III that the Halifax became the outstanding aircraft Bomber Command had hoped for.

460's conversion flight was formed at Breighton later in May and moved to Holme-on-Spalding Moor for a short period before returning to Breighton. 101's conversion flight was at Oakington in Cambridgeshire one of the squadron's former operational bases, but the impracticalities of this meant that most of its crews received their training either with 460 or with 5 Group's 1654 HCU (which operated Stirlings) at Wigsley, near Newark.

It was a hotch-potch system and it didn't last long. At Breighton there was friction between 460 and 101 Squadron crews about the amount of flying time allocated on the new aircraft and it quickly became evident that specialist units were needed for what was a complex and vitally-important step on the training ladder. On October 10, 1942 1 Group's first heavy conversion unit, 1656, was officially formed at Lindholme, with 103's conversion flight forming its A Flight and 460's B Flight. By the end of the month both had moved to Lindholme. 1 Group's second conversion unit, 1662, came into being at Blyton in January 1943 with the third, 1667, in July. Initially, 1667 operated from Lindholme but a detachment moved to the almost-completed airfield at Faldingworth, just off the Market Rasen-Lincoln road, in August followed by the remainder in October when the airfield was finally able to accommodate the headquarters staff. 1667's final move was to Sandtoft in February 1944 with Faldingworth being allocated to the Poles of 300 Squadron.

Control of all Bomber Command's heavy conversion units was passed to the newly formed 7 Group in November 1944, although it was to be something of a paper exercise, each HCU remaining in position and continuing to supply its former parent group with trained crews. 7 Group itself was reformed under the command of AVM George Hodson, a World War One fighter ace with 10 German aircraft to his credit. He was to be replaced early in 1945 by 1 Group's old air officer commanding, AVM Rice.

As we have already seen, 1 Group was initially earmarked to operate Halifaxes. But the awful problems with handling and lack of performance experienced by 4 Group squadrons coupled with the successful introduction of Lancasters into neighbouring 5 Group brought about a speedy change of heart at Bomber Command HQ. The first Halifaxes which were in squadron service with 103 were quickly withdrawn (two of these machines were, incidentally, used as test-beds for the development of the Halifax Mk III) and Lancasters began to arrive. With 3 Group also being re-equipped with the Avro bomber, Lancasters were in demand and production could clearly not cope with the re-equipment programme, the growing attrition rated and the demands of training units, so conversion units had to soldier on with their Halifax IIs and Vs.

Bomber Command's answer to this conundrum was the creation of Lancaster Finishing Schools, units where crews received an intensive two-week introduction to flying the Lancaster. 1 Group's LFS was formed at Lindholme in November 1943, by which time a few Lancasters, mainly battle-weary machines from operational squadrons which came via the repair shops of maintenance units, were already in HCU service. A Flight was formed at Lindholme, B at Blyton and C at Faldingworth, each from the Lancaster elements of the three conversion units. In January all three flights plus the headquarters staff transferred to Hemswell, where work had just finished on laying hardened runways. From there 1 LFS operated until it was finally disbanded in November 1944 by which time Lancasters were in plentiful supply and all three HCUs were equipped with them, making redundant the job of the finishing school.

The Lancaster Finishing School at Hemswell was to have an almost exemplary safety record in the 10 months it operated from there, unlike its heavy conversion unit cousins. A single Lancaster was lost in a flying accident during that time but it was to prove to be a very costly one for Bomber Command with the loss of one of its brightest young officers as well as the life of a young woman serving with the Air Transport Auxiliary, the ferry pilots who delivered new and refurbished aircraft to front-line RAF units.

On April 8 1944 a veteran Lancaster, R5672, which had been delivered to 97 Squadron almost two years earlier and in the ensuing period had recorded some 695 hours' flying with the squadron and with 1656 HCU, arrived at Hemswell. It had been completely overhauled and was delivered by 2nd Officer Taniya Whittall, of the ATA. It was customary for new aircraft to be tested following their arrival and, later in the day, R5672 took off from Hemswell. At the controls was 1 LFS's commanding officer, 23-year-old W/Cmdr Frank Campling, who had won a DFC with 100 Squadron and a DSO after completing his second tour of operations with 460 Squadron at Binbrook. Also on board was Miss Whittall, who had learned to fly at Redhill Flying Club back in May, 1939 and was by now an experienced ATA delivery pilot, along with seven of the ground crew at Hemswell, Sgt Lance Regan (20), LAC Ron Freer (22), AC1s Tom King, Harold Quinton (34), Fred Spiller (19) and Ted Stevenson (20) and 20-year-old AC2 George Killick. Some time later the Lancaster dived into the ground near Caistor, 15 miles from Hemswell, exploding on impact. There were no survivors. Taniya Whittall became one of a handful of women ATA wartime casualties and the only one to die in a Lancaster.

The casualty figures for heavy conversion units were extraordinary. 1656, 1662 and 1667 between them lost 127 aircraft in accidents and with them the lives of at least 360 men, with many more being injured. Accidents on take-off and landing were common, particularly with Halifaxes as both the Mk II and Mk V had a tendency to swing viciously in the wrong hands. Inexperience was a contributory factor to these figures but so was the inadequacy of the aircraft inexperienced crews were expected to train on. Most of the aircraft had seen extensive operational service and engine problems and structural failures were almost commonplace. Ground crews worked incredibly hard to keep these machines flying but their skills alone were not enough to offset the inherent problems with the Halifaxes.

It was those problems which were to the lead to the first, and most costly, of all the ghastly accidents which were to dog 1 Group's heavy bomber training units. On August 1, 1942 a Halifax II left Elsham for a routine training flight. At the controls was 19-year-old Welshman Sgt Bill Bagley and on board were

The Avro Manchester was used in small numbers for training purposes in late 1942 and early 1943 by 1 Group. (Author's collection)

another 11 men, 10 of them sergeants and a single officer, P/O Alex Simons. All seemed to go well until the aircraft was on its final approach. The port outer then failed, the Halifax stalled and spun into the ground from 400ft. There were no survivors.

One of the men at Elsham at the time was wireless fitter Ivor Burgess who was to witness at least three fatal crashes on or around the airfield during his time there. 'The Halifaxes we had at Elsham were horrible,' he later recalled. 'There was a problem when you applied a certain degree of bank, the tail surfaces were blanketed and the tail went up and down went the Halifax. Some of the aircraft supplied to heavy conversion units were disgraceful. They had been shot up, patched up and were mostly clapped out and no one should have been allowed to fly in them.'

A number of experienced pilots had been attached to the conversion flights to act as instructors but even they were not immune to the problems of the Halifax II. On September 22 F/O John Purcivall took off from Breighton with three 460 men on board. Purcivall, a 30-year-old New Zealander who had flown 32 operations with 103 before volunteering to become a Halifax instructor, was demonstrating a rudder stall, always a dangerous manoeuvre on the Halifax II, when the aircraft prematurely stalled, spun and crashed near Tadcaster, killing all those on board. Two hours later, W/O Reg Fulbrook DFC, who had served alongside Purcivall at Elsham, was killed when the 103 Conversion Flight aircraft he was flying, stalled and dived into the ground near the airfield, killing all five on board. Fulbrook had been one of the men specially picked to lead the intensive Halifax training programme for crews at Elsham.

103 CF had been issued solely with Halifax IIs for its training programme as the squadron was about to begin operations with the aircraft but 460 CF

received a mixture of Halifaxes, Lancasters and a few Manchesters, the problematic twin-engined aircraft from which the superb Lancaster evolved. The Manchesters were still at Breighton when 1656 HCU came into being on October 1and one was to be lost in unfortunate circumstances a few days later. Many of those who joined 1 Group units did so via 27 OTU, which was based at Lichfield in Staffordshire. On October 19 one of Breighton's Manchesters was seen making low passes over a Lichfield public house popular with 27 OTU crews when it clipped a tree and crashed into a field, killing the pilot, F/O Reg Horner, his three Australian crew members and two of the Manchester's ground crew, who had been taken along for the ride. The report into the crash stated the crew had been 'stunting' and had misjudged their height.

Conversion training got off to a slow start in 1 Group mainly because most squadrons were still flying Wellingtons and would do so well into 1943. More Lancasters were available during this initial stage of HCU work, but even these were not immune from problems and several were to be wrecked in crashes flying from both Lindholme and Blyton. Training involved the whole gamut of operational flying, from circuits to cross-country navigation exercises. It was on one of these that Sgt Eric Wright and his crew vanished on May 22, 1943. It is believed their aircraft may have crashed in the sea and all seven on board are now remembered on the Runnymede Memorial. It was a similar exercise which was to claim the lives of another seven Lindholme men a few weeks later when Sgt Mathew Brown's Lancaster collided with a 27 OTU Wellington over Brize Norton. Another crew to disappear on a navigation exercise was that of F/Sgt Ted Norman. They had only been at Blyton a matter of days before they left in a Lancaster for what should have been a relatively short flight but nothing was seen of them again.

The summer of 1943 saw a rapid build-up in activity at both Lindholme and Blyton, with flying going on virtually round the clock as demand for replacement crews for 1 Group's squadrons increased. As activity increased so did the rate of accidents. Sgt David Loop's Lancaster hit an unnamed obstruction on the main runway at Blyton as he came into land. The aircraft was wrecked but the crew walked away unscathed only to be killed three months later on operations with 103 Squadron. Many crews didn't even last that long. F/Sgt Edward Norman's Lancaster disappeared without trace shortly after he and most of his crew had arrived at Blyton from 27 OTU.

Eddie West was an airframe fitter with 1662 HCU at Blyton and was there when the unit's first Lancaster arrived, one of two the unit was to receive initially before it was joined by a number of well-used Halifaxes. It was these which were to prove so problematic for ground crews as well as those who were to fly them.

'One of the problems we had were the wing bolts which had a habit of

Frank Campling (second right), the commanding officer of 1 Lancaster Finishing School, who was killed alongside a woman ATA pilot. This photograph dates from the time he was a squadron leader with 460 Squadron at Binbrook, during which time he was awarded a DSO. (Author's collection)

moving when the air frame was put under stress, as it was every time a Halifax flew,' he recalled. 'We had to check them after every few hours of flying and it involved removing a lot of wing panels, which was a very time-consuming operation. Then I came up with an idea. Why not replace the panel over the bolts with a Perspex cover? We tried it and it worked. It was highly unauthorised but it saved us a great deal of time.'

Mechanical faults and tyre failures accounted for many of the aircraft written off at 1 Group's HCUs during the summer of 1943. Typical of them was the Lancaster of Sgt John Cromarty which suffered a complete loss of hydraulics during a night exercise from Lindholme. Cromarty showed great skill in getting his stricken aircraft back and crash landing it on the airfield perimeter. He and his crew went on to fly several operations before being eventually transferred to a Pathfinder squadron, 156 at Warboys in Cambridgeshire before being killed over Berlin in January 1944.

Bryan Bell was typical of the pilots going through the heavy conversion units in 1943. He and his crew were at Lindholme before being posted to 100 Squadron at Waltham. 'I just remember that we wanted to get qualified on Halifaxes as soon as possible so we could get our hands on a Lanc. After flying a Lancaster for the first time I remember thinking I had never flown such a magnificent aeroplane and I still think so to this day,' he later wrote.

The airfield at Blyton was very close to the village from which it took its name and this was to cause some problems for crews and villagers alike. On the night of September 7-8 the pilot of a Lancaster returning from a night cross-country exercise got his approach wrong and the wheels of his aircraft clipped the roof of a house in Kirton Road, Blyton – which backed onto one of the accommodation sites – before coming to grief on the airfield. Both crew and house occupants escaped injury.

1 Group's third HCU, 1667, was operating by the end of the summer and was to lose its first aircraft and crew at the end of September when Sgt Laurence Turley's Lancaster crashed near Doncaster, killing all seven on board. 1667 began making use of the new airfield at Faldingworth that same month to ease the pressure at Lindholme. Gordon Neale was a flight engineer posted to Faldingworth in December 1943 from St Athan. He had never flown on a Halifax before and had to find himself a crew. There was a hurried conversion course at Faldingworth on the different fuel systems, electrics, hydraulics and controls of a Halifax before starting flying, this involving mastering take-offs and landings and then six cross country exercises. He was nearing the end of his training course when the whole unit was moved, mostly by train and bus, to Sandtoft. Two days later his crew, which included a pilot from Trinidad, two Canadians and four Englishmen, left for 1 LFS at Hemswell where they completed 10hrs 40 minutes flying on Lancasters over a snow-affected fortnight before going to 12 Squadron at Wickenby.

Early autumn saw the withdrawal of most of the Lancasters still in service and the arrival of Halifaxes. This move coincided with Mk IIs and Mk Vs being withdrawn from Bomber Command's Main Force operations because of heavy losses amongst squadrons using them. Neither could match the operating ceiling of the Lancaster and were proving easy meat for both German night fighter and anti-aircraft defences and their withdrawal provided a ready supply of aircraft for training squadrons. The Halifaxes were far from ideal but Lancasters were in short supply for squadrons and the HCUs would have to make the best of it.

In the first six weeks of Halifax operations, the three 1 Group conversion units would lose nine aircraft and the lives of 40 airmen. On the night of December 16-17, when weather conditions were particularly bad over Lincolnshire and when over 30 bombers were lost in crashes on their return from Berlin, a Halifax II came down at Corringham, two miles from Blyton, killing the Australian crew of F/Sgt Gernault Vautier while a Halifax V crashed in poor visibility at Faldingworth, killing Sgt Reg Stoneman and his crew. January saw a succession of accidents: an engine fire over Devon accounted for F/Sgt Bill Wilson's crew from Lindholme, F/Sgt Eric Rayner and his crew died in the Blyton circuit, again near the neighbouring village of Corringham, while a Halifax from 1667 was believed to have been shot down by flak after drifting over London during a night exercise. The worst accident occurred when a Halifax V from Faldingworth was on a cross-country exercise at 20,000 feet over South Wales. An engine failed and, as the aircraft lost height, the starboard wing suddenly folded, struck the tail and the Halifax went into an uncontrollable spin. The 20-year-old pilot, F/Sgt Paul Bennett, died along with the other eight men on board, their bodies being scattered amongst the wreckage of the Halifax over a wide area. The youngest member of the crew, Sgt John Gibb, was just 18 years old.

Six men from Blyton were killed when their aircraft crashed near Haxey after, it is believed, the pilot, F/Sgt Wilfred Daly RAAF, took evasive action to avoid a mid-air collision. 1662 at Blyton was also tasked with training Polish crews for 300 Squadron, which was in the process of re-equipping with Lancasters and moving into Faldingworth. Seven of their men were killed when their Halifax collided with another from 1667 HCU flown by Sgt Peter Street over the Misson bombing range, near Finningley. Eight men were killed in the 1667 Halifax and another eight were to be killed the following day when a Halifax on circuits around the unit's new home at Sandtoft suddenly spun in from 700 feet. At the controls was instructor F/O Stan Burton DFC, who had recently completed a tour of operations with 625 Squadron at Kelstern.

The Halifax IIs at Blyton were proving particularly problematic and four were wrecked in as many days. One of them was written off after a force landing close to Blyton village, the pilot, Sgt Albert Slade, being praised for his skilful handling of the emergency and helping his crew escape unscathed. Less than two months later he was dead, killed on his first operation with 576 Squadron at Elsham when he went along with F/Lt Ernest Presland's crew on a mining trip off the Danish coast to gain operational experience.

At Sandtoft P/O Joe Hetherington had the misfortunate to clip overhead power lines near Crowle, not far from the airfield. His Halifax V had suffered an engine fire and he was desperately trying to make it back to the airfield when the crash happened. He was injured in the crash but eventually recovered and resumed his training two months later at Lindholme only to be killed almost immediately in another training accident. P/O John Cann was more fortunate. He and his crew walked away unscathed after their Halifax was involved in a ground collision with another aircraft at Sandtoft. Shortly afterwards the crew joined 166 Squadron at Kirmington and were shot down over France during a raid on Stuttgart. The whole crew escaped again and all seven men were to

A rare picture of a crew about to leave 1 LFS at Hemswell. This was taken in the summer of 1944 and P/O Beeson's crew went on to join 550 Squadron at North Killingholme. At the end of August their Lancaster was to be the last 1 Group aircraft to be shot down in the series of attacks on German V1 sites in Northern France, four of the crew surviving to become prisoners. (Author's collection)

evade capture, returning to their squadron after an eventful 45 days on the run. Their luck held out as they went on to complete their tour of operations.

Most trainee aircrew had little experience of combat. One man who did was 31-year-old F/O Ron 'Pat' Ross, who had served as a soldier before joining the RAF, winning a Military Medal in France and being awarded an MBE (Military Division). All that experience, however, was lost on April 1, 1944 when his 1656 HCU Halifax II flew into a hillside in Scotland, killing him and then other seven men on board.

P/O Reg Watts survived a wheels-up landing at Sandtoft to join 460 Squadron at Binbrook, where he completed his tour and won a DFC only to be killed when he was posted as an instructor to 24 Operational Training Unit at Bruntingthorpe in Leicestershire.

One man who did have a miraculous escape was Sgt Robert McDonald, a rear gunner in a Sandtoft-based aircraft. The Halifax was on a night exercise at 10,000 feet not far from Lincoln when the pilot ordered the crew to bail out following an engine fire. When they assembled on the ground there was no trace of the missing gunner and it was only eight hours later, when the wreckage of the Halifax was being inspected where it crashed near Wragby, that his unconscious body was found, still strapped in his rear turret. He was taken to the RAF hospital at Rauceby, near Sleaford, once a lunatic asylum but by now the saviour of many airmen, where he was treated for serious head injuries.

The flat areas in the Trent valley provided plenty of opportunities for low flying exercises which, in inexperienced hands, could add to the inherent dangers of HCU operations. Six men were killed flying from Sandtoft when F/O George Smyth – at 33 one of the oldest pilots in training – hit power cables near Thorne while eight were killed when P/O Edward Barley lost control of his Halifax at less than 200 feet near Alkborough. Among the dead was the instructor, F/Lt Ben McLaughlin, who had won his DFC with 12 Squadron at Wickenby. At Lindholme a Halifax flown by P/O Gilson Collins crashed when it appeared the pilot became disorientated while flying in misty conditions, while another from Sandtoft crashed at Bawtry in a bombing exercise on the Misson range. Bad weather also accounted for P/O Herbert Garthwaite's Halifax, killing him and the other eight on board, including ex-460 Squadron instructor P/O Douglas Black. The Halifax ran into a heavy thunderstorm, became iced up and crashed in Rutland.

Structural failures were still causing endless problems which even the best ground crews were unable to prevent. A Halifax V from Blyton crashed close to Swanland, near Hull after an aileron failure, killing both pilots, F/O Jack Esdale and F/Lt Leslie Cumberworth, whose family lived in Beverley five miles from the crash site. Some were more fortunate, like the Lindholme crew who's Halifax II suffered an engine failure on its final approach causing a wing to dip, hit the ground sending the bomber cartwheeling across the airfield before bursting into flames. All seven men on board walked away with nothing more serious than cuts and bruises.

Another crew walked away after their 1667 HCU aircraft struck a house in Belton village trying to overshoot at Sandtoft during dual circuit training. A few days later the same thing happened again, this time with tragic results. Australian pilot P/O Llewellyn Linklater suffered engine problems minutes into a cross country exercise, turned back and then tried to overshoot the main runway. In doing so his Halifax struck a bungalow in Sandtoft village, killing the occupants, a Mr and Mrs Wraith, the pilot and an unfortunate Sandtoft airman, LAC Tom Nixon (39), who was believed to have been passing the scene on his bicycle at the time.

Sometimes, however, it was simple mistakes which led to tragedy, none

One for the album: a new crew at Sandtoft shortly after 1667 HCU moved there. They are the crew of Gordon Markes (second left) before they went on to join, first, 550 Squadron and then 150. Others on the photograph are (left to right) Vernon Wilkes, bomb-aimer, Bill Mann (RAAF) navigator, Frank Petch (RAAF) wireless operator, Ken Brotherhood, flight engineer, Danny Driscoll, gear gunner and Les Bucknell, mid-upper gunner. (Vernon Wilkes)

more so than on the night of November 20, 1944 when, in the space of an hour, three Lindholme Halifaxes crashed and eleven men died because the wrong controls were selected. The first struck a house in Hatfield, near Doncaster, two minutes after take-off when, it was later discovered, the flaps were raised instead of the undercarriage, killing five of those on board, including the Canadian pilot F/O Michael Gleason. Ten minutes later another Halifax crashed when the bomb doors were opened by mistake. All six on board were injured, including the 19-year-old pilot, F/O Gerald Halsall, a young man who was to be killed on his first operation with 101 Squadron at Ludford the following February. The third crash came 50 minutes later and again involved flaps being raised instead of the undercarriage. Four of the six killed were Canadians, including the pilot, F/O John East.

By now operational control of the heavy conversion units had passed to 7 Group and the switch coincided with the start of the phasing out of Halifaxes and reintroduction of Lancasters. This helped speed up the pace of training, cutting out the need for crews going to the Lancaster Finishing School before progressing to their squadrons. It also saw a steady decline in flying accidents. It couldn't stop them all, however. Five men died, including the pilot F/Lt Richard Eames, when a Lancaster on night circuits bounced so heavily on landing at Blyton it flew right across the houses in Kirton Road before crashing in flames alongside the village railway station some considerable distances away.

Blyton's last fatal accident occurred in mid-March when rear gunner Sgt Jack Ellarby from Leeds was killed when the Lancaster he was in crashed while trying to overshoot. Two weeks later flying ceased at the airfield and 1662 HCU disbanded, its job done. Bomber Command was by now awash with crews. Lindholme's last fatalities had occurred back in February when a Lancaster flown by F/Sgt Robert Plante, failed to return from a night cross-country. It was last heard from in the Shrewsbury area and no trace of it or its seven-man crew was ever found. The final fatal accident involving a 1667 HCU aircraft came with the war less than three weeks from its end, the aircraft breaking up and crashing at Owston Ferry, a few miles from the airfield, killing pilot P/O Howard Speed and the other seven men on board.

1656 and 1667 HCUs did remain in being until the autumn of 1945 although flying training was rapidly wound down during the summer. Between them, the three conversion units in 1 Group fulfilled a vital, if largely unsung, role in maintaining the supply of trained crews. It was a task for which no medals would be struck although the cost, as we have seen, was a high one.

Chapter 15

One Man's Story

Thousands of young men were to fly with 1 Group during the war. Each had a different story to tell, many tragically with an abrupt ending which resulted in their documents being stamped 'Missing in Action'. Although every story was personal, there was a common theme to them all, of measured and carefully managed training followed by an intensive period of operations. If they were fortunate enough to survive that then it was back to the training regime again, this time passing on their knowledge to those that followed.

Today the best way to piece together that thread is through the log books of the men who took part, men like Keith Lewis, a wireless operator who flew with 625 Squadron at Kelstern and survived a tour of 31 operations in the spring and summer of 1944, when the bombing war was at its very peak of intensity. The story which unfolds from that log book mirrors that of many of his contemporaries. He was not one for embellishing the record, simply letting the facts speak for themselves, which makes it even more valuable to students of the bomber war.

Keith Lewis, who came from Llandeilo in South Wales, joined the Royal Air Force early in the war and, after a period of assessment, was selected for training as a wireless operator/air gunner. He was sent to the No. 3 Signals School at Compton Bassett in Wiltshire. On February 9, 1942 he qualified and was then sent to No. 2 Radio School at Yatesbury where he was instructed in the use of Marconi 1154 and 1155 radios and Morse code – he had to be able to read and transmit 15 words a minute with no errors – along with the use of the Aldis lamp and the use of flares. It was at this Wiltshire airfield where he finally got to fly in the station's Proctor and Dominie trainers, learning the art of airborne radio transmission and receiving. Sgt Lewis, as he now was, was one of 50,000 trainees who passed through Yatesbury between 1939 and 1945 and what he learned there was to stand him, and the crew of a 1 Group Lancaster, in good stead in the years to come.

After Yatesbury there came a brief gunnery course, in which he passed out top of his group, before moving on to No. 2 (Observer) Advanced Flying Unit at Millom in Cumbria in June 1943. There navigators and wireless operators/air gunners were put through intensive training, both in the classroom and in the

P/O Jeff Smith and crew pictured with some of their ground crew after they completed their tour. Note the 'S' on the wheel chock, denoting their aircraft, S-Sugar. (625 Squadron Association)

air, in Avro Ansons, on a series of cross country and navigational training exercises. Later came bombing exercises with dummy munitions, all under the careful scrutiny of 2 AFU's seasoned instructors. In less than three weeks, Sgt Lewis notched up almost 29 hours' flying time, most of it by day, on these exercises. By a strange quirk of fortune, one of his pilots on these exercises was F/Sgt Clem Koder, who was later to fly as a flight lieutenant with 625 Squadron at Kelstern and would become a founder member of the post war Squadron Association.

The next big step came when he was posted to 26 Operational Training Unit at Wing, near Leighton Buzzard, in August 1943 and it was here that most of the crew he was to fly with operationally came together. Over the next few weeks he was to fly in Wellingtons with a variety of pilots but one name, that of P/O Jeff Smith, began to appear with increasing regularity. 'Crewing-up' was an ad hoc system which worked very well, men being told to report to a certain hangar and sort themselves out into crews. Apart from P/O Smith, Sgt Lewis found himself alongside Sgts Yates (bomb-aimer) Webb and Thomas (gunners) and P/O Bancroft (navigator) and the seemingly never-ending series of circuits and landings recorded in his log book eventually began to expand into bombing, navigational and cross country exercises of ever-increasing duration. By now, P/O Smith's crew, minus its flight engineer, Sgt North, who would join later, was becoming a cohesive unit, learning to work together as well as beginning to forms bonds of friendship which, in many cases, would extend for years to come.

They flew almost daily, serving with 26 OTU's A, B and D Flights until they had completed their course on November 11, 1943, amassing 93 hours and 15 minutes of daylight flying and 44 important hours of night exercises.

P/O Smith's crew then went on leave, spending Christmas 1943 with their family and friends, before reporting to 1651 Heavy Conversion Unit at Wrattling Common in Cambridgeshire in mid-January, 1944. This was a conversion unit which served 3 Group and there they were to fly Stirlings on a series of night and day exercises, inevitably including hours of circuits and landings and the standard cross-country, bombing and air-firing exercises. Then, at the end of their two-month course, they were told them would be moving north to join 1 Group.

The crew took the train to Lincoln where they were picked up and driven to Hemswell where they were to be finally introduced to the Lancaster at 1 Group's Lancaster Finishing School. Their time at 1 LFS was to be brief: on their first day they were taken for a one-hour familiarisation flight by one of the senior instructors, S/Ldr Tuckwell, and, after Wellingtons and Stirlings, the Lancaster must have seemed a delight to them all. Solo circuits followed dual circuits, both by day and night, including three flights from Binbrook to help ease the pressure at Hemswell.

Then, finally, after two years training, Sgt Lewis was finally posted along with his crew to his first and only operational squadron, 625 at Kelstern. The crew arrived there on March 22, 1944 and were assigned to B Flight. Their first task was to be yet more circuits and landings and cross-country exercises over the next two days before three of the crew – P/O Smith, Keith Lewis and their mid-upper, Sgt Webb - found themselves down for their first operation on the night of March 24, just two days after arriving. They went together to the briefing room and sat in near darkness as the curtain was finally drawn back on their first target – Berlin. They were to fly as part of an eight-man crew that night with an experienced man in the pilot's seat, F/Lt Blackmore, while P/O Smith went along as the 'second dickey', to watch and learn. They took off from Kelstern at 18.30 as part of a force of 577 Lancasters, 216 Halifaxes and 18 Mosquitoes for what would be the final attack in what had become known as the Battle of Berlin. The raid itself was something of a failure for Bomber Command, strong winds scattering the markers and much of the bombing being spread over a wide area, some of it outside the city. Seventy-two aircraft, almost nine per cent of those sent, failed to return. Three of them were from 625 Squadron. Lancaster ND639 with P/O Smith's crew on board made it back at 1.50am on March 25. Sgt Lewis's log book simply states 'Berlin – Successful', though that probably referred to their safe return rather than the effectiveness of the attack.

They were not to fly operationally again for 16 days but were kept busy flying another cross-country exercise and taking part in a signals exercise during which they landed their Lancaster at the fighter airfield at Hibaldstow, near Brigg, one of the few four-engined aircraft to ever touch down there.

On April 9 they flew together as a seven-man crew on operations for the first time, taking part in a successful raid on the rail yards at Villeneuve St Georges, near Paris, a five hour 40 minute round trip from Kelstern. This attack marked the start of an intensive period of raids on communication targets in France prior to the coming invasion. The following day they went to Rouen, before a series of attacks on German targets, Cologne, Düsseldorf, Karlsruhe, Essen and Friedrichshafen, before hitting an ammunition dump at Maintenon in Northern France in an entirely 1 Group operation led the group's own target marking flight.

After a week's leave – during which they were fortunate to miss the debâcle of Mailly-le-Camp in which 625 lost another three aircraft – P/O Smith's crew were back at Kelstern to take part in an attack on the coastal battery at Merville. The next night they went to Dieppe and 24 hours later attacked the rail yards at Hasselt.

Despite the pace of the bomber war, they were still expected to fit in training flights, including fighter affiliation exercises and flying a couple of times on extended air tests with the squadron's commanding officer, W/Cmdr Haig. They got their first and, as it proved, only experience of mine-laying with a 'gardening' operation to Kiel Bay, returning to Kelstern with 'flak holes' according to the log book.

With their skipper now promoted to flight lieutenant they were already half way through their tour in only a few weeks and flew to Germany twice more, to Duisburg and Dortmund, before taking part in a devastating attack on the marshalling yards at Tergnier.

For the night of June 5, 1944 Keith Lewis's log book records 'Grisbeck – opening attack of Continental invasion'. His crew were back at Kelstern after four hours and five minutes in the air, taking part in the largest single Allied operation of the war. No aircraft were lost from Kelstern that night and there must have been some smiling faces at the debriefing. The end, they must have thought, was now coming into sight.

The newly promoted F/Lt Smith's crew took part in successful attacks on Vire and the road junction at Forêt de Cerisy on the following two nights before a four-day break. Then it was their first daylight attack (marked in green ink in the log book) on Le Havre, their aircraft landing at Ludford on its return. They took part in their first attack on a V1 site in the Pas de Calais on June 16 before another eight day break followed by successive daylight attacks on two further rocket sites as the flying bomb menace to the south of England grew.

By now they were among 625's most experienced crews and they carried out further attacks on Vaires on June 27, followed by Vierzon two nights later, a daylight raid on Neuville, Tours on July 12 and Revigny two nights later. This relatively short-range operation saw the crew in the air for almost nine and a half hours as crews were ordered to circle before finally being told not to bomb. To add to their misery they had to divert to Witchford in Cambridgeshire, flying back to Kelstern the following day.

By now they had 29 operations under their belt and their operational finale was to prove to be a gruelling one. At midnight on July 18 the crews were roused and by 03.35am F/Lt Smith's crew took off to take part in an attack by 942 Bomber Command aircraft on German troop concentrations around Caen as part of Operation Goodwood, Montgomery's attempt to break out of the Normandy beach head. They were back at Kelstern by 7am and then, after debriefing and breakfast, it was back to bed for the 625 Squadron crews before they were roused again for an attack that night on Gelsenkirchen. Smith's weary crew took off at 10.45pm and were back from their trip to the Ruhr shortly after 3am on July 19. Their tour was finally over.

In 31 operations from Kelstern they flew operationally for 136 hours and 20 minutes by night and 16 hours and 40 minutes by day, non-operationally for four hours by night and 43 hours and 10 minutes by day, a total of 387 hours and 10 minutes flying time with the squadron.

The crew was now simply broken up and each member went their separate way. The following month saw Keith Lewis as a wireless operator instructor at 1662 Heavy Conversion Unit at Blyton where he was to fly four times in Halifaxes.

He was later sent to St Athan where he qualified as a signals leader and in August 1945 joined 1667 HCU at Sandtoft where he flew again several times in Lancasters, including two low level 'Cook's tours' trips over Holland and Germany, taking ground crew to see for themselves the result of Bomber Command's operations against cities such as Bremen Essen, Dortmund and Krefeld. It proved to be a sobering experience for all to see in broad daylight the devastation of Germany's industrial cities.

Keith Lewis was later posted to India and Hong Kong before finally leaving the Royal Air Force. He was later among the founder members of the 625 Squadron Association. Today his son, Nic, is the secretary of the association, keeping alive the memories of all those who served at Kelstern.

Chapter 16

A Long Hot Summer

Invasion, Flying Bombs and the
Luckiest Man Alive

At 24 minutes past eleven on the night of June 5, 1944 Lancaster LL811, J-Jig of 550 Squadron, from North Killingholme, dropped its load of 14 thousand pounds bombs on a gun battery overlooking the Normandy coast. It was to be the opening salvo of Operation Overlord, the greatest amphibious operation in military history.

Aircraft from 550 and other 1 Group squadrons were in the first wave of bombers which attacked defences along the French coast only hours before the landing craft began arriving on the five invasion beaches. J-Jig, known as

Wickenby WAAF Intelligence officer Jean Noden at the debriefing following a 1 Group attack on a flying bomb site in August 1944. (Wickenby Archive)

Celebrating returning from 625 Squadron's 1000th sortie, 'Kelsey's Kelstern Kids', summer 1944.
(625 Squadron Association)

Bad Penny II, made it safely back to North Killingholme along with W/O Bowen and crew after writing its own scrap of history, something which was to be recognised over 40 years later when the crew was awarded a collective Croix de Guerre by the French Government. They all survived the war, as did Bad Penny II only to crash while being used for training at Lindholme. The invasion marked both a turning point on land and in the fortunes of air crew in Bomber Command. There were some bad days and nights ahead for the Lancaster crews in 1 Group and the next few weeks would see some of the most intensive bombing of the entire war, but from D-Day onwards their chances of surviving a tour of operations began to increase rapidly.

From the beginning of June Bomber Command was being used almost exclusively to pound coastal defences and lines of communications, not all in the Normandy area as it was essential to keep the Germans guessing exactly where the Allies would land. Among the targets was the radar station at Berneval, near Dieppe which was completely destroyed in a precision attack by over 100 1 Group Lancasters. The only aircraft which failed to make it home was P/O Bill Kay's from 100 Squadron, which hit a building at Waltham on take off, wrecking the undercarriage. After using up as much fuel as possible and dumping the bombs it later crash-landed on the extra-long emergency runway at Woodbridge. 1 Group's only loss due to enemy action in a series of intensive operations before D-Day was P/O Geoffrey Jones's Lancaster which was shot down by flak while attacking batteries near Calais. There were no survivors.

One of the key roles on the eve of D-Day in the huge operation to mislead the Germans went to 101 Squadron at Ludford. Its entire complement of 24 ABC-equipped aircraft was sent to patrol the invasion area to disrupt night-fighter communications and it was from this operation that 1 Group suffered its only loss, P/O Steele's aircraft suffering an engine failure and ditching in the Channel where the crew were quickly picked up by a Royal Navy destroyer. 101's role was to fly on a route from Beachy Head, across the Channel to Northern France, then on a line along the route of the Somme river before turning towards Paris and then follow the Seine back to the coast. Apart from

F/O B. Windrim DFC and crew pose on the wing of their Lancaster, Y2, at Kelstern 1944. Other members of the crew were F/Sgt J. Platt, flight engineer, F/O W. Porter, navigator, F/Sgt F. Tolley, bomb aimer, Sgt D. Steen, wireless operator, Sgt G. Simmonds, mid-upper gunner and Sgt J. Slater, rear gunner. (625 Squadron Association)

June 1944 at Ludford. The air and ground crew of ME837 which was delivered to 101 Squadron as an ABC-equipped Lancaster that month and was to spend the next nine months at Ludford. It was scrapped in October 1945. (P. Holway)

Bad Penny II, the 550 Squadron Lancaster credited with dropping the first bombs on D-Day. (Author's collection)

A non-ABC Lancaster of 101 Squadron, pictured on a daylight raid over France, June 1944. (Vic Redfern)

jamming any fighter signals, they were also tasked with dropping copious amounts of Window to further confuse the Germans. At the end of their seven hour operation, the 23 surviving aircraft returned to Ludford and it was only once they were on the ground they were told the significance of the night's operation.

Once the landings had taken place Bomber Command's attention switched to destroying lines of communications, and particularly targets like rail junctions and marshalling yards. Achères, on the outskirts of Paris, was one target assigned to 1 Group. It was hit on the night of June 6-7 and again four nights later. In the first attack just one aircraft was lost, one from 550 Squadron flown by P/O Michael Shervington. There were no survivors. The second attack on Achères was to prove much more costly with 1 Group losing seven Lancasters, two of them from 100 Squadron. One came down in the target area while the second, flown by P/O Harry Skinner, was badly shot up by a night fighter and headed for the coast where, once over the Allied beach-head,

The air and ground crew of 100 Squadron's L-Love pictured at Waltham, July 1944. This aircraft was lost with a different crew when it crashed into the sea while using a bombing range in The Wash in January 1945. (Author's collection)

S/Ldr Dave Robb RCAF (standing, second left) and crew of M-Mother of 100 Squadron at Waltham, 1944. (Arthur White)

Pauillac oil refinery on the Gironde estuary in France takes a pounding, August 4, 1944. This photograph was taken from F/Lt Marsden's 103 Squadron Lancaster from 7,500 feet. (Elsham Wolds Association)

F/O Ian Smith and crew, 100 Squadron June 1944. They are (left to right) F/O Smith, flight engineer Sgt J. Walsh, navigator F/Sgt M. Paff RAAF, bomb-aimer F/Sgt R. Gordon RAAF, wireless operator Sgt D.S. Sykes, mid-upper gunner Sgt D. Waters and rear gunner Sgt H.J. Taylor. One of the airfield's hangars is visible on the extreme right. (Harry Taylor)

Pilot Ivan Warmington (standing) and navigator John Clark in front of their 166 Squadron aircraft prior to an attack on the oil refinery at Sterkrade in the Ruhr, Kirmington June 16, 1944. (J. F. Clark)

the pilot ordered the crew to bail out. The bomb aimer, P/O Richard Carroll, had lost his parachute in the attack and P/O Skinner told him to hold on to him and they jumped together, only for the unfortunate bomb aimer to lose his grip and fall to his death in the sea. The pilot, rear gunner, navigator and bomb aimer all landed in the sea but made it ashore to find themselves in American hands and later returned to Waltham along with the pilot and rear gunner. The bodies of flight engineer, Sgts Ray Bott, and Richard Carroll were never found.

That same raid also cost 625 Squadron three aircraft. There were no survivors from the crews of F/O Alfred Malin and P/O Jim Dudman but five of those in the third aircraft, flown by F/O Geeson, made it back to England. With the Allies now ashore the chances of escape for those who survived increased dramatically and over the next few months hundreds of downed Bomber Command aircrew made it back to their own lines, often aided by the

I-Item, the Imp Rides Again, of 166 Squadron, Kirmington, July 23, 1944 at which time it had 28 operations to its credit. (J. F. Clark)

Shot down: three of this 103 Squadron Lancaster died when their Lancaster was shot down by a night fighter over eastern France en route to Stuttgart, July 28, 1944. They are (left to right), rear gunner Keith Kibbey (killed), mid-upper Bert Cutting, navigator Cyril Shaw, pilot Bob Armstrong (killed), bomb aimer Terry Holland, flight engineer Malcolm McCrea and the wireless operator Doug Thomas (killed). The four survivors all evaded capture. (F.S. Cutting)

Lancasters at dispersal, North Killingholme, summer 1944. (Roland Hardy)

French Resistance and by groups of SAS soldiers dropped behind German lines to organise sabotage and disrupt communications.

Another communications target hit by 1 Group on the night of D-Day was Vire, south of the American beach-heads, at a cost of three 1 Group Lancasters and the lives of 15 men. Two complete crews were lost, those of Canadian F/Lt Bill Way from 103 and P/O Fred Knight, a 21-year-old Australian who had already won a DSO with 460 Squadron. The third casualty was the Lancaster of F/O George Bain of 576 Squadron. It was shot down by a night fighter and five of the crew managed to make it to the Allied lines, including the Canadian pilot who had suffered a broken leg while parachuting to safety. His navigator was captured by the Germans but the rear gunner, Sgt Gordon Humphreys, was killed in the attack.

Two other targets were to dominate briefings at bomber airfields throughout Eastern England that summer, oil refineries and storage facilities and V1 and V2 launch and storage sites. The V1s in particular were to become a real menace to Southern England during 1944 and thousands of sorties were to be flown against launch sites, mainly in the Pas de Calais region, in the coming weeks. The first of the oil targets to be hit was the Nordstern synthetic oil plant at Wanne-Eickel, near Gelsenkirchen on the night of June 12-13 by Lancasters of 1 and 3 Groups. Seventeen aircraft were lost including 10 from 1 Group. The Poles at Faldingworth suffered their worst Lancaster losses so far when three aircraft were shot down, two by flak, with the loss of 19 lives. One of the men who survived was picked up in the North Sea by a Dutch fishing vessel and handed over to the Germans while the second briefly evaded escape only to be shot once he had been captured. This raid also cost 166 Squadron three Lancasters and there were no survivors from the crews of P/Os John Kirton, Bill Grant and Trevor Boyce.

The following day marked another change for 1 Group when they took part in a daylight attack on E-boat pens and dock installations at Le Havre. Escorted by a large number of Spitfires, the Lancasters devastated the docks area and ended the threat to the invasion fleet from the light naval vessels based there. 1 Group crews returning from the attack also reported seeing the huge explosions caused by the 12,000lb Tallboy bombs dropped by Lancasters from 5 Group's 617 Squadron. Just one aircraft was lost from the raid, a Lancaster from 3 Group.

1 Group was to escape relatively lightly from what turned out to be a disastrous attack on the synthetic oil plant at Sterkrade on the outskirts of Oberhausen. The raid involved Lancasters and Halifaxes from 1, 4 and 6 Groups and, unfortunately, the route chosen passed close by a Luftwaffe night fighter beacon. Thirty-one bombers were lost, the majority to fighters. It was the Halifax squadrons of 4 Group which suffered the bulk of the casualties but seven of the 10 Lancasters lost were from 1 Group, including three from North

Volkel airfield near Uden in Holland, pictured from P/O Twynam's 101 Squadron Lancaster during a concerted attack on German night-fighter airfields in August 1944 as Bomber Command prepared to resume attacks on Germany. (Vic Redfern)

Killingholme. One full 550 Squadron crew survived as PoWs but the other two both crashed in Holland. One was flown by S/Ldr Gavin Smith DFC, a 22-year-old flight commander, and his experienced crew included navigator F/O John Berg DFC, wireless operator, F/Sgt Ralph Townsend, who had won a DFM with 460 Squadron in 1943, and the squadron's gunnery leader, F/O St John Tizard. The second crew lost was a multinational affair, including pilot F/O Don Neilson who, although nominally in the Royal Canadian Air Force, hailed from Brazil, two Canadians and New Zealander F/Lt Alex McDonald DFC, the wireless operator. Three aircraft were also lost from Elsham, two from 576 and a third from 103, which is believed to have crashed in the Isjelmeer. Only two men survived from the three aircraft. 101 also lost a Lancaster while a second crashed at Woodbridge with battle damage, the crew escaping injury. A few nights later 101 lost two more ABC Lancasters supporting a raid on another oil target at Wesseling, near Cologne.

Maximum bombs loads were the order of the day, particularly at North Killingholme where 550 Squadron prided itself on carrying a heavier weight of bombs than other squadrons. This led to some unusual practices, including those of F/Lt Jack Shaw, a pilot with the squadron remembered by armourer Bill Marshall. Shaw would insist on starting his take off with his tail wheel on the grass at one end of the runway and then trying to delay his lift off until the last minute before climbing at a 45-degree angle. As one daylight attack got under way it was clear his landing gear had been damaged on take off as it would not retract. Shaw was ordered to land as the replacement aircraft was ready to leave. But he ignored the instruction and flew all the way to France and back with his wheels down, even drawing the attention of other Lancasters in the bomber stream. On another occasion his aircraft was seen by the legendary fighter pilot Johnny Johnson to dive on a German military column and strafe it. Not satisfied, F/Lt Shaw then made another pass over the column before heading back to Lincolnshire.

The pace of attacks grew as the month wore on. Railway targets and rocket sites were hit repeatedly and three Lancasters were lost from Wickenby in raids on Rheims and Saintes. On the first 20-year-old Sgt Bob Woolley and his crew,

A-Able's air and ground crew pictured on top of their 166 Squadron Lancaster at Kirmington. The aircrew at the rear are (left to right) F/O Don Fenn, bomb aimer, Sgt Jim Garutt, wireless operation, F/O Bill Kuyser, pilot, Sgt Trevor Wall, navigator, Sgt Doug Greenacre and Sgt Frank Attwood, gunners, and flight engineer Sgt Mick Hicks. (Doug Greenacre)

Bob Sarvis, who flew with 576 Squadron with his USAAF rank of flight officer, and five of his crew at Elsham in the summer of 1944. He was an American who was brought up in Tennessee and was a student at Tennessee Middle State University. He later joined the Royal Canadian Air Force but later transferred to the US Air Force but was allowed to remain with the squadron to complete his tour of operations. He had almost achieved this when, at the end of July 1944, his Lancaster was damaged during a raid on Stuttgart. He headed back to the Allied beachhead only for his aircraft to be shot down by American flak gunners. Six of the crew bailed out but Sarvis didn't make it, his aircraft crashing near Carentan. (Elsham Wolds Association)

who had recently joined the squadron, are believed to have been hit by flak and all were killed. On the second raid another Lancaster from 12 Squadron was again hit by anti-aircraft fire but the crew successfully ditched in the Channel where they were quickly rescued. The second Lancaster from the squadron, flown by Canadian F/O Frank Jeffrey, simply disappeared. Contact was lost soon after the raid finished and nothing more was heard from the crew.

More and more daylight raids were being undertaken, particularly against flying bomb sites. The Luftwaffe posed little threat on these thanks to the complete air supremacy enjoyed by the Allies, but flak gunners could still take their toll, as one 300 Squadron crews found to their cost. They were hit soon after bombing a site in Belgium and made it back to within a few miles of

F/O Bill Way, a Canadian pilot who was killed on the night of June 6/7, 1944 over the Normandy beach head. Note Elsham's remaining J-type hangar in the background. (Elsham Wolds Association)

An evocative picture from Wickenby as crews lounge on the grass outside flying control in readiness for a daylight operation. Pictured also is one of the station's Hillman pickups. (Wickenby Archive).

Faldingworth before their Lancaster crashed, killing all on board. A 12 Squadron Lancaster was hit in an attack on a V1 site at Siracourt, four of the crew managing to bail out before the Lancaster plunged out of control, killing the remaining three, including the pilot, P/O Ken Underwood. Flak wasn't the only problem. In an attack on a flying bomb site at Mimoyecques, F/O Strath's 166 Squadron Lancaster was struck by two 1,000lb bombs from another Lancaster, one tearing the port outer engine out of its mountings and the second leaving a five feet-wide hole in the fuselage, the aircraft managed to make it back to Woodbridge. Despite the damage, it was later repaired and flew again as a conversion unit aircraft at Lindholme. That raid also saw a mid-upper gunner on the same squadron, Sgt Stan Parrish, record his 122nd operation, a record for anyone who served in 1 Group. He had flown 21 operations in P/O Jim Dunlop's crew having already completed 101 on Wellingtons in the Middle East. He was taken off operations and became an instructor. However, when Dunlop's 166 Squadron crew prepared for their 30th and final operation to the rocket site at Wizernes on July 20, Stan Parrish was back at Kirmington to wish them well, only to stow away on the aircraft, flying without a helmet and parachute, to complete an unofficial 123rd operation.

When the bombers operated by night they still found the night fighters waiting for them. A 1 Group attack on the rail junction at Vierzon, south of Orleans, at the end of June cost its squadrons 14 aircraft and the lives of 86 airmen. Worst hit were 101 and 625 Squadrons, which each lost three aircraft although six of the men on board managed to survive and later returned to Allied lines, only one of them from 101 Squadron, P/O Harry Taylor. Wickenby was the airfield worst hit with four failing to return. There were no survivors from the 12 Squadron crews of P/Os Ormond Pollard and Leonard Honor while three survived from 626 Squadron crews of P/Os Bill Pocock RCAF and Archie Orr. The Special Duties Flight at Binbrook also lost the experienced crew of P/O Wilf Knowles.

During July Bomber Command was being called upon more and more to act as the heavy artillery for the ground campaign, which was being held up by stubborn resistance, especially around Caen. These operations called for the greatest accuracy which, although there were some exceptions leading to Allied forces being hit, was achieved. They also came at a price, one attack on July 7 costing 1 Group three aircraft. S/Ldr Ralph Weston's 166 Squadron aircraft was brought down by flak over German lines, killing all on board, while another from 550 crash-landed at Manston and the third from 626 Squadron ditched, five of the crew being rescued. It is believed both gunners had been killed when the aircraft was hit by anti-aircraft fire.

The rail junction at Revigny, which was of vital importance to the Germans, was to be attacked three times in July at great cost of Bomber Command. The first two raids, both of which were carried out by 1 Group, had to be abandoned because of poor weather conditions but not before 1 Group lost 16 aircraft with another two crashing on return. What made matters worse that many of the aircraft did not even get the opportunity to drop their bombs.

The first attack on the night of July 12-13 was particularly costly for the 13 Base Squadrons. 103 lost three in the raid with only the wireless operator in P/O John Harrison's crew, F/Sgt Greenwood, surviving. The crew of a fourth aircraft bailed out over the East Yorkshire coast as their aircraft ran out of fuel.

12 Squadron's Minnie the Moocher pictured over a heavily bombed French target, 1944
(Wickenby Archive)

576 Squadron, which shared Elsham with 103, lost one Lancaster, P/O Hart's aircraft crashing in France after straying off course and colliding with a 5 Group Lancaster engaged on another operation. Only the two gunners survived. 166 at Kirmington lost four although, remarkably 11 of those on board escaped back to Britain. Most of them were picked up either by the Resistance or by SOE or SAS members. Three were arrested by the pro-German Milice but managed to escape and made it back to Allied lines. Among the evaders was P/O Dudley Gibbons, who's exploding Lancaster had made such a mess of Kirmington's main runway earlier in the year. 13 Base's third squadron, 550, lost two aircraft on the raid while a third crashed out of fuel in Suffolk after the crew bailed out. Although this attack was not a deep penetration raid some crews spent over nine hours in the air as they 'stooged around' waiting for the visibility to improve over the target and many of those which returned reported they were very low on fuel.

Two nights later 1 Group was sent back to Revigny but once again the attack had to be abandoned because the target could not be properly identified. Yet again the Lancasters were forced to orbit the target to await instructions and the night fighters struck once more. One of the first casualties was a Lancaster from 550 Squadron flown by their CO, W/Cmdr Patrick Connolly, who had only joined the squadron in May and was flying his sixth operation from North Killingholme. He died alongside his crew, which included 550's gunnery leader, F/Lt Ken Fuller DFC. This was one of six 1 Group aircraft lost with once again Lancasters from 13 Base being hit particularly badly. 103 Squadron lost two and there were further losses from 550, 576 and 166. One aircraft from Elsham which did make it back was the veteran ED888, Mike-Squared, now flying with 576 Squadron. It had first flown with 103 back on May 4, 1943 and the second Revigny operation was its 99th. It was being flown by Scotsman P/O Jimmy Griffiths and crew who were on their 30th and final operation and their 27th in this particular aircraft. As they were circling the target the gunners spotted a Ju88 illuminated by the glow of its Lancaster victim from 156 (PFF) Squadron and immediately opened fire. The night fighter turned on its back and went down in flames, exploding as it hit the ground. It was credited to the rear gunner, Sgt 'Taffy' Langmead, his second confirmed 'kill' in Mike-Squared.

One for the album: LACW J. Clark poses in front of a Wickenby Lancaster, summer 1944. (Wickenby Archive)

When this particular crew had arrived at 576 Squadron they flew in ED888, which was by then the oldest aircraft on the squadron and one which other crews shunned in favour of newer Lancasters. But, after baling out of one new aircraft during an air test, they went back to Mike-Squared and it saw them safely through to the end of their tour. Flying with Griffiths' crew that night was P/O Jim Bell who went along for experience. He then took his own crew to the V1 site at Wizernes a few days later for Mike-Squared's 100th operation and they flew the aircraft until their tour ended in a daylight attack on Duisberg in October. Revigny was to be attacked a third time, this time by 5 Group, and they were to lose 24 Lancasters but did destroy the target area.

Bravery and good fortune often go hand in hand and nowhere was that more so than in the early morning of July 18 over Normandy and the English Channel. A huge force of RAF bombers, 667 Lancasters and 260 Halifaxes, dropped over 5,000 tons of bombs from around 8,000ft on five fortified positions around Caen. American bombers added another 1,800 tons of bombs in an operation to help the British break-out from this French city. There was little opposition and only five Halifaxes were shot down. Several other aircraft were hit and damaged, including a Lancaster from 300 Squadron at Faldingworth and it was to lead to one of the most remarkable escapes for any Allied airman.

The Lancaster of F/Sgt Stepian was on its bomb run when it was hit by at least one 88mm shell, which damaged the bomb release mechanism and the rear turret. The shell exploded just as rear gunner F/Sgt Zentar was swinging his turret, the blast forcing the turret beyond its normal limits, blowing open the steel doors behind the gunner and sucking F/Sgt Zentar out. He was only stopped from falling clear of the aircraft by his left foot, which became trapped in the doorway. The plight of the unfortunate rear gunner was quickly spotted and the flight engineer, Sgt Pialucha, and the mid-upper gunner, F/Sgt Derewienko, went to his assistance. They tried unsuccessfully to pull him back into the aircraft but, as they tried, F/Sgt Zentar's foot began to slip from his shoe as the lace snapped. F/Sgt Derewienko grabbed the gunner's trousers but these, too, began to tear.

With this F/Sgt Pialucha decided there was only one way of ensuring the tail gunner did not fall to his death. Amazingly, he climbed out of the damaged turret into the aircraft's slipstream and, holding on with one hand, managed to loop a length of rope around F/Sgt Zentar's body as they flew over the Channel. The rope was tied to the seat in the rear turret and F/Sgt Pialucha climbed back inside the Lancaster. Then, with other crew members keeping a watch on the rear gunner, who was still hanging upside down from his turret but now secured, he went back to the front of the aircraft to help the pilot get the damaged aircraft back to England. They still had a full bomb load on board but were given permission to land at the fighter airfield at Tangmere where F/Sgt Zentar, who had to swing from side to side to prevent hitting his head on the runway, was finally rescued. He was bleeding from his mouth and

The Rose turret, twin .5 guns and much better vision for the rear gunner. (Dick Preston)

209

The production line for Rose turrets in Rose Brothers factory in Gainsborough. Before the war this production line made tea packaging equipment. (Dick Preston)

ears after being inverted for so long in the slipstream of the aircraft but was otherwise unhurt.

F/Sgt Pialucha was immediately awarded a Conspicuous Gallantry Medal for what was, in any circumstances, an outstanding act of bravery in which he undoubtedly saved the life of the rear gunner. But, like so many others, the brave flight engineer was not to live long enough to receive his award. Three days after news that a CGM had been approved, he was killed while flying on operation early in September 1944 on behalf of the Special Operations Executive.

The 1 Group aircraft taking part in the Caen operation began returning to their airfields around 7am. By 11pm that night many of them and their crews were in the air again as the second operation within 24 hours was mounted, this time to the synthetic oil plants at Schloven-Buer in Gelsenkirchen and Wesseling near Cologne. Ground crews put in an enormous amount of work to make this possible. Some aircraft returned from Caen with battle damage or technical problems which could not be rectified in such a short space of time but, nonetheless, it was a very impressive effort. At Elsham, for instance, 103 Squadron provided 15 aircraft for the first attack and 12 for the second, 576 sending 16 Lancasters to Caen and 14 to Schloven-Buer. All returned safely. 1 Group was to lose four aircraft on the Schloven-Buer attack while a fifth from 550 Squadron was badly damaged by flak on the return and six of the crew managed to bail out over Norfolk. The pilot, Canadian F/O Hollis Clark, tried to land the Lancaster but it crashed and he was killed. Of the other four lost, only one man survived, the navigator of a 460 Squadron aircraft. Fourteen men from 100 Squadron were killed along with another eight from 300 at Faldingworth.

The following day attacks were mounted on flying bomb sites by day and the railway yards at Courtrai in Belgium and the synthetic oil plant at Homberg, near Kaiserlauten by night. Both proved costly for 1 Group. 101 provided ABC support for the Homberg operation and lost two Lancasters, both to night fighters. F/O Jack Harvey was killed along with his crew while P/O David Meier was one of only two survivors from his. Twenty-one Lancasters and a Mosquito were lost in this attack, seven of them from a single 3 Group squadron, 75, which was based at Mepal in Cambridgeshire. 1 Group was to lose five aircraft in the Courtai attack, all to flak gunners. Three were lost from Wickenby, P/O Norman Hagerty and his crew from 12 Squadron and two from 626, F/O Bill Wilson and crew and the aircraft of F/O Jack Bowen. Five of this crew, which included six Australians, evaded capture while a sixth, the rear gunner F/Sgt Jack Houseman, was killed. Six more evaded from the only 460 Squadron Lancaster lost. Canadian navigator W/O Geoffrey Noble, was the only survivor from P/O Sydney Smith's 101 Squadron crew but was very badly injured and was to spend most of his captivity in hospital. The other casualties of the night were F/O David Mills and three other members of his 100 Squadron crew. Low cloud again affected visibility at Waltham and his aircraft crashed after hitting a tree at Laceby Top, not far from the airfield, on its return. The crew were on their 23rd operation and their aircraft had been attacked by a night fighter and the mid-upper gunner, Sgt Wells, had been badly wounded.

Two nights later saw one of Bomber Command's true 'maximum effort' nights with 629 aircraft devastating the port area at Kiel, another 119 attacking oil production targets, 116 bombing flying bomb sites and a further 180 aircraft involved in mine laying and diversionary operations. 1 Group's contribution was to the attack on Kiel, the most successful of any on what had been one of Bomber Command's first targets back in 1939. Only two aircraft failed to return, a 300 Squadron Lancaster and another from 625 at Kelstern. There were no survivors from either aircraft.

The city of Stuttgart was to be the next major target and it was hit three times in five nights as Bomber Command's focus switched back, temporarily at least, to area bombing. Over those three nights 1,667 Lancasters and Halifaxes were to attack the city and 72 failed to return, a third of them from 1 Group. Worst affected was 103 Squadron at Elsham which lost six Lancasters, four of them in a single night.

The first raid took place on the night of July 24-25 when 1 Group lost six of the 21 aircraft which failed to return. Two came from 166 Squadron at Kirmington. P/O Gordon Heath's aircraft was probably shot down by flak gunners as was the second, flown by American pilot F/O Bill Shearer. He was one of many young Americans who had crossed the border to join the Royal Canadian Air Force. After training as a pilot he was given the option of remaining in the RCAF or joining the United States Army Air Force. He chose the former and died on his ninth operation. Two aircraft were also lost from Faldingworth and all those on board were either British or Canadians, one all British crew surviving to become prisoners while three of the four Canadians in the second initially evaded capture only to surrender in need of treatment for their injuries. An American pilot also died in a 576 Squadron aircraft lost on the same raid, F/O Bob Sarvis failing to get out of his damaged aircraft when it was abandoned over Normandy. By some cruel irony, it was later determined it was US Army flak gunners who were responsible. Another aircraft lost was E-Easy of 103 Squadron. It was hit by flak near the target and set on fire. The hydraulics were damaged which meant the crew were unable to jettison the bomb load. Losing height, the Lancaster made it back as far as Orleans before the skipper, F/Sgt John Shean, ordered his crew to jump. Four managed to get out but hit the ground before their parachutes could deploy. Two more were killed when the aircraft crash-landed, only the pilot surviving. Despite suffering a broken leg, he managed to get clear of the aircraft and was quickly found by German soldiers. The rear gunner in the Lancaster was Sgt Jack Smith, a Lincolnshire lad who was five days short of his 20th birthday.

The bombers went back to Stuttgart again the following night when losses dropped to just 12 of the 412 aircraft taking part, two of them from 166 Squadron. F/O Bernard Singleton and his crew were killed but all seven men on board P/O John Cann's Lancaster survived and evaded capture. The crew were on their 29th operation and were attacked by a Fw190 and bailed out over France. Six were quickly found by elements of the French Resistance and the SAS and were later joined by their Canadian navigator, W/O Nik Zuk. Six weeks later they were all back in England, praising the 'extraordinary French people' who helped them. Two Polish aircrew members also evaded capture from a 300 Squadron Lancaster which collided with an American aircraft over France. 1 Group's other losses came from 100 and 103 Squadrons.

The final attack on Stuttgart on July 28-29 resulted in the heaviest losses, 39 of the attacking force of 494 being shot down, most falling to night fighters helped by bright moonlit conditions as the bombers left the target area. This was the night Elsham Wolds was to suffer with a quarter of the Lancasters sent by 103 and 576 Squadrons being shot down. Each squadron lost four aircraft with a fifth from 103 crash-landing back in England and 103's historian wrote of 'many empty dispersals around the airfield, many empty places in the messes and many sad faces' the following day. Three full crews were killed in the Elsham aircraft although four men survived from F/O Bob Armstrong's Lancaster along with all those on board the fifth aircraft which crashed-landed at Little Horwood in Buckinghamshire. 576 suffered marginally fewer casualties with only one full crew, that of F/Lt Howard Smith, being killed. Six more became prisoners and another, New Zealander F/O John Archibald, eventually making it back to Allied lines after his aircraft came down near the French-German border. Three were also lost from Wickenby. F/Sgt George Ryan and his crew were on their first operation when they were shot down by a night fighter near Stuttgart, only the navigator surviving. All 14 men on

The Rose turret in service. This photograph shows just how much room the rear gunner had. (Dick Preston)

the two 12 Squadron aircraft lost were killed with the squadron's gunnery leader, F/Lt Ian Saunders DFC, being among the casualties in F/O James Downing's aircraft. There was better luck for the men on board two 625 Squadron Lancasters shot down with 10 surviving, three from the aircraft of P/O Harry Tuck DFC and all on the second Lancaster lost, flown by F/O Frank Collett.

Many 1 Group Lancasters were soon to be flying with much improved defences including *Village Inn* automatic gun-laying equipment which involved a parabolic scanning aerial being mounted in a dome underneath the rear turret. When another aircraft was picked up information was fed through a transmitter/receiver mounted in the navigator's compartment directly to the gun sight in the rear turret.

The first squadrons to receive the equipment were 101 and 460 in 1 Group and flight engineer Sgt John Andrew, who flew from Binbrook, was later to recall that his crew was selected to go to the Bomber Development Unit at

A 150 Squadron crew pictured around the Rose turret of their Lancaster, Hemswell, late 1944. Note the space afforded to the rear gunner. (Author's collection)

Newmarket for initial training. When they returned to Binbrook they were taken off operations until they had trained the remainder of the crew on the use of *Village Inn*. Like many other innovations it was good in theory but limited when used operationally. Many crews found that when it was activated while they were flying in a bomber stream it was picking up 'targets' constantly while George Toombs, who also flew with 460, found another problem. 'It was activated by two lights mounted in the dome over which was an infra-red covering. We were on ops one night in very bad weather and the coverings started peeling off. It was amazing, you could see all these aircraft flying along with what looked like car headlights behind them.' It was not surprising that crews very quickly learned to turn *Village Inn* off at the earlier opportunity.

The second innovation was the Rose rear turret, which was somewhat larger than the standard-fit Frazer-Nash turrets the production-line Lancasters came with and was equipped with twin .5 Browning machine guns which packed a far heavier punch than the normal complement of four .303s. It was an innovation planned and built in Lincolnshire and was to give the Lancasters of several 1 and 5 Group squadrons far better protection against German night fighters.

Air Chief Marshal Harris had served as a station commander at Hemswell before the war and later as AOC 5 Group and during his time in Lincolnshire got to know well a Gainsborough industrialist Alfred Rose, who lived at Fillingham Castle not far from Hemswell. Rose Brothers produced packaging machinery to a very high standard and had a highly skilled workforce. Earlier in the war Harris was very concerned about the poor defensive armament on the Hampdens of 5 Group and asked Alfred Rose if his company could help. Two weeks later drawings had been produced for a twin mounting in the aircraft's dorsal turret, effectively doubling its fire power. Within a few weeks production was under way and the first Hampdens fitted with the improved design. Harris was very impressed and the company later provided mechanical adaptations for Lancasters and were heavily involved in the work to adapt 617 Squadron's Lancasters to carry their dam-busting bouncing bombs. After the dams raid W/Cmdr Guy Gibson, wearing his newly-awarded Victoria Cross, led a contingent from the squadron to the Gainsborough factory to thank Rose Brothers' engineers for their work.

There are conflicting stories about how the idea of the new rear turret was conceived. One is that it was Harris himself who was the driving force behind the idea, another that it was it was the AOC of 1 Group, AVM Rice, who helped Rose Brothers come up with a design which won Air Ministry approval in late 1943 (some records refer to it as the 'Rose-Rice' turret). Early prototypes were built and tested in the Gainsborough factory but ran into problems with vibration. These were overcome and by June 1944 the first 10 production turrets were ready and were taken by road to Hemswell, then being used by 1 Lancaster Finishing School. One of the airfield's large pre-war hangars was set aside as a fitting shop and the first aircraft to receive them, Lancasters of 101 Squadron, were flown in from Ludford. The work was carried out by Rose Brothers engineers and RAF mechanics and within a few weeks 10 aircraft had been adapted, mostly by men from Ludford's Base Major Servicing Section. Len Brooks, who was nearing the end of his tour as a rear gunner at Ludford, was one of the first to get to use the new turret and was in the turret when his aircraft was air tested after the modification work. 'I was told to just sit there and not touch anything,' he said. But it was immediately obvious to him how much of an improvement the new turret was. It was far larger which meant that for the first time a Lancaster rear gunner could wear his parachute rather than leave it back in the fuselage. The twin .5s were down by the gunner's knees giving him vastly improved visibility. There was no Perspex panel in front of the gunner and there was so much room that the more enterprising and daring among them could actually lean out and look underneath the aircraft, a blind spot which was often exploited by night fighters. It also gave them a much greater chance of escape should they be forced to bail out. Tail gunners had long since learned to remove the Perspex panels from the old Frazer-Nash

Brothers-in-arms. The three Henry brothers, John, Gaven and David, who flew as pilots with 103 Squadron at Elsham in 1944. At Elsham they were simply known as Mk I, Mk II and Mk III and special permission was given for them to fly on the same operation, to Cologne in October 1944. They hailed from New South Wales in Australia and John joined 103 in July 1944and was to win a DFC and was followed in the early autumn by his two younger brothers. A fourth brother, Ron, served on the ground crew with a flying boat squadron. All survived the war.
(Elsham Wolds Association)

turrets, even though it meant the blast of the slipstream being sucked in. The design of the Rose turret was such that the effect of the slipstream was considerably lessened. John Faulkner, who flew in a Rose turret-equipped 166 Squadron Lancaster, said that while the new guns lacked the density of fire of the .303s, they had much greater range and hitting power. His turret was changed mid-way through his tour at Kirmington and he was convinced that many lives could have been saved had they been introduced earlier.

Rose Brothers eventually produced some 400 turrets and their design was so successful that Frazer-Nash later produced their own version, the FN82, which was fitted to later versions of the Lancaster. In a letter to Alfred Rose after the war, Harris wrote to commend the company on its 'beautifully designed' turret and added: 'It was the only turret from which gunners can escape with any real chance of getting away with it. We have had several Rose turret occupants back as the sole survivors of their crew.'

The civilian population in Lincolnshire had long grown used to the sounds of bombers taking off and of their later return. That summer they also go used to actually seeing the bombers leave and return from their daylight raids. It could be a trying time for those with sons serving in Bomber Command. Doug Greenacre, an air gunner in P/O Bill Kuyser's crew at Kirmington, remembered his mother telling him that she always counted the number of aircraft taking off from Waltham, close to her home in Grimsby, and staying awake to count the bombers back in again.

Early August was to bring more attacks on flying bomb storage sites with three 1 Group aircraft failing to return from an attack on Trossy-St-Maxim, one each from 166, 460 and 625 Squadrons, all falling to flak. Two daylight raids were also mounted on an oil storage depot at Pauillac near Bordeaux. The only aircraft lost was AS-J2 from 166 Squadron which collided with another Lancaster from the squadron soon after take-off. Both aircraft were flying over the North Sea at 450ft when the collision occurred, the tail section of F/Lt Walter Holman's Lancaster being chopped off. There were no survivors. The second aircraft, flown by P/O Strath, made it back to Kirmington with a badly damaged wing.

The battle for Normandy was coming to a close and a final attack was made in support on ground troops on August 14 when a force of 805 heavy bombers attacked German positions, a raid in which some British bombs fell amongst Canadian soldiers. The only two aircraft lost were both from 1 Group, F/Lt John Bartlett's from 103 Squadron and F/Sgt John Hough and crew from 550 Squadron.

Two days earlier 1 Group had lost seven Lancasters in a raid on Brunswick, three of them from 101 Squadron. Canadian F/O George Atyeo and five of his crew survived in one but all 16 men on board the aircraft of F/Lts Len Tugwell and Neville Marwood-Tucker were killed. The other losses were from 100, 166, 625 and 626 Squadrons.

During the late morning of August 15 1 Group took part in a series of major raids on Luftwaffe night-fighter airfields in Belgium and Holland. Over 1,000 Bomber Command aircraft were part of an Anglo-American force of 2,000 bombers taking part in an operation which it was hoped to destroy much of the remaining night fighter force. Only three aircraft were lost, none from 1 Group, but everyone who took part knew why it had been planned. Bomber Command was going back to Germany.

Chapter 17

The Highest Degree of Courage

Conspicuous Gallantry in
1 Group

Courage took many forms in wartime Bomber Command. There were those who extinguished flames inside a crippled bomber with their bare hands, one who climbed out onto the wing of an aircraft to use a fire extinguisher. There were those who, despite wounds inflicted by flak or fighter, pressed on to the target, others who led their squadron on daring raids which captured the public imagination.

There were those who needed monumental courage to simply climb into their Wellington or Lancaster and face another seven hours of absolute fear knowing full well they would have to go through it all again ten or twenty times before they could step down from operations. That was a special kind of courage indeed.

And then there were men like George Ashplant, whose instinctive courage and skill were enough to make even the King gasp in admiration but not, sadly, enough to win him his country's highest honour for bravery.

Shortly after 17.45 on the evening of February 13, 1943 F/Sgt George Ashplant lifted Wellington BK460 AS-V off the main runway at Kirmington and began climbing through cloud to join the other 13 aircraft from the squadron assigned to a force of 466 bombers to attack Lorient. It was to be the heaviest attack of the war on the port, one of the major Atlantic coast bases for Germany's U-boats. The attack was later deemed to be a success with over 1,000-tons of bombs dropped and major damage done. RAF losses were light, just six aircraft being lost on the raid. Two more crashed while landing, another hit barrage balloon cables off Plymouth while two more collided on their return. One of those was the Wellington flown by George Ashplant and his actions after the collision were to astonish everyone who learnt of them, including King George V1.

Two weeks earlier 166 Squadron had re-formed at the new 1 Group airfield at Kirmington, which lay astride the A18 Grimsby-Scunthorpe main road and close to the Earl of Yarborough's Brocklesby estate, on which some of the accommodation sites had been relocated after a German bomb had landed near the airfield while the runways were being laid. Hours later 166 had dispatched 18 Wellingtons on its very first operation, ironically to Lorient, and Ashplant and his crew were among them. They flew four more operations – a mining trip, to Lorient again and to Hamburg, when Ashplant's V-Victor was amongst six Wellingtons to abort because of severe icing – before finding themselves preparing for their third trip to the U-boat base.

George Ashplant was typical of hundreds of bomber pilots in 1943. He was born in Liverpool in April 1922, the youngest son of George and Sarah Ashplant. His father was a school teacher who, by the time George arrived at Kirmington, was headmaster of Stanley Park Primary School in Anfield and a local Justice of the Peace. His older brother Michael was in the Fleet Air Arm, where he would later serve as an observer. George himself had been a pupil at the St Francis Xavier School in the city before joining the Civil Service. In 1941 he joined the Royal Air Force and was selected for pilot training.

His first posting was to the distinctly unglamorous No 1 Overseas Air Dispatch Unit at Portreath in Cornwall. Aircraft destined for use overseas, and particularly the Middle East, were modified at Kemble in Gloucestershire and

W/O George Ashplant (second right) pictured with his crew at Kirmington. (Jim Wright, 166 Squadron Association)

then sent to Portreath where 1 OADU crews flew them out, initially to Gibraltar and then on to their theatre of operations. In June 1942 George Ashplant left Portreath for Gibraltar in a Blenheim V with a crew of two, Sgt Bill Smalley and Sgt Harry Bakewell. Over the Atlantic they noticed their fuel reserves were being depleted at an alarming rate and were forced to land in Portugal where, after they destroyed their documents and any sensitive equipment, they were arrested and handed over to the civilian police. Although officially interred, they were back in England within three weeks having been allowed to cross into Gibraltar. Later that year Sgt Ashplant was told he was being posted to join a new Wellington bomber squadron in Lincolnshire.

Bill Smalley was the bomb-aimer in Ashplant's crew at Kirmington and had successfully bombed the target before AS-V turned for home over Lorient. They crossed the English coast near Lyme Regis and reduced height to 8,000 feet above Somerset, just 200 feet above the clouds, knowing that in less than an hour they would be back in the circuit at Kirmington.

At that point something happened that was every airman's nightmare. From somewhere beneath them a 158 Squadron Halifax, returning to its base at Rufforth near York from the same raid, suddenly emerged from the clouds and struck the Wellington. The force of the impact was so great that the part of the fuselage under the nose of AS-V was sliced off and both engines wrenched from their mountings. For a few seconds the aircraft were locked together before the Halifax fell clear, turned on its back and plunged into the darkness below. With it went both Hercules II engines from V-Victor.

The Wellington went into spin but, by some means, F/Sgt Ashplant managed to level out his engineless bomber at 2,000 feet. Inside, it was a scene of utter despair. There was no power, no instruments, there was a gaping hole in the nose of the aircraft and the pilot had no hesitation in ordering his crew to jump for their lives. Sgt Smalley shouted over the noise of the wind roaring through the fuselage that his parachute had been carried away in the collision and, without hesitation, George Ashplant handed him his own parachute and told him to jump.

Once he was sure the last man had gone, he put the aircraft into what he hoped was a gentle descent, trying to make out anything on the ground beneath him. Within seconds he sensed the tops of trees flashing past, saw a hedge, pulled the stick up and then, somehow, managed a wheels-up landing in a field beyond, the Wellington coming to a halt amid a shower of mud, water and scraps of aluminium and fabric from the bomber's fuselage. He could hardly believe it but he was on the ground and still in one piece.

F/Sgt Ashplant climbed out of the escape hatch, onto the wing and dropped onto the ground. It was only at this point he realised the full extent of the damage and became aware that both engines had been torn from their mountings and had fallen from the Wellington. Suffering only from a few cuts and bruises from the landing, he climbed a nearby railway embankment and made his way along the GWR Taunton-Yeovil branch line to Thorney and Kingsbury Halt where he saw some houses. The occupants of the first refused to answer the door but he had better luck at the second.

The collision had taken place almost directly above the small town of Langport in Somerset just as the local Home Guard and ARP units were involved in a defence exercise.

Among the Home Guard members on duty was 18-years-old Roy Jones of Somerton, who was about to join the Royal Air Force. They were tasked with 'defending' the town along the banks of the River Parrett from 'attackers', including Royal Marines.

'We were lying on Hurd's Hill when there was suddenly a tremendous explosion in the sky above,' he was later to recall. At first the men thought it was linked to their exercise and only later did they discover it was the moment of impact between the Halifax and F/Sgt Ashplant's Wellington.

Shortly afterwards the Halifax spiralled down to crash at the bottom of Kennel Lane, narrowly missing the houses in that part of Langport. Soon afterwards the engineless Wellington glided over Hurd's Hill before crashing into fields between Drayton and Muchelney at Sam Quick's farm.

Debris from the two planes, including all six engines, was scattered across Langport and neighbouring Huish. One engine fell in the drive of Captain McEvoy's house in Newton Langport while another came down behind the Rose and Crown in Huish, much to the alarm of the publican, Eli Scott. Wing sections fell in Garden City, one large piece ending up in the garden behind Mrs Lisk's house.

The Langport Home Guard later joined police officers in searching for crew members from the two aircraft. They found the body of the Wellington's bomb-aimer, Sgt Smalley, beside a farm gate on the Wincanton road, just beyond Garden City, while three others surviving crew members, F/Sgt Henry Reid and Sgts Ernie Pounds, Ken Reeder and Ken Scott, were quickly located and they were later reunited with F/Sgt Ashplant at Langport police station. There they learned that Bill Smalley's body had been found, his parachute not deploying in time to save him. They also learned that the bodies of the crew of the Halifax, including the pilot, had all been found inside the remains of their aircraft.

Another young man taking part in the same Home Guard exercise was Tony Crosse, who was then 15 and lived in Drayton. He was a messenger attached to the exercise HQ at the manor house in Drayton. Late in the evening he was sent out on his bicycle on an errand and remembered hearing the sound of numerous aircraft crossing Somerset and heading north. 'I heard a prolonged burst of power, probably from the Halifax, followed by a heavy thud which made the windows rattle, and I went back into the house to report that an aircraft had probably crashed somewhere near Langport,' he said. Soon after he learned that an aircraft had come down in flooded fields near the town and an engine had fallen between a garage and a bungalow in the village of Newtown. Later they heard that a Wellington bomber had come down just north of Kingsbury Episcopi.

The following morning Tony Crosse and a friend cycled to the Wellington's crash site where they found many people standing on a nearby railway embankment to get a view of the wrecked aircraft. Tony's friend, however, knew the Quick family, who owned the land, and both boys were able to slip past a 'very casual' sentry and walk round the Wellington, marvelling at how the pilot had managed to land it. He later made detailed drawings of the wreckage (these being lost in a subsequent fire) but remembered that the front turret itself was still attached to the fuselage, although nose down and with much of the fuselage underneath missing. Both engines had clearly been torn from their mountings, one later being found at Newtown while the second was believed to have fallen into the flooded area west of Newtown and was never recovered.

'It was not until I became a professional pilot I fully realised what a magnificent piece of airmanship Ashplant had carried out in landing a crippled bomber, which must have handled like a pig, on a dark night after a devastating collision,' he later recalled.

Mrs Nancy Walker was then a 10-year-old who lived less than half a mile from the Wellington's crash site. 'I remember going down the next day to look at the Wellington. I even managed to collect a bit of the plane and had it for a few years before swapping it for a piece of a Spitfire that crashed in one of our fields!'

Olive O'Connell was just going to bed with her five-week-old baby when she looked out of the window of her parents' home and saw one of Ashplant's crew land by parachute on top of one of her father's farm buildings. The airman was rescued by some of the local ARP men and carried across the road to the house where Olive helped remove his boot from a foot he had injured. 'He was very concerned for his pilot who, he told us, had given his own parachute to another member of the crew. They were later reunited at the local police station,' she said.

Richard Lane's family were awoken by one of Ashplant's crew who knocked on their door, looking for a change of clothing after landing in a flooded field. 'I remember the man, who I think was the rear gunner, thought they had landed in Lincolnshire,' he recalled.

When the survivors returned to Kirmington and told their story there was amazement at F/Sgt Ashplant's actions, so much so that within days he had been recommended for an immediate Victoria Cross in a joint letter from his squadron commander, W/Cmdr R.A.C. Barclay, the base commander at Elsham, G/Capt Hugh Constantine, and AVM Arthur Rice, Air Officer

F/O Geoffrey Dhenin (seated centre) pictured during his time at Kirmington. With him are (back row) S/Ldr 'Uncle' Spence, intelligence officer, F/Lt Dennis Walker, engineering officer; (front) F/Lt Harry McGhie, 166 Squadron signals leader, and F/Lt Fred Fitton, 166 Squadron gunnery leader. (Jim Wright, 166 Squadron Association)

Commanding 1 Group at Bawtry Hall. W/Cmdr Barclay described F/Sgt Ashplant's actions 'an act of extreme gallantry worthy of the highest recognition'. He wrote: 'It is considered that this NCO, by his action in deliberately giving away his parachute to enable all his crew to abandon the aircraft, whilst he himself remained in the wreck without any lights or any means of escape other than the almost hopeless chance of surviving the inevitable crash, displayed most outstanding courage, devotion to duty and complete disregard for his personal safety'. In his endorsement, AVM Rice said F/Sgt Ashplant had acted in accordance with the highest traditions of the RAF and added: 'I strongly recommend that he should be awarded the VICTORIA CROSS', with the latter in capitals to emphasis just how he felt.

On March 14 a note was added to the letter: 'Awarded the Conspicuous Gallantry Medal (immediate award).' It was signed *A. T. Harris, Air Marshal, Commander-in-Chief, Bomber Command*. It was later explained that the Victoria Cross would have been awarded had George Ashplant's actions taken place over enemy territory but because the collision had happened shortly after the aircraft had crossed the English coast, it was appropriate that the award be the recently-introduced CGM (Flying), the equivalent of the DSO for non-commissioned officers. It is believed George Ashplant was only the second man in Bomber Command to receive the award and was the only man to fly in 1 Group to be recommended for a VC.

Two other men were to be decorated after their actions that night. The Halifax had crashed into a field between Yeovilton and the hamlet of Limington. Gladys Little's husband worked on nearby Rugg Farm and she recalled that the farmer, Charlie Elford, who was milking his cows at the time, a young army officer, Lt John Bartholomew of the Royal Engineers, and another farm worker, Mr Duke, all tried in vain to get to the rear gunner, who they could see was still trapped in his turret. Later Mr Elford, who suffered serious burns in the incident, and Lt Bartholomew were to be awarded George Medals for their actions.

There was a footnote to the incident later in the month when an aide to King George VI wrote to Sir Louis Greig, whose duties at the Air Ministry including the overseeing of awards, to explain that when the King read the submission concerning F/Sgt Ashplant he was most interested to know more about the incident. 'He would like to know,' the letter went on, 'what type of aircraft Sergeant Ashplant was flying and just what is meant by the phrase "both engines were torn from their bearers". The King said he could not imagine how, in the circumstances, Sergeant Ashplant ever got the machine out of its spin.'

By mid-April George Ashplant (by now a Warrant Officer) and his crew, with a new bomb aimer and wireless operator, were back on operations and were to have another fortunate escape the following month when, as they were about to take off from Kirmington for a raid on Duisburg, a photoflash ignited in the aircraft's flare chute. The crew hastily abandoned their Wellington which was destroyed by the resulting fire.

But George Ashplant's crew's good fortune finally ran out on the night of July 24-25 over Hamburg. Their aircraft was coned by searchlights and crashed in Buchholz, just north of the city. Although the aircraft was later claimed by the pilot of a Fw190 flying a 'wild boar' sortie, it was credited to the Hamburg flak. George Ashplant was later buried alongside his crew, F/Sgts Reid and Jeffery and the two recent additions, Sgts Cyril Land and Alex Wells. Their graves were later moved to the British war cemetery in Hamburg where all five rest today, the inscription on George Ashplant's grave reads: *"We salute him; Whose course is run."* The day after the raid a notice arrived at Kirmington promoting both George Ashplant and his navigator Henry Reid to the rank of pilot officer.

He was never to receive his CGM nor was the King able to ask how he had landed that Wellington. Instead, it was presented to his father at a ceremony at Buckingham Palace in December 1945.

F/Sgt Ashplant was later commemorated on three war memorials in Liverpool, at Halewood Parish Church close to his family's home, at the St Francis Xavier School in Woolton and at St Charles RC Church in Aigburth.

His CGM remained with the family in Liverpool until the early 1980s when it was stolen during a burglary at his sister-in-law's house. It was never recovered.

The crew that went alone

It was courage of a different sort which led to another act of extraordinary bravery by a Lancaster crew from Elsham Wolds just a few weeks after George Ashplant won his CGM.

They were led by S/Ldr Charles O'Donoghue, a regular RAF officer who had spent part of the war in India and had flown Blenheims before arriving at Elsham Wold early in 1943 where he joined 103 Squadron. There he was to make a reputation for himself as something of a maverick, a man who liked to do things his own way. He told his crew he disliked night operations and would prefer to operate as he had done in Blenheims, by day, something he was to put into practice before very long in dramatic fashion.

March of 1943 was a stormy month and Elsham wasn't a good place to be in those conditions. There was heavy rain, low cloud and banks of fog alternating with storm-force winds which led to operations being cancelled and nerves becoming frayed as crews steeled themselves for yet another sortie over only to be stood down at the last minute. At times the winds were so strong even the Lancasters parked at their dispersals could be seen to be moving slightly, straining against their chocks as their wings flexed in the wind.

It was in these conditions that S/Ldr O'Donoghue asked to do something quite extraordinary, carry out a single-aircraft surprise daylight attack on Germany.

Another operation had been scrubbed on the night of March 19th and it was then that O'Donoghue, who had recently replaced the tour-expired S/Ldr Kennard as 'A' Flight commander, went to see the squadron CO, W/Cmdr Carter, with his idea for a solo nuisance raid. Carter consulted Group HQ at Bawtry and, after reviewing O'Donoghue's plans, gave the go-ahead.

Early the next morning O'Donoghue and his new crew, flight-engineer Sgt Jim Callaghan, a 20-year-old Londoner, navigator Sgt Tony Fry (21) from Grantham, bomb-aimer F/O Eric Ashcroft (20) from Worthing, wireless operator Sgt John Winn (22) from Northampton and gunners F/O Ian Burns DFM, a 22-year-old Glaswegian who had won his medal on his first tour with 144 Squadron in Hampdens, and Sgt Sefton Stafford (33) from Blackpool, climbed aboard Lancaster ED612. It was still very dark at the dispersal but, as the only RAF bomber flying that morning, there was nothing to delay their take-off at 4.20am.

Their target was the small port of Leer, near Emden and they carried 11 1,000lb bombs, the first with a six hour delayed fuse. The squadron's operation record book recorded: 'It was a target of S/Ldr O'Donaghue's own choosing and he bombed from 3,200ft at 0645. As this was a surprise raid, he was, of course, the only aircraft attacking. The first stick of bombs fell within 100 yards of the town's railway station and the second stick fell parallel to the town's main street.' The report added that the attack was made 'in foul weather' and the Lancaster returned safely, landing at Elsham at 0842.

O'Donoghue's raid was judged a success so when he requested another solo raid eleven nights later permission was readily granted.

In the interim his crew had taken part in an inconclusive attack on Duisburg on the night of March 26/27 and Berlin three nights later when 21 bombers were lost and most of the bombs fell in open country. In between O'Donoghue had to abort a raid on St Nazaire when two engines on his Lancaster cut on take-off. He managed to get the aircraft clear of the airfield and was ordered to dump his bombs in the North Sea before making a successful two-engine landing back at base. During the Berlin raid O'Donaghue's Lancaster dropped its bombs from 16,000ft, some four thousand feet below the other Elsham Lancasters.

His second and final single-Lancaster nuisance raid began in the early hours of April 1. O'Donoghue and his crew were allocated Lancaster ED626, a virtually new aircraft which had only been delivered to the squadron earlier that month.

They took off at 4.30am and their target this time was the little town of Emmerich on the Rhine which they planned to reach at dawn. The weather was again foul with strong winds lashing Elsham and the cloud base so low it seemed to be pressing down on the airfield. O'Donoghue again hoped to catch the Germans napping and it appears that, initially, he was successful. The Lancaster was believed to have reached its target and bombed at first light but it was then that his luck ran out.

The whole of Northern Europe was covered by the world's most sophisticated air-defence system and, once the Lancaster was picked up on radar, a chain of event began which was to lead to the destruction of ED626 and the deaths of all those on board.

One of the Luftwaffe's crack day fighter units, 3/JG1, was based at Arnhem/Deelen in Holland, and its Fw190s were scrambled to intercept the Lancaster as it turned for home. It is likely they took only minutes to find the bomber and the ensuing fight would have been a grossly unequal one. At around 7.20am an RAF listening post picked up a distress call and two minutes later the bomber crashed in flames five miles east of Harderwijk, a small town in the centre of Holland. The 'kill' was later credited to Ofw Fritz Timm, one of JG1's least experienced fighter pilots. Timm was to go on to become a Luftwaffe ace with five Allied aircraft to his credit before he, too, was killed in combat at the end of May, 1944.

Back at Elsham there was an ominous silence. Crews who had been woken early that morning by the sound of O'Donoghue's take-off began to look at their watches and wonder whether this time his luck had finally run out.

At the station tannoy summoned all crews to the briefing room where they were told that a distress call had been picked up from a single aircraft which had been hit as it was believed to be crossing the Dutch coast on its way back to England. There was a chance, the men were told, that the Lancaster had ditched in the North Sea.

Australian Don Charlwood, who flew as the navigator in Geoff Maddern's crew, later recalled: 'We were ordered out on a square search in the area east of The Wash but our chances of success were negligible. Met had forecast waves of 30 to 40 feet high and the gale was still blowing.

'All that morning we flew, scanning the changing mountains and valleys of the grey North Sea. White-caps rose and broke, lashed by squall after squall before eventually we flew back across the scudding clouds and the windmills of Norfolk with little hope that anyone would have anything to report.

'When we reached Elsham it was to learn that the German radio had claimed a single heavy bomber shot down. All members of crew had been killed. Perhaps the listening post had heard O'Donoghue's last call.'

The confusion over the location of the crash probably emanated from that last message from the dying Lancaster. Harderwijk is some distance from the North Sea but the town is bordered by the Veluwe Meer, one of the inland waterways which are a feature of this part of Gelderland and, in the murk of that terrifying morning, perhaps the crew of ED626 mistook that for the coast.

Today six of the crew, O'Donoghue, F/Os Ashcroft and Burns, and Sgts Callaghan, Fry and Winn, lay side by side in the British military section of Harderwijk General Cemetery. The rear gunner, Sgt Stafford, is buried some 15 miles away in the Amersfoot (Oud Leusden) General Cemetery, suggesting that somehow he became separated from the rest of his crew in the final seconds of Ofw Timms's attack.

Whatever did happen, Bomber Command learned a simple message that All Fools' Day morning, four-engined bombers were not suited to daylight nuisance raids whatever the weather. There would be no repeat of S/Ldr O'Donoghue's exploits nor would there be any medals for him and his crew.

The hero who took his Lancaster home for tea

Medals were not always awarded for a single act of courage. Many went to airmen who showed outstanding courage and determination over long periods of operations. Once such was Arthur Harrington Jefferies, one of the most colourful characters to fly with 1 Group. He was a man destined to fly on some of the most harrowing operations during the long, hard winter of 1943-44 and was to be awarded a Conspicuous Gallantry Medal. But his devil-may-care attitude to authority and his disciplinary record meant that when he was killed on his 29th operation he was still an NCO, something almost unheard of for a pilot of his experience and undoubted ability.

F/Sgt Jefferies had joined the RAF at 18 and was to have numerous brushes with authority during his short career in Bomber Command. He had already had one spell on a disciplinary course before going to 1662 Heavy Conversion Unit at Blyton in April 1943. He then joined 101 Squadron at Holme-on-Spalding Moor where he flew four operations before the move to Ludford. From there he was to fly on a number of raids, including Hamburg where he nursed his badly damaged Lancaster back to Ludford.

At the end of August 1943 he appears to have run into problems once more and was sent to the RAF disciplinary centre in Sheffield. He finally returned to Ludford in November but was immediately sent to Lindholme where he joined a new crew which was posted to C Flight of 100 Squadron.

Soon after they arrived at Waltham they became part of the new 550 Squadron and later moved to North Killingholme. There a blind eye was often turned to his disregard of RAF discipline. He wore his cap at a jaunty angle, left more than the regulation number of buttons unfastened and walked everywhere with his hands firmly in his pocket, which is perhaps why he died on the Nuremberg raid still a non-commissioned officer. Ted Stones, who served on Jefferies' ground crew, later recalled: 'One cold winter's day Jefferies and I were walking past the guardroom when the Station Warrant Officer, 'Lavender' Yardley, stepped out, told him off and said he ought to be setting an example. Arthur replied: "I am. Its bloody cold and they ought to keep their hands in their pockets too!'"

One day in December 1943, with the Battle of Berlin at its height, Arthur and his crew were detailed to fly their aircraft LM425 N-Nan on an air test and then a practice bombing operation on one of the coastal ranges. This didn't go down too well with Jefferies and his crew. They had been planning a night out in Grimsby but, instead, it looked like they would be stuck at Waltham after returning from their bombing exercise. This was when Arthur Jefferies came up with the idea of a slight diversion in their flight plan, to the USAAF airfield at Grove, just a few miles from his parent's home in Wantage, Berkshire.

They took two or three of their ground crew with them and, once they landed at Grove, they were only too happy to guard their Lancaster, N-Nan, taking it in turns to visit the nearby American PX to stock up on supplies that were all too rare at Waltham. In the meantime, Jefferies and his crew talked the Americans into lending them a jeep and they promptly drove off to his home where his mother was only too pleased to serve a splendid tea for her son and his friends.

On their return to Waltham they left N-Nan at its dispersal and went to their billet only to be summoned over the station tannoy for an official dressing down. Their failure to return from their exercise had led to the Observer Corps being asked to report any crashed aircraft and air-sea rescue units being alerted to be on the look-out for ditched aircraft while all the time they had been tucking into Mrs Jefferies' tea in distant Wantage.

The following night they were on operations again and left Waltham for Berlin, one of the eight raids the crew was to complete on the German capital.

At both Waltham and North Killingholme, senior officers saw beyond the lack of discipline, the uniform buttons left unfastened. They saw an outstanding young pilot who never failed to press home an attack and, following a raid on Stuttgart in March, he was recommended for a CGM. 'His coolness and deliberation in driving home his attacks have at all times been an inspiration to his comrades,' wrote his CO, W/Cmdr Jimmy Bennett. Notification of his award of the CGM arrived at North Killingholme on the very day that F/Sgt Jefferies died along with three members of his crew when they were shot down on their way to Nuremburg. He was just 21 years of age and it was his parents, George and Bertha Jefferies, who later received his medal and were left to mourn the young man who once flew 150 miles to bring his entire crew home to tea.

Binbrook's one-legged gunner
Flying Officer Roberts Dunston was awarded the Distinguished Service Order after completing 30 operations flying as rear gunner in a 460 Squadron Lancaster at Binbrook. What made Bob Dunstan extraordinary was that he did it with just one leg.

Bob Dunstan (third left) with his crew at Binbrook, 1944. (Laurie Wood)

Dunstan had joined the Australian Army straight from school at the age of 17 in 1940 and was part of 2/8th Field Company which was sent to Egypt to fight the Italians. His company was quickly absorbed into the 6th Division Engineers and took part in the successful attack on Bardia in January 1941. A few days later his unit was tasked with checking the Italian minefields, pill boxes, machine gun posts and tank traps prior to the Australian assault on Tobruk when their vehicles were fired on by Italian artillery. A shell burst 50 yards from his truck and, by some cruel stroke of misfortune, young Roberts Dunstan was hit in the right knee by a splinter.

He was taken to a first-aid post and then endured an agonising overnight drive in a field ambulance to a casualty clearing station. After a brief stop, he was transferred by the hospital ship *Dorsetshire* to an Australian military hospital in Alexandria. Medics there examined his wound and told him he'd nothing to worry about. But the wound became infected, he later remembered being given anaesthetic and waking up in agony in a different ward. Four days later he was told his right leg had been amputated.

In May that year he returned to Australia and nine months later was discharged from the Australian Army with £50 back pay and a new aluminium leg. He returned to his home in Mount Eliza, Victoria to recuperate and, still only 18, went back to school to complete his studies. By now he realised most of his old chums in the 2/8th were either dead or in German PoW camps while he was living in a peaceful suburb of Melbourne. 'I found myself impatient,' he later recalled, 'wanting like hell to be in it again.'

That's when he spotted a recruiting poster for the Royal Australian Air Force, proclaiming 'It's a Man's Job!' At first he dismissed the idea. After all, he'd only got one leg. But then he thought more about it. He met the educational standards, he had been in the military and he had a good knowledge of gunnery. So, trying to put a swing into his somewhat lop-sided step, he went to the local recruiting office where, initially, no one seemed interested in taking on a one-legged flyer. But Dunstan was a persistent young man and kept trying, returning day after day after his classes in law at Geelong High School ended. Then, much to his surprise, a letter arrived at the family home telling him he'd been accepted and, because of his previous service, recruit training was waived. A year to the day after arriving back in Australia he reported for duty at the No 2 Bombing and Gunnery School at Port Pirie.

After a four-week course which involved numerous flights in Fairey Battles shooting at drogues, he was one of 70 wireless operators/air gunners to receive their brevets and was promoted to sergeant air-gunner. In November 1942, he was among 800 young RAAF officers and NCOs to arrive at Avonmouth on the troopship *Highland Brigade*. He was to spend time looking up distant relatives and spent time in Bournemouth and London where he was intensely proud to see so many Aussie uniforms.

He went to 27 OTU at Lichfield where most Australian crews received their initial training on Wellingtons. Here he joined the crew of Tom Clayton, a 20-year-old pilot from Liverpool, Aussie bomb aimer Colin Francis, wireless operator Eric Clemens and navigator Laurence (Tich) Richards, both Londoners who had gone through the blitz before joining the RAF. Then it was on to 1 Group's 1656 HCU at Lindholme in South Yorkshire, where Tom Clayton was replaced by F/Lt John (inevitably 'Nobby') Clark while two Australian sergeants, Ian Murray from Western Australia and Vin Hegarty from Adelaide, joined as flight engineer and mid-upper gunner respectively. Now with five Australians in the crew they found themselves posted to 460 Squadron RAAF, which had recently moved from Breighton to Binbrook.

Lancasters were not easy aircraft to get around in, even if you had two legs. Dunstan found the easiest way to get to his rear turret was to unstrap his leg and then crawl along the fuselage before climbing into his gunner's seat, leaving the leg back in the fuselage with his parachute. Quite how he would have coped in an emergency is not recorded. No doubt given his determination he decided it was a bridge he would cross when he came to it.

At Binbrook his crew were allocated a veteran Lancaster Mk 1, W4927, which had been given the squadron code AR-C but which was, for some reason, always referred to as Dog-2. It was to prove a lucky aircraft for Nobby Clark and his crew. Their first operation was on June 11, 1943 when they were part of a force of 783 aircraft which attacked Dusseldorf. Over the target they were caught by several searchlights and spent a hair-raising few minutes trying to escape. Their aircraft was hit numerous times by shrapnel and the bomb aimer Colin Francis had his helmet blown off by one small shell fragment. Back at Binbrook, the holes were patched up and Dog-2 took them to Bochum and back the following night.

The Binbrook crews were to get a taste of what it was to be on the receiving end when they spent a night in the shelters as nearby Grimsby suffered a heavy attack from the Luftwaffe. The Battle of the Ruhr was at its height and Dog-2 joined the bomber streams for attacks on Oberhausen, Cologne, Krefeld and Mulheim before the crew were given six precious days of leave. Dunstan took the opportunity to go to Edinburgh with Vin Hegarty, who had relatives there and who he was keen to show a piece of Happy Valley flak which had hit him in the shoulder but had failed to penetrate his leather flying jacket.

Turin, Hamburg, Mannheim, Nuremburg.... the raids went on. Early in August Dog-2's crew was stood down briefly from operations and planned a raucous night out in Grimsby. But as they went into the mess for lunch, Dunstan was pulled to one side and told he would be flying as a replacement rear gunner with the station CO, the legendary Australian Group Captain Hughie Edwards VC DSO DFC, whose courage was almost matched by his reputation for hairy Lancaster take-offs and landings. Dunstan joined Edwards' crew and they made their way out to E-Edwards' dispersal where the group captain joined them ready for what proved to be an uneventful trip to Berlin and back. The landing, however, was far from faultless, Edwards missing the runway as he thumped the Lancaster down, later offering his apologies to his crew. Dunstan, however, was later to recall that that night's entry in his log book was the one he was most proud of. The following night he got his reward from Edwards, an invitation to dance with actress Vivian Leigh who was visiting the station.

In October Dunstan was promoted to pilot officer with just two operations to go before he would complete his tour. That afternoon the crews at Binbrook were briefed for a raid on Kassel, a city they had been to before and a target which held no particular terrors for them. Of all the Ruhr targets, this was one of the easy ones, or so they thought.

As they approached the target they saw the night-fighters at work, with first one bomber go down and then another. Searchlights were everywhere; it was one of those nights crews would later recall they could walk on the flak, it was that intense. But then disaster struck Dog-2 from an unexpected source, incendiaries dropped from another Lancaster above them. At least five struck their aircraft, one landing in the lap of the flight engineer before he managed to throw it out. The navigator and flight engineer were told to go and find the others and they dealt with four more just before Dog-2 was attacked by a night fighter. The port tail plane was shredded by cannon shells, one of which exploded close to Dunstan's turret, fragments ripping the sleeve of his heated suit.

With Vin Hegarty directing things from his turret, Nobby Clark managed to evade a second pass by the fighter but it was to take all his skill to keep Dog-2 flying. The port elevator was damaged, the rudder and elector trims were damaged as were the hydraulics and the oxygen supply to both turrets, leaving both gunners incapacitated. Dunstan was later told he spent much of the homeward journey swearing profusely over the intercom system

It took all the efforts of the pilot to keep the Lancaster flying, Clark flying most of the way back to England with his feet on the instrument panel to give him the leverage to keep the stick back and the nose up.

Back over England they descended to 8,000 feet, which allowed both gunners to recover their senses. The wireless operator, Eric Clemens, went back through the fuselage to chop a way through to the rear turret to allow Dunstan to crawl out to take up his crash position before Dog-2 made a perfect wheels-up landing in a field close to the neighbouring bomber airfield at Kelstern. The

Arthur Jefferies (marked with a cross) pictured with five of his 550 Squadron crew a few days before he died on the Nuremburg raid. (Author's collection)

following morning the crew returned to the crash site to say a fond farewell to Dog-2, the Lancaster that had taken them on 29 bombing operations. The aircraft was second only in 460 Squadron longevity to the legendary G-George, which now resides in Australia's national war museum.

The crew completed their 30th and final operation over Dusseldorf on the night of November 3-4, 1943. After being screened from operations Dunstan was awarded his DSO and went back to Lindholme as an instructor before returning to Australia as something of a national hero. He was to be reunited with 460 Squadron's G-George when he was invited to fly in the veteran Lancaster on a war bond promotional tour around the country at the end of the year.

After leaving the air force, he became a journalist, the author of a best-selling autobiography before going into politics where he became Minister of Water Supply and Public Works in the Victorian Legislative Assembly. He died in 1989 at the age of 66.

The doctor who risked his life

Bravery, of course, was not restricted to air crew. Many of those who served on ground crew or staff risked their lives to save men trapped in burning aircraft.

Among them was Dr Geoffrey Dhenin who, in the summer of 1943, found himself at Kirmington as 166 Squadron Medical Officer. The MO was a vital cog in the machine that was a wartime bomber squadron. Apart from dealing with day-to-day ailments and injuries, it was his job to determine whether an airman was fit to fly, either after being wounded or, on occasion, getting the 'shakes'. But he was to be faced with something far more daunting in the early hours of October 9, 1943.

Three hours earlier 13 of the squadron's Lancasters had taken off for Stuttgart but one of them, AS-C flown by 21-year-old W/O Reg Rabett DFC, turned back when the port outer engine failed. As W/O Rabett was on his final approach into Kirmington shortly before 2am, the port inner failed as well, the aircraft going into an uncontrollable spin and crashing into the ground almost on the airfield boundary, broke in two and burst into flames. Five of the crew, including the pilot, were killed but gunners were trapped, Sgt Ted Croxon in the mid-upper and Sgt Les Davidson in the rear turret which itself had become wedged under part of the fuselage. Nearby was part of the bomb load.

F/O Dhenin was quickly on the scene in the station ambulance and, after helping free Sgt Croxon, set about trying to save the trapped rear gunner. His turret had been crushed under wreckage from the Lancaster and part of the bomb load was only a matter of feet away. Helped by Cpl Bill Rush, who had been manning one of the station's anti-aircraft guns, he managed to crawl under the debris and spent half an hour trying to free Sgt Davidson. Finally, the station's mobile crane arrived and managed to lift the wreckage sufficiently for F/O Dhenin to help drag the injured gunner clear.

For his bravery that night F/O Dhenin was awarded the George Medal while a BEM went to Cpl Rush. Dhenin himself went on to become the Deputy Principal Medical Officer (Flying) at Bomber Command HQ after the war, took part in the atom bomb trials in Australia in the early 1950s, was knighted for his work and finished his career as an air vice marshal. Both Sgt Davidson and Sgt Croxon, who he helped save that night, are believed to have survived the war.

Ablaze over Italy

Courage could also take a collective form and this was to be displayed on the night of February 14-15, 1943 when the crew of a 101 Squadron Lancaster won a DSO and no fewer than five Conspicuous Gallantry Medals between them.

Sgt Ivan Hazard and his crew were part of a force which attacked Milan, a long flight but a lightly-defended target, or so it was for most of the force of 142 bombers from 1, 5 and 8 Groups. Over the target area Sgt Hazard's Lancaster was attacked by a single CR42 fighter, which raked the fuselage with cannon and machine-gun fire, igniting a canister of incendiary bombs which had 'hung up' in the bomb bay.

The fuselage became a mass of flames and quickly spread to the upper gun turret, exploding ammunition adding to the crew's problems. Despite the inferno nearby, the gunner, F/Sgt George Dove, stuck to his position and, although suffering burns to his face and hands, opened fire on the attacking aircraft. The fighter had already been hit by a burst from the rear turret, which was manned by Sgt Les Airey, and disappeared in flames.

F/Sgt Dove then climbed down from his position and managed to get through the flames to the rear turret where he found Sgt Airey had been wounded in the attack. The pilot had already warned the crew to be ready to jump but, on learning of Sgt Airey's injuries, he decided to attempt a force landing.

In the meantime, the wireless operator, P/O Fred Gates, the navigator, Sgt Bill Williams, and the flight engineer, Sgt Jim Bain, tackled the fire with the aircraft's extinguishers and managed to bring it under control. By now the badly damaged Lancaster was down to 800 feet but, with the fire almost out, Sgt Hazard conferred with the rest of the crew and they decided to attempt to get home. They managed to regain sufficient height to cross the Alps but shortly after doing so one of the engines failed.

For the remainder of the journey home P/O Gates gave what help he could to the pilot and then climbed over the gaping hole in the fuselage to tend to the wounded rear gunner. With the flight engineer nursing the engines and the navigator keeping a careful check on their course, Sgt Hazard managed to get the Lancaster back to England where they made an emergency landing.

There was an immediate award of a DSO to P/O Gates, the only officer in the crew, and Conspicuous Gallantry Medals for F/Sgt Dove and Sgt Hazard, Williams, Bain and Airey, the highest number of awards for a single aircraft's crew.

Only the two gunners, F/Sgt Dove, and Sgt Airey, would live to collect their medals. Sgt Hazard, Sgt Bain and Sgt Williams were all killed the following month when they crashed on the beach near Hornsea during an air test. P/O Gates survived them by only a few weeks, failing to return from an operation a few weeks later.

'Johnny Garland Didn't Come Back Last Night'

There were to be no gallantry medals for Johnny Garland. Simply a Portland stone headstone in the Berlin War Cemetery, one of 3,576 in the suburb of Charlottenburg, the vast majority of them the final resting place of men of RAF Bomber Command.

Johnny Garland was a teenager when he died, too young even for a serious girlfriend. He was a sergeant, a rear gunner in a Lancaster bomber, killed along with his seven companions in a 101 Squadron aircraft during the Battle of Berlin.

No one survived to tell the final story of Lancaster LM364, SR-N[2], which left Ludford Magna at 5pm on the afternoon of Thursday, December 2, 1943 bound for Berlin along with 457 other Lancasters, Halifaxes and Mosquitoes. All that is known is that the aircraft crashed near the small town of Rehfelde, 19 miles east of Berlin. Seven of the crew were buried in a communal grave in the parish cemetery in the town. It appears that Sgt Garland's body was not found immediately (this sometimes happened with rear gunners, isolated as they were at the back of the aircraft) but eventually all were reunited in what was known in the official German *Tödenliste* as 'Comrade's Grave No. 425'. The bodies were later moved to the British War Cemetery at Heerstrasse in Berlin in 1948, five of the crew being buried together and three, including Johnny Garland, in separate graves, all in plot 8, row G.

So what made Johnny Garland special? What did was the very fact that he volunteered for the war's most dangerous job, flying night after night over the world's most heavily defended cities knowing full well that he was unlikely to survive the 30 operations that would mean he had earned a rest from front-line duties.

He was born in the Nottinghamshire village of Fiskerton, which had the Trent on one side and the Newark-Nottingham rail line on the other. He went to school in nearby Southwell. His father ran a market garden in the village and, after leaving school, Johnny worked for him before he joined the RAF. His best friend joined the same day – he went off to Southern Rhodesia to train as a pilot and returned too late to fly operationally. Johnny's first and only posting was to 101 Squadron where he joined the crew of 22-year-old F/Sgt Laurence Murrell. He would return frequently to the village – there were regular trains to Fiskerton from Market Rasen, the nearest station to Ludford – and would pick up his bike there and cycle into the village where he would enthral his friends and worry his family with stories of squadron life and how his crew's greatest fear was crashing near a town they had bombed and then being attacked by angry residents.

On the morning of Friday December 3, 1943 the bad news came: the village postman in Fiskerton, who obviously had inside knowledge on the special telegrams delivered to the families of missing aircrew, told those he met: 'Rumour has it that Johnny Garland did not come back last night.' The rumour was true. Johnny Garland was dead alongside pilot Laurence Murrell, his navigator Sgt Richard Webb, wireless operator Sgt Ron Hayes, flight engineer Sgt Ted North, bomb aimer Sgt Bob Kibby, mid-upper gunner Sgt John Cockroft and special operator Sgt Terry Bramley. This was to be one of two tragedies for the Murrell and Bramley families, the pilot's brother dying in a Japanese prisoner-of-war camp while the special operator's brother, Alan, was killed while serving with the Royal Army Service Corps at Dunkirk.

There were no gallantry medals for any of them but no one would deny they were all heroes.

Chapter 18

Where it Hurts Most

Hitting Hitler's Oil Supplies

During the summer of 1944 Bomber Command had been under the control of Supreme Headquarters Allied Expeditionary Force and had played a significant part in ensuring the success of the D-Day landings and, eventually, the break-out from Normandy. Its bombers had also played a major role in the destruction of V1 launch sites and V2 storage sites. The late summer was to see the RAF's Lancasters and Halifaxes pounding German defensive positions around those Channel ports still to be taken by the Allies and, in September, supporting the airborne landings at Arnhem.

By mid-September Bomber Command was once again under the direct control of the Air Ministry with the caveat that it could be used whenever necessary to support ground operations. Bomber Command was to be given a new primary role, the destruction of Germany's synthetic oil industry which, it was argued, would cripple its armed forces. Bombers would also be used to attack transport networks and factories still producing armoured vehicles and trucks at almost record levels for the Wehrmacht. It was a policy, it was believed (and was to be proved correct), that would hit Germany 'where it hurts most'. Harris, in the meantime, still believed his bombers would be best employed wearing the Germans down by returning to the destruction of their major cities and industrial areas, in a return to area bombing. His orders, however, were clear: fuel production and storage had to take precedence. But those same orders did allow him some leeway when the weather or tactical conditions made precision bombing impossible, and it was something he was to exploit to the full.

1 Group itself was to become the major element in Bomber Command's main force. 5 Group, with its own target marking and precision bombing squadrons, was operating virtually independently (it was known, rather disparagingly outside 5 Group circles, as 'Cocky's Private Air Force' after its AOC, Sir Ralph Cochrane) as was 3 Group, newly-equipped with Lancasters fitted with *G-H*, the new and very effective blind bombing equipment. This left 1 Group along with the Yorkshire-based 4 and 6 Groups, supported by

target-marking squadrons of 8 Group, to act as Bomber Command's heavy artillery. During the autumn 1 Group was also to expand substantially with the addition of three new squadrons, 150 (one of the original 1 Group squadrons, now returned from the Middle East), 153 and 170 and three new airfields, Scampton, Fiskerton and Dunholme Lodge, all transferred from 5 Group. Dunholme was used only briefly, closing within a month of its transfer simply because the skies around Lincoln had become too crowded.

Another major change was the transfer of training duties to the newly-formed 7 Group in November. It was reformed with its headquarters at Grantham to oversee training throughout Bomber Command and on November 3 the 1 Group training airfields, Lindholme, Blyton and Sandtoft, became 71 Base, the first to be set up under the auspices of the new training command. Sturgate near Gainsborough, which had arrived too late for an operational role, was also put under the base's control although, once more, it was not to be used operationally before the war ended. By this time Bomber Command was awash with newly-trained crews and many of those who went through courses at 71 Base airfields never got to fly operationally, being classified as 'supernumerary', and were allocated menial jobs. Lancasters were also in plentiful supply and 1 Group's Lancaster Finishing School was moved

626 Squadron's outdoor radar section, June Wade, Joe Goode, Kit Thompson, Bud Currie and Gordon Sturrock (Wickenby Archive)

Digging out a snow-bound Lancaster, Kelstern winter 1944. (625 Squadron Association)

from Hemswell to Lindholme in November and disbanded altogether in January 1945.

One of the men to join 1 Group that autumn was Clem Koder, an experienced pilot who had spent the previous two years with Flying Training Command. He went through an operational training unit with the intention of joining a Mosquito squadron but was then offered a place alongside a 'headless' 100 Squadron bomber crew at 1667HCU at Sandtoft. They had arrived there from Waltham after their pilot lost his nerve after just three operations. F/O Koder already had the requisite time on night and instrument flying, albeit mainly on Ansons, but jumped at the chance. He spent a couple of weeks with his new crew at Sandtoft before they were all posted to 625 Squadron at Kelstern.

His story there mirrors that of many young men in Bomber Command is best told in his own words: 'Duties with Flying Training Command, although a most necessary function, called for no relaxation but lacked the excitement and great spirit that one found on an operational squadron. Always when asked if I was frightened on operations I would say no, I was more frightened that I would not keep up the high standard set by the other squadron personnel. This also applies to the ground crews whose servicing was of the highest quality at all times of the day and night regardless of the weather conditions. It was the magnificent spirit of all that helped me and I shall always feel proud to be one of those who operated in Bomber Command.

'I found it a great thrill to taxi out in my Lancaster, G-George, with others around the perimeter track at Kelstern and to be signalled onto the runway to prepare for take-off. Then we would be lined up, looking straight down the main runway, brakes on with increasing revs, the whole aircraft shuddering, yearning to be released, and then, at the moment of take-off, away we went, backs pressed against our seats, a quick glance to port to give a wave to the station commander and others gathered giving us an encouraging send-off.

'Very often take-off would be at dusk and the usual practice would be to circle the base gradually to about 5,000 feet and as one did so 460 Squadron RAAF at Binbrook, some four miles to the west, could be seen similarly circling base and climbing. To the northwest 100 Squadron at Waltham, just south of Grimsby, could also be seen, and so too could we see 101 Squadron climbing from Ludford Magna, a few miles south of us, and beyond them was 300 Squadron at Faldingworth and 170 at Dunholme Lodge.

'At 5,000 feet the aircraft, still climbing, headed towards Reading, and in the fading light the concentration of Lancasters would be seen forming a long stream and picking up other squadrons from South Lincolnshire and Huntingdonshire. At Reading there was still sufficient light to pick out many aircraft in the bomber stream as it turned to port in a south easterly direction towards Beachy Head. By the time the Channel coast was reached the light had gone and so had the comforting sight of all those other Lancasters.

'As the English coastline receded and the blackness of the water took over, one felt somewhat isolated in spite of the confidence I had in my navigator,

Clem Koder (third left) and his 625 Squadron crew. Others on the photograph are Sgt H. Bulman, flight engineer, P/O T. Donahue RCAF, bomb-aimer, F/O H. Zlotnik RCAF, navigator, F/Sgt K. Stewart, wireless operator, W/O K. Sheehan, RCAF, mid-upper gunner, and F/S A. Avery RAAF, rear gunner. (625 Squadron Association)

PA177 of 100 Squadron pictured at Waltham soon after the aircraft was delivered. It was named 'Jug and Bottle' and a public house built in the 1990s close to its dispersal was named after the aircraft. (Arthur White)

Hal Zlotnik, a Canadian from Vancouver, and the confidence in the navigators of other aircraft I knew were nearby. Strangely enough, some of those navigators had been pupils of mine only months earlier at the Observers' Advanced Flying Unit in Cumberland.

'After some 20 minutes, the blackness below would be broken by the pale line formed by a sandy beach of a chalk white cliff on the French coast, some 17,000 or 18,000 feet below. Still feeling on one's own, a check with Hal seemed necessary. As usual, he gave me the assurance I was looking for – we were on track.

'Time went on and through the darkness no friendly aircraft appeared to be keeping us company. At about 20 minute intervals I called up Hal for the usual check and while I received the usual comforting response, he knew my reason for doing so.

'After three or perhaps four hours, there was suddenly 30 seconds to H-Hour, and the first illuminators could be seen falling over the target area followed by the mixed coloured target indicators. Within a very short space of time a large area of the ground and air space became a scene of brilliance, supplemented by searchlights and flak. It was then that I knew I had not been alone and was in good company for now I could see discipline and determination epitomised by the bomber force over the target area. For me, this impressed me more than anything I had seen or taken part in during the Second World War, crews flying for many hours unseen by one another, yet to arrive over the target area right on time, just as they had been instructed at briefing.

'When home on leave, my father was keen to know about our operational flying and he quite touched me by asking if he could be one of my gunners. As for my mother, I said very little but there was one moment when she said: "Your father told me that a German night fighter came so close to you one night that you could read the number on it." Now mother was known for exaggerating stories and became quite indignant when I explained it would have been impossible to read the number on the side of any aircraft at night. However, when father joined us she asked: "Didn't you tell me that a German fighter flew so close over the top of his cockpit that he could read the number?" To this, I responded: "Oh, that was an Fw190". "Yes, yes, that's the number!" came mother's reply.'

Clem Koder and his crew went on to complete 36 operations with 625 Squadron between September 1944 and March 1945 before moving to Nottinghamshire where he flew Hurricanes on fighter affiliation exercises. His flying career was ended after a heavy landing when he was told by a doctor that because of his height (he was just 5ft 4ins tall) he must never fly heavy aircraft. He then explained he had just completed 36 operations on Lancasters but always sat on a cushion to help his forward visibility!

The autumn of 1944 was also to see a dramatic increase in the survival chances of the young men in 1 Group. The Luftwaffe's night fighter force, although still highly capable, was hampered by lack of fuel, aircraft and crews, and the Allied advances meant the bombers' time over hostile territory was greatly reduced. In the period from mid-August to the end of December, 1943 1 Group had lost 190 aircraft and 921 men had been killed: in the same period in 1944 the figures were down to 154 aircraft lost and 823 men killed, despite a big increase in the number of sorties flown. In September 1944 460 Squadron recorded its first loss-free month since being formed while 100

E-Squared of 170 Squadron pictured during an air test. The squadron was based briefly at Dunholme Lodge before moving to Hemswell. (Author's collection)

Squadron at Waltham was to go from the night of September 12 until Christmas Eve without losing a single aircraft. One of 100 Squadron's favourite haunts was the King's Head pub in Waltham village. The aptly-named Lancaster family lived a couple of doors down from the pub and their daughter, Sally, had been knitting small 'good luck' dolls which she would hand out to aircrew as they arrived at the pub. Canadian Peter Bennett wore his pinned to his battle tunic collar, as did many 100 Squadron aircrew at the time. Almost all were to survive. Years later some still returned to see Sally Lancaster, by then married and living in Grimsby, to thank her for those knitted dolls.

Losses amongst aircrew were awful for the families of those involved at any time but when uncertainty was added to the mix, the effects on the wives, the children and the parents must have been almost beyond our comprehension. Even in the darkest hours of the war there was a mechanism in place which permitted the names of those killed in action and whose bodies were found to be transmitted back to this country and the information passed to relatives as quickly as possible. It was a process which often took weeks, some times months and occasionally years. Aircraft crashed in the most inaccessible of places and, until the bodies of the occupants could be found and identified, they were simply listed among the 'missing'. However, a very large number of aircraft and their crews were never found at all, they were simply 'lost without trace' and confirmation of their deaths had to wait, in the majority of cases, until the war was over.

Among them were the seven-strong 625 Squadron crew of 21-year-old P/O George Curless. They had taken off from Kelstern during the evening of August 26-27, 1944 as part of a 370-strong force to attack Kiel, an area which was to attract the attention of Bomber Command regularly between 1939 and 1945. Nothing more was heard from their Lancaster, K-King. It simply vanished. The crew's wireless operator was Sgt John Knight and the following morning his parents, Michael and Nora Knight, who lived in Redcar, received a telegram from Kelstern telling them their son was missing. It was in July 1945, 11 months after Lancaster LM168 CF-R had lifted off from Kelstern for Kiel, they were finally told by the Air Ministry that, in the absence of any further news, their son's death had been presumed on the night of August 27, 1944. It must have been one of thousands of similar letters sent out to families across the country but its effect, however much expected, must have been devastating. They also received a parcel containing their son's personal effects, including two photographs, two collar studs, a safety razor, shaving brush and a set of darts. The names of John Knight and his fellow crew members, George Curless, Frank James, Cyril Connolly, Albert Windle, Cyril Plant and Tom Smith, now appear alongside those of 20,000 other airmen on the Runnymede Memorial alongside the Thames, near Windsor. They were all simply lost without trace.

Sgt Les Bucknell in the mid-upper turret of IQ-B of 150 Squadron pictured in clouds over Mannheim in the winter of 1944. (Vernon Wilkes)

That attack on Kiel was to cost 1 Group three other crews, two of them from 12 Squadron. Again, no trace was ever found of the crews of F/O Brian Leuty and F/Lt Charles Taylor RNZAF. A Lancaster from 576 Squadron was attacked and set on fire over the target. F/O Jack Linklater's crew dropped their bombs and turned out over the sea but it was evident their aircraft would not survive for long and the crew, which included six Canadians, were ordered to bail out. Six were later picked up but the pilot drowned. The Elsham squadron was to lose a second aircraft that night. A small force of Lancasters had followed the bomber stream towards Kiel before diverting to drop mines in the Baltic. Nothing was heard from P/O Harold Murray and his crew and they were presumed to have crashed in the sea. That same operation also cost 166 Squadron two Lancasters and their crews.

Another 'casualty' that night was 550 Squadron's BQ-N. It had first flown back in 1943 with 460 Squadron and was one of the ageing Lancasters passed on to 550 when it was formed the previous November. N-Nan, as W5005 was known, was the squadron hack and was disliked by every crew which flew it. Nan could never reach the heights of other Lancasters and was prone to engine problems. But it soldiered on and that night, in the hands of a mainly Australian crew, left Killingholme on its 94th operation with already over 600 hours of operational flying. Once again problems were encountered and on its return it ditched in the River Humber, only a couple of miles from its home airfield, the crew making it back to base in time for their post-op eggs and bacon. In a letter to the author many years later the aircraft's Australian mid-upper gunner Bob

100 Squadron's the Ruhr Rover with the air and ground crew of F/Lt Trueman, Waltham, November 1944. (Author's collection)

Sloan explained they were on their approach into North Killingholme when, probably due to flak damage, the flaps would not go down and the aircraft spiralled to port, splashing down in the river before completing 360-degree turn in the water. Near empty tanks helped the aircraft float until the crew could get clear. The dinghy failed to release and the five Australians and one RAF men on board who could swim helped the British flight engineer, Sgt Walters, as they inflated their Mae Wests and swam about three quarters of a mile before they were found by an army unit and the alarm was raised. The story went round North Killingholme that the crew was so fed up with N-Nan's performance that the Humber ditching might not have been the accident it seemed. And when their replacement aircraft arrived, they were amused to see some squadron wag had named it 'SS Nan'. It, too, was later to be written off on its return from Merseburg.

The last week of August was to be a particularly bruising one for 1 Group squadrons. A highly successful attack on the Opel works in Russelheim cost 1 Group eight Lancasters and the lives of 51 young men. 101 lost two ABC Lancasters, each carrying a crew of nine, while 626 also lost two aircraft and their crews. Another two failed to return to Faldingworth, with only a single Polish airman amongst the 14 men on board, an indication of how difficult it was becoming to find replacements for the 300 Squadron men lost during the summer. A few nights later 300 were to lose another three aircraft in an attack on Stettin. Six members of an all-Polish crew died when they were attacked by a night fighter over Denmark while the other two carried all-RAF crews, one crashing in the Baltic and the other being abandoned over Sweden after suffering battle damage.

Briefing at Kirmington late August, 1944. Amongst those pictured is the future actor Donald Pleasence, who was not to return after this particular operation, spending the remainder of the war in a prison camp. (Jim Wright, 166 Squadron Association)

The Stettin raid also proved to be another black night for 101 Squadron with only a single man escaping from the 24 on board the three Lancasters lost, two crashing in the Baltic off the Swedish coast and the third being shot down by a fighter over Denmark. At least two more 1 Group Lancasters crash-landed in Sweden, one from 460 Squadron and the other from 626 at Wickenby. The Wickenby Lancaster was badly damaged by a night fighter and after crash-landing in Sweden, the crew was repatriated the following month. When they returned and told their story the mid-upper gunner, F/Sgt Harry Allison was immediately promoted and awarded a DFC for his actions that night. The Lancaster had been attacked by a pair of Ju88s, which wrecked the rear turret and damaged the hydraulics. Allison hand-cranked his turret before firing a long burst at one of the night fighters which was seen to catch fire and explode. His citation read: 'This officer's gallantry and presence of mind have always been of the highest order.'

Fifteen of the 23 aircraft lost by Bomber Command that night were from 1 Group with another, from 166 Squadron, failing to return from a mining operation in the Baltic. 166 had also lost a Lancaster over Stettin, F/Lt Fred Dunton's aircraft being shot down near the target. It was the first operation of his second tour with 166 Squadron. It was to be the last operation of the year in which losses on that scale were to be suffered by 1 Group.

August ended with a concerted daylight attack on V2 storage sites. Many of these were in tunnels and the Bomber Command's job was to block the entrances, something they were able to achieve with considerable efficiency. This required relatively low level bombing and the German flak gunners brought down six Lancasters, five of them from 1 Group. 550 Squadron lost its CO on the raid. W/Cmdr Alan Sisley, a 27-year-old Australian who had joined the RAF before the war, was flying with F/O Peter Siddall's crew, who were new to the squadron, when their aircraft was hit by flak during an attack on the storage site at Agenville. There were no survivors. Two Lancasters from Kirmington and a third from Elsham were lost over the same target. Five were killed, six evaded and three more became PoWs including the navigator in F/O Bryan Tutty's 166 Squadron crew, F/O Donald Pleasence, later to become one of Britain's best-known actors, not least for his portrayal of F/Lt Colin 'Forger' Blythe in the film *The Great Escape*. A 460 Squadron Lancaster and its crew were lost while attacking a storage site at Raimbert while a 625 Squadron Lancaster was damaged and its crew later safely bailed out.

It was in September that the fortunes of bomber crews in 1 Group turned dramatically. Just nine aircraft were to be lost on operations during the month with three more written off in crashes. All three of these involved 101 Squadron, two aircraft being written off without injury to their crews on their return from a daylight attack on Le Havre. The third, flown by F/O Edward

The crew of 550 Squadron's N-Nan, which ditched in the Humber. They are (left to right) R. Hopman, pilot, K. Sharpe, navigator, C. Stocks, bomb aimer, E. Kenny, flight engineer, F. Ferguson, wireless operator, R. Sloan, mid-upper gunner, and R. McKenzie, rear gunner. Five of the crew were Australian while the bomb aimer and flight engineer were British. (Bob Sloan)

Brooks, broke up in mid-air while on the training flight over Scotland, killing all seven on board, including the rear gunner, Sgt Jimmy Watt who, at 18, was one of the very youngest Canadians killed in Bomber Command.

Numerous operations were flown during the month to attack German defensive positions around Le Havre and later Calais, both being finally bombed into submission. Oil and industrial targets in Germany were also hit and it was during one of these, against Frankfurt, that F/O Ken Cole's 100 Squadron aircraft was lost with all nine men on board. Flying with him that night was P/O Clement Brown and his bomb aimer. Their crew had just joined 100 Squadron and they flew to Frankfurt that night to gain experience. This was to be the squadron's last loss until Christmas Eve. Two Lancasters were lost from Kelstern. F/Lt Robert Banks' aircraft was shot down over Germany and all on board killed, including 625 Squadron's gunnery leader, F/Lt Dennis Webber DFC, who had taken the place of the crew's regular rear gunner. A second Lancaster from the squadron, flown by F/O Howard Cornish, was lost along with its eight-man crew when it collided with a Lancaster from 622 Squadron from Mildenhall over Germany.

626 Squadron also lost a Lancaster on the Frankfurt raid, F/O George

F/Lt Tom Greenslade and crew, 625 Squadron. (Gus Hallgren)

Bolderson's Lancaster crashing in the Eiffel region. All the crew managed to bail out but three of them, the 22-year-old Canadian pilot along with Sgt Francis Foster and F/Sgt Stan Dunnett, were captured by civilians and murdered.

The good fortune which often seemed to accompany 100 Squadron crews around this time was in evidence when the new CO, W/Cmdr Ian Hamilton, led aircraft from Waltham in an attack on German flak defences on island of Walcheren. S/Ldr Hedley Scott's Lancaster was hit repeatedly by flak on its bomb run but, despite being wounded, the bomb aimer, P/O John Sanderson, continued to give instructions to his skipper. As their Lancaster, ND356, left the target it was hit again, rupturing the fuel tanks in the starboard wing and knocking out an engine. It was then hit a third time, badly damaging the nose and wounding the bomb aimer yet again. They made it back across the North Sea on three engines but, with no hydraulics, were diverted to the emergency airfield at Carnaby. There were immediate awards of DFCs for S/Ldr Scott and for P/O Sanderson while their aircraft, which was found to contain 120 flak holes, was repaired at Carnaby and rejoined the squadron early in 1945.

A Distinguished Service Order and Conspicuous Gallantry Medal were awarded to S/Ldr Tom Rippingdale and his navigator Sgt Francis Cridge of 166 Squadron that same night when they were involved in an attack on the docks and industrial area of Neuss, just across the Rhine from Düsseldorf. Their aircraft was attack by a Ju88 while they were on their bomb run. The night fighter was engaged by both gunners and was seen to explode but, in the exchange of fire, the rear gunner, 19-year-old Sgt Ron Hallett, was killed and Sgt Cridge badly wounded. The aircraft itself had been badly damaged, both turrets put out of action and many of the instruments destroyed. Damage to the hydraulics meant the bomb doors would not open but S/Ldr Rippingale estimated that if the bombs were released their combined weight would force the doors open. It worked and the bombs fell away. Sgt Cridge had been hit in the face, arm and body by shell fragments and had lost a lot of blood. Nevertheless, he stayed at his navigator's table and managed to plot a course back to Manston in Kent where S/Ldr Rippingdale was able to crash-land their crippled Lancaster.

Two other Lancasters failed to return to Kirmington from Neuss. F/O James Davies and his crew were lost without trace. F/O Raymond Miller's aircraft crashed in Düsseldorf and four of the crew were killed. The pilot and wireless operator were taken prisoner along with their navigator, the unfortunate W/O Ralph Watson, who had only returned to Kirmington a week earlier after being shot down during the Mailly-le-Camp raid in May and evading capture. This time he had to wait until the following May to make it home. Two other 1 Group aircraft were lost in the attack, those of F/O Robert Bamberough of 12 Squadron and F/O Stanley Durrent of 576 Squadron. They were aged just 20 and 21 respectively.

AS-O of 166 Squadron at Kirmington. This aircraft was lost on a mining operation off the Frisian Islands in late October, 1944. (Peter Green Collection)

NG264 of 150 Squadron pictured over Lincoln Cathedral. The aircraft flew with the squadron during its time at both Fiskerton and Hemswell. (Martin Nichol/David Briggs collection)

460 Squadron at Binbrook managed to go through September without losing a single aircraft but their run of good fortunate ended in another highly successful daylight operation to Emmerich, on the west bank of the Rhine. One was hit by flak, the crew bailing out successfully. The second had the misfortunate to be hit by incendiaries dropped by another Lancaster, killing the wireless operator, F/Sgt Keith Potter, and starting a serious fire in his compartment. The flight engineer and navigator bailed out but the rest of the crew got the fire under control and the aircraft later crash-landed at Hawkinge in Kent. F/Lt Geoffrey Fulford and crew from 166 Squadron were lost on this operation.

It was during early October that the next and final series of major changes to 1 Group came into operation. Three further squadrons were to be added to its strength along with three airfields, all transferred from neighbouring 5 Group. The first of the new squadrons, 153, came into being on October 7 when it was formed from C Flight of 166 at Kirmington. Hours after its formation 11 aircraft of 153 took part in the attack on Emmerich. On October 15 153 moved to what was perhaps Lincolnshire's most famous bomber station, Scampton. Its last occupants had been 617 Squadron during their dambusting days. It had closed in the late summer of 1943 for the laying of concrete runways and, on its re-opening, had been transferred as 15 Base headquarters to 1 Group along with the airfields at Fiskerton and Dunholme Lodge.

A week after the creation of 153 the second of the new squadrons, 170, was formed from 625's C Flight at Kelstern with additional aircraft and crews being drafted in from 12, 103 and 626 Squadrons. Its first CO was W/Cmdr Peter Hackworth and it was to move to Dunholme Lodge. The airfield's proximity to the ring of airfields around Lincoln, including Scampton and Wickenby, Fiskerton, Skellingthorpe, Waddington and Bardney meant that within a month of 170's arrival they were on the move again, this time to Hemswell with Dunholme Lodge closed to operational flying. At Hemswell 170 would be joined by the third new squadron, 150, which was reformed in Bomber Command at Fiskerton on November 1 and moved two weeks later. 150 were 1 Group 'old boys', flying Battles and Wellingtons from Newton, Snaith and Kirmington before being transferred to the Middle East Air Force.

153 Squadron was to suffer its first casualties in one of the most ambitious bombing operations of the war. Operation Hurricane was directed at the city of Duisburg and launched on October 14. The first phase involved a mass daylight attack by 1,013 Lancasters, Halifaxes and Mosquitoes. They were followed by more than 1,200 American bombers and the third phase involved a second Bomber Command attack, this time by 1,005 aircraft. Over 9,000 tons of bombs and incendiaries fell on Duisburg in less than 24 hours at a total cost to the Allies of just 20 bombers. Most of those were lost in the first wave of the first attack and eight of them were from 1 Group.

F/Lt George Wood pictured with his 576 Squadron Lancaster, Rub-A-Dub-Dub. (Elsham Wolds Association)

The first aircraft began leaving Kirmington shortly after 6.15am with 'H' hour at 8.45am. Duisburg was well defended by flak batteries and it was these that took their toll on the 1 Group aircraft leading the first wave. F/O Joe Brouilette's 153 Squadron Lancaster was hit and crashed in the Rhine while a second from the new squadron, flown by P/O George Draper, crashed near the city. There were no survivors from either aircraft.

Frank Woodley was a mid-upper gunner with 550 Squadron and watched with something approaching astonishment as his aircraft headed towards the target in the centre of some 700 RAF bombers. It was, he said, a sight which was to remain with him long after the war.

Four aircraft were lost from Wickenby. Two from 12 Squadron, flown by F/O Theo Sorensen and Canadian F/Lt Roy Clearwater, and one from 626, flown by F/Lt Reg Aldus, all fell to the flak gunners while a fourth, Q-Queenie of B Flight, ditched off Donna Nook soon after take off, the crew being picked up by a rescue launch. The wireless operator, F/Sgt John Penrose, later recalled that the port outer caught fire within minutes of the Lancaster becoming airborne and they were ordered to jettison their bombs over the sea and then ditch, which they did, the Lancaster sinking within a minute, by which time all seven men on board had got out through the escape hatches. The dinghy had come out of the starboard wing the right way up so most of crew didn't even get their feet wet. They fired off a flare and 25 minutes later saw a Morse signal being flashed in the distance 'Help coming'. A few minutes later an air sea rescue launch from Grimsby pulled alongside and the seven men clambered aboard.

An all-Polish crew was lost from Faldingworth on the same raid along with the crews of F/O Andrew McNeill (166 Squadron), F/O Harry Dodds and F/O Alan Abrams (both 550 Squadron). Only five men from all those brought down survived. 1 Group's final loss was the Lancaster of P/O Lloyd Hannah and his crew from 625 Squadron at Kelstern, who were on their first operation. They were flying CF-S, a veteran Kelstern Lancaster, and took off at 6.30 am and within a minute an engine burst into flames and the aircraft began to lose power. P/O Hannah, one of six Canadians on board, immediately ordered his crew to bail out and they jumped from less than 600 feet. Five landed safely but the bomb aimer, F/Sgt Lloyd Bennett, was killed when his parachute failed. The pilot died when the aircraft crashed and exploded near the village of Little Grimsby, just five miles from the airfield. Villagers were convinced he deliberately remained at the controls and managed to prevent the heavily-laden aircraft hitting houses and some years ago a plaque in his memory was unveiled in the local church. His crew were back in action within a fortnight and were to survive after bailing out on another operation in February 1945 after an incident which led to their new wireless operator winning a CGM.

The surviving 1 Group aircraft were back at their Lincolnshire airfields later that morning and many were immediately warned they would be back

F/Lt Colin Henry's 12 Squadron crew pictured at Grimsby with the skipper of the port's air sea rescue launch after they were fished out of the North Sea after ditching during the Duisburg raid on October 14, 1944. (Wickenby Archive)

over Duisburg again that night. After a few hours sleep1 Group crews were again in the first wave but this time flak opposition was light and only three were lost, the crews of P/O James Campbell (626 Squadron), F/O George Shaw (166) and an ABC Lancaster from 101 flown by P/O Colin Hunt.

A Lancaster from 626 Squadron at Wickenby came to grief as it returned from a raid on Stuttgart later in the month. In attempting to land, F/O Robert Clements' aircraft overshot, hit some trees and crashed close to the Market Rasen-Lincoln railway line in Stainton-by-Langworth. Rescuers were quickly on the scene and helped extricate the crew from the wreckage. Six of them survived with varying degrees of injuries but the flight engineer, Sgt Bob Terry, died while being taken to Lincoln County Hospital. Three other 1 Group aircraft were lost in this raid, two from 460 and one from 550 Squadrons with only one man surviving.

Three days later Essen was attacked by a record number of RAF heavy bombers, 1,055, in an early evening raid. Just eight aircraft were lost, three of

'We Dood It Too' of 150 Squadron, which flew three operations from Fiskerton before the squadron moved to Hemswell. (Martin Nichol/David Briggs collection)

them from 625 Squadron. F/O Owen Morshead's Lancaster disappeared without trace while that flown by Canadian P/O Lloyd Tweter crashed in Essex on its return. The third aircraft collided with a Halifax of 462 Squadron, which operated from Driffield, over Belgium. Both aircraft exploded and the only survivor was Lancaster pilot S/Ldr Hamilton, a flight commander, who was blown clear and was back at Kelstern inside a week. Also lost on the same raid were F/O Denis Ritchins' crew from Binbrook, F/O Douglas MacLean's from 12 Squadron and F/O Tom Dawson whose crew were the last 576 Squadron casualties from Elsham before the squadron moved to its new home at Fiskerton, near Lincoln.

When S/Ldr Hamilton returned to Kelstern he found a new squadron CO in charge. W/Cmdr John Barker was one of the very few men to command both a Spitfire and a Lancaster squadron and when he arrived at Kelstern had never been at the controls of a four-engined bomber before. John Barker, a graduate of Brasenose College, Oxford, and later to become an air vice marshal, was a remarkable airman and, after an hour's instruction on a Lancaster at Kelstern, volunteered to take a new crew on their first operation. He arrived at 625 Squadron from a staff job at the Air Ministry after flying both Army Co-operation and Spitfire operations earlier in the war. At Kelstern he proved enormously popular, flying regularly and thoroughly earning the DFC he was awarded in 1945. Squadron records note he was regarded as an 'incredibly brave' airman. He also kept a Spitfire MkV at Kelstern for fighter affiliation work and would spend many hours flying it around Lincolnshire.

Two back-to-back raids on Cologne at the end of October cost Bomber Command just two bombers out of the 1,398 taking part. Both of them were from 1 Group. One was flown by 21-year-old Australian F/O Edward Reid who, along with his 18-year-old navigator, P/O Arthur Emery, had been awarded a DFC for an operation earlier in the autumn. They were one of the youngest crews at Binbrook and all died that night. The second aircraft lost was PM-H from 103 Squadron at Elsham, flown by a young Canadian, F/Sgt Jackson Cooke, and he was to be awarded a CGM for his bravery that night.

F/Sgt Cooke's Lancaster was hit by anti-aircraft fire just after the bombs were released. The rudder controls were wrecked and fuel tanks in both wings holed. The flight engineer reckoned they had enough fuel to keep them airborne for 10 minutes and F/Sgt Cooke immediately headed for the Allied lines in Belgium. Once they were over friendly territory he ordered the crew to bail out but, as they were doing so, the mid-upper gunner, F/Sgt John McCoubrey, accidentally opened his parachute inside the fuselage. When he saw what had happened, F/Sgt Cooke went back into the cockpit of the Lancaster, determined to land the aircraft and save his gunner's life. As he tried to land in a field near Namur two engines failed. His CGM citation went on: 'Coolly and skilfully, this intrepid pilot achieved his purpose and made a crash-landing, incurring little further damage to the aircraft. This airman set a magnificent example of skill, courage and captaincy in the most difficult circumstances.' Sadly a month later F/Sgt Cooke and five of his crew (his bomb aimer had landed behind German lines but eventually managed to escape) were killed in a daylight raid on Dortmund.

Another man who received an immediate bravery award, in this case a DFC, was P/O Lawrence Woods, the bomb aimer in F/O Ted Owen's 460 Squadron crew. During a daylight attack on the refinery at Wanne-Eickel in the Ruhr their aircraft was hit by flak and the pilot was badly wounded. P/O Woods, whose only previous 'flying' experience was a few hours he had spent on Binbrook's indoor Link trainer, took over the controls and, despite high clouds and severe icing, flew the Lancaster back to England. By this time the pilot had recovered sufficiently to land their aircraft, K-2 The Nazi Killer, at Manston.

A raid on Düsseldorf early in November saw both 153 and 576 Squadrons lose aircraft from their new bases. 153, which was commanded by W/Cmdr Francis Powley, formally of 166 Squadron, had only been at Scampton for a few days when P/O Robert McCormack, one of many RCAF aircrew now serving in 1 Group, and his crew failed to return, the first of 22 Lancasters the squadron was to lose on operations from Scampton, sadly including one flown by their CO. Of the two 576 crews, only one man survived while 550 also lost the crew of F/Lt Don Foster. Two nights later six aircraft from 1 Group were lost in an attack on Bochum, including the 166 Squadron crew of F/O Joe Wilson who were on their 29th operation.

1 Group was to spend much of November attacking oil targets and providing support for the Allied advances. The attack on Dortmund at the end of the month in which F/Sgt Cooke lost his life cost the group six aircraft. Sgt Cooke's Lancaster was involved in a mid-air collision with another from 550

Squadron and crashed out of control, killing all those on board, the second Lancaster making it safely back to North Killingholme. The raid cost 153 another aircraft and the crew of F/Lt William Pow. The rear gunner survived from the 101 Squadron crew of F/O John Lyons as did the rear gunner in F/O Ron Fennell's 12 Squadron Lancaster. The sixth aircraft lost was that of F/O Maurice Gray from 460 Squadron. Mid-air collisions were every crew's nightmare and another occurred on the night of December 6-7 when 475 Lancasters from 1 and 3 Groups attacked a synthetic oil plant at Leuna in eastern Germany. On the approach to the target P/O Peter Walter's Lancaster from 460 Squadron collided with another from 635 Squadron at Downham Market, both aircraft exploding in the air moments later. The only survivor was the Binbrook aircraft's pilot who was blown clear. 1 Group's other losses that night were the crews of F/O Harry Johnson from 103 and F/Lt Joseph Morris from 550 Squadron.

Acts of bravery such as that which earned F/Sgt Cooke his award often went unrecorded. On the night of December 12-13 1 Group was involved in what was to prove to be the last heavy night attack of the war on Essen. F/O Philip Picot's 103 Squadron Lancaster was hit by flak and he ordered his crew to bail out. However, the rear gunner, 19-year-old Canadian F/Sgt Prince Yates, had been badly wounded and F/O Picot is believed to have remained at the controls of his aircraft and tried to land to save the life of F/Sgt Yates, only for the Lancaster to crash. This was the story the surviving members of the crew managed to piece together and were able to tell when the war ended. 150 Squadron lost its first Lancaster on this raid (and, incidentally, the first four-engined bomber lost on operations from Hemswell) when F/Lt George Devereau's aircraft was shot down. 460 Squadron also lost one of its most experienced pilots. S/Ldr James Clark, who had already earned a DFC and AFC and had been mentioned in dispatches, was on his 53rd operation when his aircraft was hit by flak. At least two other members of his crew, the navigator F/O Brian Reid and rear gunner F/O John Scott, were on their second tours.

12 Squadron also lost an aircraft that night, three of F/O Reg Veitch's crew surviving. They would lose another two nights later when P/O Eric Gillingham's Lancaster burst into flames and dived into the ground near Holbeach as it was heading back to Wickenby. The American pilot of a 153 Squadron Lancaster, F/O Harry Schopp, was killed along with three of his crew when their aircraft collided with another Lancaster in Bomber Command's only raid of the war on the town of Ulm, mid-way between Stuttgart and Munich. 101 Squadron lost an ABC Lancaster in the same raid along with F/O Don Ireland and his crew.

One 550 Squadron crew had a remarkable escape during a raid on a refinery at Merseberg, south of Berlin when their aircraft, N-Nan, was hit by a shower of incendiaries. One stuck in the wing root and ignited. The mid-

F/O Les Cameron, his crew, ground crew and 550 Squadron personnel at North Killingholme. Behind them is Lancaster LM273 BQ-O in which the crew did most of their tour with the squadron. The aircraft was lost in February 1945 durring a raid on Pforzheim. On the photograph are (doorway) F/Lt Avery (squadron navigation leader), F/Lt Bill Peek (bombing leader); (back row) Sgt Dave Eldridge, Sgt Frank Popple, F/Lt Jock Shaw, F/O Peggy Burnside (intelligence officer), F/O Cameron, Sgt Joe White, Sgt Glen Sutherland, P/O Joe Rigby, Sgt F. Piertney and S/Ldr B. Redmond. In front are the ground crew of LM273. (Jim Cameron, via 550 Squadron Association.

upper gunner, Sgt Frank Woodley, raised the alarm and immediately the flight engineer, F/Sgt John Allen and the wireless operator used the escape axe to chop a hole in the fuselage. The flight engineer put his gloved hand outside the aircraft and snuffed out the incendiary. Back at North Killingholme it was discovered the Lancaster had been hit by no fewer that 50 incendiaries while a 1,000lb bomb had gone clean through the tailplane.

At Binbrook the whole station turned out to say farewell to G/Cpt Hughie Edwards VC, who had been station commander there since February 1943. During that time he had flown on at least 15 operations and marked his departure by taking the new crew of P/O Arthur Whitmarsh to Essen on their first operation. He was succeeded as station commander by 460's CO, W/Cmdr Keith Parsons, and left 1 Group to take up a post in Ceylon.

There was to be no Christmas respite for 1 Group five aircraft were lost late on Christmas Eve in a relatively small-scale attack on railway targets and an airfield around Cologne. One of those lost was from Waltham, F/O Oscar Griffiths and crew being 100 Squadron's first casualties since mid-September. A second aircraft from the squadron crashed while trying to land at Squire's

Gate at Blackpool after an order diverting them to the USAAF airfield at Bungay in Suffolk. The crew survived the crash but not, perhaps, the ridicule over a 200 mile diversion error! Of the other four 1 Group aircraft lost, two from 166 and one each from 103 and 460 Squadrons, just one man escaped with his life.

170 Squadron, which had moved from Kelstern to Dunholme and finally to Hemswell since its formation, had flown over 300 sorties with 1 Group during December and was to suffer its first loss in a highly-accurate attack on the synthetic oil refinery at Schloven-Buer near Gelsenkirchen on the night of December 29-30. The crew lost was that of 27-year-old Geordie F/O Harry Ross, their Lancaster, known as 'Mama's Madhouse', crashing after being hit by flak near the target. The squadron was to lose another dozen aircraft before the war ended.

1944 had begun for 1 Group with an attack on Berlin and was to end with an attack on the railway yards at Osterfeld, near Leipzig. It was a wholly 1 Group raid, with 149 Lancasters taking part supported by 17 8 Group Mosquitoes. Two bombers were shot down and their crews killed, those of F/Lt Charles Hyde from 150 and F/O Jim Sherry from 166 Squadrons. Three of the crew of a 626 Squadron Lancaster were killed when their aircraft was shot down by 'friendly fire' over the Allied lines and a second from the Wickenby squadron crash-landed at Manston on its return.

By the time the aircraft taking part in the Osterfeld raid had returned to Lincolnshire the new year was dawning. Victory was a little over four months away yet the war was far from over for the men of 1 Group.

Nose art on 150 Squadron's IQ-B Baker, Hemswell, 1944. The idea came from the character of Captain Reilly Ffoul, from the Daily Mirror's *'Just Jake' cartoon* (Vernon Wilkes)

Chapter 19

'They Were All Mad Buggers!'

The Poles who Flew in 1 Group

During an attack on Cologne in late July 1941 a homebound Wellington from all-Polish 300 Squadron was hit by flak as it crossed the Dutch coast and caught fire. The hydraulics were shot away, a wing tip was missing and, as the crew later reported, 'things kept falling off'.

But the engines were undamaged and F/Sgt Pietrach's crew reckoned they could make it back to England. More bits fell off, the fire spread to the navigator's compartment, the bomb doors suddenly went down, leaking fuel caught fire and then an engine failed.

By now the stricken Wellington had crossed the Norfolk coast and F/Sgt Pietrach pointed the nose north, in the direction of 300's base at Hemswell. A few weeks earlier Pietrach and his crew had had another hairy night when they were hit by flak over St Nazaire and on that occasion had decided to land at the first available airfield. Back at Hemswell they came in for some ribbing from other crews about their safety-first attitude. So it was perhaps not coincidental that their radio should 'fail' as they reached the English coast just as they were ordered to divert to the nearest airfield.

On the fighter airfield at Sutton Bridge in south Lincolnshire those on the ground were astonished to see a burning Wellington fly over with sections of fuselage and wing flapping behind it. An urgent message was passed to Hemswell followed by another from Grantham telling much the same story, this time with the added information that the surviving engine also appeared to be misfiring. By the time Pietrach's B-Baby reached Hemswell most of the station personnel turned out to watch as he carefully prepared for a wheels-up landing on the grass runway. Just as he did the complete tail section of the Wellington came away and was left attached to the fuselage by the rudder cables. Pietrach and his crew emerged from the pile of wreckage unscathed. No jokes were told after that at Hemswell about diverted landings.

1 Group was to be the wartime home of all the Polish squadrons to serve

Faldingworth 1944: a 300 Squadron crew in a posed picture with their Lancaster. (D. Lyons)

with Bomber Command. And it was courage and determination like this which was to win them the admiration of their contemporaries. 'They were all, simply, mad buggers. I'm just glad they were on our side,' one Bomber Command veteran was to tell the author many years after the events at Hemswell that night.

In September 1939 the Polish Air Force had been destroyed in a matter of days by the Luftwaffe. It was outnumbered four-to-one, its aircraft were outclassed but it was certainly not out flown. Relatively few Polish fighters were shot down by the Luftwaffe while those that were accounted for a creditable number of German fighter, bomber and reconnaissance machines. Most of the Poles' aircraft were to be destroyed on the ground.

Before the war the British air attaché in Warsaw, G/Capt A.P. Davidson had a very high regard for the men of the Polish Air Force and, in the days before Poland capitulated, there had been some preliminary discussions on the formation of Polish units within the RAF if events led to Poland's capitulation. As the Germans swept eastwards to meet the advancing Russians, many of those in the 10,000-strong Polish Air Force fled to neutral Romania, a country which quickly found itself under pressure from the Germans to intern the Poles and from the French and British to let them go. The Romanians appear to have done both: interred the airmen and then turned a mostly-blind eye to their escape. By now the Polish government had set up camp in Paris and provided fake documents which were taken into Romania by a team of special couriers whose task it was to speed the repatriation of Polish soldiers and airmen. The first shipment of some 800 men, crammed onto a small Greek ship, left the Black Sea port of Balchik on October 15, 1939 heading for Beirut. Once there they switched ships and the following day were on their way to Marseille.

Times for a break for a 300 Squadron crew at Ingham. (Peter Green Collection)

In France the airmen quickly began to be assimilated into the French Air Force, but not without some misgivings. General Sikorski, who was to lead Polish forces until his death in a plane crash off Gibraltar in 1943, wanted his men to go to Britain as he had a much higher regard for both the RAF and the aircraft it flew. He was not alone. His men found the level of bureaucracy in the Armee de l'Air 'terrifying' and, after seeing the French forces at first hand, gave them little chance if the Germans chose to invade.

Eventually three Polish fighter squadrons were formed within the French air force and by May 1940 there were some 7,000 Polish Air Force personnel serving in France. They continued to be appalled at the quality of some of the French aircraft and, in particular, at their poor maintenance and the tactics they were told they would need to adopt. The Poles themselves repeatedly warned their French hosts what would happen if aircraft were left unprotected, parked in neat rows on airfields. But even after the Blitzkrieg began and whole swathes of aircraft had been destroyed on the ground, the French insisted on lining up their replacements in just the same way. Because of this, the Poles lost a third of their entire fighter strength in just one Luftwaffe attack on May 10, 1940 at Luxeuil. Within a few days Sikorski was preparing to order his men to leave for Britain.

The British, in the meantime, were still somewhat wary of the Poles. The first contingent had arrived in Britain in December 1939, having chosen not to fight with the French. Instead they found themselves subject to a military diet of endless parades, form-filling, medicals and English lessons.

In June 1940 a formal agreement was reached with the Polish government (which had moved yet again, this time to London) to form two Polish squadrons in Bomber Command, to be paid for by the Poles through a loan from the British. It was agreed they would be subordinate to a British station commander, quartermaster and paymaster and would serve subject to King's Regulations. They would receive the same pay as their RAF counterparts, wear the same uniforms – with a 'Poland' flash on the sleeves – and their aircraft would carry RAF markings with a small red and white chequer on the fuselage. Those first two squadrons, 300 (Masovian) and 301 (Pomeranian), were formed at Bramcote in Warwickshire in July, 1940 and were to be followed by two more, 304 (Silesian) and 305 (Ziemia Wielkopolska), the following month. 300 would serve with 1 Group until the war ended, 301 was disbanded in 1943 because of a shortage of Polish aircrew while 304 later transferred to Coastal Command and 305 to the 2nd Tactical Air Force. The missing number in that sequence, 303 Squadron, became perhaps the most famous fighter squadron in the Battle of Britain and was to forever cement the Poles' reputation in Britain as tough fighting men.

Typical of the Polish airmen who flew with 1 Group was Zygmunt Bednarski, a student at Krakow University before the war, where he was

Polish aircrew pictured at Hemswell in 1942. In the background are some of the officers' married quarters, buildings still there today incorporated in the new village of Hemswell Cliff. (D. Lyons)

studying electrical engineering. During his time there he was called up for national service and chose the Polish Air Force. From an intake of 240 he was one of just six to qualify as a pilot.

His period of national service was due to end, by some cruel irony, on Friday September 1, 1939. Five days earlier, as the noises from neighbouring Germany grew ever more menacing, the Polish armed forces were put on a war footing and Bednarski was told to forget about demobilisation. By that time he was flying Czapla RWD-14s, single-engined, high-winged reconnaissance aircraft which, in Polish terms, was modern, having only entered service earlier that year. But they were slow, equipped with only a pair of machine guns and were hopelessly outclassed by everything in the Luftwaffe arsenal.

The Polish air force had just 35 Czaplas in service, spread over seven squadrons. Within days they had all gone, 24 shot down or destroyed on the ground while the remainder were flown to either Romania or Hungary.

Zygmunt Bednarski survived the German onslaught and together with the remainder of his unit ended up in the east of the country where they fell into the hands of the Russians, who had taken the opportunity to stage their own invasion of Poland.

Many of those around him were relieved to have been captured by the Russians but Bednarski, who was multi-lingual and fluent in Russian, was not so sure. When he and thousands of his fellow officers were ordered to board trains heading for Smolensk and told they were being taken east for 'interviews' he became deeply suspicious. He and another Polish airman cut a hole in the

A 300 Squadron Wellington which made it back to Ingham from Bremen in September despite intensive fire damage. (D. Lyons)

floor of their railway truck and, as the train slowed, dropped onto the track and made for the nearest woods.

Later they came into contact with some Russian peasants who gave them food and advised them to stay well clear of any young Russians they came across because all, they were told, were committed Stalinists. The two men headed south and eventually found their way into Romania where they were promptly arrested and accused of spying. Neither had identification papers, which had been taken by the Russians, and, despite their protestations, were taken to a prison camp near Ploesti.

Both were determined young men and within days were on the run again, this time making it as far as Bucharest where they were arrested a second time, this time as they attempted to get into the French embassy. They were sent to an internment camp where conditions were simply awful but security was lax. The two young Poles were there only a matter of days before they escaped again, this time knocking out one of the guards and later evading a search party by hiding in a river, up to their necks in water, as the banks were searched.

The pair later came across a railway line and managed to smuggle themselves onto a train hauling timber from the nearby forest. When the train halted near a village they went into a small cafe in the hope of finding something to eat. The local police were quickly alerted but a local woman took pity on them, hiding them, providing them with fresh clothes and eventually helping them onto another train, this time heading for the Black Sea port of Balchik. There they came into contact with a Romanian who was able to provide them with fake passports and identity documents and they were able to board a ship bound for Marseille. On board were a number of other Polish escapees and once in France they were quickly recruited into the French forces, desperate for men as the German invaders were sweeping aside the country's army and air force. Days later France capitulated and the Poles were gathered together and told: 'La guerre et fini'. But Bednarski and his colleagues had not travelled thousands of miles just to end up in a German prisoner-of-war camp and decision to join the fledgling French Resistance movement.

Then a radio message was received telling them that all trained aircrew were badly needed by the British. A dozen Poles immediately volunteered, including Bednarski, and they were assembled on the coast where they were told they would be taken out to sea in small boats in the hopes of being picked up by a passing British ship.

The first party was intercepted by a naval patrol and their boat sunk by machine-gun fire. Bednarski was in the second vessel, a small fishing boat. It was to spend four long days adrift in the Mediterranean before they were found by a British tanker which later landed them in Oran. There they were told by the British consulate to make their way to Casablanca, some 400 miles away, from where they would be taken to England. When they asked how they were to get to Casablanca they were allocated a small truck, several cans of petrol and simply pointed in the right direction. With that they set off with no map or compass, in a hostile terrain with little or no knowledge of the local language

BH-G of 300 Squadron pictured during an air test, 1943. (Peter Green Collection)

Zygmunt Bednarski (centre) with his Lancaster and crew at Faldingworth. (Z. Bednarski)

in either Algeria or Morocco, their eventual destination. Three hundred miles into their journey they stopped at a roadside village to buy food only to find when they returned to their truck that all their petrol had been stolen. The hardy band of Poles completed the remainder of their astonishing journey on the backs of camels.

Once in Casablanca they were found room on a British ship, the *Arandora Star*, bound for Liverpool. By now German U-boats were strengthening their grip on the shipping lanes and Bednarski insisted on spending the whole of the five-day voyage on deck. He was one of 6,200 Polish airmen to make it out of a total of 6,863 in France, an astonishing achievement of organisation, bravery and endurance.

He was later to spend time training in Scotland, at Cranwell in Lincolnshire and Hucknall in Nottinghamshire before being posted to 305 Squadron, which had flown with 1 Group from 1941 until 1943 before being transferred to the 2nd Tactical Air Force. He was to fly 12 operations flying Mosquito fighter-bombers on low-level operations over Northern France before being wounded when his aircraft was badly shot-up by a Me109. After a spell recuperating, he was posted to a Polish OTU as an instructor but quickly tired of that and volunteered for service in Bomber Command.

He went to the Poles' own bomber training unit, 18 OTU at Finningley near Doncaster, where he teamed up with four other Poles, a Canadian of

Polish descent and an Irishman as a Lancaster bomber crew. Later they made the short move to 1656 Heavy Conversion Unit at Lindholme and then to the last remaining Polish squadron in Bomber Command, 300 at Faldingworth.

There he and his crew would complete 22 operations before the war ended, a tour which included a hair-raising night over Kiel where he later recalled having to fly his Lancaster at low level like a Mosquito to escape the searchlights. On another occasion he landed his Lancaster on two engines at Manston and on a raid on Bremen suffered shrapnel wounds in his hand and leg but still managed to land his Lancaster back in Lincolnshire.

One of those who flew with him was wireless operator Eugene Kassakowski, a Canadian of Polish descent and the crew's 'interpreter'. He had lied about his age and had joined the RCAF at the age of 16 and flew with 'Ziggy' Bednarski during his time with 300 Squadron. 'He was an absolutely great pilot and could do just about anything with a Lanc,' he remembered.

Like many other Polish airmen and soldiers who served with the British, Zygmunt Bednarski was later to settle in England. During his time at Faldingworth he would cycle to nearby Market Rasen and then catch train to Cleethorpes where the sea front cafes, pubs and dance halls were popular with aircrew. There he was to meet a pretty young lady who told him her surname, Croft, was a very old Cleethorpes name. They later married and, when he was finally demobilised in 1948 (by which time he had over 3,000 hours in his RAF

A 300 Squadron Lancaster undergoing maintenance at Faldingworth, 1944. (Peter Green Collection)

log book), they settled in Cleethorpes where he opened a small electrical business under the name John ('because it seemed the most popular name') Croft. Years later he added '-Bednarski' to this, becoming a popular member of the large Polish community in the area, which included many former Polish airmen and soldiers from the Carpathian Lancers, which was disbanded in Grimsby in 1947.

It was only long after the war that he realised how fortuitous his decision was to escape from that train bound for Smolensk. The men with him at the time were among the 6,000 Polish officers shot on Stalin's orders and buried in the Katyn Forest.

Among the very first batch of Polish airmen to reach Britain was John Prochera. He had joined the Polish Air Force in 1938 and was a gunner on Krasa light bombers. His unit was destroyed in the early days of the fighting, most of the aircraft being destroyed on the ground. By February 1940 he was in England and, after passing through the Polish OTU at Bramcote, joined 301 Squadron, flying his first few operations on Battles. His Swinderby crew then converted to Wellingtons and he flew from there and Hemswell before completing his first tour of operations. John Prochera then did something unusual, he applied to serve in the Royal Air Force. He joined a crew of three Australians, a New Zealander, a Scotsman and an Englishman at 1656 Heavy Conversion Unit at Lindholme before being posted to the newly reformed 100 Squadron at Waltham, thus becoming one of the first Poles to fly in Lancasters. By October 1943 he completed his second tour of operations and was always to remember the friendliness and comradeship he found at Waltham, both on the station and in the local community. John Prochera was never to fully master the complexities of the English language (although his command of swear words was prodigious) but the welcome he was given at Waltham transcended simple linguistics and it was to stay with him for the rest of his life. After leaving 100 Squadron he had a spell instructing before volunteering for operational flying again, this time with the Pathfinders of 156 Squadron at Warboys. There he went on to amass a total of 93 operations and finished up as the squadron's gunnery leader. After the war John Prochera left the RAF and decided to settle in Grimsby, renewing the friendships he had made in the area during his time with 100 Squadron. In later years he became a stalwart member of the Aircrew Association and ran a successful motor repair business. His command of the language improved only slightly but his affection for his adopted country never diminished.

It wasn't just Polish men who served alongside the RAF in 1 Group. In 1941 the Soviet-Polish Pact was signed (perhaps two years too late for Poland) following Hitler's invasion of Russia. This allowed for the freeing of large numbers of Poland's armed forces from prison camps, including a large number of young women. They had been rounded up by the Russians and

Four holders of Poland's equivalent of the Victoria Cross at Faldingworth. (Z. Bednarski)

shipped to labour camps in the east. When they were freed many chose to join the British and were moved by train from Siberia to the Middle East. There 1,436 of them were recruited into the newly-formed Polish Women's Auxiliary Air Force and brought to Britain where they were trained in all the WAAF trades, everything from cooks to parachute packers, from drivers to telephonists. Virtually all of these young women served with Polish squadrons first at Ingham and then Faldingworth.

They were not universally welcomed by the Polish air and ground crews as two years in labour camps had left both mental and physical scars and many of the Poles far preferred the more flirtatious and prettier British WAAFs.

The Polish contribution to 1 Group was significant. Their squadron numbers were limited by the shortage of replacements, a problem which grew more acute as the war progressed. Unlike other overseas squadrons, particularly the Australians and Canadians, there was no replacement pool to draw on the make up for those lost on operations. Towards the end of the war men like Zygmunt Bednarski switched from flying fighters to bombers to keep the squadron as near all-Polish as possible. The squadrons themselves were relatively small, never more than two flights, and certainly by 1943 the Poles of the final squadron in 1 Group, 300, felt they were being marginalised. They were the last to be re-equipped with Lancasters (not until the beginning of 1944, two years after the first Lancs went into service) and the last in the whole of Bomber Command to operate the ageing Wellington. In the autumn of 1943 as the bombing campaign reached its intensity they were relegated to mainly mining operations which proved intensely frustrating for the young Polish airmen desperate to kill Germans. Not even a glowing testimony to the effectiveness of their work from Arthur Harris could make up for not being able to drop bombs on Berlin.

But the Poles made their own history. They were to fly on some of the very first 1 Group operations against German invasion barges in the late summer of 1940 and the very last, to Berchtesgaden on April 25, 1945.

Mad buggers they may have been, but they were true warriors of the bomber war.

End of the line for a 300 Squadron veteran. (Z. Bednarski)

Chapter 20

Daylight at Last

1945: The Final 124 Days of Hostilities

The final year of the war dawned with high expectations and heavy snow blanketing Lincolnshire's airfields. Those final four months were also to see the heaviest bombing of the war and the lightest casualties amongst aircrew, despite 1 Group losing 24 aircraft in a single night. It was to witness the controversy of Dresden and the compassion of the food drops to the starving population of Holland and was a period which saw 1 Group reach the peak of its powers with 368 Lancasters on its strength, the highest number in Bomber Command, but paradoxically with fewer and fewer targets to attack. Ironically one of the final tasks many bomber crews were to undertake before demobilisation was dumping unused bombs in the sea.

Victory always seemed so close at hand in those closing months yet the resilience and tenacity of the Germans, the rigors of the weather and the vulnerability of their aircraft took their toll on the Lancasters and men of 1 Group. Among the first losses of the year was a 100 Squadron Lancaster with New Zealander F/Lt Verrell Weatherley at the controls which inexplicably plunged into The Wash during a bombing exercise, taking with it the pilot and his five-man crew. A couple of days later P/O Christopher Weight was killed along with the other five men on board a 103 Squadron Lancaster which crashed into the Humber in a blizzard.

Despite the awful weather which had led to the cancellation of a raid on New Year's Day, 1 Group Lancasters went to Nuremburg on the night of January 2 and lost six aircraft with two more being involved in a collision over Subrooke, near Lincoln on their return. There were no survivors from the 150 Squadron crew of F/O Geoffrey Russell and the 153 Squadron Lancaster of F/O Daniel Reid, one of five Canadians in the crew. Two others were lost from 100 and 300 Squadrons while the other three were from 166 Squadron. P/O Richard Chittim's aircraft was hit by flak near Nancy and only the rear gunner survived while P/O Stephen Buck and five of his crew parachuted to safety over the Allied lines after being shot down, the rear gunner, Sgt Ned Baker, being killed when he struck the tailplane. There were no survivors from the

Smiling faces at Wickenby in the spring of 1945. Among the 626 Squadron personnel identified are 'Fish', Beryl, Alan, wireless operator A. Lloyd, Kath, air gunner E. Duncan, Athel, D. Tucker, Charlie, T. Martinez, Dennis, Arthur, Franks, flight engineer D. Butler, 'Red' Livingstone, Scottie, Geoff and Wes. (Wickenby Archive)

third 166 Lancaster, which was again hit by anti-aircraft fire. The pilot was 30-year-old F/O Henry Burgoyne from New Cumnock in Ayreshire. He had joined the Metropolitan Police before the war and during the London Blitz won a George Medal together with Pc John James for rescuing a number of people from a collapsed block of flats in Marylebone, the two police officers at one time supporting part of a collapsed roof with their backs while a man and an unconscious woman were pulled out. Pc Burgoyne was already a member of the RAFVR and later trained as a pilot and arrived with his crew at Kirmington in the autumn of 1944. They were shot down on their 20th operation.

Heavy snow blanketed the area over the next few days but it barely affected operations. Wickenby and Kirmington were among the stations where all non-essential personnel were put on snow clearing operations after a blizzard swept across Lincolnshire on January 7. They worked in shifts to clear the main runways, being supplied with hot soup and tea every half hour. After clearing the runways they watched as Lancasters left for an attack on Munich and then had to start all over again to keep the runways clear for the bombers' return. Conditions at Elsham were so bad that snow was accumulating *inside* the hangars, blown through cracks in the walls. There, as at Binbrook, Ludford and Kelstern, conditions were considerably worse than on the airfields at lower altitudes. At one stage drifts around Binbrook were reported to be 21 feet high.

The raid on Munich, the last for over a week because of the weather, cost 1 Group nine aircraft, one of them a 626 Squadron Lancaster from Wickenby which collided with a 150 Squadron Lancaster over France. The pilot, F/O Bob Smith, was killed along with his rear gunner, Sgt Bill McLean, while the 150 Squadron aircraft returned safely to Hemswell. Collisions and strikes from 'friendly' bombs were now almost as much of a hazard as the German defenders in the crowded skies over Europe. Another 1 Group Lancaster involved in a collision that night was O-Oboe of 460 Squadron, flown by F/O Art Whitmarsh, whose crew Hughie Edwards had accompanied on their first operation and his last from Binbrook. They were outbound over the Vosges mountains and were climbing through clouds when they hit another Lancaster. Their aircraft fell back into the clouds in a spin and it took the entire pilot's strength to regain control. A quick inspection of the aircraft revealed that the trailing edge of the port wing was badly damaged, the aileron and wing tip were missing and much of the bottom of the fuselage had been torn away along with the H2S assembly. The mid-upper gunner, Sgt Ken de la Mare, used a rope to escape from his position into the relative safety of the front of the aircraft but the rear gunner, Sgt Dave Fellowes, was trapped inside his turret, which was vibrating fiercely but he declined an offer to bail out and opted to trust Whitmarsh to get the bomber home. After jettisoning their bombs, they were ordered to make for the emergency airfield at Manston where they made a safe landing. The following morning they walked through the snow at Manston to inspect O-Oboe. 'It wasn't a pretty sight,' Sgt Fellowes was later to recall. They were given rail warrants to return to Binbrook only to be stopped on the journey back by RAF service police and admonished for being 'incorrectly dressed'. It was later reported that the police personnel involved learned some new Australian phrases relating to their ancestry!

626 lost a second aircraft during the raid, F/O Ken Stroh's Lancaster being shot down near the target. Wickenby, like most other bomber airfields, was a very multinational place in 1945. Of the two Lancasters lost that night, 10 of those on board were Canadians and one Australian. There were five Canadians lost in F/O Charles Clarke's 550 Squadron crew while the 19-year-old wireless operator, Sgt Lois Precieux, was from Mauritius. There were also five Canadians in F/O Edward Saslove's Lancaster from 576 Squadron at Fiskerton which was lost with three of its crew and six Canadians in one of two 103 Squadron aircraft which failed to return to Elsham. Another six Canadians died in F/O Walter Soper's 166 Squadron crew while the pilots of the remaining two 1 Group aircraft lost, F/O Bob Hanbidge of 12 Squadron and F/O Norman Dunlop of 170 Squadron were both Australian.

Nose art at Kelstern. Clockwise from the top left, Wee Wally Wallaby, We Drop 'Em, Joe's Kite and Our Kid. (625 Squadron Association)

The snow relented sufficiently to allow 1 Group to take part in a highly accurate attack on the synthetic oil plant at Leuna, near Leipzig on the night of January 14-15. Three 1 Group aircraft were lost on the raid, two of them from Wickenby. F/O John Murray and two of his crew from 12 Squadron survived after they fell victim to a night fighter while F/Lt Don Nelson was the only survivor from his 626 Squadron crew, which was on its 30th operation in an ex-300 Squadron Lancaster on its 41st trip. The third Lancaster to be shot down was F/O Herbert Hazell's from 625 at Kelstern. Two other Lancasters, one from 300 Squadron and the second from 460, crashed on their return. A second plant in the same area at Zeitz was hit a few days later with the loss of six more 1 Group aircraft, one each from 100, 166, 300 and 153 Squadron and two from 12 Squadron with only 14 of the 42 men on board surviving. A seventh from 576 at Fiskerton was abandoned by its crew over Belgium. On the same night F/O Fred McGonigle's 101 Squadron Lancaster was lost while supporting a 5 Group attack on the Brüx refinery in Czechoslovakia, 101's first loss of 1945.

Operations were limited for the rest of the month but 153 Squadron at Scampton continued to suffer. An attack on Duisburg cost the squadron two aircraft, those of F/Lt Alan Jones DFC and F/O Ken Winder, while another, flown by 32-year-old F/Lt Owen Jones DFC was lost in an attack on Stuttgart. There were no survivors. The Stuttgart attack also saw 300 and 460 Squadron each lose a Lancaster. The pilot of the Faldingworth Lancaster was F/Lt Zigmund Zarebski, who had flown Spitfires and Hurricanes with the Polish Air Force in Britain before transferring to Bomber Command.

February opened with another very bad night for 1 Group. The target was Ludwigshafen, just across the Rhine from Mannheim. Two 101 Squadron Lancasters collided over France, killing 14 of the 16 men on board. A third from the squadron, flown by New Zealander F/O Bob Clark was shot down near the target. F/Lt Francis Conn DFC, who was on his second tour, had left Waltham with two newcomers to 100 Squadron, F/O Bob Dukelow and his navigator F/O Geoff Blackbourn, going along for experience. All nine men on board were killed when they were shot down close to the Rhine. 166 Squadron lost three Lancasters on the raid, those of F/Lt Ed Spankie DFC and F/Lt Edward Pollock and their crews. The third aircraft, flown by F/O Mike Smithers, was attacked by a Ju88 which raked the Lancaster with cannon fire, killing four of the crew and wounding the pilot. After a second attack he managed to bail out together with his bomb aimer, Sgt Ray Storey, and flight engineer, Sgt Eric Bradshaw, and all three landed in the Black Forest. Later, when he was being interrogated, Smithers was astonished how well the Germans were informed about 166 Squadron, his captors even asking about the well-being of the Kirmington CO, G/Cpt Vivian, whose foot had been injured at particularly boisterous Christmas party! The final aircraft lost that

Bombs away. A dramatic photograph taken from a 101 Squadron Lancaster during the daylight raid on Bremen on March 23, 1945. The aircraft directly below is also from 101 and, on the original, it is possible to make out the shadow of one of the ABC aerials falling across the fuselage. (Vic Redfern via Peter Green)

night was a 550 Squadron Lancaster which collided with a Hemswell-bound 170 Squadron aircraft over France, killing two of the crew.

The next victim of a mid-air collision was a Lancaster flown by the popular station commander at Binbrook, G/Cpt Keith Parsons. He had taken a new 460 crew on Bomber Command's only attack of the war on the town of Wiesbaden. After leaving the target area his Lancaster collided with an aircraft from 626 Squadron at 19,000 feet, the collision sheering off the canopy just above his head and knocking out both port engines. His Lancaster rolled and went into a spin and he ordered the crew to jump. When the altimeter went past 7,000 feet G/Cpt Parsons realised he wasn't going to have time to get out through the escape hatch so, breaking off chunks of Perspex with his hands, he climbed out through the shattered canopy and pushed himself out. 'The spin on the aircraft was so tight that I actually stood on top of the canopy quite comfortably before giving one hell of a push and pulling the ripcord,' he was later to recall. It was only when he reached the ground he realised his parachute had been torn as he made his escape and was about to collapse as he reached the ground. He was the only survivor from his aircraft while the only one casualty in the Wickenby Lancaster, was the rear gunner, Sgt Henry Norton, who died in the collision. A second Lancaster lost from 460 was flown by F/O John Maguire, a 21-year-old Australian who had only recently married a girl he met in Doncaster while at 1656 HCU at Lindholme. There was only one survivor from his crew. The three other 1 Group aircraft lost included one from 300 Squadron and two from Fiskerton, F/O Richard Sowerbutts and his crew being killed when their Lancaster crashed in Luxemburg. The second was abandoned when an engine caught fire over France and the crew landed safely.

Oil targets were being hit with great frequency and accuracy and the next on the list was the Prosper benzol plant at Bottrop, near Gelsenkirchen. Luftwaffe night fighters accounted for several of the six 1 Group Lancasters lost, one each from 12, 100, 153, 170, 460 and 550 Squadrons, 33 men losing their lives. Military targets were also being hit and on the night of February 7-8 285 Lancasters from 1 and 8 Groups virtually destroyed the town of Kleve, close to the Rhine in support of a British attack on the town. So badly was Kleve bombed that military vehicles were held up by the mountains of rubble. It was an attack which was to cost 1 Group a single aircraft, that flown by F/Lt John Somerville and crew from 12 Squadron. Clem Koder, who completed 36 operations as a pilot with 625 Squadron at Kelstern, later remembered this as one of the operations his crew enjoyed best because they were told at their

January 1945 at Kirmington. The 166 Squadron aircraft is one of those fitted with a Rose turret.
(Peter Green Collection)

W/O Lake and five members of his crew about to board their Lancaster at a muddy Kelstern prior to an air test. (625 Squadron Association)

briefing that their bombing was intended to provide close support for Canadian troops and for the Durham Light Infantry.

Dresden. The very word now unfairly haunts the memory of Bomber Command. Over the years it has been used to despoil and denigrate the achievements and sacrifices of all who served in the RAF's bomber squadrons. In a single night a raid of the highest efficiency and accuracy provided the bombing campaign's opponents and the post-war revisionists with exactly what they were looking for: civilian casualties and unnecessary destruction on an almost unimaginable scale.

The raid took place on the night of February 13-14 and was part of the long-planned Operation Thunderclap, aimed at undermining the will of the German people in the closing stages of the war. Dresden was one of four cities selected as Thunderclap targets (the others were Chemnitz, Leipzig and Berlin, all close to the front line with the Russians). At the Yalta conference earlier in the month the Russians themselves had pushed for something on the scale of Thunderclap and the idea had been enthusiastically backed by Churchill. The Americans, too, were keen in the idea and were to follow up the RAF's Dresden raid with a bombing attack of their own. In his latest history of the Second World War, historian Max Hastings maintains that the bombing was approved at a joint Western Allied Combined Chiefs of Staff meeting in Malta, held prior to the Yalta summit and adds: 'The heavy bomber forces were directed to assault Germany's transport infrastructure, including such rail centres as Dresden and Leipzig *in the path of the Russian advance*' (author's italics)

Dresden was to be the first Thunderclap target and two separate raids were mounted by Bomber Command that night. The first, involving 5 Group, produced scattered bombing. The second, involving Lancasters of 1, 3, 6 and 8 Groups, came exactly one hour and 35 minutes after the first and was the one which was to obliterate the city, creating a firestorm killing perhaps as many as 50,000 people (although Hastings maintains the actual figure was around

F/O Windrim DFC (centre) and crew with their aircraft Y2 of 625 Squadron. (625 Squadron Association)

Wickenby's MT office staff, Sgt Munyard, F/O Corbette, Cpl Shaw, Anne Pew and Ivy Adams.
(Wickenby Archive)

half that estimate). It had been purposely timed to catch fire crews and rescue workers out in the open. When they reached the city the master bomber, whose call sign on the night was King Cole, ordered crews to bomb visually on the fires started by 5 Group. Those towards the end of the stream simply dumped their bombs into the conflagration below, Lancasters rearing up in the turbulence caused by the overheated air over Dresden 20,000 feet below.

An American raid the following day did little more than turn over the smouldering embers of the once-beautiful city of Dresden although, controversially, the B-17s' long-range Mustang fighter escorts were ordered to strafe roads leading away from the city, killing many of those who had managed to escape the flames.

There were many post-war theories about the choice of Dresden as a target, with the one suggesting it was a demonstration to the Russians of the might of Allied air power amongst the most widely used. But for the bomber crews who assembled in their briefing rooms in Lincolnshire on the afternoon of February 13 it was just another long-range attack on a German city. According to which briefing you listened to it was an 'assembly point for the Russian front', 'a centre of lines of communication', 'an important evacuation area for government departments from Berlin' or 'a vital transport centre for troop movements'. Geoff Robinson was a flight engineer at Wickenby and recalled that at their briefing they were told the Russians had requested the raid because the Germans were using the city in which to mass troops ready for a counter-attack. The success of the raid, they were told, could hasten the end of the war, something those who had been around Bomber Command had heard several times before. At the time few men on the squadron knew anything about Dresden or its history. It was just another target. Eric Thale, who flew with 625 Squadron that night, remembered the highly accurate marking of the target from 1,000ft by Bill Topper in his 5 Group Mosquito and the controlling of the attack by Maurice Smith, again of 5 Group. 'It was so good that our master bomber merely told us to bomb the fires, and that's what we did,' he said.

At Hemswell, crews from 150 and 170 Squadrons were briefed that the raid was in direct support of the rapidly-advancing Russian armies. The aircrew, however, were more aware that they faced a 10-hour operation at a time when the war was clearly nearing its end. Over at Binbrook, 460 crews regarded Dresden as just another target. They were told at their briefing the city was a

W/Cmdr Frank Powley (centre) CO of 153 Squadron, who was killed on a mining operation in March 1945. He had a premonition he would not return. Before joining 153, W/Cmdr Powley commanded 166 Squadron. (F. Fish)

F/O Peggy Burnside and S/Ldr Bruce Derner in the briefing room at North Killingholme prior to the attack on Nordhausen, April 3, 1945. (Roland Hardy)

major road and rail junction between the eastern and western fronts. Crews at North Killingholme, meanwhile, were briefed that the city contained vital industrial and communications targets.

Only at Faldingworth was there any real sign of dissent about Dresden. Earlier that day the decision to cede large parts of Polish territory to Russia, agreed at Yalta, had been announced on the BBC's Home Service. It came as a hammer-blow to the Polish airmen who had been fighting with the RAF for almost five years and the news was not helped at the Faldingworth briefing where crews were told the raid was intended to support the Russian advance in eastern Germany. The crews wanted to know why they should risk their lives when Poland had clearly been betrayed at Yalta.

In the event, a seven-man Polish crew from Faldingworth were among the first casualties of the Dresden raid. Shortly after take off at 9.45pm that night, W/O Mykietyn's Lancaster collided with another aircraft from 550 Squadron near Wragby, both bombers exploded in mid-air, killing the Polish crew and that of F/Lt Eric Allen from North Killingholme. Just half a dozen Lancasters were lost on the raid itself, including two from 1 Group, flown by F/O Roland Young of 576 Squadron and P/O Doug Rimmington of 103.

Before take off all crews were issued with small silk squares with a Union Jack on one side and the words 'I Am English' in Russian on the reverse in case they were forced down near Russian lines. They were to carry the same silk squares the following night when the second part of Thunderclap was enacted, an attack on Chemnitz, another two-part raid, this time involving the Halifaxes IIIs of 4 Group. 1 Group's Lancasters were once again in the second attack but this time found the target covered in cloud and could only bomb on sky markers. Parts of the city were damaged but most of the bombs fell in open country. Thirteen aircraft were lost, four of them from 1 Group. There were no survivors from the Lancasters of F/Lt Bob Cunliffe (625 Squadron), F/O Dennis Kemp (166) or F/Lt Clement Mills (153) but all seven men in the 100 Squadron crew of P/O Tom Townley bailed out on what was their first and only operation from Waltham.

F/Lt Jimmy Marsh, 12 Squadron's gunnery leader, who was killed in an attack on Zeitz, January 16, 1945 as part of F/Lt Stuart Whyte's crew. He had already completed one tour of operations with 460 Squadron. (Author's collection)

Many crews flew to both Dresden and Chemnitz, a total flying time of some 19 hours, some keeping going on the benzedrine 'wakey-wakey' tablets freely handed out after briefings. Geoff Robinson was the flight engineer in 'Dicky' Bird's 626 Squadron crew at Wickenby and remembered that after leaving Chemnitz for the flight home his skipper switched on the automatic pilot. The next thing he remembered was waking to find the rest of the crew fast asleep. He woke the skipper and they discovered they were down to 2,000 feet over Spalding in south Lincolnshire!

1 Group was stood down for the next five days but was to suffer heavily when its aircraft took part in the last attack of the war on the Ruhr city of Dortmund, losing 11 Lancasters with another crash-landing on its return. Worst affected was again 166 Squadron which lost three Lancasters. One was

625 Squadron's B Flight commander, F/Lt Lennox and his crew pictured at Kelstern with their Lancaster, spring 1945. They include F/Sgt Ron Wilsden, wireless operator, an unknown friend of the crew, F/Lt Lennox, F/O M. Brook, navigator, F/Sgt D. Abbott, flight engineer and Sgt W. Birkby, rear gunner. (Author's collection)

being flown by A Flight's commander, S/Ldr Ken Collinson whose crew had already completed their tour but volunteered for 'one more'. Killed along with him that night were the squadron's gunnery leader F/Lt John Barritt and the bomb-aimer, F/O John Sinclair DFC, a former Metropolitan police officer who had become a father that very day. Another of the squadron's flight commanders, S/Ldr Ron Waters, managed to get his crippled Lancaster back to Manston on two engines after being hit by flak over the target and then by a fighter on the return leg. 166 also lost the aircraft and crew of F/Lt David Hall, six of whom were Canadians. Another flight commander lost was S/Ldr Tom Warner from 101 Squadron, although he survived along with four of his crew.

286

The following night Duisburg was attacked and another eight 1 Group Lancasters failed to return, three of them from 576 Squadron at Fiskerston. The crew of F/Lt Charles Living were killed but 11 of those on board the other two managed to bail out over Allied lines. 550 lost its CO, W/Cmdr Bryan Bell but he survived to be taken prisoner along with five members of F/Lt Derek Luger's crew. Bell had previously served as a flight commander with both 100 and 550 Squadrons at Waltham before moving to 1656 HCU at Lindholme as Wing Commander Training under A/Cmdr George Banting. After a spell of leave he returned only to find out that he was going back to 550 as commanding officer. Thus it was that he had put himself on the battle order for the Duisburg raid.

He had just handed over controls to F/Lt Luger when a fighter came up unseen from astern. 'His first burst hit the rear gunner and started a fire,' he later wrote. 'We heard his screams and then the intercom burnt out.'

The mid-upper gunner got in a 'good burst' at the fighter as they carried on with their bomb run but it soon became clear that the Lancaster wasn't going to make it. The fire had spread and all the hydraulic fluid had been lost and the order to abandon the aircraft was given. As the crew started to bail out

625 Squadron's veteran V-Victor pictured with air and ground crew soon after the squadron moved from Kelstern to Scampton in the last month of the war. (Clem Koder)

287

the blazing tail section of the Lancaster parted from the main section of fuselage, blowing the fortunate wireless operator clear.

W/Cmdr Bell landed safely and, after getting his bearing from the stars, set off in what he hoped was the direction of the Allied lines only to meet up with a platoon of German soldiers and spent the remaining weeks of the war in a Bavarian prison camp. Two members of the crew were killed in the fighter attack, the rear gunner, 19-year-old Sgt Fred Jones, and the bomb aimer, Sgt Gordon Hancock.

Only three men died in two 170 Squadron Lancasters lost on the Duisburg raid, the pilot, F/Lt Tom Smith and his flight engineer in one, and the rear gunner, F/Sgt Franklyn Paterson, in the second. His aircraft was hit by flak and partially abandoned and he had the misfortune to fall through an open escape hatch before he could attach his parachute when the aircraft was attacked seconds later by a night fighter.

Two nights later 1 Group was to be involved in what proved to be the third most destructive raid of the war after Dresden and Hamburg when they bombed the picturesque Black Forest town of Pforzheim, the centre of Germany's pre-war watch-making industry. It was because of this and the likelihood that precision instruments were being made there that it was selected as a target. Much of the town was timber-built and at least 17,000 people are thought to have died when the 367 Lancasters involved, the majority from 1 Group, bombed from as low as 8,000 feet. It was later estimated that 83 per cent of the town had been destroyed in the raid, which lasted just 22 minutes. It was another terrifying display of the power of Bomber Command. Thirteen Lancasters failed to make it back, all but one of them from 1 Group. In one of them wireless operator F/Sgt Jack Bettany was to win a CGM. He was flying as a replacement in F/Sgt 'Basher' Paige's 625 Squadron crew on his 16th operation with his third different squadron in a much-interrupted Bomber Command career when their aircraft was hit by a shower of incendiaries. The aircraft was badly damaged and F/Sgt Bettany managed to throw at least 15 out of holes in the fuselage. He also ensured both gunners managed to get out before baling out himself, using the aircraft's spare parachute after his own inadvertently opened inside the fuselage. When the crew arrived back at Kelstern and told their story the squadron CO, W/Cmdr John Barker, immediately recommended F/Sgt Bettany for his bravery award. Jack Bettany himself thanked his lucky stars that he had checked the position of the reserve parachute before they left Kelstern.

Although losses had tailed off dramatically, accidents still took their toll and six young men relatively new to 12 Squadron at Wickenby died when their Lancaster dived into the ground at Stainton-le-Vale on the Lincolnshire Wolds during a training exercise. The pilot, P/O Keith Lindley, was just 20 and his elder brother Arthur had been killed flying over Holland in a 107 Squadron

Grog's-the-Shot, 100 Squadron's Z2, pictured after the move from Waltham to Elsham, March 1945. This aircraft led Bomber Command's Main Force on the final operation of the war to Berchtesgaden. Pictured are (left to right) P/O McQuaid DFC, P/O Sanderson DFC, F/Sgt Johnson, S/Ldr Scott DFC, F/Lt Harwood DFC, F/Sgt Nelson and P/O Jones, together with members of the ground crew. (Author's collection)

Boston in August 1942. P/O Lindley was later buried in Newport Cemetery in nearby Lincoln. A few nights later two more crews from 12 Squadron were to be killed on training flights but this time their deaths were no accidents.

This was the night in early March 1945 when the Luftwaffe staged Operation Gisela, when over 100 He219 and Ju88 night fighters shot down 20 bombers as they returned to their bases from raids on Kamen and Landbergen. On a number of nights during the previous month night fighters had followed the bomber streams back to England to check their approach and landing procedures. On the night of March 3-4 the intruders struck just as the tired bomber crews began to relax with the beacons and landing lights in view. Airfields in Yorkshire were hit particularly badly with half the losses occurring there. 1 Group escaped relatively lightly, although a Lancaster from Binbrook was caught by a Ju88 not far from the airfield at Wickenby. Five of the crew managed to bail out but both the flight engineer, Sgt Alan Streatfield, and the wireless operator, F/Sgt Bob Davey, the only Australian in the crew, were killed. The two 12 Squadron aircraft were both on night exercises. P/O Arthur Thomas' Lancaster was caught near Gainsborough and crashed between

Blyton and East Stockwith close to the River Trent. The second, flown by F/O Nicholas Ansdell, was attacked further south in Lincolnshire and came down at Ulceby Cross, near Alford, a roadside memorial stone now marking the location of the crash site. There were no survivors from either crew. At least one Lancaster was attacked in the circuit at Ludford but escaped, cannon shells hitting the home of the local vicar, the Rev Ravins, narrowly missing his two young children, one of whom later became a school friend of the author.

There was another tragic loss that same night when a 153 Squadron aircraft vanished without trace on a mining operation over the Baltic. The aircraft was flown by P/O Leo Gregoire, a Canadian who had recently been awarded a DFC. His fellow Canadian bomb aimer, W/O Ken McCoy, was the only survivor of a 626 Squadron Lancaster shot down over Belgium in May 1944 and had evaded capture, returning to operational duties with 153 at Scampton. 153 was to lose two more aircraft and their crews in exactly the same circumstances a month later.

Bomber Command returned to Chemnitz on the night of March 5-6 on a night which saw nine Halifaxes of 6 Group crash on or soon after take-off because of heavy icing, one of them coming down in the city of York. There were no such problems for the Lancasters of 1 Group but eight of them failed to return. Two were from 625 Squadron at Kelstern but of the 14 men on board only two would be killed. One, flown by Canadian F/O Jim Alexander, had suffered engine problems on the outward leg and could barely climb above 15,000ft before it was attacked by a Ju88 soon after they had dropped their bombs. The aircraft lost its hydraulics and then caught fire and the skipper ordered his crew to bail out. The rear gunner, Sgt Joe Williams, struggled to get out of his turret only to find his parachute was on fire. He recalled a conversation in the Waterloo Inn at Laceby the night before when the pilot had talked about stowing the aircraft's spare parachute behind his seat and he quickly made his way to the front of the aircraft where F/O Alexander was about to make his exit from the burning Lancaster. The pilot quickly climbed back into his seat, allowing the young tail gunner to strap on the spare 'chute and jump before finally going himself. It was an experience very similar to that of Jack Bettany at Kelstern. Another 1 Group casualty that night was the 460 Squadron Lancaster of F/Lt John Holman DFC, who was on his 40th operation. He was killed along with the other seven men on board, including another second tour officer, F/Lt Tom Morgan DFM.

The 1 Group Summary of Operations for this raid makes interesting reading. It states that 239 Lancasters were detailed for the raid, nine aborting for various reasons. Apart from the eight missing aircraft, another from 101 Squadron, had diverted to Juvincourt, east of Paris after being damaged. 'Ground opposition was very slight in the target area,' the summary went on, 'but the Leipzig defences were active. Only three aircraft were damaged, two

Tom Tobin and crew, 153 Squadron, Scampton 1945. (Tom Tobin)

over the target and one over Leipzig. Fighters were in evidence in the target area and along the first two legs of the route home. Ten aircraft were engaged in combat, one on the outward leg while crossing the battle lines, one near Leipzig and the others in the target area. One Ju88 is claimed destroyed and one Me110 damaged.' The summary concluded that while the target was covered in cloud, the bombing was concentrated and a 'big red explosion was reported'.

Those defences referred to were still a major threat to bomber crews despite the near-collapse of the German military. Forty-eight hours after the Chemnitz raid 1 Group was to lose another 13 Lancasters and the lives of 67 men on the 1,850 mile round trip to Dessau. Three of those were from North Killingholme and included 550's veteran 'The Vulture Strikes' which was being flown by F/O Cyril Jones. Four of his crew survived along with six others from the crews of F/O Bob Harris and P/O Searn Nielson. 103 Squadron also lost three aircraft, two crashing near the target area while the third, flown by Canadian F/O Bill

550 Squadron's last commanding officer, W/Cmdr J. C. McWatters (pictured seated centre). On his right is S/Ldr Peter Sarll. This pictured dates from the late spring of 1945. (Peter Sarll)

Nightingale, survived attacks by two Ju88s and, although badly damaged, made it back to the Allied lines where the crew bailed out, the pilot being killed when his parachute failed. 101 Squadron was still flying ABC duties and lost one of its aircraft, flown by S/Ldr Monty Gibbon DFC, a flight commander at Ludford, This was one of only 11 aircraft lost by the squadron on operations in 1945. 170 Squadron at Hemswell lost the aircraft of F/O John Walker and F/O Harry Fuller while 576 also suffered two losses, the aircraft of F/O George Paley and F/O Charles Dalziel, the only 1 Group pilot shot down that night to survive.

Allied ground forces were now poised to cross the Rhine and the final raids on the much-bombed Ruhr cities of Essen and Dortmund (the latter involving a new record of 1,108 RAF bombers) took place on March 11 and 12. 1 Group's final loss over Essen was the Lancaster of F/O Eric Gibbins of 153 Squadron which went down in the target area. P/O George Burgess and five of his 460 crew were lost on the Dortmund raid while a second aircraft from 103 Squadron crashed near Elsham village on its return with a bomb embedded in the tail. The only fatality was the 19-year-old flight engineer, Sgt

Francis Carter. 153 lost another Lancaster and an experienced crew when F/O Ken Ayres' aircraft crashed off the Danish coast while on another mining operation. His aircraft may have fallen victim to a pair of night fighters which also accounted for S/Ldr Slater's 103 Squadron Lancaster. He managed to evade capture along with four of his crew but his two gunners died in a battle with a Ju88. Another aircraft failed to make it back to 153's home at Scampton a few nights later in an attack on the Duerag refinery at Missburg, the pilot, P/O Edward Parker being the only survivor. The same raid also claimed F/O Russell Wallace's Lancaster from 550 Squadron.

The Nuremburg raid at the end of March 1944 claimed 22 1 Group Lancasters among the 96 bombers lost in this disastrous attack. Almost a year on, on the night of March 16-17, 1 Group staged its own attack on the city, sending 231 Lancasters accompanied by 16 Mosquitoes from 8 Group to provide the target marking. No fewer than 24 of the Lancasters failed to return from a raid which cost the lives of 123 men and left another 43 to spend the remaining few weeks of the war in captivity.

Casualties were especially severe at Wickenby where five Lancasters from 12 Squadron and another from 626 failed to return. One of the 12 Squadron aircraft landed with battle damage in France but the remainder were shot down, almost all by night fighters which attacked the bomber stream on its way to Nuremburg and on the homeward leg in an awful repeat of the events a year earlier. 103 and 166 each lost three aircraft and two each were lost by 170, 576, 625 and 100 Squadrons with other single losses from 153, 460 and 550.

One of the aircraft lost that night was the 166 Squadron Lancaster flown by F/O Kevin Muncer, whose pregnant wife was living in Kirmington village, close to the airfield. He and his crew were on their 22nd operation and were attacked by a night fighter and went out of control. F/O Muncer was thrown through the overhead escape hatch and, although his parachute opened, he landed with such force in some trees that his left arm was literally ripped off. He was quickly found by a German farmer and a French PoW and taken to the farmer's home where he and his wife gave the injured pilot treatment before help arrived. After the war Kevin Muncer was surprised to receive his watch back. Another French PoW working on the farm had found his severed arm and, on removing the watch, saw the pilot's name engraved on the back. He later contacted the International Red Cross who arranged to have the watch, a birthday present from his sister, sent back to him. Two years later Kevin Muncer was able to repay the kindness of the farmer and his wife by helping arrange the repatriation of their son, who was a PoW in Scotland, to help the elderly couple out on their farm.

One of the other 166 Squadron aircraft lost that night was flown by F/Sgt Bill Hylder, whose flight engineer, F/Sgt Ron Guscott, was a 'supernumerary' pilot remustered as an engineer. Both were killed as was another flight-

C Flight, 550 Squadron pictured at North Killingholme, spring 1945. (Peter Sarll)

engineer/pilot, Sgt Derek Jones, who was lost in F/O Patrick Rolls' crew from 625 Squadron.

Frank Woodley was the mid-upper gunner in a 550 Squadron Lancaster that night and witnessed at first hand the terrible toll of 1 Group Lancasters. At one stage in the raid he spotted a Ju88 250ft above them flying at the same speed and the same course. His pilot ordered the gunners not to fire and, after three minutes or so, the night fighter peeled off and disappeared. A few minutes later a Me210 crossed their path, little more than 50ft away.

Two of the aircraft which went to Nuremburg that night from Waltham were the veterans Able Mabel and N-Nan, both of which had taken part in the 1944 attack. Mabel made it back safely but Nan, which was being flown by F/O George Dauphinee, was attacked by a night fighter and two engines set on fire. As the crew prepared to bail out the Lancaster exploded and only two members of the crew, the wireless operator P/O Roy Bailey and the navigator, F/O Bruce Douglas, survived, although, like Kevin Muncer, they were injured falling into trees. Nan had been the last Waltham aircraft to take off that night and it was to be the last Lancaster lost from the airfield.

What made the losses that night particularly hard was that it was clear to all that the war in Europe was almost over and every crew now with 1 Group had high expectations of survival, something those who had flown in 1942, 1943 or 1944 certainly didn't have. Those expectations must have been uppermost in the minds of 23-year-old Canadian F/O Alf Lockyer and his crew when they arrived at North Killingholme on the eve of the Nuremburg raid. The following day they took Lancaster Fox-Two on their first training operation with 550 and they were almost in sight of the airfield when they were attacked by a Luftwaffe intruder and crashed on Sunk Island in the Humber, only the flight engineer survived. They had been with the squadron barely long enough for anyone to get to know them.

Bomber Command was to drop more bombs in the six weeks up to the end of March than in the entire first two years of the Second World War and 1 Group was in the forefront of that, priding itself on its squadrons carrying a heavier bomb load than in other groups. Daylight operations were by now virtually the order of the day with only occasional attacks being staged at night. 550 Squadron was always at the top of the Group bombing tables thanks largely to the work of the station Armaments Officer, S/Ldr Hugh Gardiner and the Engineering Officer, S/Ldr George Cooper, two men the former CO, W/Cmdr Bryan Bell, remembered as 'outstanding officers'.

It was one of these daylight raids which was to claim one of 101 Squadron's veteran Lancasters and see a flight engineer from the squadron win 1 Group's final CGM of the war. It went to Sgt Jeffrey Wheeler who was seriously wounded by a fragment of an anti-aircraft shell while his aircraft was involved in the raid on an oil refinery near Bremen. He didn't report his injuries until the aircraft was well clear of the target and then insisted on remaining at his post to help get the damaged Lancaster back to Ludford. Two other aircraft failed to return to Ludford from that attack, including the veteran SR-R 'The Saint', which was on its 122nd operation, with the loss of the crew of F/O Ralph Little, an American serving in the RCAF. Three crew members from the second 101 aircraft survived after it exploded after being hit by flak.

The end of March brought a significant event in 1 Group's wartime history, the end of operations from Waltham. 100 Squadron flew its last operation from the airfield on March 31 when its aircraft went to Hamburg. When the squadron returned it was told to prepare to pack up and leave for Elsham where it was to spend the remainder of the war, celebrating its move by what must have been a spectacular 'beat-up' of one of the best-loved of all RAF bomber airfields. The end of flying at Waltham was quickly followed by the closure of Kelstern as 12 Base was disbanded. 625 Squadron flew its last operation from there on the afternoon of April 3 when 247 1 Group Lancasters bombed Nordhausen, where V2 rockets were being assembled by slave workers in underground tunnels from the adjoining Mittelbau concentration camp. Two aircraft were lost, those of F/O Leslie Driver RNZAF of 626 Squadron, and F/Sgt Tom Collier and crew, who had only recently joined 625 at Kelstern. After the raid the remainder of 625 moved to Scampton for the final month of the war.

One of 1 Group's last night raids of the war was staged on the synthetic refinery at Lutzkendorf, near Leipzig on the night of April 4-5. Two aircraft were lost and a third crashed on its return. One of the Lancasters shot down was F/Lt Walter Kroeker's from 12 Squadron at Wickenby. In January 1944 this crew had crash-landed their Lancaster in Sweden after a raid on Stettin and spent much of the year in internment before being repatriated and rejoining the squadron in the autumn. Six of those were to be killed on the Lutzkendorf raid with 35-year-old F/O Charles Biddlecombe joining them as a replacement mid-upper gunner.

On the same night 30 Lancasters were detached for mine-laying duties off the Norwegian coast and in the Kattegat and that particular operation was to lead to the loss of eight aircraft. One of them was being flown by 153 Squadron's CO W/Cmdr Francis Powley, a much-decorated Canadian who had been a pre-war regular in the RAF. He was a former CO of 166 Squadron and had a DFC and an Air Force Cross to his name. These operations were hated by aircrew, not least because of the higher-than-average losses incurred with the ever-present threat of fighters, flak ships and the dangers inherent in low-level flying. That night, despite having a premonition that he would not return, W/Cmdr Powley put himself on the Battle Order in an effort to lift morale at Scampton. He flew with S/Ldr John Gee's crew and his aircraft was believed to have been shot down off the Danish coast. Another Lancaster from 153, flown by F/Lt Art Winder, also failed to return along with two from 626 Squadron and one each from 103, 550 and 576 Squadrons, with just six men from the Fiskerton Lancaster surviving.

These were to be the last significant losses suffered by 1 Group. Two aircraft, one from 170 Squadron at Hemswell and the second from 300 at Faldingworth, were shot down in an attack on the harbour at Kiel which saw the battle cruiser *Admiral Scheer* capsize and the *Hipper* and *Emden* wrecked. All 1 Group's aircraft returned safely from an attack on Potsdam, the first time most crews had been over the Berlin area, while the last casualties occurred on April 22 in an attack on Bremen in support of an assault by British infantry. F/O Arthur Cockcroft and his crew, whose average age was just 21, had only recently joined the squadron at Scampton. They took off shortly after 3.30pm on the afternoon of March 22 and it is likely their aircraft was hit by flak near the target, the Lancaster crashing close to the coast near Wilhelmshaven. There were no survivors.

Three days later 1 Group's Lancasters were bombed up for the last time in the war. Their target was to be Hitler's 'Eagle Nest' building and the nearby SS barracks at Berchtesgaden in southern Bavaria and they joined 5 Group in an all-Lincolnshire raid on a target more symbolic than strategic. Crews were woken at around midnight for the pre-op briefing and the first aircraft were airborne before 5am. Two Lancasters were lost, one from 5 Group's 619 Squadron with its crew and the second from 460 at Binbrook, the six Australians and the British flight engineer in F/O Harold Payne's crew spending the next few days as prisoners. It was a fitting finale for the Aussies at Binbrook, Anzac day.

There were no celebrations when the Lancasters arrived back at their airfields. There almost certainly would have been had the men of 1 Group known that, for them, the bombing war was finally over.

Chapter 21

'Living in a Sea of Mud'

Life on a 1 Group Airfield

Today little remains of most of the 26 heavy bomber airfields which were scattered right across Lincolnshire by summer of 1944. Some have been turned to other uses while others have vanished completely, swallowed up by developers, industrial users or simply returned to the soil from which they grew.

Yet during wartime they were all virtually small towns in their own right, each populated by more than 2,000 young men and women dressed in regulation blue, all doing a job which almost nightly brought back-breaking work in the harshest conditions, fear and courage in almost equal measure and more tragedy than today we can ever imagine.

Some notable attempts have been made at scattered museums to capture the essence of what it was like to serve on those airfields, where pre-war King's Regulations and service traditions were often stretched and twisted to meet the demands of the bomber war. But the real essence of what life was like on those airfields almost 70 years ago is best viewed through the memories of the dwindling number of survivors and the letters the men and women of Bomber Command left behind.

As we have seen, the airfields themselves varied widely, from the solidly built pre-war bases at Hemswell, Binbrook and Lindholme to the near gerry-built aerodromes at Sandtoft, North Killingholme and Faldingworth. Ludford and Kelstern were at the highest altitude of any Bomber Command airfield and conditions there at times were, at times, awful. In between came the airfields constructed early in the war, Waltham, Kirmington and Elsham Wolds, each relatively well-built and, by RAF standards, reasonably comfortable. Blyton bucked the trend by falling into both the second and third category by being built badly early in the war. The Yorkshire airfields 1 Group used early in the war, Breighton, Holme-on-Spalding Moor and Snaith were all rather cheerless places and then there was Ingham, the only airfield in 1 Group not to get hardened runways and, as such, never to progress beyond Wellington operations, ending the war as home to a small support unit.

Aircrew tended to find conditions better than ground staff. For a start, they

It wasn't just aircraft that were given names. An unidentified driver poses before his lorry at Wickenby in 1944. (Wickenby Archive)

were only usually at a particular airfield for a few months, if they were lucky to survive that long. Ground crews and station staff could find themselves stuck at an airfield for years at a time.

John Wilkins flew as a navigator with both 12 and 101 Squadrons before ending up in pathfinders at Warboys. During his time at Wickenby, 12 Squadron went through a period of heavy losses and he remembers seeing tearful groups of WAAFs on his arrival there following a particularly bad night for 12 Squadron.

'Conditions at Wickenby were bloody awful most of the time,' he remembered, 'but not as bloody awful as Faldingworth, where we spent some time on detachment with 101 Squadron. It was generally regarded as the worst station of all in 1 Group. It was built on a bog and, as a result, the runways went up and down like nobody's business. Pilots always said that if you had to make a force landing chose anywhere but Faldingworth.'

His recollections of Faldingworth were shared by Audrey Brown, who served there as a WAAF driver during the winter of 1943-44. Wet was the norm, she recalled, and that extended even to the inside of the Nissen huts in which the WAAFs lived. Several were built actually into the ground, meaning a step down once you got inside. The ground was either saturated or frozen for much of that winter and her hut was almost permanently flooded, so much so that the bottom bunks were unusable and boxes containing clothes and personal possessions would often be found floating around the building. Wellington boots were prized possessions and were worn constantly.

Her work involving driving crews to and from dispersals, driving the ration and coal trucks and occasionally helping out getting bombers down on foggy nights. These were in the days before fog-dispersal equipment and in misty conditions the WAAFs were sent out to set paraffin-filled 'goose lights' along runways to increase visibility. When the mist turned to fog they had to drive the trucks out, line them up alongside runways and turned on the headlights to help get aircraft down.

B Flight ground crew pictured on a Lancaster's Merlin engine, 103 Squadron, Elsham Wolds.
(Elsham Wolds Association)

A typical scene on a Lincolnshire bomber airfield. This was Ludford Magna where the water arrived in buckets (or from the sky), Nissen huts were everywhere and a bike was essential. (Vic Redfern)

The local pub played an essential part in the lives of thousands of airmen. This was the Marrowbone and Cleaver in Kirmington – or 'The Chopper' as it was better known – around 1944.
(Jim Wright, 166 Squadron Association)

Almost a home-from-home – one of the huts at North Killingholme came complete with its own fireplace. (Roland Hardy)

Audrey's time at Faldingworth coincided with the station's period as a heavy conversion unit and this involved aircrew only being there for a few weeks at the most. This meant that for the WAAFs the few romantic liaisons that were struck up were very short-lived indeed, not that there was much time for socialising with the girls working 12-hour shifts and being expected to help out whenever any snow needed clearing.

The first WAAFs to arrive at North Killingholme when the station opened in January 1944 had a particularly bad time. May Peet was a mess waitress and had been posted into 1 Group from Syerston where her 'customers' had once included Guy Gibson in his pre-Dambusters days. She spent her first fortnight in 1 Group at Waltham, where she found conditions very good, but was then posted to North Killingholme and was in for something of a shock. Her work was in the officers' mess and it was a long trek from the temporary WAAF quarters, which were in the neighbouring village of East Halton, particularly during the heavy snowfalls which were a feature of her first few weeks with 550 Squadron. Conditions did improve later, particularly after the opening of a new WAAF site closer to the airfield but North Killingholme always remained something of a rough-and-ready airfield. The spirit was good, she recalled, and the WAAFs were able to enjoy regular nights out at the nearby American fighter airfield at Goxhill – 'we only went for the grub, it was so much better than ours' – and visits to May Gabriel's fish and chip hut in nearby South Killingholme.

The conditions on airfields like Wickenby and Faldingworth were in stark contrast to those on the pre-war airfields at Hemswell and Binbrook. Ken Penrose served as a wireless mechanic in 1941 with 12 Squadron at Binbrook and later volunteered for aircrew and, after a hair-raising time at Sandtoft flying worn out Halifaxes, found himself posted back to 12 Squadron, this time as the wireless operator in a Lancaster crew. 'I was delighted,' he said, 'because I remembered what a great base Binbrook was with brick buildings which were well heated and excellent messes. It was therefore a shock when we got our rail warrants and found we were going to Wickenby. I hadn't realised the squadron had moved! Wickenby was in the middle of nowhere and we were just living in a sea of mud. There was a good spirit about the place, though.'

Perhaps the worst time to serve at a particular airfield was when it had just opened. At Kirmington, which eventually became one of the better wartime airfields, the first arrivals found no heating whatsoever in any of the accommodation huts. The stoves had not been delivered and there was no sign of them. Thankfully, resourceful members of the ground crew rounded up all the empty oil drums they could find, punched holes in them and fitted them in huts as coke-burning braziers.

Arthur Miles was an electrician in the advance party which moved from Holme-on-Spalding Moor to Ludford in the summer of 1943. Little did he know it but he was to see Ludford at its best, relatively free of the mud for

Although Waltham was a relatively well-drained airfield, Wellington boots were still the order of the day in this picture of ground crew assembled alongside 100 Squadron's HW-V Vergeltungswaffe – Waltham's own version of a V-weapon. (Author's collection)

which it would become infamous. Accommodation, however, was a different matter. The place was still far from finished and Arthur and his section had to spend six months sleeping on 'biscuit' mattresses in the camp cinema. They were the lucky ones, others had to make do with bell tents.

Ludford Magna earned the unfortunate nickname 'Mudford Magna' and conditions there came as a bit of a shock to newcomers. Among them was Gerry Parfitt, a radar mechanic posted to Ludford from Linton-on-Ouse in the summer of 1943 shortly after the station opened. 'It was a bit of a shock after serving on a peace-time station like Linton,' he recalled. 'They were all prefab buildings and Nissen huts with precious little in the way of heating, just a small stove and a ration of coke or coal which didn't last long. After that, it was just a case of scrounging.'

He remembers Ludford as being a very large airfield, even by Linton-on-Ouse standards. Most of the accommodation sites were north of the Louth to Market Rasen road which runs through the villages of Ludford Magna and Ludford Parva, while the airfield lay to the south and then it was a case of a long cycle ride through the village, turning down by a path at the side of the

Black Horse pub, onto the aerodrome, past the Astra cinema and the WAAF site, through the main entrance, past the headquarters buildings and on to the radar section, a white concrete block building behind the main hangar.

Herbert Harrison flew as a flight engineer with 101and remembers being given some sound advice when he arrived at Ludford – get yourself a good pair of Wellington boots. 'It was a quagmire, like living in a sea of mud,' he recalled. 'It was good advice to get some gum boots, you even needed them to get to the toilets in the middle of the night. There's no doubt Ludford could be a grim place, but it had its good points. Some of the villages round there were the most beautiful I have ever seen.' Tealby was a favourite with 101 personnel, not the least because of the King's Head, one of the most attractive pubs in the Lincolnshire Wolds. Local landowner Lord Heneage also opened up his tree-lined fishing pond at Benniworth for the squadron to use as a swimming pool.

Gordon Neale was one of many ex-1 Group men who always remembered the welcome given by Lincolnshire people to the RAF. He served with 12 Squadron at Wickenby and whenever his crew were not flying they were out looking for new pubs and new dance halls in the county. On one occasion they hitched a lift in an army lorry to Lincoln where they decided to board the first local train to leave St Marks Station. It went to Boston, somewhere they hadn't been before and the first pub they went into was full of Royal Navy personnel.

The officers' mess of 550 Squadron – like everything else at North Killingholme, it was in a prefabricated hut. (Roland Hardy)

Ground staff of A Flight, 166 Squadron at Kirmington.
(*Norman Ellis*)

One way of cleaning a Lancaster's Merlin engine was to wash it out in high octane fuel, which is what Dave Price and Tommy Guest are doing in this photograph taken at an A Flight dispersal at Kirmington in 1944. (*Norman Ellis*)

Snow clearing operations at Binbrook. (*Peter Green Collection*)

As he made his way to the saloon bar he spotted a familiar face – his old next-door neighbour from Dodsworth, near Barnsley. It turned out he was commanding a small flotilla of landing craft being made ready for the invasion later that spring. After closing time he and his crew were invited back on board the landing craft in Boston docks for pink gins in the ward room. By this time the last train for Lincoln was long gone and they had to do with the hard deck of an infantry landing craft for the night.

On another visit, this time to Skegness, they had a night to remember when they met a group of seaside landladies on a night out. Once the landladies discovered the seven young men were operational aircrew they got the freedom of Skegness for the night, free drinks and free accommodation.

Wickenby was a little off the beaten track and often men would have to walk back from Lincoln after a night out. On one occasion he and a couple of his crew fell in with another airmen, who turned out to be F/Lt Bradbury, who had just taken over as 12 Squadron's engineer leader. He was a determined type and kept them going through a long night of walking by promising them something to eat in the officer's mess on their return. When they arrived it was still the small hours of the morning and he had to rouse the duty cook who could only offer them cold rice pudding. 'But we were hungry so we ate it with our bare hands and we were thankful,' he recalled.

Bryan Bell flew from Waltham with both 100 and 550 Squadrons and remembered it as a happy station where there was always a welcome for aircrew in the pubs in neighbouring Grimsby and Cleethorpes. His particular favourite was the Ship Hotel in Grimsby's Flottergate where the publican, Sam Muscat and his wife, always had a pint waiting for his crew on the bar and a steady supply of chicken and much-prized Dover sole to eat. Rations at Waltham were also enhanced by his bomb aimer, F/O Dickie Rice, who was a crack shot with a .22 rifle or a 12 bore shotgun. Whenever the opportunity arose he would be off on his bicycle to the nearby woods, looking for roosting pheasants. Eventually, the village policeman called at the airfield to ask the station commander if he would stop one of his men cycling through the village with a rifle on his back. Dickie Rice's fame as the newest Lincolnshire poacher was then brought to an abrupt halt.

Pubs were an integral part of life on a wartime bomber airfield and each squadron had its favourites. 166 at Kirmington adopted the village's Marrowbone and Cleaver (dubbed 'The Chopper') as its second home while some crews at 103 Squadron favoured The Dying Gladiator (which earned the nickname 'The Dying Navigator') in nearby Brigg. Ludford's Black Horse was a popular spot for 101crews as was The Wheatsheaf in Louth, one of several pubs in the town used regularly by airmen from Ludford and Kelstern. There was always a welcome for the bomber boys in Scunthorpe and, for those who missed the last train, 'Irish Maggie' kept spare beds for stranded airmen.

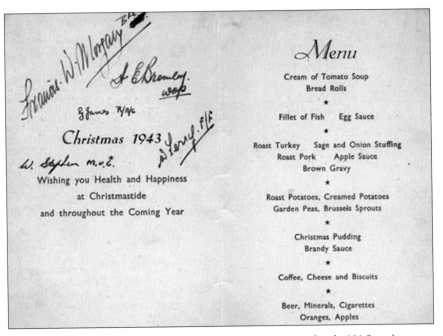

The Christmas menu at Ludford Magna, complete with the autographs of a 101 Squadron crew.
(Vic Redfern)

At Wickenby the 'local' was the White Hart in Lissington although many there made the journey into Lincoln where the RAF's favourite Lincolnshire pub, the Saracen's Head – know to all as 'The Snake Pit' – was on the city's High Street. 550 Squadron had The Cross Keys at South Killingholme on its doorstep with East Halton's Black Bull also nearby while 100 Squadron was spoiled for choice with the King's Head in the village on its doorstep and the myriad of public houses in Grimsby and Cleethorpes just a short bus or bike ride away. In Binbrook, 460 Squadron's unofficial secondary headquarters was the Granby Inn in the village where there was always a welcome from the landlady Renee Trevor and where the ceiling in the bar was decorated by the signatures of hundreds of men who served with the squadron, a ceiling unceremoniously replastered by one of the pub's post-war owners. Nights out could also be brought abruptly to an end. Gordon Neale recalled being at a dance hall in Lincoln on a night 12 Squadron had been stood down. Suddenly the music stopped and RAF Police went on stage to announce that all air and ground crews were to return to Wickenby immediately. His crew, all of whom had already downed five pints of beer, then set off on their bicycles, making it back to the airfield just in time for briefing. Four hours later they were over Normandy.

Ground crews had a particularly tough time in bad weather as they had to do much of their work out on the dispersals. They were a resourceful lot and would knock up make-shift huts from old packing cases to give themselves some shelter when they were not working.

Ted Manning served as an engine fitter with 103 Squadron and later with 1656 HCU at Lindholme and remembered how tough it was to work at dispersals on aircraft in all weathers. One particular night stands out in his mind, helped perhaps by the damage it did to his hearing.

He recalled: 'Can you imagine a blizzard night at Lindholme, lying stretched out on top of a Merlin engine, the cowlings removed, the roaring airscrew a few inches from my head, pulling in the snow and sleet in a vortex and hurling it back at me. The only comfort I had was the heat from the engine. There was a small valve at the front end of the engine which controlled the automatic pitch of the airscrew blades. The best way to adjust this was to shove an engine stand under the Merlin, scramble up, adjust it with the engine stationary, climb

The crew of F/O Richard Bastic of 576 Squadron at Fiskerton early in February 1945. A few days later all seven men, F/O Bastic, Sgt Fred Martin, F/Sgt Bill Frost RAAF, F/Sgt Bill Bibby, F/Sgt Jack Coates and Sgts Henry Sargent and Bob Swaffer, were killed when their Lancaster, UL-J2, disappeared on a raid to Dortmund. (Martin Nichol/David Briggs collection)

13 Base 'brass' at a boxing tournament at Elsham in 1945. They are (left to right) G/Cpt Hugh Constantine (station commander), G/Cpt McIntyre (station commander Kirmington), A/Cmdr 'Ferdy' Swain (Base commander) and G/Cpt Lindgard (station commander North Killingholme).
(Elsham Wolds Association)

down, get into the engineer's seat in the aircraft, start the engine and check whether it was right. If it wasn't, you had to start the whole weary business again. The quick way, however, was to ask a mate to run the motor while you adjusted it while it was running. It was hard enough on a fine summer evening but, in bad weather like it was that night, it was very unpleasant. But that aircraft was needed that night, not in 24 hours."

Eddie Halton was an airframe fitter with 1662 HCU, arriving at the Blyton shortly after 199 Squadron departed, leaving behind a single Wellington. He was to spend a happy summer at Blyton despite the conditions. He lived with other members of the ground crew in an isolated hut just off the Northorpe road. There was no running water or electricity but, thankfully, there was a farmhouse nearby where the farmer's wife always had a pot of tea on the go and a plate of home baking for any airmen to sample.

In October 1943 he was posted to the new airfield at Kelstern to join 625

Squadron where he found himself in a totally different war. At Blyton there had been little time to get to know air crew before they moved on (or were killed in flying accidents) whereas at Kelstern he was part of a team responsible for three disperals, serving aircraft lettered Q, T and X. Now there was great affinity between ground- and aircrew and they always took it badly when one of 'their' aircraft failed to return. In one week alone they lost two 'Qs'.

Conditions at Kelstern were uncomfortable to say the least. He was allocated a bed in a Nissen hut which had been erected on a slope with one end of the hut standing clear of its concrete base by a good six inches. During his time there the airfield was virtually cut off by heavy snow (although the station staff, helped by aircrew, managed to keep it operational) and food had to be rationed. Ground staff were told they would have to put up with soup and hard tack while what food stocks remained would be saved for aircrew. When the flyers heard about this there were some angry protests and the catering arrangements were hastily changed. Eddie West later went on to work for the Imperial War Museum and helped restore an ex-428 Squadron Lancaster which is now on display at Duxford.

Routine work and small repairs to Lancasters were handled by station staff but major servicing was carried out at Base level where additional facilities were available. Additionally, there was some direct support from the Lancaster's manufacturer, Avro. In 1941 the company acquired the old First World War

MT driver Joyce Stammers, Elsham Wolds, in her Dodge truck. (Elsham Wolds Association)

Living at the dispersal: ground crew with their home-made hut at a Wickenby dispersal, 12 Squadron 1943. (Wickenby Archive)

airfield at Bracebridge Heath, south of Lincoln and it was here that many badly damaged Lancasters were repaired and returned to their Lincolnshire squadrons. Bracebridge was Avro's central repair depot for Lancasters and Ansons (and later the Lancaster's transport derivative, the Avro York), employing at its peak some 3,000 people. It was also the hub of a network of repair facilities, which supported by 70 mobile workshops. Typical of its workers seems to have been a fitter named James Stockdale of 8 Lucy Tower Street, Lincoln. In December 1944 he was issued with a three-month pass to enable him to work on Lancasters at Fiskerton. His original pass is now in the possession of a group of enthusiasts doing a sterling job in keeping alive the wartime spirit at this particular airfield.

Kelstern was only in use for 18 months and its resident squadron, 625, operational for only a week or two more yet both were to be endowed with affection by all those who served there. There is no village of Kelstern, just a scattering of houses and farm buildings on one of the highest points of the Lincolnshire Wolds yet it was here that the first post-war memorial to a Lincolnshire bomber squadron was to be unveiled. Clem Koder flew from Kelstern as a pilot and later became a leading figure in the 625 Squadron RAF Memorial Association said the only real fear he had while serving there was not keeping up the highest of standards set by all who flew from there. In a letter to the author in 1990 he wrote: 'This also applied to the ground crews whose working was of the highest order at all times of night and day regardless of the weather conditions. It was the magnificent spirit of all that help me through those days and I shall always feel proud to be one of those who operated in Bomber Command.'

The heavy losses that squadrons suffered in 1943 and 1944 had an inevitable drain on morale. Ivan Health served in an A Flight crew with 460 Squadron at Binbrook in the summer of 1943. They arrived at Binbrook from 1656 HCU at Lindholme and, as was the practice, their names went at the bottom of the Flight list. Three weeks later they found themselves at the top of that list. 'It was a frightening time for all of us,' he remembered. 'We were losing two or three aircraft every time we went out. I had a good mate and we had a two bob bet on who would last the longest. He went after 13 ops.'

There was an increase in the sickness rate amongst crews. 'You only had to sneeze and you wondered, or perhaps hoped, you wouldn't be fit to fly.' He recalled trips into Grimsby where they would see girls waiting outside the town's Savoy cinema in Victoria Street for airmen who had gone missing the night before.

It wasn't all bad. 626 Squadron aircrew relax in the Lincolnshire sunshine, 1944. (Wickenby Archive)

At times there was tension between the crews but he remembered only one case of LMF – 'lack of moral fibre', the RAF's label for cowardice – during his time at Binbrook. It involved a young Scottish pilot who repeatedly returned from operations with photo-flash pictures clearly showing the Dutch coast. He was stripped of his rank and posted away with 'LMF' stamped on his documents. It was harsh treatment intended to deter others from seeking the easy way out of operations. That young pilot survived the war: Ivan Health met him some years later on a train. Health himself completed a total of 36 operations with 460 and then, remarkably, another 46 with a pathfinder squadron. At Wickenby one pilot who feigned illness and turned back from a raid was immediately declared 'LMF', stripped to the ranks and, within 24 hours, had been sent to the RAF psychiatric hospital at Matlock where he was treated as 'a malingerer and a coward'. He later was sent down the mines.

Discipline of a different form was administered at Wickenby during Gordon Neale's time as a flight engineer with 12 Squadron in the spring and summer of 1944. Aircrew from both 12 and 626 Squadrons were ordered to parade on the main runway to witness a disciplinary incident involving a sergeant air gunner who had been court martialed for striking an officer in a pub in Market Rasen. The decision of the court martial was read out, as was the sentence, demotion and 56 days' detention and the unfortunate air gunner was marched away.

Lincolnshire airfields were toured several times by the King and Queen while Harris himself was a regular visitor to squadrons, handing out pep talks which were almost universally well received. During his time at Waltham Bryan Bell remembered a number of crews, his included, being taken to Binbrook where they crammed into one of the messes to hear Harris speak. Weary crews always found post-op briefings tiresome but Harris stressed the importance they played and told them: 'We at Bomber Command HQ are like a bunch of eunochs – we know what it's all about but we can't do it ourselves!' He also told crews to respect what the Americans were doing. There was some derision amongst Lancasters crews when they saw what miniscule bomb loads Americans Fortresses and Liberators were carrying in comparison with RAF bombers. Harris told them: 'If the Yanks can shoot down as many fighters as possible during the day, it makes our job at night that much easier.'

Aircrew were a superstitious lot. Percy Miller, who completed a tour with 625 Squadron, remembered Kelstern as being a particularly superstitious station. 'No one would take over a dog or a car left by crews who had bought it,' he said. 'It was said to be the surest way of following them and it was usually left up to the ground crew to get rid of any pets or cars left behind.' At Waltham crews always reckoned 'ops' were imminent when they saw the sails turning on the nearby windmill.

Superstition also extended to loaning out flying kit. Percy Miller was part

Maintenance work on Lancasters at Fiskerton, 1944. (Martin Nichol/David Briggs Collection)

of the crew of M-Midge (named after Percy's wife) and the pilot loaned out his Sidcot suit just before they were due to take off for a mining trip off Kiel, usually such a 'piece of cake' that it only counted as one-third of an operation. Both Lancasters accompanying M-Midge were shot down and Miller's own aircraft only just managed to avoid a flak ship when it dropped to 60ft to lay its mine. No Sidcot suit was ever loaned out again.

He also remembered the pressure on crews to complete operations whatever the odds. Kelstern came under the control of neighbouring Binbrook and the Base CO, the indomitable A/Cmdr. Arthur 'Hoppy' Wray, took a dim view of any crews who aborted trips in all but the direst circumstances. Miller's crew suffered engine problems soon after taking off for the Ruhr with flames and sparks shooting back past the tail from the recalcitrant engine but, after a hurried intercom conference, the crew decided to press on to the target rather than face the wrath of Wray on their return. They flew low over the North Sea in an effort to burn up fuel to help them gain altitude but were still unable to get above 15,000 feet. They were late over the target and got the full attention of the local flak gunners but managed to drop their bombs. 'When we got back we were told our engine problems had been spotted after we took off and no one thought we would make it home again,' he said.

Jim Lord flew as a pilot with 550 Squadron, completing a tour during the summer of 1944. He had fond memories of his time at North Killingholme, helped perhaps by his time there not coinciding with the harsh winters of 1943-44 and 1944-45 which left much of the airfield either flooded or buried in snow. It was a hard time for everyone on the squadron – his own crew had to abandon their Lancaster over Suffolk on its return from Revigny – but lightened by the sense of camaraderie on the squadron and the social life they enjoyed. The Cross Keys in South Killingholme was only a short stroll from the airfield and there was transport available for trips into Grimsby and, in particular Cleethorpes, where the sea-front Cafe Dansant was a beacon for aircrew from a wide area. 550's favourite public house in the resort was The Lifeboat. 'We had a lot of fun and games there,' he recalled.

F/O Mills and crew at dispersal with their aircraft UL-D2, Fiskerton 1945. (Martin Nichol/David Briggs collection)

Bomb aimer Reg Francis remembered North Killingholme for the friendly spirit which existed on the station. He had just arrived at the airfield when, on the morning of March 12, 1945, he enjoyed a good breakfast with his crew members after a night cross-country exercise, one of the routine exercises designed to ease new crews into squadron life. The crew expected to get the rest of the day off and discussed the possibility of catching the bus into Grimsby. In the meantime, Reg decided to visit the clothing stores for a change of battledress. It was a particularly windy morning and this, together with the somewhat frail nature of the station tannoy, meant he was unable to make out the garbled announcement he heard on his way to the stores.

'When I got there the LAC behind the counter looked at the paperwork and saw my name. He said they had been calling for me over the tannoy for the past five minutes telling me to report to the ops rooms immediately.' He ran across the airfield to the briefing room where he was greeted by an RAF Police corporal who told him to report to the bombing leader, F/Lt Peek, immediately.

'By this time I was in a blue funk and didn't know what to expect.' He went on. 'When I found him he told me I'd missed my very first briefing and added: "Never mind, I've drawn the tracks on your chart – you're going to Dortmund". Then he proceeded to give me an individual briefing. What a nice chap to come to the aid of a sprog bomb aimer!'

Blyton had a particularly bad reputation. It was shoddily built and life on an HCU could not match that on an operational squadron for the ground staff. John Allison was a wireless operator whose crew spent some time there on 1662 HCU during the winter of 1943-44 before going on to 101 Squadron. 'It really was a bloody awful place,' he recalled. 'Our Nissen hut had matchboard ends and they fitted so badly that the resulting cracks had to be filled with rolled up newspapers and old socks. Even so, the draughts howled through whenever it was windy.'

The nearest town was Gainsborough which his crew found a particularly miserable place. 'Our navigator, Steve Wall came from Kent, which he kept reminding us was the garden of England. He would go on alarmingly about Lincolnshire. I was born and bred in Lincolnshire but I had to agree that the Blyton area was pretty bleak. However, once we got to Ludford and were able to cycle to some pretty villages like Tealby and Walesby, Steve quickly changed his tune about Lincolnshire, much to my satisfaction.'

Most of those who served at Elsham left with fond memories of the time they spent there. It was built in the early days of the war and the contractors did a good job. It was well drained and didn't suffer from the problems its neighbours did.

Mike Stedman flew from there as a pilot in B Flight of 576 Squadron in 1944 and remembered particularly the easy cycle ride down the hill to Barnetby station to catch the train to Scunthorpe where he had a girl friend waiting and a pint or two to look forward to in the Oswald Hotel.

'There was also the night we had a trip up the hill to camp from a dance at the Waafery in Barnetby village in the Wing Co's car. There was a full load with our bomb aimer standing in the boot pretending to throw out 'Window'. Then someone shouted: 'Fighter, fighter, corkscrew left!' The car swerved, pitching our luckless bomb aimer out of the boot and over the hedge. Happy days!'

Elsham, like most other airfields, had been carved out of Lincolnshire farmland and, war or no war, some agricultural work had to go on. Cutting the grass and providing hay for local farms was part and parcel of airfield life. Elsham was unique in that one farm worker, Ernie Hatcliffe, continued to live on the airfield throughout the war with his wife Gladys. Mr Hatcliffe had actually helped survey the site for an airfield in the summer of 1940 and by the time 103 Squadron arrived he was living in a farm workers' cottage around which the airfield had been built. The Hatcliffes were issued with Air Ministry permits to get on and off the station and, as time went by, became an integral part of life at Elsham Wolds. Apart from his routine work Ernie helped tend the vegetable gardens which were dug around the airfield and to look after the pigs which provided a source of fresh meat. His wife, in the meantime, was only too happy to help young airmen with their laundry though she found it upsetting on the days when someone else would come round to collect the freshly-ironed shirts and starched collars with the news that the owners were missing on operations. The Hatcliffes became firm favourites with all who served at Elsham and what other farm worker and his wife had a cinema on their doorstep where they went three times a week for just three pence?

Elsham could still be a cold place in winter. Gwen Richardson served there as a cook and lived in one of the huts on the WAAF site adjacent to the Melton Ross road. The winter of 1944-45 was particularly bad and with their water supply frozen, the WAAFs had to heat snow in order to wash.

Wickenby was another base where the 'dig for victory' campaign got full backing from the station CO. The camp had its own piggery and a large area around one of the technical site buildings was turned into a potato patch, the rule being that those returning from leave had to spend their first day back at Wickenby tending the area.

Emily Warwick spent most of the war in the WAAFs and in 1943 was posted to Wickenby as a clerk in the headquarters office. One of her tasks was to type letters to the families of those missing in action. She was given a book of sample letters, some for British aircrew and others for Australians, Canadians and New Zealanders, and it was usually left to the clerk to decide which was most appropriate. It was then left to the squadron commanding officer to sign them. She, too, recalled the grim winter conditions on the airfield. 'We had long icicles hanging from the roof of our hut and our towels would freeze overnight if we left them damp over the backs of chairs. Often we would have to go out and collect snow in a bucket, heat it up and then the 10 of us in the hut would get washed in it. What water was left then went into our hot water bottles."

Whatever the conditions, there were still a few for whom the importance of pre-war 'bull' was never forgotten. One such was Station Warrant Officer 'Lavender' Yardley at North Killingholme, who was a stickler for regulations. Woe betide anyone who appeared in front of him with his tunic not buttoned correctly. Ted Stones, who served with 550 Squadron, remembered Yardley as 'a real sod'. He explained: 'There was a path running through a particularly muddy area to the NAAFI. It wasn't wide enough so he decided something had to be done about it and it became known as our 'Burma Road'. It was built solely on fatigues. He had a big Irish sergeant who went around with him and they used to stand outside the airmen's mess. Anyone who came out without his hat on correctly or a button out of place was on fatigues that night and that meant a spell helping build the Burma Road!'

Wireless fitter Ivor Burgess served on most 1 Group airfields, meeting and marrying his wife, a WAAF, at Wickenby. The airfield was as spartan as most bomber stations in North Lincolnshire and there was no provision for married couples but he remembers it being a happy station. 'Much of that was down to the man at the top, the station CO, G/Cpt Crummy. He was a gentleman of the old type and treated everyone under him as gentlemen. The same applied to W/Cmdr Craven, the CO of 12 Squadron.'

Ivor Burgess is not alone in singling our G/Capt Crummy for praise, nor the first to mention that station morale had much to do with the station or base commander. But sometimes the opposite could occur as those stationed at Kirmington with 166 Squadron early in 1945 were to discover.

In mid-December 166 Squadron's popular CO W/Cmdr Don Garner, who had won a DSO the previous September, was posted to a staff job and his place at Kirmington was taken by W/Cmdr R. L. Vivian, a pre-war RAF officer who

Life was so much better with transport. Wickenby aircrew and one of the station WAAFs, 1944.
(Wickenby Archive)

had commanded an Army Co-operation squadron in England before taking over 60 Squadron in Malaya in 1941 and then a training unit in Rhodesia. When he arrived at Kirmington he had no experience of flying Lancasters and, despite the best efforts of a number of pilots who took him on training sorties, it seemed it would be some time before he got the hang of it. It also seemed he hadn't got the hang of the almost complete lack of 'bull' on a wartime bomber airfield which led to what became a virtual threat of mutiny, the story of which appears in the wonderfully detailed wartime history of 166 Squadron, *On Wings of War*, by S/Ldr Jim Wright, who was a wireless operator with the squadron at the time.

On December 29, the day after he flew his first operation as a second pilot, W/Cmdr Vivian issued an order that was to shock every aircrew member at Kirmington: they were to parade every morning at 8am for inspection. This was an absolute anathema to everyone who flew Lancasters. Yes, there had to be discipline but daily parades for aircrew? That was just too much for the men of 166, in fact it was virtually unheard of in Bomber Command in 1945. Every morning air crew had the far more important job of carrying out detailed checks on their aircraft, checks that were vital to their own and their crew's well being.

The first of the parades was due to be held on Monday January 1. Over the weekend there had been talk of little else and most aircrew had decided they were not going to turn up. They gathered that morning in the section huts around the perimeter track and watched as the flight sergeant in charge of discipline waited and waited for the reluctant airmen to fall in. By 8.30am less than 10 per cent of the squadron had assembled. At this point W/Cmdr Vivian marched out carrying a Malacca cane and looking distinctly displeased with what he saw. He stood waiting for 15 minutes but no further aircrew turned up so, after a brief word with the flight sergeant, he marched back to station HQ and summoned the three flight commanders and five section leaders. The popular bombing leader with 166, F/Lt Arthur McCartney, set out to explain to the CO exactly why daily parades were low down on the priority list for aircrew at Kirmington but W/Cmdr Vivian was in no mood to listen and accused him of being a trouble-maker and said he would have him posted away from the squadron.

Later, the news was passed on to aircrew that not only were the daily parades to continue and that those who failed to turn up would be on a charge, but the man who had spoken for them at the meeting was under threat of being posted. There was an angry response from the Lancaster crews. F/Lt McCartney was not only popular at Kirmington, he was also highly regarded by all who flew with the squadron and the men quickly made it clear to their flight commanders and section leaders that if 'Mac' was posted then they would refuse to fly. As the word spread, news came that the ground crews were also threatening to down tools if W/Cmdr Vivian went through with his threat.

The situation was now spiralling out of control and the three flight commanders asked for another urgent meeting with the CO. What was said behind closed doors was never disclosed but later that morning F/Lt McCartney was told his threatened posting had been withdrawn and an order went round the airfield cancelling daily parades for aircrew. There was to be no more 'bull', pre-war style, at Kirmington.

S/Ldr Dutton (centre) and crew pictured at Fiskerton shortly after a raid on Bottrop in February 1945. This aircraft, UL-02 of 576 Squadron, was one of three lost from Fiskerton on the Nuremburg raid on 16/17 March. (Martin Nichol/David Briggs collection)

Chapter 22

The Veterans

The Lancaster 100-Club and
the Lone Survivor

Between 1941 and 1945 some 7,374 Lancaster bombers were built. Of those 3,349, or slightly more than 45 per cent, were lost on operations and many more in crashes and training accidents. The average life of a Lancaster was around 17 operations, about the same life expectancy of the young men who flew them. Just 34 of all those built were to complete 100 or more operations. What is surprising is that 1 Group, which lost almost a third of all Lancasters shot down, had half of those on its strength at one time or another.

This statistic alone says a lot about the skill, dedication and hard work of the ground crews who cared for 1 Group's Lancasters. Much has been recorded in this book about the exploits or air crew and the dangers they faced, but none of this would have been possible without the men assigned to look after each aircraft, men who would often assemble at the side of a runway to watch their charge take to the air and, as often as not, would be there waiting with fingers crossed for the safe return of 'their' Lancaster and the crew who had, after all, only borrowed it for the night. There was a real bond between the air and ground crews and Joe Clark, a flight engineer with 100 Squadron in 1943, recalled that before every operation one of his Lancaster's airframe fitters always gave him his wedding ring 'just to keep me safe'. The good luck charm worked and the crew completed their tour at Waltham.

It was a hard life for these men. Most of their work had to be carried out on the dispersal pans in all weather. Only occasionally were Lancasters towed into the hangars when major work was required. Routine jobs, of which there were very many, had to be done out on the edge of the airfields, and those airfields could be damnably cold and uncomfortable places to work. There they would have to check each engine carefully, make any repairs necessary, patch up holes in the fuselage, inspect the hydraulics, test the electrics and so on and so on. Then there was the armament work to do, cleaning, checking and rearming guns, refuelling and, of course, the back-breaking job of 'bombing up' before every operation.

It wasn't surprising that a firm bond was quickly established between air and ground crews. The men who flew the Lancasters and the Wellingtons before them knew their lives depended on the men with oil-stained fingers, faces chapped from the cold and often with a Woodbine clamped between their lips. The ground crew themselves mostly had a similar high regard for the men who flew the Lancasters. They saw at first hand the looks on the faces of aircrew when they returned from a particularly tough operation. They saw, too, the damage caused by flak and fighters to those fortunate enough to make it back. And often they had to help with the wounded and swill away the blood after another night over the Ruhr.

G-George's 80th bomb tally is added at Binbrook after an attack on Stuttgart in February 1944.
(Laurie Wood)

The dedication of the ground crew and the skill of those who flew the Lancasters were not, of course, enough. It was largely down to good fortune that a crew and a Lancaster survived. That's why so many men carried mascots with them. For some it was a 'lucky' scarf, a child's toy or a rabbit's foot. Others went through a regular routine before they flew. One 1 Group airman always made a habit of urinating on his Lancaster's tail wheel before he flew. He survived so it must have worked.

Good fortune certainly flew with those 17 1 Group Lancasters which made it into the record books although, in the case of four of them, it was to run out shortly after they flew their 100th operation. The average life expectancy of a Lancaster was around 17 operations, and for every one which was able to chalk up 100 operations, very many more never made it into double figures. Some squadrons did seem to be luckier than others. Four of the Lancasters which recorded 100 or more operations flew at one time or another with 100 Squadron which, as we have already seen, suffered fewer losses than some of its neighbours. 460 Squadron, just up the road at Binbrook, did not have a single centenarian, although it did have one Lancaster which made it to 90 operations. 626 and 300 were the other two squadrons operating before the autumn of 1944 not to have a Lancaster with 100-plus operations.

The grand dame of all Lancasters was ED888, Mike-Squared/'Mother of Them All', which flew with 103 and 576 Squadrons from Elsham. It was delivered to 103 in April 1943 and was finally retired after returning from Cologne late on Christmas Eve 1944, its 140th operation. It left Elsham early in 1945 for Tollerton, near Nottingham where many hundreds of Lancasters were to be reduced to scrap. At the controls for that last flight was F/Lt John Henry, one of three Australians brothers who served with 103 Squadron as pilots at the same time. After take-off he flew several low passes over the airfield where Mike-Squared/Mother had amassed an astonishing 974 operational hours and had undergone no fewer than 19 engine changes. At Tollerton, John Henry did manage to salvage a few mementoes from ED888 before it was finally towed away to await its fate, which eventually came about over two years later. Among the items he did take was the bomb release cable which was later mounted and presented by the Henry brothers to the Elsham Wolds Association, which represents air and ground crews who served with 103 and 576 at the airfield. One man who flew in 'Mother' was Charlie Baird, a Scotsman who was mid-upper gunner in Sgt Denis Rudge's crew. They had

A classic photograph of Elsham's most famous Lancaster, ED888, as it was 'awarded' a bar to the DFC it had already been bestowed with. This photograph dates from its time with 576 Squadron. (Elsham Wolds Association)

Ground crew of 460 Squadron pictured at Binbrook with G-George before the aircraft left for its flight to Australia. (Laurie Wood)

joined 103 in April 1943 and took over ED888 after five operations, flying all but one of their next 25 in 'Mother', completing their tour over Berlin at the end of August.

ND458, 'Able Mabel' of 100 Squadron ended the war with 127 operations to its credit plus six 'Manna' drops of food to the civilian population in Holland and one 'Exodus' flight to pick up British PoWs, making a total of 134. The Manna flights did take place over territory still occupied by the Germans although a tacit agreement had been struck that the aircraft would not be fired on. Able Mabel was delivered to the squadron in January 1944 and had a number of close shaves, including a damaging combat at high altitude with a Me410 over Russelheim in August 1944. It was also scrapped without ceremony in 1947.

At Waltham Abel Mabel often flew alongside two other veterans, JB603 'Take It Easy', and ND644, 'Nan', all of which were to record 100-plus operations. JB603 had been delivered to the squadron in November 1943 and was to be lost on its 111th operation to Hanover early in January 1945, all seven of F/O Reg Barker's crew being killed when it crashed in Holland. ND644 was also lost, the aircraft failing to return from a raid on Nuremburg in March 1945 when only two of F/O George Dauphinee's crew survived. Record-keeping was not meticulous in Bomber Command and in his excellent book, *Claims To*

Fame: The Lancaster, Norman Franks points out that Nan's total at the time was either 115 or 128 depending on a variety of factors.

One other 100-plus Lancaster to fly from Waltham was EE139 'Phantom of The Ruhr'. It was delivered to 100 Squadron in May 1943 and was transferred to 550 Squadron when it was formed there in November before moving with 550 to North Killingholme where it went on to complete 121 operations. Its ghoulish nose art depicted a skeletal figure clasping a bomb and was the work of Sgt Harold 'Ben' Bennett, its first flight engineer in Ron Clarke's crew. Earlier in the war he had been on the receiving end of German bombing raids and was perhaps inspired after he and other crew members saw the film Phantom of the Opera at a cinema in Grimsby. Clarke and his crew flew their first 20 ops in the Phantom before it was damaged, the crew completing their tour in another aircraft. Phantom was to fly its 100th operation to Le Havre in September 1944 and was retired after its 121st to Aschaffenburg in November. Phantom of The Ruhr finished the war at 1656 HCU at Lindholme and was scrapped early in 1946. Its artwork and codes were later to be worn by the Lincolnshire-based Battle of Britain Memorial Flight's sole remaining flying Lancaster. Another

JB603 Take It Easy of 100 Squadron, pictured at Waltham in early October 1944 after its 85th operation. (Author's collection)

The Vulture Strikes of 550 Squadron pictured with the squadron's aircrew on its return from its 100th operation to Chemnitz on March 6, 1945. The following day it left North Killingholme on its 101st and failed to return from a raid on Dessau. (Roland Hardy)

550 Squadron veteran Lancaster sporting garish nose-art was PA995, 'The Vulture Strikes!' which was lost in March 1945 on its 101st operation. It had arrived at North Killingholme the previous May and had a near trouble-free life, completing its 100th operation in the raid on Chemnitz on the night of March 5-6, 1945. On its return most of B Flight congregated for a photograph in front of The Vulture to celebrate its 100th operation and the completion of F/O George Blackler's crew. Thirty-six hours later The Vulture left North Killingholme on another long-distance operation to Dessau with the new crew of F/O Cyril Jones. It is believed to have been shot down by a night fighter, four of the crew surviving to become, briefly, prisoners of war.

Two Lancasters which completed a similar number of operations were a pair of 101 Squadron veterans, DV245 'The Saint' and DV302 'Harry', both of which were delivered to Ludford within a few days of each other at the end of September 1943. The Saint first flew operationally early in October 1943 and was to be lost on its 122nd sortie along with its pilot, F/O Ralph Little RCAF and two of its crew, in a daylight attack on Bremen in March 1945.

Harry first flew operationally three weeks after The Saint and survived the war, flying its last of 121 ops to Heligoland in April 1945.

The only Lancaster flying from Wickenby to make it to the 100 mark was 12 Squadron's ME758, 'Nan' which completed its 106th on the Heligoland raid on April 18, 1945 with F/Lt Tom McPherson and crew on board. On its return an impromptu ceremony was held at Wickenby when the aircraft was 'awarded' a DSO and DFC. Nan was to fly another two bombing operations with 12 Squadron plus six Manna and two Exodus flights before being retired and scrapped within weeks of leaving Wickenby.

576 Squadron, which had ED888 on its strength for some time during 1944, had three other Lancasters which achieved 100-plus operations flying with the squadron from Elsham and Fiskerton. LM227 'I-Item' completed its 100th on the final operations to bring home PoWs, having flown 93 bombing operations. LM594 'A-Able' completed 95 bombing operations plus five Manna and two Exodus while ME801, yet another 'N-Nan', recorded its 100th bombing

This display board can be found in the Australian War Museum listing the pilots and them operations flown by 1 Group's only surviving Lancaster, G-George of 460 Squadron. (Fred Bury)

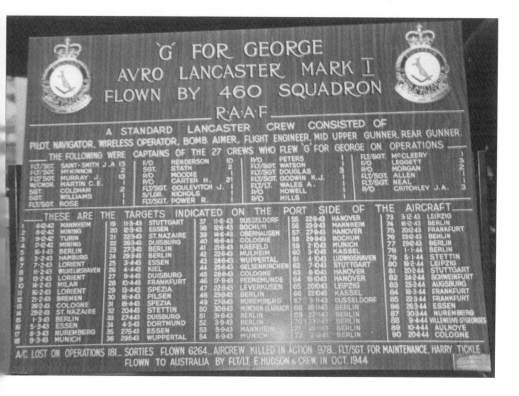

F/Lt Jack Playford shakes hands with Sgt Bill Hearn, ground crew chief for 100 Squadron's Able Mabel after it completed its 100th operation following an attack of Ludwigshaven on February 1, 1945. (Author's collection)

operation in March and ended the war with 109 plus four Manna and Exodus sorties. It was scrapped after a crash-landing in the late summer of 1945.

Yorkshireman Les Brown flew as a wireless operator in both A-Able and N-Nan, in the latter on its 99th operation to Essen in March, 1945 and on A-Able's 105th on a Manna drop over Holland. He recalled that the number of operations a particular aircraft had done meant little to crews at the time. 'As long as a particular aircraft flew all right we were happy with it,' he said. He does remember the Manna drop well, not particularly because of their veteran Lancaster, but because of the 'scary' sight of looking down on German anti-aircraft gunners as they flew at a few hundred feet over Holland.

'At first it did seem like a scary op,' he recalled. 'We were told the Germans had agreed not to fire at us but, at the same time, were told the Yanks weren't going because of the danger to their aircraft. On our last Manna drop the rear gunner said he did see flashes from the ground as though someone was firing a rifle at us' Their other concern was avoiding injuring Dutch civilians. Relief supplies were dropped in either bags suspended inside the bomb bay or from SBC canisters, designed to scatter incendiary bombs. 'So many people turned out that we were worried we were going to hit them.' He flew as a flight sergeant in P/O Bill Holmes' crew. They had joined 576 late in 1944 and were to complete 32 operations before the war ended.

Three of the 100-plus Lancasters flew with 166 Squadron, although only one would serve exclusively at Kirmington. This was ME746 'Roger-Squared', which first flew with 1 Group when F/Sgt Fred Mander and crew took the aircraft to Cologne in April 1944 and topped the 100 mark 11 months later with a daylight attack on Essen. Roger-Squared went on to complete 116 bombing operations plus another nine Manna and Exodus trips. Two of its contemporaries at Kirmington were LM550 'Let's Have Another' B-Beer and ME812 'Fair Fighter's Revenge', both of which finished the war with 153 Squadron at Scampton. Both arrived at Kirmington in May 1944. B-Beer was the aircraft in which gunner Sgt Stan Parrish flew his record 122nd operation. 153's new CO, W/Cmdr G.F. Rodney, took B-Beer (which now had the 153 codes P4-C on its fuselage) on the final major bombing operation of the war to Berchtesgarden, its 101st. The aircraft completed four Manna and two Exodus flights and was finally scrapped in 1947. Fair Fighter's Revenge was allocated to F/Sgt Sid Coole and his crew at Kirmington in June 1944 as a replacement for their previous aircraft, 'Fair Fighter', which had been written off after a crash. As ME812 also bore the codes AS-F the crew decided it would be Fair Fighter's Revenge and that was the name it bore for 105 bombing operations with 166 and 153 plus five Manna and Exodus trips.

ED905 was another real 1 Group veteran, having first been issued to 103 Squadron in April 1943 and was first flown by the squadron's legendary Belgian pilot F/O Vincent Van Rolleghem. Belgian and British flags were painted on the nose by a member of the ground crew, John Lamming, one of the many Lincolnshire men serving at Elsham. Its codes were PM-X but it was to have a troubled time at Elsham, suffering battle damage and numerous

The Saint of C Flight, 101 Squadron pictured at Ludford in the spring of 1945 being prepared for operations. It was lost in a daylight attack on Bremen, March 1945. (Vic Redfern)

Ninety-nine to go. I-Item of 576 Squadron leaves Elsham Wolds on its first operation on July 4, 1944. It completed its one hundredth with the squadron at Fiskerton. (Mike Stedman)

engine problems and was out of action for several lengthy periods. After a major overhaul in the spring of 1944 it was allocated to 550 Squadron at North Killingholme where it became the squadron's F-Fox. It completed its 100th operation in November and was then retired and ended its days at 1656 HCU at Lindholme where it was written off in a heavy landing in 1945.

1 Group's final Lancaster official centenarian was PB150 which flew with 625 Squadron at Kelstern as CV-V. It first flew with 625 in June 1944 but Norman Franks casts some doubt on claims that it reached its 100th sortie with a Manna drop near The Hague in May 1945 and suggests the true total may have been nearer 92.

Between the end of 1942 and May 1945 1 Group was to lose 1,016 Lancasters on operations and another 199 in crashes. Of those that survived almost all had been reduced to scrap within two years of the war ending. Just one survives to this day and, remarkably, it was one of the very first to fly on operations with 1 Group back in November 1942.

Lancaster W4783 was built at the Metro Vickers factory at Manchester and then taken by road to Woodford in Cheshire, not far from what is now Manchester Airport. There, it was assembled alongside other Lancasters before being test flown and signed off as a finished aircraft. On October 22, 1942 it was flown by a pilot of the Air Transport Auxiliary from Woodford to Breighton, one of the first to be delivered to 460 Squadron, which was still in the process of converting to Lancasters after flying Wellingtons and then briefly beginning to convert to Halifaxes.

At Breighton, W7483 was given the squadron codes AS-G, G-George, and assigned to the crew of F/Sgt J.A. Saint-Smith, who were mid-way through their tour of operations. The aircraft was also, crucially, in the care of F/Sgt Harry Tickle and his ground crew. They had already established something of a record in not losing a Wellington or a Halifax with the 'G' code and Harry was to take very great care of his new charge.

On the night of December 6-7 G-George was part of a force of 101 Lancasters involved in an attack on Mannheim. With the target covered in clouds most of the force bombed on dead reckoning and virtually every bomb dropped by the 272 aircraft on the raid missed Mannheim altogether. On his return to Breighton, F/Sgt Saint-Smith asked his ground crew to paint a bomb symbol on the fuselage just below the cockpit and to add a touch of his own, a tiny figure with a halo, showing 'the Saint' had been at the controls. Fourteen of the next 15 sorties flown by G-George were accompanied by the tiny figure with the halo before the Lancaster passed to another crew.

The Phantom of the Ruhr of 550 Squadron being bombed up at North Killingholme in readiness for its 100th operation to Le Havre in September 1944. (Les Browning)

460 Squadron lost aircraft regularly during that winter and the following spring but each time G-George returned safely to Breighton, once showing the scars of incendiaries which had struck the aircraft's tail. When the squadron left Breighton for Binbrook G-George was among the first aircraft to arrive at the big North Lincolnshire airfield where new concrete runways had recently been laid. The bomb tallies on the fuselage continued to mount up. One, curiously, was accompanied by a small red flag complete with hammer and sickle. It later transpired that the George's pilot at the time, F/Sgt Jack Murray, was fond of saying 'All for Joe', a reference to Joe Stalin, each time the aircraft dropped its bombs over Germany. When his tour ended the ground crew added the tiny flag to mark his crew's achievement.

During the winter of 1943-44 G-George was to fly to Berlin no fewer than 10 times. Once, the bomb-aimer wasn't satisfied with the bomb run and the Lancaster flew a wide circuit of the city before going over the target area a second time and, despite being the first to take off, was the last to land at Binbrook. There, standing at the end of the runway as it touched down, was Harry Tickle, worried that 'his' Lancaster had come to some harm. The closest it did was on the night of December 16-17, 1943 when it was attacked by a night fighter over Berlin but, despite being holed several times, made it safely back to Lincolnshire, landing safely despite the foggy conditions.

On April 20, 1944, G-George flew its 90th operation to Cologne. When the aircraft returned it was taken off operations, in need of a major overhaul before it would be fit to fly again. Soon afterward Binbrook was visited by the Australian Prime Minister, Mr John Curtin, as part of his tour of Australian forces in Britain. 460 was the RAAF's premier squadron in Bomber Command and, at the end of the tour, he was officially presented with Lancaster W4783 G-George by the RAF as a gift to the Australian people and arrangements were made for it to be flown back to Australia where it would be used to raise funds for the Victory War Loans scheme.

That summer G-George underwent a major overhaul at Binbrook including fitting four new engines, all under the watchful eye of Harry Tickle. A tour-expired crew of highly-experienced and decorated Australians, led by F/Lt Eddie Hudson DFC, was selected for the 12,000-mile flight from Binbrook to its destination, Amberley in Queensland. Added to their strength was, appropriately, F/Sgt Tickle, the man who had cared for G-George for the past two years. The aircraft left Binbrook a few days short of its second anniversary with 460 Squadron for Prestwick in Scotland where further modifications were carried out and then, on October 10, left to fly the Atlantic, landing on Canada's eastern seaboard. Then it was on via Montreal, San Francisco, Hawaii, Fiji and New Caledonia before arriving in Australia on November 10.

Over the next few months G-George visited most of the major cities in Australia and, among the passengers it carried during that time was one of the most

F-Fox of 550 Squadron is waved off by ground staff at North Killingholme. It completed 100 operations with 103, 166 and 550 Squadrons. (Roland Hardy)

remarkable men to have served with 460 Squadron at Binbrook, F/O Roberts Dunstan DSO, the one-legged gunner whose story is told in an earlier chapter.

Its job done, G-George ended the war parked on the edge of an airfield near Canberra and there it remained for the next 10 years. There were moves to reduce the aircraft to scrap but, thankfully, it was decided that G-George should have pride of place in a new museum then being planned for the city to commemorate Australia's role in the Second World War. In 2003 G-George underwent another major overhaul as the museum was revamped and is now the centre-piece of a display entitled Striking By Night, set around a night raid on Berlin in December 1943. G-George was also to figure in the lives of thousands of schoolboys in the post-war years as it was chosen as the one of the bombers depicted in the Airfix plastic model kit.

G-George is not the oldest surviving Lancaster. That honour belongs to R5868 Q-Queenie of 83 Squadron and S-Sugar of 467 Squadron, another Australian unit, which flew from Scampton, Bottesford and Waddington with 5 Group, completing 136 operations. Unlike Elsham's Mike-Squared, which recorded even more operations, it was saved from the scrap dealers, spent some time as the 'gate guardian' at Scampton and now resides in the RAF Museum at Hendon. The only other surviving Lancasters to see operational service are five Canadian-built Mk X aircraft which served very briefly in 1945 with the all-Canadian 6 Group in North Yorkshire before being returned to Canada where, it seemed, there was more a sense of history than existed in Britain at the time, or perhaps less of a need for scrap metal.

Chapter 23

Aftermath

Manna, Exodus and Disbandment

There were no more bombs to drop, at least in anger, but the work of 1 Group's Lancasters wasn't quite over yet. Earlier in April the group's squadrons had been warned that they may be required to carry out food drops over Holland. Part of the country had been by-passed by the war and the civilian population, and quite a few of the German occupiers, were nearing starvation. An unofficial agreement had been made between the British and Canadian armies and the Germans that if the drops were carried out they would not be opposed.

No doubt there were many Lancaster crews sceptical about the arrangement but towards the end of the month they began carrying out dummy drops on their own airfields and, on April 29, Operation Manna began. Over the next eight days Lancasters from 1 and 3 Groups dropped 6,672 tons of supplies in four designated areas in western Holland.

Waltham airfield was used as one of the collection points for the supplies of tea, sugar, dried milk and eggs, peas, flour, powdered potatoes, chocolate,

300 Squadron Lancasters in formation over Lincolnshire. (Peter Green Collection)

550 Squadron's 'The Stalker' low over Holland during a Manna drop on May 5, 1945. This remarkable photograph was taken by a Dutch civilian at Puttershoek, near Rotterdam and was supplied by John Carson, who was 'The Stalker's' navigator.

and bacon. The large sacks were suspended from hooks in the bombs bays while others were packed into canisters designed for incendiary bombs. Once the bomb doors were closed the bags were gently released and then, over the 'target', dropped from as low at 200ft.

The dropping zones were marked with large white crosses and Pathfinder Mosquitoes used red target indicators to help the accuracy of the drops.

Once the word got around in Holland large crowds turned out to watch the food drops and white stones were laid, spelling in English: 'Thank You Boys', 'Thank You RAF' and 'God Bless You'.

Operation Manna concluded with the German surrender and then another happy task befell the Lancaster crews of 1 Group, flying home British PoWs in what became known as Operation Exodus. The aircraft were used to fly 24 men at a time, mainly from the airfield at Melsbroek, near Brussels, to airfields in the south of England. Many of those who returned in the Lancasters were Bomber Command crews, some of whom had been captured long before the Avro Lancaster came into service. Exodus was a major undertaking and the 40 Lancasters supplied by 12 and 626 Squadrons at Wickenby, for instance,

The last aircraft written off in 1 Group during the war: NN806 M-Mike of 576 Squadron suffered an undercarriage collapse as it was about to take off from Fiskerton on a Manna operation on May 8, 1945. There were no injuries amongst the crew of F/O Scott. (Martin Nichol/David Briggs collection)

625 Squadron bomb aimers pictured after the squadron moved to Scampton, where it was disbanded. (625 Squadron Association)

ferried 960 men back to England in a single day. Later in the summer some aircraft were used in Operation Dodge, flying soldiers back from Italy. 300 Squadron at Faldingworth was given the job of flying supplies to the Polish Red Cross, initially in Belgium and later in Germany itself, a task they undertook with some relish. For the Polish airmen the end of the war was not greeted with the same unbridled enthusiasm as it was by neighbouring squadrons. Their country was not free and many would never return to Poland, choosing to stay in England.

Of 1 Group's 14 Squadrons only three were still flying at the end of 1945. 12, 100 and 101 re-equipped with the Lancaster's replacement, the aptly-named Avro Lincoln. 12 and 101 moved to Binbrook where they were joined by 5 Group's two elite squadrons, 9 and 617 as part of the new 1 Group. 460 Squadron went the other way, transferring to East Kirkby in 5 Group in readiness to take part in Tiger Force, the RAF's contribution to the assault on Japan. However, the atomic bombs ended that and in the autumn 460 was disbanded along with the remaining 1 Group squadrons. Two would be reformed, 103 in 1954 as a Canberra squadron in Germany and later as a helicopter squadron and 153 as a Meteor night-fighter squadron in the following year.

Chapter 24

The Airfields and Squadrons
of 1 Group

Between the summer of 1940 and the late spring of 1945 1 Group Bomber Command was to use 23 different airfields in a variety of roles, some for the whole of that period and others only briefly.

BINBROOK

The only 1 Group airfield to be operational from the summer of 1940 until the end of the war, Binbrook was planned as part of the second phase of Britain's pre-war airfield building programme and opened in the early summer of 1940. It became the home of 12 and 142 Squadron, which returned from France where they operated Fairey Battle light bombers which were used in some of the first 1 Group operations of the war. Both squadrons were to re-equip in the autumn with twin-engined Wellingtons, 142 Squadron moving to Waltham in November 1941 while 12 Squadron remained at Binbrook until September 1942 when contractors moved in to lay hardened runways. In January 1943 it became 12 Base headquarters and in May that year became fully operational again when 460 Squadron moved in from Breighton in East

Binbrook village pictured from the sergeants' mess. Note the air raid shelter. Binbrook was bombed on at least one occasion. (Author's collection)

The sergeant's mess at Binbrook in 1943. The building had been camouflaged back in 1940. (Author's collection)

A dedication service for the 460 Squadron memorial in Binbrook village in 1974. It was attended by many ex-460 Squadron personnel, including the former station commander Hughie Edwards VC. (Grimsby Telegraph)

Yorkshire with Lancasters and remained there until the end of the war. It also flew the most sorties and suffered the highest losses in 1 Group. In the post-war years Binbrook housed three Lincoln bomber squadrons. It was later to be used by Canberra bombers and Javelin fighters before becoming, most famously, the final home of the RAF's Lightning jet interceptor force. It finally closed in the summer of 1988 although it was to be used as a relief landing ground for Scampton until the mid-1990s. Binbrook was also to be used as the location for David Putnam's 1990 film 'Memphis Belle' which depicted the last wartime sortie of a USAAF B-17.

Today many of the original buildings remain, including the C-type brick hangars, and are used for light industrial and storage purposes. The houses built as part of the original airfield, much added to in the post-war years, have now been incorporated into the 'new' village of Brookenby. A memorial to 460 Squadron, unveiled in 1974, can be found in Binbrook village.

BLYTON

Opened in November 1942, Blyton was among the first of the new wartime airfields in 1 Group and was briefly used by a Polish operational training unit before being occupied by 199 Squadron which flew Wellingtons between November 1942 and February 1943 before transferring to 3 Group. Blyton then became the home of 1662 Heavy Conversion Unit, flying mainly Halifaxes and Lancasters until being disbanded in April 1945. It was then used by No 7 Aircrew Holding Unit until the early autumn, processing the demobilisation of more than 5,000 men. It was later allocated to the USAF but never used and finally closed in 1954.

Today little remains of the airfield, which lies to the north of the village of Blyton, apart from sections of the runway and perimeter track which are used for motor sports events.

BREIGHTON

One of three Yorkshire airfields to be used by 1 Group until new airfields in North Lincolnshire were ready for occupation, Breighton opened in January 1942, part of the first phase of the major wartime building programme. At the same time 460 Squadron RAAF was formed at the airfield and began operations with Wellingtons two months later. During the late summer 460 Conversion Flight was formed to begin the transition to Halifaxes but within a few weeks began converting to Lancasters. 460 operated Lancasters from Breighton until it moved to Binbrook in May 1943. Breighton was later used by 1656 HCU during the summer of 1943 before being transferred to 4 Group, 78 Squadron flying Halifaxes from the airfield until the end of the war.

Breighton, which lies a few miles north-east of Selby, closed after the war but was reopened in 1959 and housed Thor and Bloodhound missiles before finally closing in the mid-1960s. Today Breighton is still one of the best preserved airfields from this era with many of the original buildings, including a T2 hangar, remaining. Parts of the airfield are used for storage and light commercial use while flying continues through the Real Aero Company which specialises in restoring and flying a whole variety of vintage aircraft.

DUNHOLME LODGE

Dunholme Lodge (which took its name from a nearby house rather than the village of Dunholme) was to have the shortest life of any 1 Group bomber airfield, just six weeks. It lay between the village of Welton and the old Ermine Street running north from Lincoln and within only a few of miles of Scampton. It had opened as a 5 Group satellite airfield to Scampton in the summer of 1943 and was used by 44 and 619 Squadrons during the period when Scampton was non-operational while runways were being laid. In the autumn of 1944 it was transferred, along with Scampton and Fiskerton, to 1 Group and was used by 170 Squadron following its formation at Kelstern on October 15, 1944. Dunholme lay within the circuits of Scampton, Wickenby and Fiskerton and, with the danger of mid-air collisions very real, it was decided to close Dunholme to operational flying at the end of November. 170 Squadron moved to Hemswell and for the remainder of the war Dunholme Lodge was used for the modification and testing of gliders. The airfield was later used to house the RAF's Polish record office and as a Polish resettlement centre. In the late 1950s it became a Bloodhound missile site, protecting the V-bomber bases at Scampton and Waddington before closing finally in 1966. Today very little trace remains of Dunholme Lodge.

ELSHAM WOLDS

Elsham was to be a corner-stone of 1 Group operations from the day it opened in July 1941 until the end of the war. It had been built on the site of a First World War fighter airfield, the solitary remaining building of which was incorporated into the new airfield. Its first occupants, 103 Squadron, was one of the group's founder squadrons and was to remain at Elsham until the war ended, a period of occupation almost unique in Bomber Command. It was a large airfield built on top of the northern-most section of the Lincolnshire Wolds north of the village of Barnetby. As 13 Base headquarters, it eventually handled all the major Lancaster engineering work for its resident squadrons as well as those at its satellites, Kirmington and North Killingholme and had no fewer than six hangars, two of the utilitarian T2s, three B1s and one of the far more substantial J1. A second squadron, 576, was formed at Elsham in November 1943 and flew from there until the end of October, 1944. 103 was joined for the last month of the war by 100 Squadron following the closure of

A wartime photograph of the control tower at Elsham. In later years it was turned into a house before being demolished. (*Sid Finn*)

Waltham. 103 remained at Elsham until it was disbanded in November and Elsham passed to the control of 23 Group Flying Training Command. It was used for glider training and later by Flying Training Command's Instructors School until the end of 1946 when Elsham Wolds closed.

Today the airfield is cut in two by the A15 Barnetby-Humber Bridge road but traces of its former occupants can still be seen, particularly the J1 hangar which has been incorporated into a sizeable industrial estate. A water treatment plant was also constructed on the south-western boundary of the airfield, close to the end of the end of the main runway and this is now incorporated a memorial garden to both 103 and 576 Squadrons.

FALDINGWORTH

Work on the construction of Faldingworth on the site of the old Toft Grange decoy airfield began in August 1942 and, even though it was far from finished, Faldingworth was used from July 1943 as a satellite of Lindholme and for use by the newly-formed 1667 Heavy Conversion Unit. In March 1944 Faldingworth became operational for the first time with the arrival of the Poles of 300 Squadron from Ingham. They were in the process of converting from

340

Wellingtons to Lancasters and initially flew as only a single flight squadron. A second flight was later formed, mainly made up with RAF personnel who were replaced by Poles as more replacements became available. 300 flew its Lancasters from Faldingworth until the squadron was disbanded in October 1946 and the airfield was later used briefly by a second Polish squadron, 305, which had been flying its Mosquitoes in Germany. When it was disbanded the airfield was taken over by Maintenance Command and its resident units, 93 and later 92 MU, stored and supplied munitions to other RAF airfields in Lincolnshire, including nuclear warheads for Thor missiles and nuclear bombs for the V-bombers at Scampton and Waddington. So much secrecy surrounded Faldingworth's role that, between 1956 and 1980 in did not appear on Ordnance Survey maps. The airfield buildings were later briefly used for accommodating Asian families displaced from Uganda and parts of the airfield were then acquired by British Manufacturing and Research which used facilities there for the development and testing of weapons and munitions. In the later 1990s part of the airfield was sold for agricultural purposes although some weapons and munitions storage and testing is still carried out.

Today some buildings remain along with sections of perimeter tracks, dispersals and the main runway, at the end of which is a memorial to those who flew from Faldingworth.

FISKERTON

Another of the airfields transferred to 1 Group in the autumn of 1944, Fiskerton had opened in November 1942 within 5 Group and was used by 49 Squadron until problems with the main runway ended operational flying briefly in September 1943, 49 moving to nearby Dunholme Lodge and returning five weeks later after repairs had been carried out. A year later Fiskerton, which was one of the handful of airfields in Lincolnshire to be fitted with FIDO fog-dispersal equipment, was part of 5 Group's 52 Base which was transferred to 1 Group and it was immediately occupied by 576 Squadron which brought its Lancasters from Elsham Wolds. A second squadron, 150, was formed at Fiskerton in November 1943 before moving to Hemswell. 576 flew as a two flight squadron until the closing stages of the war when it was joined by C Flight of 625 Squadron at Kelstern. Flying ended at Fiskerton in the late autumn of 1945 and, after a period of care and maintenance, the airfield closed, although some accommodation was used as emergency housing for homeless families. Later part of the airfield became headquarters of 15 Group Royal Observer Corps.

Now little remains apart from some sections of the perimeter track and one or two of the dispersals. A memorial stone stands close to the old airfield (see *On Hallowed Ground*).

HEMSWELL

The oldest of the airfields in 1 Group, Hemswell was first in use (as Harpswell) in the First World War. During the early 1930s the site was chosen for one of the major Expansion Scheme airfields and it opened in 1936 and was used by first by 144 and 61 Squadrons flying Ansons and Hawker Audax biplanes. In 1937 it came under the control of 5 Group and both squadrons re-equipped with Blenheims which, in turn, were replaced by Hampdens in 1939. It was with these aircraft that the first bombing raids were carried out on September 26, 1939 when both squadrons took part in attacks on German shipping. 61 and 144 Squadrons continued to operate from Hemswell until July 1941 when it was transferred to 1 Group and occupied by 300 and 301 Squadrons, which moved in with Wellingtons from Swinderby. A third Polish squadron,

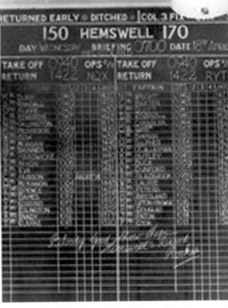

The Battle Order board for 150 and 170 Squadrons at Hemswell, April 1945. (Martin Nichol/David Briggs collection)

305, later arrived while 300 moved to Ingham before returning in January 1943. A shortage of Polish replacements to make up the squadrons' losses meant that by April 301 Squadron's personnel were absorbed into 300 Squadron, which then moved to Ingham once again. The airfield closed for runway construction and when the airfield reopened in January 1944 it was to become home to No 1 Lancaster Finishing School which itself was disbanded in November that year. Hemswell then became operational again with the arrival of, first, 150 Squadron from Fiskerton followed by 170 Squadron from Dunholme Lodge. After the war Hemswell was used by 109 and 139 Squadrons, flying Mosquitoes. The airfield then became a base for the new Lincoln bomber flown by 83, 97 and 199 Squadrons, which flew alongside the Mosquitoes until the early 1950s when both 109 and 139 began to convert to Canberras. When the Lincolns were phased out Hemswell passed to the control of 3 Group and was used by the Nuclear Weapons Task Force, its specially-adapted high altitude Canberras being used for air particle sampling in the Christmas Island H-bomb tests. In 1957 Hemswell became a Thor missile base, the airfield housing three of the missiles in specially built bunkers. The missiles were removed in 1963 and Hemswell was then earmarked as a ground training base for the proposed TSR2 supersonic bomber. When development work on

Hemswell post war. The control tower has long gone but the brick-built hangars are still there today. (Scunthorpe Telegraph)

that was halted Hemswell provided overspill accommodation for the School of Recruit Training at Swinderby before finally closing in 1967. Some light aircraft flying continued from Hemswell along with a thriving glider school while the airfield's huge brick hangars were used for storage while the married quarters were used by nearby RAF Scampton.

Today the site hosts a busy market while many of the buildings have been redeveloped for commercial use. Little remains of the runways or perimeter tracks. The extensive accommodation areas have now turned into a village in their own right – Hemswell Cliff - while a memorial to all those who flew from the airfield during wartime is on the old station parade ground.

HOLME-ON-SPALDING MOOR

One of the raft of airfields built in the early days of the war, Holme-on-Spalding Moor, which lies a few miles south-west of Market Weighton, was one of four Yorkshire bases used by 1 Group. It opened in August 1941 and was briefly used by the Wellingtons of 458 Squadron before the squadron was transferred to the Middle East. 101 Squadron, which had flown Blenheims and Wellingtons in 2 Group, then moved in from Stradishall and later began training, alongside 460 Squadron, on Halifaxes before being re-equipped with Lancasters. They left for Ludford Magna in June 1943, Holme-on-Spalding Moor transferred to 4 Group control and was used by the Halifaxes of 76 Squadron until the end of the war. It was later used for flying training and for bomb storage before being mothballed in 1954. Three years later it was briefly reactivated for the United States Air Force before being leased to the Blackburn Aircraft Company which had a major factory at nearby Brough. The company was in the process of developing the Blackburn Buccaneer for the Fleet Air Arm and its own runway at Brough wasn't long enough for the aircraft. Blackburn, and its successor British Aerospace, used the airfield for trials work with the Buccaneer and for design changes to the RAF and Royal Navy's American built F4 Phantom until 1984 when the airfield finally closed.

INGHAM

The smallest of all 1 Group airfields, Ingham opened in 1942 as a satellite airfield for Hemswell and was to be the only airfield in the group to have grass runways throughout the war. It was less than three miles from neighbouring Scampton and occupied a relatively small site between the A15 and B1398 Lincolnshire Cliff road, making it unsuitable for heavy bomber operations. The airfield, which was to get a concrete perimeter track, was to be used mainly by Polish squadrons, flying Wellingtons, although one RAF squadron, 199, spent four months there in 1943. When the Poles of 300 Squadron left for Faldingworth in the spring of 1944 Ingham, it was used by 1687 Bomber Defence Training Flight and 1481 Bomber Gunnery Flight, which was later disbanded. In the autumn of 1944 the airfield was renamed Cammeringham to avoid confusion with another RAF station and flying ended in December when control switched to 15 Base at Scampton. It was to be used by a variety of non-operational RAF and Polish units before it finally closed at the end of December 1946.

A number of original buildings from the airfield still remain, including one hangar, which had been reskinned and extended, and the old control tower, which has been refurbished and is now used for domestic purposes.

KELSTERN

Visitors will find it difficult to find anything that remains of Kelstern, apart from the impressive roadside memorial to the men of 625 Squadron who flew from there from late 1943 until the spring of 1945. There was an airfield there in the First World War but the new bomber base was built some distance away, a mile or so north of the hamlet from which it was named. 625 Squadron formed from a nucleus of experienced 100 Squadron crews at the end of September 1943 and was in action within a matter of days. Kelstern was part of 12 Base and 625 flew initially as a two flight squadron. A third was formed in 1944 and part of it was detached in September to help form 170 Squadron, which later moved to Dunholme Lodge. In the spring of 1945 625 left Kelstern for the last time, A and B Flights moving to Scampton and C Flight to Fiskerton where it merged into 576 Squadron. Later that year the airfield closed and the land was put under the control of the Ministry of Agriculture before being sold to tenant farmers in the 1960s.

Kelstern saw the erection of the very first bomber squadron memorial in Lincolnshire in 1964, followed by an annual roadside ceremony attended by 625 Squadron veterans from all parts of the world. Today some scattered buildings still survive together with sections of perimeter track.

KIRMINGTON

RAF station Kirmington still survives today in the guise of Humberside Airport although very little of the original bomber airfield remains apart from a few buildings on the old dispersal sites on the edge of the nearby Brocklesby Estate. Kirmington opened in January 1942 but was not used by 1 Group until October of that year, allowing 150 Squadron to move in with its Wellingtons from its base at Snaith, near Goole. The squadron was only to be at Kirmington for a matter of weeks before one element moved to the Middle East. The remainder was later to merge with the home echelon of 142 Squadron to form the bomber squadron which will always be synonymous with Kirmington, 166. The squadron continued to fly its Wellingtons from Kirmington until September 1943 when it began to convert to Lancasters. The squadron's C Flight was detached in October 1944 to help reform 153 Squadron before a new C Flight, formed at Faldingworth, moved to Kirmington a few days later. Operational flying ended at Kirmington in April 1945 and 166 Squadron disbanded later that year. After the war Kirmington was used to stage a number of disposal sales of military vehicles and equipment, events which drew huge crowds. The airfield returned largely to agriculture although there was some limited private flying. In the late 1960s and early 1970s flying increased and in 1974 the then Lindsey County Council, with the financial backing of the British Steel Corporation whose own airstrip at Scunthorpe had been swallowed up in the development of the Anchor Steelworks, opened the airfield as Kirmington Airport. Days later, Lindsey County Council vanished as part of local government reorganisation and the new Humberside County Council rebranded Kirmington 'Humberside (Hull) Airport', the name 'Hull' quickly being dropped after vigorous local protests.

Today the airport operates flights to numerous destinations as well as being the base for busy helicopter operations to North Sea gas installations. The A18 runs alongside the airfield and it is worth noting that just north-east of the present airport buildings a section of the wartime runway can be seen on the opposite side of the road. During wartime barriers were dragged across the road while flying was taking place.

A handsome memorial to those who flew from Kirmington is situated in nearby Kirmington village together with a stained glass window in St Helen's Church in the village, the distinctive copper-sheathed spire of which proved to be a welcome site for homebound Wellington and Lancaster crews.

LINDHOLME

Built as part of the 1930s Expansion Programme, Lindholme in South Yorkshire opened as a 5 Group airfield in June 1940. It was then known as Hatfield Woodhouse, being renamed in August 1940, and was built with five brick-built C-type hangars. Its first occupants were the Hampdens of 50

Squadron which were joined in June 1941 by a second Hampden squadron, 408 of the Royal Canadian Air Force. 408 was only there for a month before Lindholme was transferred to 1 Group. 50 Squadron went to Swinderby and 408 to Syerston in Nottingham, exchanging places with two Polish squadrons, 304 and 305. They were to fly operationally from Lindholme until 1942 before 304 was transferred to Coastal Command and 305 went to Hemswell. Lindholme closed for flying until two runways were laid (there wasn't room for the standard third runway) and from October of that year became the headquarters of 1 Group's heavy conversion training. 1656 HCU was formed there and Lindholme was later to host 1667 HCU and No 1 Lancaster Finishing School.

Lindholme was to have important role to play in the post-war history of the RAF, operating first Lincoln bombers of 50 and 100 Squadrons and later Lincolns, Varsities and Hastings of the Bomber Command Bomber School. Adaptations to Canberras were also conducted at Lindholme and later the airfield was to house Northern Radar, part of a chain of similar centres providing radar cover across the country for both military and civilian traffic. In 1985 the site was sold and is now occupied by Her Majesty's Prison Lindholme. Virtually all trace of the old airfield has disappeared although the old hangars were incorporated into the prison buildings.

LUDFORD MAGNA
Built by Wimpeys, Ludford came to epitomise all that wartime airfields were about. It was wet, cold and muddy yet its only occupants, 101, were to write themselves into RAF history. Ludford, constructed at one of the highest points on the Lincolnshire Wolds with a north-south main runway, opened in June 1943 and within days 101 Squadron moved in with its Lancasters from Holme-

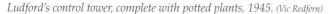

Ludford's control tower, complete with potted plants, 1945. (Vic Redfern)

Nissen huts being dismantled at Ludford in the late 1940s. Most were sold for industrial or agricultural use. In the background is one of the airfield's seven hangars. (Grimsby Telegraph)

on-Spalding Moor. The airfield was built on the south side of Magna Mile, the road running between the twin villages of Ludford Magna and Ludford Parva while most of the accommodation sites lay to the north side. It later became 14 Base headquarters and was eventually to have seven hangars, handling as it did major servicing for squadrons at its satellite airfields at Faldingworth and Wickenby. In the autumn of 1943 101 Squadron's aircraft were fitted with ABC electronic equipment intended to disrupt German night fighter transmissions and, as such, was required to fly on virtually all major bombing attacks until the end of the war, with subsequent heavy losses. Ludford was also to be fitted with FIDO fog-dispersal equipment. After the war 101 Squadron moved to Binbrook and Ludford was mothballed and much of the site returned to agriculture. It was reactivated and housed Thor missiles between 1959 and 1963 before finally closing.

Today a few buildings remain together with sections of perimeter track. The runways themselves were torn up and used as hardcore for industrial development along the Humber bank. A memorial to 101 Squadron and the 1,176 men it lost in action – the highest figure in Bomber Command – can be found in the village.

NEWTON

Another Expansion plan pre-war airfield, Newton, which is only a few miles from the centre of Nottingham, was one of the first two airfields to be used by 1 Group, 103 and 150 Squadrons arriving there with their Fairey Battles from France in July 1940. Both squadrons later converted to Wellingtons during their time at Newton and moved the following July to Elsham Wolds and Snaith respectively, ending 1 Group's direct association with the airfield. However, in its next role, Newton was to house a flying training school for Polish aircrew, many of whom went on to fly with 1 Group squadrons. Newton continued in its training role from its grass runways throughout the war. Flying continued at Newton until 2001 when most of the land was sold for light industrial purposes.

The brick built hangars still remain, as does the original control tower while one of the ancillary buildings is still used by the local air cadet unit. The village sign for Newton incorporates an image of JN-X, a 150 Squadron Wellington.

NORTH KILLINGHOLME

One of the last operational airfields to open in 1 Group, North Killingholme's first and only occupants was 550 Squadron which flew in from Waltham on January 3, 1944. The squadron, which was to earn itself an outstanding reputation during its time at North Killingholme, began operations almost immediately and was finally disbanded in October 1945. The RAF had no long-term use for it and much of it was sold for agricultural purposes

The airfield lays adjacent to the villages of both North and South Killingholme and East Halton and today is a major industrial estate. One of the original hangars still exists together with a few buildings while large sections of runway and perimeter tracks remain and are now used for storage purposes.

There is a memorial to those who flew with 550 Squadron at the main entrance on the road between South Killingholme and East Halton.

SANDTOFT

RAF station Sandtoft officially came into being at about the same time as North Killingholme but it was never to play an operational role in 1 Group. It was in February 1944 that its first and only occupants, 1667 Heavy Conversion Unit, arrived from Faldingworth and was to fly a mixture of Halifaxes and Lancasters from there in its training role, suffering its share of accidents and crashes. At the end of 1944 it passed into the hands of 7 Group and was yet another airfield for which no military use could be found in the post-war years.

Today Sandtoft is home to a large industrial estate, including vast areas of imported car and van storage alongside the M180 motorway which now runs alongside the old airfield. Some buildings, runways and perimeter tracks do remain.

SCAMPTON

An airfield which is perhaps the most famous of all Bomber Command bases was to play a role in the final months of 1 Group's wartime history. Scampton, then known as Brattleby, was a major Royal Flying Corps airfield in the First World War but flying ended in 1920 after which virtually all trace of the old airfield disappeared. In the early 1930s the site was chosen for one of the first of the RAF's major new airfields and Scampton, as it was now called, reopened in August 1936. It was home first to 9 Squadron with its exotic Handley Page Heyfords and later 214 Squadron's Vickers Virginias and Handley Page Harrows. Other pre-war aircraft to fly from Scampton included Audaxes, Wellesleys and Hinds before the new Hampden made its debut there in the hands of 49 Squadron with 83 Squadron converting soon afterwards. These were the aircraft with which Scampton, and 5 Group, went to war. Two of the RAF's first wartime VCs were won by men flying Hampdens from Scampton, F/Lt 'Babe' Learoyd and Sgt John Hannah. Both squadrons later flew Manchesters from Scampton before 57 Squadron arrived with Lancasters in November 1942. In the spring of 1943 617 Squadron was formed at Scampton and its CO, W/Cmdr Guy Gibson, was to win a third VC from the airfield leading the raid on the Ruhr dams in May 1943. Shortly afterwards the station closed for flying for the laying of hardened runways and the next operational unit to operate from there was 1 Group's 153 Squadron, which moved in during October 1944 from Kirmington following the transfer of the airfield

The dedication of the 625 Squadron memorial – the first airfield memorial in Lincolnshire – in 1964 at Kelstern. (Clem Koder)

to1 Group. It was joined in the last month of the war by 625 Squadron. Both squadrons were disbanded there after the war before Scampton became the home to a succession of Lincoln squadrons. During the Berlin blockade crisis in 1948 and 1949 it was used by two USAF B29 units. Scampton was later used by several Canberra squadrons before being closed in 1955 for major redevelopment, including lengthening the main runway with the resulting loop in the otherwise dead-straight A15 Lincoln-Caenby Corner road. The airfield reopened in 1958 and became home to the Scampton Wing, three squadrons of Vulcan bombers, providing a major element of Britain's Cold War defences. The Vulcan remained in service until the 1980s and the Scampton became home to the RAF's Red Arrows aerobatic team.

At the time of writing, the Red Arrows are still flying from Scampton but the future of the base, the last remaining airfield with links to 1 Group still in RAF hands, remains very much in doubt.

SNAITH

Opened in July 1941, Snaith was to be used by the Wellingtons of 150 Squadron for 15 months before the airfield was transferred to 4 Group and became home to 51 Squadron, which arrived with its Whitleys after a six-month detachment to Coastal Command. It converted to Halifaxes and remained at Snaith until the end of the war. The airfield was always known locally as 'Pollington' after the village which it bordered. It closed for flying in April 1945 when 51 Squadron moved to Leconfield and the land was later sold for agricultural purposes.

Today the remains of RAF Snaith can just be glimpsed from the M62, which cuts across one of the old runways. Still there is the airfield's distinctive J-type hangar together with a few remaining buildings.

STURGATE

Sturgate was the very last wartime airfield built in Lincolnshire. Built between the villages of Heapham and Upton, near Gainsborough, it was intended for 1 Group but by the time it opened in September 1944 it was redundant. It was used briefly by No 1 Lancaster Finishing School at Hemswell and was later allocated to 71 Base HQ at Lindholme and used occasionally by its heavy conversion units. After the war Sturgate was used by the USAF as a fighter airfield before finally closing. Today the airfield is used by the Lincoln Aero Club.

SWINDERBY

Among the first airfields to be used by 1 Group, work of Swinderby began in the late 1930s and it opened in August 1940, being occupied almost immediately by the Poles of 300 and 301 Squadron, who flew their first operations in Battles. They later converted to Wellingtons and both squadrons flews from there until the summer of 1941 when they moved to Hemswell. Swinderby then passed to 5 Group and was used by 455 and 50 Squadrons before it was allocated to 1660 Heavy Conversion Unit. In the post war years Swinderby was used for both piston and jet-engined training before becoming the home of the RAF's School of Recruit Training. It finally closed in 1996.

Large areas of the airfield – which lays alongside the A46 Lincoln-Newark road – still remain, including the three hangars. The large accommodation site has now been incorporated into the new village of Witham St Hugh's.

SYERSTON

Opened in December 1940, Syerston, which lays between Newark and Nottingham, was used for a little over six months by 1 Group until the two squadrons there, the Poles of 304 and 305 Squadrons, were found a new home at Lindholme. Syerston itself went on to earn fame as a 5 Group bomber airfield, 49, 61, 106 and 408 Squadrons operating Manchesters and Lancasters from the Nottinghamshire airfields. Guy Gibson led 106 Squadron there before moving to Scampton to form 617 and it was from Syerston that F/Lt Bill Reid was awarded a Victoria Cross after a raid on Dusseldorf in November, 1943. The airfield was also home to No 5 Lancaster Finishing School in 1944. After the war it was used by RAF Transport Command and then for training purposes and for gliding.

The J-type hangars remain together with most of the runways and perimeter tracks.

WALTHAM

Its official name was RAF Grimsby, but to all it was simply known as 'Waltham'. The airfield lay on the outskirts of Grimsby between the villages of Waltham and Holton-le-Clay and before the war had been Grimsby's municipal airport, a place where Alan Cobham's flying circus had performed to the delight of thousands. The RAF link began in 1938 with the setting up of Bomber Command's 25 Elementary and Reserve Training School and that, together with the local branch of the Civil Air Guard, was to provide the RAF with many aircrew recruits in the coming years. Work on building the bomber airfield began in May 1940 and by the following summer it was already being used as a relief landing ground by neighbouring Binbrook, which lacked Waltham's concrete runways. 142 Squadron finally moved in during the autumn of 1941 and flew from there for just over a year, part of the squadron moving to North Africa and the remainder to Kirmington. It was immediately replaced by 100 Squadron, which was reformed at Waltham after suffering a hard time in the Far East. They soon took charge of their first Lancasters and the squadron was to operate them for the remainder of the war from Waltham.

In April 1945 100 Squadron moved to Elsham and Waltham closed. Attempts were made in the post-war years to resurrect civilian flying but came to nothing.

Much of the airfield remains today, including two of the hangars and large sections of runway and perimeter track. A memorial to those who flew from Waltham stands alongside the A16 to the east of the airfield, close to the spot where, during the war, traffic lights were installed to halt vehicles on the Grimsby-Louth road while flying took place.

WICKENBY

Wickenby had the standard three-runway, three-hangar configuration yet, despite its comparatively modest size, was to accommodate two Lancaster squadrons in the last 18 months of the war. The airfield was built on flat farmland between the villages of Wickenby and Holton Beckering, north-east of Wragby, and opened in September 1942 when it was immediately occupied by the Wellington IIs and IIIs of 12 Squadron on its move from Binbrook. Soon after their arrival 12 Squadron began converting to Lancasters and flew them for the first time operationally in January 1943. In November that year the squadron's C Flight was detached to form 626 Squadron and both operated from Wickenby with great distinction until the war ended. In November, 1945

Mishap at North Killingholme. 550 Squadron's Q-Queenie went off the perimeter track and became bogged down as the squadron was about to depart for Caen on the evening of July 7, 1944. (550 Squadron Association)

12 Squadron returned to Binbrook, 626 was disbanded and the airfield was turned over to 93 Maintenance Unit for the dismantling of munitions. It finally closed in 1956 but seven years later parts of the airfield, including the runways, were acquired for civilian flying.

Today the runways are shorter and the aircraft smaller, but Wickenby is still a thriving airfield. One of the wartime hangars is still used for aviation purposes and, most significantly, there is small museum and visitors' centre, staffed by volunteers, who keep the memories and spirit of Wickenby alive. The airfield has a striking memorial, topped by a figure of Icarus, to all the 1,080 men who flew from Wickenby and never returned.

THE SQUADRONS

12 SQUADRON: Flew throughout the war with 1 Group after its return from France in the summer of 1940, initially from Binbrook and later from Wickenby. Operated Battles, Wellingtons and Lancasters and lost a total of 189 aircraft. Later flew Lincolns, Canberras, Vulcans and Buccaneers before becoming a Tornado squadron. At the time of writing operates Tornado GR4s from Lossiemouth.

100 SQUADRON: Flew Lancasters from Waltham from December 1942 until April 1945 before moving to Elsham Wolds. Lost 113 Lancasters. In the post-war years flew Lincolns, Canberras, Victors, Canberras again before becoming a Hawk squadron. Currently operates from Leeming in Yorkshire.

101 SQUADRON: Served with both 2 and 3 Groups before joining 1 Group. Flew Wellingtons and Lancasters from Holme-on-Spalding Moor before moving to Ludford Magna where it operated ABC-equipped Lancasters until the war ended. Lost one Wellington and 147 Lancasters in 1 Group service. After flying Lincolns, 101 became the RAF's first jet bomber squadron when it converted to Canberras from Binbrook. Later operated Vulcans before converting to VC10 tankers, which it currently flies from Brize Norton .

103 SQUADRON: Operated with 1 Group from the summer of 1940 until the war ended, initially from Newton and from 1941 at Elsham Wolds. The only 1 Group squadron to fly Halifaxes on operations, it also operated Battles, Wellingtons and Lancasters and lost a total of 201 aircraft, the highest number in 1 Group. Disbanded in November 1945 when it was renumbered 57 Squadron, 103 was reformed in Germany in 1954 where it flew Canberras before becoming a helicopter squadron, operating in the Middle and Far East before being finally disbanded in August 1975.

142 SQUADRON: Arrived at Binbrook after service in France in July 1940, it flew Battles and Wellington from both Binbrook and Waltham before the bulk of the squadron was transferred to the Middle East. Later operated as a Mosquito squadron. Lost 51 aircraft. Disbanded October 1944 only to be reformed briefly the following year. The squadron was reformed once again in 1959 as 142 Strategic Missile Squadron at Coleby Grange in Lincolnshire and was equipped with Thor missiles before being finally disbanded in May 1963.

150 SQUADRON: Also flew in France before joining 1 Group. 150 flew from Newton, Snaith and, briefly, Kirmington before being transferred to the Middle East. Rejoined 1 Group as a Lancaster squadron, flying from Fiskerton and Hemswell. Lost 58 aircraft. Disbanded November 1945.

153 SQUADRON: Reformed as Lancaster squadron at Kirmington in October 1944 after service in the Middle East, it later operated from Scampton until the end of the war. Lost 22 Lancasters. Disbanded September 1945.

166 SQUADRON: Reformed in 1 Group at Kirmington in January 1943 after service in 4 Group, it flew exclusively from Kirmington. Lost 39 Wellingtons and 114 Lancasters. Disbanded November 1945.

170 SQUADRON: Reformed at Kelstern in October 1944, it operated Lancasters from Dunholme Lodge and Hemswell. Lost 14 aircraft. Disbanded November 1945.

199 SQUADRON: Formed in November 1942, 199 flew Wellingtons from Blyton and Ingham before transferring in 3 Group in June 1943. Lost 12 aircraft while with 1 Group. Later served with 100 Group before being disbanded in July 1945. Reformed in the early 1950s and flew Lincolns and Valiants before being disbanded again in 1958.

300 (MASOVIAN) SQUADRON: Formed in 1940, the Polish squadron which operated with 1 Group throughout the war. The last squadron in Bomber Command to fly Wellingtons operationally, it also flew Battles and Lancasters and served at Swinderby, Hemswell, Ingham and finally Faldingworth. Lost 83 aircraft. Disbanded January 1947.

301 (POMERANIAN) SQUADRON: Formed at Swinderby alongside 301, it flew Battles and Wellingtons before moving to Hemswell. Disbanded in 1943 because of a shortage of Polish crews. Lost 29 aircraft. Later reformed as 301 (Special Flight) as part of 138 Squadron. Finally disbanded December 1946.

304 (SILESIAN) SQUADRON: Formed in August 1940, it flew Wellingtons from Syerston and Lindholme before being transferred to Coastal Command in 1942. Lost 18 aircraft. Later flew with Transport Command and was disbanded in December 1946.

305 (ZIEMIA WIELKOPOLSKA) SQUADRON: Formed alongside 304, it flew Wellingtons from Syerston, Lindholme, Hemswell and Ingham before being transferred to the 2nd Tactical Air Force. Lost 30 aircraft. Disbanded January 1947.

458 SQUADRON RAAF: The very first Australian squadron within Bomber Command operated briefly from Holme-on-Spalding Moor before being transferred to the Middle East. 458 lost three Wellingtons during its short stay at Holme. Disbanded at Gibraltar June 1945.

460 SQUADRON RAAF: One of eight Australian units to serve in Bomber Command, 460 established itself as one of the outstanding of all wartime bomber squadrons. It was formed in March 1942 and flew Wellingtons and Lancasters from Breighton before transferring (largely by Horsa glider) to Binbrook in the summer of 1943. It lost 200 aircraft, the highest of any Australian squadron in Bomber Command. Disbanded October 1945.

550 SQUADRON: Formed at Waltham in November 1943, it flew Lancasters from there until moving to North Killingholme in January 1944. Lost 73 aircraft. Disbanded October 1945.

576 SQUADRON: Formed from 103's C Flight at Elsham Wolds in November 1943, it flew from there until the autumn of 1944 when it moved to Fiskerton. Losses amounted to 75 Lancasters. Disbanded September 1945.

625 SQUADRON: One of only two squadrons to fly from Kelstern, 625 was formed there in October 1943 and flew 188 operations from there before moving to Scampton for the last few weeks of the war. Lost 74 Lancasters. Disbanded October 1945.

626 SQUADRON: Flew from Wickenby alongside 12 Squadron from November 1943 until the end of the war. Lost 60 Lancasters. Disbanded October 1945.

Chapter 25

1 Group Today

All but one of its wartime airfields have gone and only three of the squadrons that flew Lancasters from Lincolnshire remaining in being, but 1 Group itself remains an integral part of the modern Royal Air Force.

When the war ended there was a major re-organisation within the RAF but 1 Group remained in being at its wartime headquarters at Bawtry and was to oversee Bomber Command operations until the creation of Strike Command in 1968.

The immediate post-war years saw a major reduction in the size and scale of the bomber force with the aptly-named Lincoln gradually replacing Lancasters before it, too, gave way to the first of the new jet-age bombers, the English Electric Canberra.

Britain's nuclear defence force also fell under the aegis of 1 Group, with the new V-bomber force of Valiants, Victors and, especially, Vulcans providing the back-bone of the country's strike force. 1 Group also had responsibility for introduction of the American-built Thor missile into Britain's defences. These were based at 10 airfields, including Ludford Magna, Hemswell and Breighton, all former 1 Group stations, while the nuclear warheads for the missiles were stored in great secrecy at Faldingworth along with the nuclear weapons for the V-bomber force. Ten RAF squadrons were reactivated to operate the missiles, each adding the initials SM - strategic missile – to their squadron code. Hemswell was occupied by 97 (SM) Squadron, Ludford by 104 and Breighton by 240. Each squadron was equipped with three missiles, stored horizontally in large concrete bunkers, most of which still remain today. Hemswell was also used as the delivery hub for the missiles, each flown in on USAF C-124 Globemasters. By the summer of 1963 the missiles had become obsolete and Hemswell was once again used, this time to fly them back to the United States.

During this period 1 Group was also responsible for the Bloodhound missile defence system, which was set up to primarily protect the V-bomber bases, including Scampton, Waddington and Finningley. Dunholme Lodge, which had such a brief life within wartime 1 Group, was re-activated to take some of the missiles while others were based at Breighton and at Misson, near Bawtry, which had been used during the war as a 1 Group bombing range.

With the creation of Strike Command in 1968, 1 Group also assumed responsibility for the RAF's jet fighters, including the Javelins and later the Lightning force at Binbrook before it was disbanded in the late 1980s, and Binbrook closed.

From its headquarters at Bawtry 1 Group was to oversee several major overseas operations, including Malaya and Suez, and it was 1 Group Vulcans which carried out the epic Black Buck raids on Port Stanley during the Falklands War in 1983.

In 1984 Bawtry Hall closed and 1 Group headquarters moved first to Upavon in Wiltshire and later to Benson in Oxfordshire, along the way absorbing the operational duties of 2 Group when that was disbanded in 1996, at which point the headquarters moved to High Wycombe, where they remain today. In 2000 there was another major restructuring of the RAF and 1 Group assumed its present role of overseeing Britain's air defences with quick reaction alert aircraft being on permanent readiness at Leuchars in Scotland and Coningsby in Lincolnshire. Its aircraft have also seen service in operations in the Gulf, the Balkans, Afghanistan and, most recently, Libya. In 2007 the RAF underwent another major reorganisation with Strike Command and Personnel and Training Command coming together under a single Air Command.

The links with wartime 1 Group still remain. Scampton is still operational and currently houses the Red Arrows display team, although its future is, at the time of writing, clouded with uncertainty. And three of the wartime squadrons which flew 1 Group Lancasters from Lincolnshire are still operational – 12 Squadron with the GR4 Tornado at Lossiemouth, 100 Squadron which flies Hawks in a variety of roles from Leeming in North Yorkshire and 101 Squadron, which operates VC10 tankers from Brize Norton in Oxfordshire. Bawtry Hall, 1 Group's headquarters for 44 years, is now a busy conference and training centre.

1 Group itself will continue to be a key component of Britain's air defences and strike capability for the foreseeable future. It still retains its original panther's head badge and its motto – *Swift to Attack*.

On Hallowed Ground

Close to what was one of the runways at Fiskerton stands a memorial stone to the men of 49 Squadron (5 Group) and 576 Squadron (1 Group) which flew from the airfield during the war. Flanking it are two stones carrying individual dedications. This is one of them dedicated to 576 Squadron's aircrew killed flying from Fiskerton.

LISTEN TO THE WIND

Stranger – pause here a little while,
And listen to the West wind's sigh,
With it's tales of long-gone men –
Earth shall not see their like again.

Stand by this stone and lend an ear,
And I'll show you ghosts of yesteryear;
The windsock's creak, the cold wind's moan,
Long-dead men crowd around – we're not alone.

Look on this empty, lonely place,
Do the shadows, unseen, still cross my face?
Listen! Far-off thunder – or a Merlin's roar,
Borne on the wind, from Time's remoter shore.

Abandoned, quiet, here I lie,
Time stands still, though years roll by;
Runways broken, dispersals gone,
The only sound the skylark's song.

Half a hundred years have passed,
Half a century since I saw them last;
Lancasters, black against the sky,
Aircrews young, so many soon to die.

They came from England and far distant shores,
Volunteers, each one, to defend Liberty's just cause;
These fractured runways know how many went,
Silent witnesses to Youth's blood, spent.

ON HALLOWED GROUND

I was created from the very earth for which they fought,
My rich, dark soil with their sacrifice they bought,
In Lincoln Cathedral, yonder, their names are to be found
And know this – by their blood, you stand on hallowed ground.

Let the tangled weeds that cover me remain,
Shrouding my memories of hope and pain;
And, as I return slowly to the land,
Let this proud stone in perpetual homage stand.

So, stranger, continue now upon your way,
But forget not those who – it seems but yesterday –
Gave all their tomorrows that you might live,
For your Freedom they gave all they had to give.

Cedric Keith St George Roberts, May 1995

Mascots were an essential part of many 1 Group crews and this one was no exception. 'Ethel' was an elephant knitted for this 550 Squadron crew by one of the barmaids in the Cross Keys public house in South Killingholme. On the photograph are: back row(left to right) Ron Digby (pilot), Johnny Walker (flight engineer) Ernie Lewis (navigator); front row, Don Crabtree (wireless operator) James Perrigo, holding 'Ethel' (mid-upper gunner) and Ray Hagar RCAF (rear gunner). Missing from the photograph is the bomb aimer, Sgt A. McLeod RCAF. The crew and 'Ethel' safely completed their tour at North Killingholme. (Brian Perrigo, via 550 Squadron Association)

359

Bibliography

Ralph Barker – *The Thousand Plan,* Airlife

Ron Blake, Mike Hodgson, Bill Taylor – *Airfields of Lincolnshire since 1912,* Midland Counties

Chaz Bowyer – *Wellington at War,* Ian Allen

Don Charlwood – *No Moon Tonight,* Goodhall Publications

Bill Chorley – *Bomber Command Losses (Volumes 1 to 8),* Midland Counties

Alan Cooper – *Air Battles of the Ruhr,* Airlife
—— *Bombers over Berlin,* William Kimber

Oliver Clutton-Brock – *Massacre over the Marne,* Patrick Stephens

Pat Cunningham – *Bomb on the Red Markers,* Countryside Books

Roberts Dunstan and Burton Graham – *The Sand and the Sky,* Robertson and Mullins

Jonathan Falconer – *RAF Bomber Airfields of World War Two,* Ian Allen

Sean Feast, *Carried on the Wind,* Woodfield Publishing

Sid Finn – *Black Swan,* Newton
—— *Lincolnshire Air War 1939-45,* Aero Litho

Peter Firkins – *Strike and Return: 460 RAAF Heavy Bomber Squadron,* Australian Military History Publications

Norman Franks – *Claims to Fame: the Lancaster,* Arms and Armour

Leslie Frith – *What a Way to Win a War,* Swann

Bruce Halpenny – *Action Stations 2 : Military Airfields of Lincolnshire and the East Midlands,* Patrick Stephens
—— *Action Stations 4: Military Airfields of Yorkshire,* Patrick Stephens

Max Hastings – *Bomber Command,* Michael Joseph
—— *All Hell Let Loose,* HarperPress

Harry Holmes – *Avro Lancaster: The Definitive Record,* Airlife

Arthur Hoyle – *Hughie Edwards VC, The Fortunate Airman,* Australian Military History Publications

Mike Ingham – *The Air Force Memorials of Lincolnshire,* Midland Counties

Richard Knott – *Black Night for Bomber Command,* Pen & Sword

Martin Middlebrook and Chris Everitt – *The Bomber Command War Diaries,* Penguin

Martin Middlebrook – *The Berlin Raids,* Viking
—— *The Nuremburg Raid,* Allen Lane
—— *The Battle of Hamburg,* Allen Lane
—— *The Peenemunde Raid,* Allen Lane

BIBLIOGRAPHY

Philip Moyes – *Bomber Squadrons of the RAF,* McDonald & Jane's
Patrick Otter – *Maximum Effort (Volumes 1, 2 and 3),* Archive, Manor, Hutton
    Press
    — *Lincolnshire Airfields in the Second World War,* Countryside Books
    — *Yorkshire Airfields in the Second World War,* Countryside Books
Brian Rapier – *Halifax at War,* Ian Allen
Ian Reid – *To Fly Over Waltham,* Ashridge Press
Stewart Scott – *Airfield Focus: Ludford Magna*
    — *Airfield Focus: Swinderby*
Stewart Scott & John Jackson – *Offence to Defence: the History of RAF*
    Binbrook, GMS Enterprises
Eric Taylor – *Operation Millenium,* Robert Hale
Dennis West – *To Strive and Not to Yield,* Woodfield Publishing
Jim Wright – *On Wings of War: A History of 166 Squadron,* 166 Squadron
    Association
Adam Zamoyski – *The Forgotten Few,* John Murray

Index

Advanced Air Striking Force – 1-3, 6-7
'Airborne Cigar' (ABC) – 107, 112-114,
   121, 125, 136, 138, 154, 168, 195,
   203, 211, 246, 254-55, 258
   Development – 107-8
Air Transport Auxiliary – 178, 329
Airey, Sgt Les – 235-36
Airspeed Oxford – 16, 27, 145
Allison, John – 155, 314
Arbuthnot, G/Capt Terrence – 16
Ashcroft, F/O Eric – 226, 228
Ashplant, W/O George – 91, 218-25
Armstrong Whitworth Albemarle – 85
Armstrong Whitworth Whitley – 3, 17,
   33, 41, 57, 59, 73, 114
Augsburg – 141
Avro Anson – 145, 189, 310
Avro Lancaster – 15, 43, 50, 60, 65, 67,
   69, 70-74, 76, 78, 80, 81-83, 89-91,
   94, 98, 101, 104, 105, 109, 113-14,
   119, 121-128, 130, 133-39, 140-43,
   148, 152, 154-58, 161-64, 168, 171,
   174-75, 177, 179-83, 187, 190-91,
   197, 201, 208-17, 225, 240-41, 248,
   253, 269, 271-72, 277-89, 309-10,
   313
Avro Lincoln – 335
Avro Manchester – 67, 70, 179
Avro repair depot Bracebridge Heath –
   310

Bain, Sgt Jim – 235-36
Baldwin, Air Vice Marshal – 49
Banting A/Cmdr George – 287
Barclay, W/Cmdr R.A.C. – 222-23
Barker, W/Cmdr John – 256, 288
Baxter, Sgt Robert – 55-56
Bednarski, F/O Zymunt – 265-69
Belford, F/Lt Bill – 136, 138
Bendall, Colin – 129-130
Bennett, W/Cmdr Jimmy – 132, 230
Bennett, Lowell – 129-130
Bell, W/Cmdr Bryan – 182, 287-88, 295,
   305, 312
Berchtesgaden – 272, 327
Berlin – 32-33, 38, 53, 76, 77, 80, 97-98,

100, 114-145, 167, 180, 190, 226, 229,
   280, 322, 329
Bettany, F/Sgt Jack – 288, 290
Bickers, S/Ldr Ken – 142
Bilton, P/O – 19
Birbeck, F/O Eric – 94
Birch, Sgt Bill – 139-140
Black, P/O Douglas – 185
Blackbourn, F/O Geoff – 277
Blackden, W/Cmdr Vivian – 19, 26
Blucke, Air Vice Marshal Robert – 14
Bochum – 82, 86, 257
Bomber Command – 1, 3, 9, 11, 28, 47,
   51, 62, 67, 78, 80, 101, 116, 160, 194,
   218
   Area bombing directive – 49
   Base system – 43, 85, 102
   'Black Thursday' – 131, 145
   Operation Dodge – 334
   Operation Exodus – 322, 325-27, 333-
      34
   Group HQs
      Hucknall – 1, 12
      Bawtry Hall – 12, 26, 78, 162, 226
   Battle of the Ruhr – 80,
   Operation Fuller – 147
   Operation Hurricane – 253
   Operation Gomorrah – 91
   Operation Manna – 322, 325-27, 332-33
   Operation Millennium – 56, 58
   Operation Neptune – 172
   Operation Overlord – 174, 193
   Operation Thunderclap – 280
   Pathfinder Force – 51, 78, 123
   Transportation Plan – 153
Boston – 303, 305
Bott, Sgt Ray – 199
Bottomley, Air Vice Marshal Norman –
   49
Bottrop – 279
Boyce, G/Capt Clayton – 59
Boyce, P/O Trevor – 201
Bradshaw, Sgt Eric – 277
Bradbury, F/Lt – 305
Breakspear, S/Ldr Harold – 162, 168
Brest – 27, 28, 72, 148,

INDEX

Breen, Air Commodore John – 1, 11,
Bremen – 20, 22, 26, 27, 34, 61, 192,
  295-96, 324
Bristol Blenheim – 3, 24, 62, 220, 225
Brown, Audrey – 299, 301
Bryant, Sgt Cec – 94-96
Brunswick – 112, 124-125, 137, 217
Burgess, Ivor – 179, 316
Burns, F/O Ian – 226, 228
Butler, Sgt Bill – 124, 125

Caen – 206, 208, 210
Campling, W/Cmdr Frank – 50, 178
Cant, W/O Bob – 117, 118
Caistor – 118, 138, 178
Calais – 8, 195,
Callaghan, Sgt Jim – 226, 228
Carter, G/Capt Nick – 133, 152, 226
Catlin, P/O Jim – 139, 140
Chafer, F/Sgt Ron – 110, 111
Châlons – 147
Charlwood, Don – 149, 152, 227
Chemnitz – 280, 285, 290
Cherbourg – 118
Cheshire, W/Cmdr Leonard – 167
Cochrane, AVM Sir Ralph – 238
Clark, S/Ldr James – 257
Clark, F/Lt John – 231, 233
Cleethorpes – 61, 79, 94, 100, 269, 306,
  313
Clemens, Sgt Eric – 231-32
Coastal Command – 18, 37, 42, 56-57
Cohen, S/Ldr Lionel – 61
Collins, S/Ldr Ken – 286
Cologne – 25, 27, 34, 37, 49, 53-54, 56-
  59, 62, 78, 87-89, 94, 163, 191, 232,
  261, 327, 329
Connolly, W/Cmdr Patrick – 207
Constantine, Air Commodore Hugh –
  14, 28, 58, 148, 222
Conway, F/Sgt Norman – 117,
Corser, S/Ldr Ted – 130
Craven, W/Cmdr – 316
Crich, Sgt W. R. – 22-24
Cross, S/Ldr Ian – 50, 148
Crummy, G Capt – 136, 316

Davidson, G/Capt A.P. – 263
Dauphinee, F/O George – 294, 322
Davison, G/Capt A. P. – 9

De Havilland Mosquito – 80, 100, 122,
  130, 141, 162, 167, 174, 190, 211,
  236, 253, 269, 293, 333
Deane, W/Cmdr L.C. – 167
Dessau – 291, 324
Dhenin, F/Lt Geoffrey – 234-5
Dickens, W/Cmdr T. C. – 5
Dieppe – 167, 191
Dilworth, W/Cmdr John – 141
Doncaster – 12, 182
Donkin, G/Capt R.H. – 104
Dornier 215 – 47, 48,
Dortmund – 84, 85, 114, 173, 192, 257,
  285, 292, 314
Dresden – 54, 58, 273, 280-85
Dripps, F/Sgt Don – 97, 135
Dunstan, F/O Roberts – 230-234, 331
Düsseldorf – 49, 68, 77, 85, 114, 122,
  148, 191, 232, 234, 251, 257
Duisburg – 34, 49, 56, 61, 82, 173, 191,
  208, 253-55, 287
Dunkirk – 53, 147

Edinger, S/Ldr Peter – 34
Edwards, G/Capt Hughie VC – 80, 91,
  232, 259, 275
Ellis, W/O Ted – 135-36
Emden – 26, 30, 48, 53
Emmerich – 226, 252
Essen – 49, 52, 53, 54, 60, 61, 75, 76-78,
  80, 81, 191-92, 292, 326-27

Fairey Battle – 1-8, 11, 29, 41, 101, 231
Fielden, S/Ldr – 34
FIDO – 16, 134, 135
Finn, Sid – 57,
Floryanowski, S/Ldr S. – 21
Focke-Wulf 190 – 81, 143, 212, 227
Forêt de Cerisy – 191
Francis, Sgt Colin – 231-32
Frankfurt – 32, 33, 61, 73, 82, 249
Franks, S/Ldr A.D. – 53
Frazer-Nash turret – 214-16
French Resistance – 117, 138, 141, 170,
  172, 201, 207, 212, 267
Friedrichshafen – 165, 191
Frith, Sgt Les – 6, 29, 30, 31
Fry, Sgt Tony, 226, 228
Fulbrook, W/O Reg – 68, 179
Fuller, S/Ldr Harry – 292

Fussell, Sgt Marcel – 71-72

Gainsborough – 215, 289, 315
Gardiner, S/Ldr Hugh – 295
Garlick, S/Ldr John – 130
Garner, W/Cmdr Don – 316
Gates, P/O Fred – 235-36
Gosman, F/Lt Doug – 29, 31
Gee, S/Ldr John – 296
Geffen, Sgt Harry van – 111, 114
Gelsenkirchen – 87, 88, 150, 192
Gibbons, P/O Dudley – 162, 207
Gibbons, S/Ldr Monty – 114
Gibson, W/Cmdr Guy VC – 215
Gilbert, S/Ldr Colin – 53, 55, 60
Golding, W/Cmdr Albert – 53
Goodman, W/Cmdr Hubert – 172
Gneisenau – 26, 28, 49, 50, 51, 147
Graham, S/Ldr 'Bluey' – 132, 133
Grant, P/O Cy – 88, 89
Greig, Sir Louis – 224
Gibbon, S/Ldr Monty – 292
Gibbons, P/O Dudley – 162, 207
Grieg, Capt Nordahl – 129
Grimsby – 4, 79, 98, 130, 133, 217, 232, 244, 305, 311, 313-14, 323

Hackworth, W/Cmdr Peter – 252
Hamburg – 27, 32, 36, 54, 56, 58, 61, 76-77, 89, 107, 146, 219, 232, 295, Battle of – 91-96
Hamilton, W/Cmdr Ian – 250
Handley Page Hampden – 3, 17, 28, 29, 41, 48, 50, 114, 147, 175-177
Handley Page Heyford – 15
Handley Page Halifax – 17, 67, 69-70, 78, 104-105, 114, 123, 138, 142, 154, 157-58, 190, 201, 220-22, 236, 253, 256, 285, 290
Hanover – 23, 27, 32, 112-114, 118, 119, 121, 124, 322,
Harris – Air Chief Marshal Sir Arthur – 11, 49-50, 56, 57, 90-91, 114, 121, 150, 153-54, 214-15, 224, 238, 272
Hasselt – 172, 191
Hatcliffe, Ernest and Gladys – 315
Hawker Hart – 145
Hawker Hector – 6
Hawker Hurricane – 150, 243
Hazard – Sgt Ivan – 235-36

Heath, F/Sgt Ivan – 89, 98, 311-12
Hegarty, Sgt Vin – 231, 233
Heinkel 219 – 289
Herman, F/Sgt George – 112
Herscovitz, F/Sgt Reuben – 112
Hirzbandt, W/Cmdr – 60
Hodson, Air Vice Marshal George – 177
Holford, W/Cmdr David – 50, 67-68, 132-133, 137, 141, 145-51, 176
Homberg – 211
Hubbard, W/Cmdr A.L.G. – 53
Hull – 33, 78,
Hull, F/Lt Bill – 162, 168

Ijselmeer – 26, 202
Ivelaw-Chapman, Air Commodore Ronald – 172

Jarman, S/Ldr Eric – 165
Jefferies, F/Sgt Arthur – 159, 228-30
Johnson, W/Cmdr Johnny – 203
Johnson, Sgt Johnny – 149, 152
Jones, F/O Cyril – 291, 324
Junkers 88 – 32, 47, 48, 123, 208, 248, 251, 277, 289-91, 293-94

Kammhuber, Generalmajor Josef – 47,
Karlsruhe – 191
Kassell – 232
Kaufmann, W/Cmdr Keith – 69
Kennard, S/Ldr – 226
Kiel – 27, 51, 53, 191, 296, 312
King George VI – 218, 224
Kleve – 279
Koder, F/Lt Clem – 189, 240-43, 279, 310
Krefeld – 87, 192, 232

LMF ('lack of moral fibre') – 111, 312
Lamming, John – 327
Langille, F/Lt Alan – 88, 89
Langmead, Sgt Taffy – 208
Lawrence, S/Ldr Philip – 23
Le Havre – 191, 248, 323
Leighton, S/Ldr John – 60
Leipzig – 115, 121, 130, 132, 139, 280-81
Lewis, Sgt Keith – 188-192
Lincoln – 46, 65, 82, 113, 142, 185, 289, 303, 305-306, 310

Lindo, S/Ldr Harold – 139
Little, F/O Ralph – 295, 324
Littler, W/Cmdr Charles – 26
Liverpool – 26, 219
Lorient – 218-19
Longcluse, Sgt Norman – 7
Louth – 103, 305
Lowe, S/Ldr – 19
Lübeck – 54
Ludwigshafen – 114, 277
Lutzkendorf – 295-96

Macleod-Selkirk, S/Ldr Ian – 114
Mahaddie, W/Cmdr Hamish – 149
Mailly-le-Camp – 167-71, 251
Manahan, S/Ldr Jim – 86
Mannheim – 15, 27, 37, 83, 112, 232, 329
Marigny, F/O Galton de – 142
Market Rasen – 34, 65, 237, 269
Meadows, Sgt George – 127, 128
Messerschmitt 109 – 1, 269
Messerschmitt 110 – 21, 25, 47-48, 139, 291
Messerschmitt 210 – 294
Messerschmitt 410 – 322
Miller, Percy – 312-13
Miller, Sgt Stan – 123-124
Mills, Sgt Alan – 34, 37
Misson bombing range – 162, 185
Mönchengladbach – 97
Mulheim – 232
Mulholland, W/Cmdr Norman – 33

Nash, Sgt Harold – 96
Namur – 257
Neale, F/Sgt Gordon – 182, 303, 306, 312
Nissen huts – 40, 85, 87, 163, 299, 302, 309, 314
Nicholls, S/Ldr John – 52
Nicholls, S/Ldr Tom – 159
Norman, W/Cmdr Bob – 121
Norman, Sgt Edward – 180
Nottingham – 23, 27
Nuremburg – 153-56, 158, 160, 167, 230, 232, 273, 293-94, 322

Oberhausen – 232
O'Donoghue, S/Ldr Charles – 225-28

Oldenburg – 94
Ostend – 20, 37
Oxland – Air Vice Marshal Robert – 11, 12, 78

Parrish, Sgt Stan – 206, 327
Parsons, W/Cmdr Keith – 259, 278-79
Peenemünde – 98
Peirse, Air Marshal Sir Richard – 26, 49
Pforzeim – 114, 288
Pialucha, Sgt – 209-10
Playfield, Air Vice-Marshal 'Pip' – 1
Portal, Sir Charles – 149
Powdrell, S/Ld Walter – 78
Powley, W/Cmdr Frank – 162, 257, 296
Prinz Eugen – 49, 50, 147
Prochera, F/Lt John – 270

Quinton, AC1 Harold – 178

RAF Stations 1 Group

Binbrook – 3-7, 17-18, 23, 26, 33-35, 40, 45, 57-59, 61, 65-66, 80-81, 84-85, 89-90, 92, 94, 98, 100, 102, 105, 116, 122, 128-30, 132, 138, 150, 159, 161, 163, 165, 178, 190, 206, 213, 230-32, 241, 252, 256-57, 275, 283, 289, 296 - 297, 301, 306, 311-13, 330, 336, 338
Blyton – 46, 56, 66, 72, 77, 102, 105, 134, 175, 180,182-83, 185, 187, 192, 239, 297, 308-309, 314-15, 338
Breighton – 45, 52-53, 60, 70-71, 80-81, 85, 148, 175-76, 179, 231, 297, 329-30, 338-39
Dunholme Lodge – 46, 102, 239, 241, 252-53, 339
Elsham Wolds – 27, 36-37, 45, 57-58, 67-68, 72-74, 79, 81, 83, 88, 90-92, 100, 102, 105, 117-118, 122, 130-131, 141, 147, 149, 156, 172, 179, 183, 207-8, 210-13, 225, 248, 256-57, 274, 295, 297, 315, 325, 339-40
Faldingworth – 16, 102, 104-105, 119, 134, 163, 175, 183, 201, 204, 209, 211-12, 241, 247, 269, 271, 284, 296-98, 301, 340-41
Fiskerton – 16, 46, 102, 135, 239, 252, 256, 275, 277, 279, 287, 310, 325, 341

Hemswell – 3, 28, 36, 40, 45, 53, 54-55, 57, 60, 76-77, 81, 86, 102, 105, 150, 177-78, 182, 190, 214-15, 240, 253, 258, 261, 270, 275, 278, 283, 292, 296-97, 301, 342-43

Holme-on-Spalding Moor – 15, 33, 46, 65, 70-71, 79, 81, 83-84, 86, 134, 175, 229, 297, 343-44

Hucknall – 268

Ingham – 45, 55, 60, 76-77, 86, 92, 97, 102, 105, 119, 134, 297, 344

Kelstern – 44-45, 102-104, 121, 125, 128, 133-134, 138-139, 142, 159, 167, 171, 183, 188-92, 211, 233, 240, 243, 252, 275, 277, 279, 290, 295, 297, 305, 308-10, 312-13, 328, 344

Kirmington – 46, 58, 66, 72, 76, 82, 84, 94-95, 102-103, 122, 127, 132, 134, 138-139, 161-62, 166, 171, 174, 183, 206-7, 212, 217-18, 220, 225, 234, 248, 251-54, 274, 297, 301, 305, 316-18, 327, 345

Lindholme – 26, 28, 30, 36, 40, 45, 53, 57, 60, 74, 76, 79, 102, 104-105, 111, 134, 137, 149, 175, 177, 180-83, 185, 194, 206, 229, 231, 234, 239-40, 269-70, 279, 287, 297, 307, 311, 323, 345-6

Ludford Magna – 15-16, 43-45, 86-87, 102-104, 106-107, 109, 111-114, 116, 119, 121-122, 132-34, 136, 138, 154, 157, 186, 191, 195, 197, 215, 229, 236, 241, 276, 290, 295, 297, 302-303, 305, 315, 346-47

Newton – 4-8, 17-19, 21, 23, 28, 45, 253, 348

North Killingholme – 46, 102, 126, 138, 157, 159, 162, 193-94, 202-3, 229-30, 245-47, 258, 284-85, 291, 294, 297, 301, 313-14, 316, 324, 328, 348

Sandtoft – 46, 102, 105, 175, 177, 182, 184-85, 192, 239-40, 297, 301, 348

Scampton – 3, 40, 45, 48, 102, 162, 173, 239, 252, 258, 290, 295, 327, 331, 349-50

Snaith – 28, 32, 45, 52, 55, 61, 66, 72, 136, 253, 297, 350

Sturgate – 46, 102, 135, 239, 350

Swinderby – 10, 17, 21, 25, 27, 45, 270, 350

Syerston – 26, 27, 40, 45, 301, 351

Waltham – 33-36, 42-43, 45, 50-51, 54, 57-59, 60-61, 72, 78-81, 85, 97, 102, 104-5, 107, 122-123, 126, 130-131, 133, 138, 143, 145, 150, 160, 195, 199, 211, 217, 229-30, 240-41, 244, 250, 270, 277, 285, 295, 297-98, 301, 305, 312, 322-23, 332, 351-52

Wickenby – 16, 46, 65, 71, 76, 83, 85, 98, 100, 102, 105, 115-16, 121-22, 125, 127, 130, 134, 136, 138, 141, 159, 171, 182, 185, 203, 206, 211, 213, 248, 252, 254-55, 258, 274-275, 277, 279, 283, 285, 288-89, 293, 295, 297-98, 301, 303, 305-306, 316, 325, 333, 352-53

RAF Heavy Conversion Units 1 Group

1656 – 70, 76, 79, 104, 110, 137, 149, 175, 177-78, 180, 184, 231, 269-70, 279, 287, 307, 311, 323, 328

1662 – 104, 175, 177-78, 180, 182, 187, 192, 229, 308, 314

1667 – 104, 175, 178, 183, 187, 192, 240

RAF Units

1 Group Aircrew School – 46

1 Group Lancaster Finishing School – 46, 50, 70, 104, 110-11, 177, 182, 190

1 Group Target Towing Flight – 46, 105

1 Group Special Duties Flight – 162-63, 167, 169, 207

7 Operational Training Unit – 13, 46, 177

18 Operational Training Unit – 57, 60, 66, 137, 268

22 Operational Training Unit – 57, 58

27 Operational Training Unit – 180, 231

1481 Bomber and Gunnery Flight – 57, 102, 105

1687 Bomber Defence Training Flight – 105

RAF Squadrons 1 Group

12 – 2-5, 7, 19, 21, 23, 29, 34-35, 48, 54, 57-58, 61, 71, 76, 83, 85-86, 94, 98,

100, 121, 125, 127, 130, 134, 136, 138-39, 140, 142, 161, 171, 182, 204-6, 213, 245, 251-52, 254, 256-57, 275, 277, 279, 288-89, 293, 298, 301, 312, 316, 333, 335, 353

100 – 79, 83, 85, 94, 97-98, 104, 107, 121-122, 125, 130, 132, 135, 138, 141, 145, 159, 161-62, 171-72, 217, 229, 240-41, 243-44, 250, 270, 273, 277, 279, 285, 293, 295, 319-320, 335, 353

101 – 15-16, 48, 62, 65, 71, 76, 82-84, 86-88, 92, 94, 105-107, 111-114, 116, 126, 130, 134, 136, 142, 154, 155, 157, 162, 165, 169, 186, 202-3, 206, 211, 213, 215, 229, 235-236, 241, 247-48, 255, 258, 273, 277, 286, 292-93, 295, 298, 314, 322, 324, 335, 353

101 Halifax Conversion Flight – 70

103 – 2-6, 8, 10, 17, 20, 22, 26-27, 29, 33-34, 45, 50, 57, 67, 69, 71, 78, 83, 88, 90-92, 99, 105, 116, 126, 130-132, 136, 139, 142, 147-49, 159, 161-63, 172-73, 176, 180, 201-2, 208, 210-12, 225, 258, 285, 291-93, 296, 307, 320-21, 327, 353

103 Halifax Conversion Flight – 67, 68, 148, 179

142 – 2-8, 19, 29, 31, 33, 35-36, 43, 48, 50, 54, 60-61, 71-73, 79, 354

150 – 1-4, 6-8, 10, 17, 19, 20, 28, 32, 45, 52, 55-56, 58, 61, 71-73, 136, 239, 253, 273, 275-76, 283, 354

153 – 173, 239, 252-54, 258, 273, 277, 279, 285, 290, 293, 296, 327, 354

166 – 73, 76-77, 81-82, 83, 85, 88, 91, 94, 96-97, 105, 125, 127, 134, 137, 142,161, 165, 167, 169, 174, 201, 205-8, 212, 216-18, 234, 248, 252, 254-55, 258, 273-75, 277, 285-86, 293, 296, 305, 316-18, 327, 354

170 – 239, 241, 276, 279, 283, 288, 291, 293, 296, 354

199 – 66, 72, 77, 81, 82, 85, 86, 96, 308, 354

300 (Masovian) – 8, 10, 17, 28, 36, 45, 53-55, 60, 76-77, 81, 82, 85, 92, 97, 105, 164, 177, 204, 209, 211-12, 241, 261, 269, 273, 277, 296, 320, 335, 354

301 (Pomeranian) – 8, 10, 17, 21, 28, 36, 53-54, 76, 354

304 (Silesian) – 8, 10, 17, 26-28, 30, 37, 355

305 (Wielkopolska) – 8, 10, 17, 26-28, 30, 37, 53-54, 60, 76-77, 81, 86, 91, 97, 268, 355

460 – 50, 52, 55, 60, 69, 76, 80-85, 90-92, 98, 100, 121, 125, 127, 129, 130, 132, 136,138, 140, 142, 165, 169, 178, 184, 201-2, 211, 213-14, 217, 230-31, 234, 241, 243, 245, 248, 255, 258, 275, 277-79, 283, 292-93, 296, 306, 311-12, 320, 329-30, 335, 355

460 Halifax Conversion Flight – 148, 179

550 – 105, 126, 130-131, 135-136, 138, 157, 159, 173, 193, 197, 202-3, 206-8, 211, 229, 245, 248, 254-55, 258, 279, 284, 287, 291, 293-96, 306, 316, 328, 355

576 – 105, 130-131, 135-136, 138, 140, 159, 172, 201-2, 208, 210, 212-13, 245, 251, 256-57, 277, 285, 287, 292-93, 296, 315, 320-21, 355

625 – 104, 121-122, 133, 138-139, 142, 159, 162, 171, 188-89, 192, 199, 206, 211, 213, 217, 240, 244, 248-49, 254, 256, 277, 285, 288, 293-95, 308, 310, 312, 328, 355

626 – 105, 127, 130, 134, 138, 159, 162, 171, 173, 206, 211, 217, 247-49, 252, 254-55, 275, 277-78, 285, 293, 295, 312, 320, 333, 355

Raimbert – 248

Reid, F/Sgt Henry – 221, 225

Revingy – 206-8, 313

Rice, Air Vice Marshal Edward – 12, 13, 78, 162, 172, 177, 215, 222-23

Rippingdale, S/Ldr Tom – 251

Robertson, S/Ldr Ian – 136

Rodney, W/Cmdr G.F. – 327

Rogers, Sgt Handley – 19, 59,

Rolleghem, S/Ldr Vincent Van – 172, 327

Rose, Alfred – 215-16

Rose Brothers – 215

Rose turret – 14, 214-17

Ross, W/Cmdr Quentin – 142

Rostock – 53, 54

Rotterdam – 5, 26, 32, 124

Ruhr – 75, 86, 89, 173, 192, 232, 313
Rush, Cpl Bill – 234-35
Russelheim – 247, 322
Ryan, W/Cmdr – 34

Saundby, Air Vice Marshal Robert – 56
Scharnhorst – 26, 49, 50, 51, 147
Schibor, S/Ldr – 30
Schloven-Buer – 210-11
Schweinfurt – 140, 154, 159
Scott, S/Ldr – 250
Scragg, W/Cmdr Colin – 137, 152
Scunthorpe – 43, 305, 315
Searby, G/Capt John – 99
Shannon, W/Cmdr Dave – 167
Short Stirling – 17, 58, 67, 77, 78, 86, 114, 123, 175, 190
Simmons, W/Cmdr Don – 59
Sisley, W/Cmdr Alan – 248
Skarzynski, G/Capt Stanislaw – 60
Skegness – 96, 305
Slade, S/Ldr Fraser – 100
Slater, S/Ldr – 293
Smalley, Sgt Bill – 220-21
Smith, S/Ldr Gavin – 202
Smith, F/Lt Jeff – 189, 191-92
Smith, F/O Jimmy – 85, 86
St John, W/Cmdr J.R. – 172
St Nazaire – 6, 80, 119, 226, 261
Stachon, G/Capt B. – 27
Stafford, Sgt Sefton – 226, 228
Stedman, F/O Mike – 163, 315
Stettin – 83, 136, 247-48
Stockton, Norman – 129
Stuttgart – 71, 113, 140, 141, 211-13, 230, 255
Supermarine Spitfire – 7, 8, 49, 201, 222, 256
Swain, W/Cmdr James – 83

Tait, W/Cmdr Willie – 149
Taylor, Sgt Frank – 124-125
Terschelling – 48, 60,
Tickle, F/Sgt Harry – 329-330
Turgle, S/Ldr Philip – 85
Turin – 71, 72, 80, 232
Tyler, S/Ldr Edward – 84

Ulm – 258
Utz, S/Ldr Eric – 158

Vickers Vilderbeest – 79
Vickers Wellington – 3, 8, 9, 12, 22-29, 32-34, 36, 41, 45, 48, 50, 52-53, 56-58, 60-61, 66, 71, 72, 76-77, 80-81, 83-85, 91-92, 94, 96-97, 101, 105, 139, 145, 175, 190, 206, 225, 270, 272, 308,
Vierzon – 192, 206
Vire – 197, 201
Vivian, G/Capt R.L. – 277, 316-18

Wallis, P/O Ken – 33, 34
Wallis, Sir Neville Barnes – 17
Wanne-Eickel – 201, 257
Warner, S/Ldr Tom – 286
Watson, F/Sgt Ralph – 170, 251
Wedderburn, S/Ldr Bill – 86, 92
West, Eddie – 180, 309
Weston, S/Ldr Ralph – 206
Westland Lysander – 6, 172
Westland Wapiti – 11
Wheeldon, Sgt Rex – 2, 19, 21
Whipp, Major Sydney – 171
White, W/O Claude – 121, 122
Whitmarsh, P/O Arthur – 259, 275
Whittall, 2nd Officer Taniya – 178
Wiesbaden – 278
Wilhelmshaven – 296
Winn, Sgt John – 226, 228
Williams, Sgt Bill – 169-70
Williams, Sgt Bill – 235-36
Wizernes – 206, 208
Women's Auxiliary Air Force – 271, 298-99, 301, 303, 315-16
Wood, S/Ldr Clifford – 122
Woodley, Sgt Frank – 259, 294
Wray, Air Commodore Arthur – 13, 104, 313
Wright, Sgt Barry – 139, 140
Wright, S/Ldr Jim – 317

Yardley, Station W/O 'Lavender' – 229, 316

Zeitz – 277